=AN=
AMERICAN
HISTORY PRIMER

AN
AMERICAN
HISTORY PRIMER

Richard L. Mumford

Elizabethtown College

HARCOURT BRACE JOVANOVICH, PUBLISHERS
San Diego New York Chicago Austin Washington, D.C.
London Sydney Tokyo Toronto

ISBN: 0-15-502344-6

PREFACE

The genesis of this textbook has been the history classroom. I have used nearly all of the contents, in various forms, in actual classroom situations. The book has grown out of thirty years of teaching at levels ranging from senior high school to graduate school. The field testing for the exercises has been gradual, semester by semester, before the final merger into book form. Each of the exercises and questions has been modified, according to its success or failure in classroom use. I have experimented and revised and a different syllabus has emerged each semester. But the central goal has remained the use of history as a mechanism to develop meaningful, worthwhile analytical and reflective thinking skills.

Three convictions have grown out of this experience of teaching history. First, students need to go beyond the memorization of historical data (not *avoiding* knowledge of data, but going beyond it). Second, students have difficulty going beyond the data on their own. Analytical thinking is not automatic. Students cannot be expected merely to follow a professor's analytical thinking process in a lecture or to draw out a textbook author's thinking processes just by reading the text. Students need guidance, encouragement, challenge, models, practice, and evaluation in order to develop insight and critical thinking skills. They need exercises aimed at encouraging these skills. Third, this training is best accomplished within the context of a coherent body of data—a historical period or topic, for example.

Of course, history is enjoyable on its own. Intrinsic is the delight in learning, in following a good story. Those who have read much history know that it is often more unusual, more ironic, and more fascinating than fiction. Historians have always aimed at presenting history accurately, with clear prose. However, students of history need to reach beyond entertainment and pleasure to see the usefulness of applying their minds to historical data through analysis, criticism, evaluation, comparison, and insightful connections. In an open, democratic society, these skills are indispensable.

This textbook was not put together in the stacks of a research library. Colleagues and students suffered through a multitude of learning designs and structured assignments—the students as subjects and the colleagues as critics—and I appreciate their suggestions and insights. Other debts are numerous. My family, especially my wife Keiko, has put up with my physical absences and mental preoccupations. Elizabethtown College, of Pennsylvania, offered encouragement in many ways. An enthusiastic dean, Frederick Ritsch, was very supportive. When he asked, "How is it going?", he expected a specific answer. This was helpful. An indispensable editor at Harcourt Brace Jovanovich, Drake Bush, was not only willing to speak out in favor of the publication of this book, but rendered insightful advice about content, structure, and format. The Manuscript editor, Kay Kaylor, helped shape the manuscript into a clear and precise form. Her insights and suggestions improved the textbook considerably. I also appreciate very much the fine professional work of the production editor, Cynthia Sheridan; the designer, Don Fujimoto; and the production manager, Kim W. Turner.

I bear ultimate responsibility for this textbook and for any inadequacies. My final hope is that in a world of conflicting belief systems, of constant struggle within the minds of millions, of tenuous uncertainty about reasonable solutions to ill-defined problems, and of continual misunderstandings caused by shallow, impressionistic thinking, these exercises will encourage and train some students to define problems clearly, to collect and classify relevant evidence, to critically analyze data, to reflect judiciously on beneficial courses of action, and to exhibit quality thinking in both private and public matters.

RICHARD MUMFORD

TO THE INSTRUCTOR

"Intellectual ability, on which history rests, can, without question, be enhanced by further education, not indeed through theoretical precepts, but only through practical exercises."

THEODORE MOMMSEN

This textbook is meant to assist students in developing many of the analytical and reflective thinking skills employed by historians. Each chapter covers a specified time period and is divided into several parts.

In Part I, students examine critically and with reflection some of the essential data contained in history textbooks and in lectures by instructors. Of course, the data are not complete, and not all of the information about the period of history is provided in this section. But it furnishes a foundation for some of the essentials common to nearly all United States history courses. The data are presented in a format that demands analysis and reflection as well as memorization. In this way critical thought accompanies the student's encounter with each item of data. Not only is the item more likely to be remembered, but it also becomes impregnated with meaning, a combination of a student's judgment, prior knowledge, and experience.

Part II promotes the development of specific thinking skills. Eight important analytical thinking skills commonly used by historians are first identified and explained to students. Then, the exercise format enables students to practice these skills and to check on their mastery of them by comparing their answers with those suggested by the author. Only through repetitive practice can these skills be finely honed and made a part of the student's normal reaction to a body of information.

In Part III, students use the knowledge of essential data and the analytical thinking skills developed in Parts I and II to answer actual problems encountered by historians, problems that relate especially to the period of history under scrutiny and to recurring issues that challenge historians. Students will need to examine the questions carefully and critically, to search other sources (standard textbooks, lecture notes, library sources), to reflect on the issues, and then to write answers with justifications. Students can then compare their answers with the author's thoughts. Ideally, students should compare answers with one another, and if the class format allows, share them with the instructor in classroom discussion. Most of the questions in this third section are open-ended, with no final, "true" answers. This does not mean that all possible opinions are equal in value. Those answers with more supporting evidence and more reasonable arguments are obviously more useful.

Format

The author has chosen about ten dates and ten concepts as essential data for each chapter. These are followed by specific "thinking-skill" exercises that progress from simple to complex. Two different skills are introduced in each of the first four chapters. These eight skills are repeated, with more challenging exercises, throughout the book. Finally, a varying number of open-ended "thought" questions related to controversial historical issues and decisions are provided at the end of each chapter. The three parts correspond to educator Benjamin Bloom's six levels of objectives and to other patterns of thinking. (Bloom's concept of levels of educational objectives implies that levels of thinking also may be developed.)[1]

This textbook uses the following nine analytical and reflective thinking skills, presented here in order of complexity, and provides exercises at each level.

1. The student must first distinguish between factual and inferential and opinionative statements. This distinction between fact and inference is essential for choosing data as evidence. The student is asked to identify and distinguish data, not manipulate them.

2. At the next level, the student can compare ideas and attitudes by picking out similarities and differences in two essays on similar topics.

3. In the third exercise, the student must determine the relevance of evidence by breaking down information and distinguishing between data that apply directly to the thesis and data that may be interesting and important but not related to the thesis.

4. At the next, questioning level, the student selects techniques to acquire data. Scientists use experiments to acquire data. Social scientists use polls, surveys, clinical observation, and similar techniques. Historians must ask questions about specific *unique* events and then search for answers to those questions. This requires the skill of developing questions that are clear, that drive to the heart of causation and penetrate the hidden area of motivation. Questions are essential to historical investigation, both in the beginning study of a topic or thesis and in evaluating related evidence.

5. The student must learn to organize data—to assemble, classify, and place into categories diverse data usually offered in a random manner—and these exercises address that skill. Historians most often classify data into five categories: political, economic, social, diplomatic, and cultural. And although the synthesis of data can sometimes be contrived, it allows historians to deal with a mass of data by forming it into a useful design. This skill also involves analysis, since random information is separated and examined individually before being placed under the appropriate heading.

6. The final three skill exercises require the student to move to a higher level of thinking—evaluation. For the sixth exercise, the student must evaluate the type of arguments being used by those who make statements about events and situations in history. Historians consider as evidence not only facts and statistics, but arguments made by people involved in an event, by experts, and by historians who later investigate the event.

   Identification of the type of argument determines its degree of reliability. The five types of arguments used in the exercises cover all those that circulate in the nonmathematical, nonscientific fields. The student must distinguish the more powerful empirical arguments from those of reason and the less reliable ones of anecdote and intuition. Thus the student becomes aware of the quality of support for different historical interpretations.

7. The next skill exercise centers on the evaluation and application of evidence and provides practice in deciding how the evidence applies to a thesis—as a challenge, as a refutation, or merely as significant but neutral data. Since historians usually operate on the basis of a thesis (revealed at the outset or somewhat hidden in a narrative account), it is important that history students develop the ability to recognize the proper placement of data and arguments both in favor of and against the thesis statement. Through these exercises, students will learn to evaluate the relevance of evidence and to divide data into supportive and nonsupportive categories.

8. The last exercise cultivates the skill of drawing inferences from statistics. The student must also react to inferences drawn from quantitative data and must think both analytically and reflectively about their accuracy. Numerical data can be deceptive, in that they

[1] Benjamin S. Bloom, editor, *Taxonomy of Educational Objectives; The Classification of Educational Goals, Handbook I: The Cognitive Domain*, David McKay Company, Inc., 1956, pp. 201–7.

seem exact and indisputable; and determining supportable implications from statistical data can therefore be hazardous. Normally, statistical data is eventually converted into descriptive language. However, drawing inferences requires imagination and insight to determine meaning beyond verbal description. Drawing inferences also demands sound judgment and impartiality—thinking beyond the obvious. The student must be content with what seems to be a reasonable and reliable interpretation of the quantitative data.

9. Finally, the thought-provoking questions in Part III combine the highest cognitive levels—evaluation and synthesis—with the affective domain of emotions, feeling, and attitudes. These open-ended questions call for the application of individual values and encourage personal conclusions requiring students to make decisions based on their own attitudes, outlook, and beliefs. Each question is presented with enough information to allow for some immediate judgments, and yet each leads the student to a search for additional data. The student is not left without criteria by which to compare his or her personal conclusions. The "Thoughts for Questions" provide additional data and reflections, as well as a personal perspective on particular issues. The skills developed by the open-ended questions are suited to the less precise humanities and the nonmathematical segment of the social sciences.

These exercises lead students through an organized, step-by-step process, reinforced by practice and covering all aspects of analytical and reflective thinking. From the simple level of memorization (essential dates and concepts) through the higher levels of evaluation, synthesis, and affective thought, students can develop specific skills and use them to consider significant issues and problems in United States history. Simultaneously, with data revolving around a chronological arrangement of the traditional subject matter of a survey course in American history, students sharpen these skills while absorbing the complex data, ideas, and interpretations of American history.

TO THE STUDENT

This textbook can be used in private study for the development of thinking skills, as a preparatory overview of United States history, and as a review of subject matter presented in a standard textbook or through lectures. It can be used alone, with any United States history survey textbook, or with other sources of data on United States history available in the classroom or in the library.

Ideally, the instructor should, in designated class periods, use the material within this textbook as a basis for discussion. Students should do the exercises before class. During class, the students should compare answers, discuss choices, debate, challenge, supply evidence, explain arguments, and react to the variety of viewpoints presented and defended. As a result, discussions become more than superficial, disorganized statements of opinions. Such discussions would involve important, specific topics and issues that had been examined before class with the help of this textbook and the main textbook or other sources. Students would use the analytical thinking skills that were being refined and sharpened in chapter after chapter.

Through classroom discussion, students also develop the oral and aural skills of orderly debate and careful listening. Although the primary skills referred to in this book are the analytical and reflective thinking skills of historians, most of them apply equally well to other academic disciplines, and indeed, to life beyond the academic world.

Some Practical Hints

1. *Write in the book.* It is an exercise book. Students may think that transactions "in the head" are sufficient, but the act of writing both reinforces mental transactions and comits students to definite viewpoints. Writing down responses both enhances learning and avoids the psychological deception that "I have thought about it, so I know it."

2. The author's answers, explanations, reflections, and suggestions are not the authority. Students should develop the healthy habit of questioning the author's choices and statements. Bias, personal beliefs, background experiences, limitations of knowledge, and the exclusion of important considerations are apt to creep into the author's answers. Disagree. Argue your positions with evidence and reason.

3. Develop the habit of *self-analysis.* What are the reasons for reaching your conclusions? What are the personal beliefs and background experiences in your life that may have influenced your viewpoints? Are your conclusions based on inadequate or incomplete evidence? Scientists can, in most cases, detach themselves from experiments. Historians and history students must be at least cognizant of background factors that impinge on objectivity and shape reasoning.

4. *Be confident.* It is not true that all answers to open-ended questions are equally valid, that it "all depends on your point of view." Some answers have greater validity—they are backed by stronger arguments and supported by more relevant and significant evidence than other answers. The fallacy of accepting all answers to controversial questions as equal is damaging to sincere efforts at reaching judicious, reasonable solutions to difficult problems. However, be confident that your judgments, after consideration of evidence and careful reflection, have merit. Your judgments can, no doubt, be improved by acquiring more evidence and considering opposing arguments, but your viewpoints should be presented and defended with vigor. Therefore, propose, argue, debate, defend, and support your conclusions, not with prejudice, or emotion, or a closed mind, but with confidence tempered by openness and a willingness to listen, to modify, and to reconsider.

5. *Use different sources.* Obviously this textbook does not contain all the facts and ideas necessary for a thorough understanding of United States history. Even the standard United States history textbook (perhaps twenty-five in print) is only a concise reduction of the overwhelming abundance of data and resources available about United States history. Students should always be aware that much more information, and significant information, is available about each topic or issue covered in this textbook or in the standard survey textbook. Get in the habit of looking at other sources and searching for additional information. Libraries are open long hours, instructors are available, and a variety of resources are in print.

All instructors expect students to remember information and ideas about United States history. Research indicates that a large amount of information, available as recall data to students at the time of final examinations, is lost within one year of the examinations (some research shows the 90 percent is lost). This author hopes that students will develop, along with a retention of *some* important information, an approach to learning, with (1) an attitude of confidence in the ability to think clearly, (2) an instinctive attitude of applying incisive questions to accumulated data, (3) a habit of organizing and categorizing knowledge, (4) an ability to reflect and analyze, (5) a willingness to make judgments and reach tentative conclusions, and (6) a development of respect for relevant evidence and reasonable arguments. These habits and approaches are lasting, and if they are encouraged and developed, this book will have been a successful vehicle for a lifetime of reflective and analytical thinking. In the sixteenth century, Yang-ming observed, "To know is to know how to know and to know what one ought to know."

CONTENTS

CHAPTER

1

THE AGE OF DISCOVERY, EXPLORATION, AND SETTLEMENT

"The goal of history will make good the evil of history."

St. Augustine

"History is a collection of irrational decisions and actions explained rationally."

Dick Mumford

PART I
Acquiring Essential Data

ESSENTIAL DATES

Often students remember the distasteful process of memorizing dates in history classes. It is not necessary to know the date of every event in history. All dates are not of equal importance; nor is it necessary to remember the exact year of each event. For some developments the approximate time is sufficient. However, certain dates of events and developments ought to be committed to memory. Also, many events can only be understood in their proper place in a sequence of events. Placing the outbreak of the Civil War "sometime in the 1860s" and the southern secession "sometime at mid-century" fails to capture the sequence of events and their relationship in time. "Before" and "after" are important adverbs for the historian. Once data like the outbreak of the Civil War is established in the mind, it becomes a collecting place for remembering other events by their relationship to these few essential ones. The mind organizes and automatically structures data in chronological categories.

For each chapter in this book, certain key events, decisions, or developments will be listed. The student should place these in their proper sequence. Then, check the correct sequence and learn the date of each.

Place these key events in proper chronological order by numbering each from one to ten, first to last. Write when you think the event approximately took place by writing a date after each event. Check your sequence with the correct ordering, listed after "Essential Concepts" in each chapter. Or, if you wish to use this for review, write the correct sequence on another paper, check your answers, and then give it another try later.

1. Cortez conquers Mexico. _____

2. Puritans arrive in New England. _____

3. First human settlers arrive in America. _____

4. Protestant Reformation begins. _____

5. Columbus sets sail across the Atlantic. _____

6. Magna Carta is signed in England. _____

7. Jamestown settlement founded in Virginia. _____

8. Smallpox epidemic devastates the Indian population of America. _____

9. Dutch found New Netherlands (later New York). _____

10. Spanish Armada fails in its attempt to invade England. _____

ESSENTIAL CONCEPTS

Examine carefully the following concepts or ideas. After each, explain in what ways the concept is useful in understanding the period. Also consider whether the concept is "dead"—important for that time only—or whether the concept is "alive"—still has importance in contemporary society even if in a slightly different or modified form.

1. *agricultural revolution*   The introduction of technology and practices—iron plows, nailed horseshoes, reclaimed lands, horses replacing oxen—that resulted in a large increase of available food. Also new crops from America—potatoes, corn, beans, manioc, and sweet potatoes—were spread worldwide.

   _____

   _____

   _____

2. *superimposed parts*   The process of absorbing the beliefs, institutions, and structures of two or more societies into a new culture (for example, American Indian traditions into Spanish culture and Catholicism).

   _____

   _____

   _____

3. *biological exchange*   The interchange of disease between two groups of people without previous contact—caused devastating results as measles, mumps, smallpox, and other diseases wiped out Indian villages and when syphilis spread throughout Europe.

   _____

   _____

   _____

4. *encomienda*   Spanish rights over the land and labor of groups of Indian villages that led to a wealthy Spanish elite and a poor Indian peasantry.

   _____

   _____

   _____

5. *"Protestant wind"*   The storm that destroyed many Catholic Spanish ships during the invasion of Protestant England in 1588.

   _____

   _____

   _____

6. *mercantilism*   The economic theory that encourages a nation to export more goods than it imports, thereby establishing a favorable balance of trade. Colonies help this process.

_____

_____

_____

7. *joint-stock company*   Business organization that allows a merchant or investor to join with others in a commercial enterprise and risk only the share invested in the company.

_____

_____

_____

8. *indentured servant*   The contractual relationship whereby a person could receive passage to America in exchange for an agreement to work for four to seven years for the person who paid for the passage.

_____

_____

_____

9. *enclosures*   The practice by English landowners of fencing off agricultural lands in order to raise sheep, thus forcing farmers off the land.

_____

_____

_____

10. *marine technology*   Those inventions and developments that enabled European ships to sail long distances across the Atlantic and Pacific out of sight of land: chronometers, astronomical instruments, charts of ocean currents, accurate maps, and new arrangements of sails.

_____

_____

_____

ANSWERS

The correct sequence of events and their dates.

1. 3; 75,000–10,000 B.C.
2. 6; 1215
3. 5; 1492–1504
4. 4; 1517
5. 8; 1518–30

6. 1; 1519–21
7. 10; 1588
8. 7; 1607
9. 2; 1620
10. 9; 1624

PART II
Developing Thinking Skills

SKILL EXERCISE ONE: FACT, INFERENCE, OR OPINION

Although visual and material history and the analysis of artifacts have recently become of increasing importance to those who study history, historians spend most of their time using written historical records and statements made about them in books and articles. There are three basic classifications of all statements made about history. It is an important skill for the history student to be able to distinguish among the three, described here.

Factual-Descriptive Statements   These statements are presented in a form that claims to correspond to reality. They describe events, developments, and situations about which, through careful research, the historian can determine the truth or falsity beyond a reasonable doubt. The form of the statement lends itself to verification. An example is, "The Civil War battle at Gettysburg took place in July of 1863."

Inferential-Analytical Statements   Inference can be defined as a logical conclusion from given data. The writer goes beyond the statement of fact to interpret, draw inferences, and project implications from the fact or facts. These statements contain elements of the historian's own viewpoint or logical induction, an attachment of insightful meaning to the inert facts. An example is, "The battle of Gettysburg was the decisive turning point of the Civil War." This may be considered "true" by many historians, but it remains an interpretation, open to questions and to disagreement.

Opinion-Conviction Statements   Although in some cases difficult to separate from the inferential statements, these sentences tend to be generalizations or moral and ideological viewpoints that stretch beyond the possibilities of gathering convincing supportive evidence. They often involve a very subjective judgment with which there may be widespread disagreement. These statements emanate not from careful research, but from a religious, philosophical, or political ideology, and contain an appeal to authority, to intuition, or even to prejudice. They appear among the general public, among politicians, and from those with a strong ideological bent. An example is, "Divine Providence gave the North the victory over the South at the battle of Gettysburg."

For each of the statements below write the type of statement (factual, inferential, or opinion) and explain why you consider it to be that type. Check your choices with those suggested. (*Note:* The answers offered are not always to be taken as the only possible answers. You may disagree and present arguments and evidence to support your judgment.)

1. The fact that two large continents were situated between Asia and Europe was slow to dawn upon the Europeans.

   _____

   _____

2. The Incas of Peru controlled a thousand-mile empire connected by an elaborate system of roads.

   _____

   _____

3. Since the Aztecs were barbaric savages, Cortez took the only course open to him and destroyed their power.

_____

_____

4. The plants and animals of Europe and America revealed as much, if not more, variety than the people and the cultures of the two areas.

_____

_____

5. New World foods that were unknown in Europe included the potato, corn, manioc, the peanut, the avocado, and the tomato.

_____

_____

6. Cortez's subjugation of the Aztecs with only six hundred men plus some Indian allies represents the greatest military accomplishment in history.

_____

_____

7. The Spanish writer Lope de Vega in his play *The New World* has a character argue that the motivation of the conquistadors was a selfish desire for gold and silver.

_____

_____

_____

ANSWERS AND EXPLANATIONS

The student should feel free to disagree and argue against the suggested designations. (*Note:* We are not interested in whether the statement is indeed true or false, but in classifying the statement in one of the three categories.)

1. Even though this statement uses the word "fact," the essence of the statement is the words "slow to dawn." Historians may indeed gather evidence to support this statement, but it is an *inference,* not a fact. It is, perhaps, drawn from many facts, but could not be proven with any degree of certitude. "Slow to dawn" is vague and open to many questions.

2. Although the word "thousand" may not be the exact distance and the word "elaborate" implies some subjective interpretation, the statement is a *factual-type* statement. Research can substantiate the essence of this statement.

3. Too many generalizations and loaded words are included to make this anything but an *opinion.* The words "barbaric savages" are very subjective and the word "only" cuts off various other possibilities that were open to Cortez.

4. This sounds like a factual statement except for the words "as much, if not

more." It is a judgment and a generalization for which much evidence could be gathered. It is an *inference* from facts.

5. This is a *factual-type* statement. Research can be done (and has been done) to establish the validity of this statement.

6. This may be true. But the words "greatest" and "in history" make it an *inference* from the facts. Whenever the words "greatest . . . in history" appear the historian is wary of the claim.

7. This is somewhat tricky. Of course the statement on motivation is an inference. But since the writer *did* have his character argue the source of motivation, it becomes a *factual-type* statement. The main thrust of this statement is what Lope de Vega had his character argue, not whether the argument itself was a fact.

Using a textbook or another history book and your imagination (especially for the opinion statements), write below another example of each of the three types of statements used in the above exercise. Use the same historical period and topic.

Factual Statement _____

_____

Inferential Statement _____

_____

Opinion Statement _____

_____

FURTHER QUESTIONS

1. Would an article containing only factual statements be interesting reading? Why or why not?

_____

_____

_____

2. Cruelty is defined as "causing, or fitted to cause, pain or grief . . . inhuman treatment." Would the following statement be a fact, an inference, or an opinion? Explain your choice. "The Spanish were cruel in their treatment of the Indians."

_____

_____

_____

SKILL EXERCISE TWO: PERCEIVING SIMILARITIES AND DIFFERENCES

The ability to make comparisons, to identify similarities and differences in two sets of data, is a fundamental thinking skill. The successful thinker is one who is alert enough to notice resemblances between distinct and seemingly unrelated events and developments and, at the same time, is aware of variances in two events that, on the surface, seem very much alike. This is a discrimination that encourages acute observation and thoughtful insight.

No two historical events are the same. Yet many are similar, so much so that often historians make an effort to form generalizations covering several events or they elicit lessons from what seems to be a repetition of very similar events. Drawing forth generalizations and lessons can be a deceptive enterprise. The careful historian will be quick to point out the elements of dissimilarity in two events or situations that seem to be almost identical. Noticing these differences and pointing out similarities in what is presented as two diverse situations is a sign of mature thinking. This skill enables the student to compare phenomena and yet retain the ability to perceive contrasts. Also, placing events and situations side by side in a comparative analysis often results in insights into each of them that cannot be gained by studying them separately.

Below are descriptions of the Spanish and of the English expansion into and colonization of America in the sixteenth and seventeenth centuries. Read each carefully looking for similarities and differences. Then answer the questions based on the two descriptions. Some items of comparison are suggested.

The Spanish

In the beginning of the sixteenth century, the Spanish brought their European culture to the New World. They fought the Native Americans and forced them to work for long hours in mines and later on plantations. A large number of Spaniards then came to America, and people from other areas of Europe were not allowed. Missionaries from Spain built mission stations and converted large numbers of Native Americans to Catholic Christianity, but the Native Americans were still kept in an inferior position in society. Religion became a strong tie to bind the colonies to Spain. The Spanish intermarried with the Native Americans and soon produced a large population of *mestizos*, part Native American and part Spanish. The government and economy were directly controlled by Spain in an authoritarian manner and did not allow for representative institutions or for much economic enterprise outside the government-sanctioned system. Gold and silver from America in the sixteenth century added $30 million annually to the Spanish economy. On a local level wealthy landowners dominated the government, and in most cases purchased their positions on the town council from the Spanish king. The Spanish way of life—language, dress, customs, architecture, and religion—became a part of life for the transplanted Spaniards and for the Native Americans. Blacks were brought in as slaves and large numbers were worked to death on sugar plantations in the West Indies.

The English

The English first settled in America on a permanent basis in 1607. They attempted to maintain their English traditions in their small settlements and to preserve their protestant Christianity. Numerous battles against the Native Americans resulted, in nearly all cases, in the Native Americans withdrawing further inland to the West. The English did not live among the Native Americans. They soon opened up settlement to people from other European nations. There were very few English missionary enterprises to the Native Americans and hardly any offspring between the English and Native Americans. Many of the English settlers had left England because they refused to conform to the established church, the Church of England. The English government formed a very loose connection with the colonies and allowed representative decision-making bodies (assemblies) to emerge. Local governmental structures varied, but were often under the control of local citizens—sometimes with decisions taking place by all male residents of a town or area. Private companies established the colonies and both settlers and the companies sought profits from trade. Tobacco became the earliest cash crop and farm produce, lumber, and naval stores were also sold. Although these settlers were at first predominately English, later German, Dutch, French, and Scotch-Irish habits and ways influenced the culture. Blacks were introduced as servants and increased in number throughout the seventeenth century. Soon they and their families were legally bound as slaves and worked mostly on southern plantations. They increased in number largely through natural births. The English struggled against the Spanish to the south and the French to the north and west.

QUESTIONS

1. What do you observe as the most important *differences* between the Spanish involvement in America and the English experience in America? List these and explain under each what might be some of the results of these differences.

   _____

   _____

   _____

2. What are some of the important *similarities* in the involvement of the Spanish and the English in America? List these.

   _____

   _____

   _____

3. Use your textbook and other sources, along with some insightful analysis, to find other similarities and differences not evident in the above descriptions (for example, climatic factors or the level and types of Native American culture in the two regions of settlements).

   _____

   _____

   _____

4. Would you consider the similarities greater than the differences or the differences greater than the similarities? Why?

   _____

   _____

   _____

5. What were the major *consequences* in subsequent history and cultural development that stem from these early differences between the English and Spanish experiences in America? Use your knowledge of North America and Central and South America in contemporary times.

_____

_____

_____

SUGGESTED ANSWERS

Differences

1. Intermarriage with Native Americans

2. Century of settlement

3. Missionary activity

4. Foreign rivals

5. Governmental system—colonial and local

6. Type of resources

7. Economic systems and policies

8. Culture of each region

9. Religion and religious connection with the European country

Similarities

1. Treatment of the Native Americans

2. European culture

3. Christianity

4. Profits and economic gain

5. Slavery

6. "Invasion" of Indian lands rather than building trading posts and peaceful relations with the Indians

PART III
Debating Historical, Social, and Moral Issues

QUESTIONS FOR THOUGHT

There are no definitive or correct answers to most of the questions that appear at the end of each chapter. But they are worthy of consideration because they stir up our minds to think, to imagine, to ponder, to debate, to search for evidence, to formulate reasoned arguments, and to form tentative opinions. These questions lead us to consider issues encountered by the historian. They challenge us to extend our minds beyond the memorization of the logical arrangement of data. They place us in the psychological mode of deliberating about an open-ended problem or issue, and as a result, accumulating data and arguments as evidence to help formulate temporary answers. Students must think seriously about these questions and, with the appropriate gathering of and use of evidence and arguments, develop their own answers. These answers might then form a basis for class discussion, an interchange of viewpoints with other students and with the instructor.

1. The "Black Legend" view of Spanish colonization involves a condemnation of Spanish behavior as cruel and brutal, and as a case of ruthless exploitation of the Native Americans. Proponents of this view conclude that in the encounter between the two cultures it was the Spanish who were uncivilized and barbaric. It was the Spanish who committed genocide (wholesale killing of a race of people). Is this view valid? Could an argument be made that the Spanish, in the construction of missions, their evangelism, and their intermarriage with the Native Americans, dealt with the Native Americans in a more humane manner than the English treatment of the North American Indians (a refusal to intermarry, few efforts to convert them, and continual warfare and confiscation of their lands)? Explain.

   _____

   _____

   _____

   _____

   _____

2. Is it valid for the historian to argue that Columbus has received more praise than he deserves because someone would have eventually discovered America anyway? Explain. Is Columbus a "hero" in history or an inaccurate cartographer (misjudging the size of the earth) who was very persuasive and stubborn, and who happened to be in the right place at the right time? Explain.

   _____

   _____

   _____

   _____

   _____

3. Some historians have argued that the biological exchanges—potatoes, corn, tomatoes, beans, and so forth—were more important than the extraction of gold and silver from Mexico and Peru. Do you agree? Why? Is this a case in which the unintended results of an enterprise (biological exchanges) are just as important as the intended results (gold and silver)? Explain.

_____

_____

_____

_____

4. Should the Christian religion (Catholic and Protestant) be considered an important cultural contribution of the Europeans to the Native Americans? Why or why not? Does an affirmative answer here reflect a cultural bias in favor of a "superior" European outlook on life? Explain.

_____

_____

_____

_____

_____

5. In this chapter two designations have been used for the people who inhabited America before Columbus—Indians and Native Americans. Which titles are preferable? Why? Do decisions about designations such as this reflect attitudes, assumptions, and interpretations about history? Explain. Should we label Cortez and Pizarro "explorers" or "conquering soldiers"? Why?

_____

_____

_____

_____

6. One historian's view is that the arrival of Europeans in America should be considered an "invasion" of America, which contained an advanced civilization with a large population. Do you agree or disagree? Why?

_____

_____

_____

_____

7. Columbus decided to embark across the Atlantic due to an error in his calculations of the size of the earth. Cortez arrived in Mexico just as suppressed Indian groups were rebellious against the Aztecs. The Pilgrims found friendly Indians who helped them survive at Plymouth. How much does luck, timing, coincidence, and chance play in the developments of history? Is this "blind" fate or is there some grand design for history? Explain.

_____

_____

_____

_____

_____

8. How does the historian deal with the concept of a "Protestant Wind" or the sentence, "God's breath dispersed a thousand ships" in reference to the storms that contributed to the destruction of the Catholic Spanish fleet in the Spanish effort to invade Protestant England in 1588? Is divine intervention a factor to seriously consider? Why or why not? Should the historian consider religious beliefs as an important factor in history, but not include the supernatural intervention in history that is often a fundamental part of that belief? Explain.

_____

_____

_____

_____

_____

9. Certainly great suffering occurred when Europeans arrived in the New World in the sixteenth and seventeenth centuries. Historians have debated the element of guilt and the degree of accountability for that suffering. Consider the following views:

A. Francis Parkman viewed the European exploration and colonization as a sign of progress. A backward, primitive people were defeated. Civilization advanced with the founding of cities, the spread of Christianity, the establishment of universities, and the development of the economy, especially the proper use of land for crops. There was room for pride of accomplishment in the activities of soldiers, missionaries, and settlers. Other historians supported Parkman by noting the respect and honesty of many Puritans and Quakers in their relations with Native Americans. They emphasized that often violence between the two cultures was based on efforts by the Europeans to defend themselves.

B. Several historians, especially in the 1960s and 1970s, have attempted to revise this view. They point out that the Native Americans practiced a sophisticated viable culture and actually assisted Europeans to survive in America. The Europeans were aggressive, disregarded the culture and rights of Native Americans, and the proper word for exploration is really "invasion." In essence, the colonization was a criminal act of fraud and violence to destroy a highly developed culture.

With which of these views do you most agree? Why?

_____

_____

_____

If the second view is the correct one, do governments now owe "reparations" to Native Americans and should they attempt to make amends in the return of land and the payment of compensation? Why or why not?

_____

_____

_____

What is the place of judgment in history? Can the modern historian apply current moral standards to the period of exploration and colonization? Why or why not?

_____

_____

_____

10. Consider the quotations at the beginning of the chapter. Explain their meaning and implication, and whether you agree or disagree with each quote.

_____

_____

_____

_____

_____

THOUGHTS FOR QUESTIONS

Compare these reflections with your own answers to the Questions for Thought. Feel free to agree or disagree.

1. Civilization is a difficult term to define. The Spanish, because of superior military ability and the biological weapon of disease, were able to exploit the Native Americans. However, to say that the Aztecs were not cruel or would have treated the Spanish with brutality had they had the opportunity is to be shortsighted. Behavior is uncivilized and barbaric, not a culture or a people.

The Spanish at least lived among the Indians and made an effort to integrate them into their culture albeit at a lower rung in the social ladder. Intermarrying shows acceptance. Warfare ended rather quickly in Spanish areas. Conversion is a type of cultural imperialism when viewed from today's standards, not from the standards of the sixteenth century. The history of the behavior of both the English and the Spanish remains a "black legend."

2. Ultimately this latter statement is true of every hero or great man (or woman) in history who is in the right place at the right time. Even though developments may evolve in much the same way, their courage, foresight, and perseverance can be praised. Columbus's act was a catalyst for a host of other developments; he set off a gigantic chain reaction, much of which might have occurred differently had the discovery been made years later. Yet one should be cautious in attributing too much influence to the single act of *one* individual. Consider Isabella, the charts of Henry the Navigator, the ninety crewmen, the supporters at the Queen's court, and so forth.

3. Certainly the ingots of silver attract more attention than the bag of seed potatoes; the gold basket is more alluring than a basket of yellow corn. Yet in the long run, the worldwide distribution of potatoes and corn probably influenced more people in positive ways than the gold and silver. Historians are doing more and more research on the influence of the normal, average, mundane items that have impact on the mass of people. Diet and health is one of these areas. Better health meant more babies survived and people had longer life expectancy. This dramatically increased population worldwide and had a variety of repercussions on politics, economics, diplomacy, and cultures.

4. A statement supporting one religion over another does indicate a "bias." It is obvious that at that time, most Europeans considered their Christian faith to be the only truth, superior to all other religions. However, the Christian religion also served as a vehicle to introduce ideas and art to America. The Spanish established schools and universities in America in the sixteenth century. Concepts and forms of art, music, and literature were developed and spread. One can question the degree to which the native population was actually introduced to this culture, other than in relation to the church routines. Even in this case the Church spread music, new moral principles, and philosophical ideas among the surviving native population. To what degree this means the emasculation of cultural values of the Indians and the Africans is debatable. Many of these values survived both outside the Church and even inside the Church.

5. Names do reflect inner attitudes. In a sense, there are no Native Americans— all migrated to the continent, earlier or later. "First Americans" might be an appropriate designation for those humans who were here first. The term "Native American" is bulky and long. The word "native" has a connotation of backwardness in some contexts. "Indian," in its derived etymology, is inaccurate, but as a commonly understood term is useful. Probably a revision of history-book terminology for this period is necessary. The perspective tends to be that of the European and the words to describe the period reflect this perspective. Labels often reflect bias, sometimes unconscious bias, and should be examined carefully. Should Aztec ceremony be called a "bloody, cruel human sacrifice" or a "priestly function to assure the sun's progression"?

6. A description of what took place in the one hundred and fifty years after Columbus would fit the dictionary definition of "invasion." Whether Europeans had a right to settle in America in what they considered to be sparsely populated areas (ecologists and demographers might view it differently) is debatable. The American nations have allowed immigration for centuries and are often criticized as nativists if they try to raise barriers to immigration. Assuming that the migration of people is a natural right, the question of forceful penetration and violent resistance in specific

cases is an issue. William Penn learned an Indian language, treated Indians fairly, and paid them for land. But he was exceptional. "Invasion" seems an adequate descriptive noun.

7. We often notice the coincidence when it is successful, but ignore the times when the elements of luck or timing fail. The first efforts at English colonization failed. But either way the element of chance raises its head in most historical contexts. Like the physical scientist, the historian believes that eventually the meticulous details of history will yield rational explanations rather than "luck," but in both disciplines, probability prevails. Both Columbus and Cortez showed courage and resolve. The pilgrims were a friendly people sharing a thanksgiving meal with the Indians. Success may not be due so much to chance as to the character, behavior, and planning of participants, and man-made circumstances. A storm helped defeat the Armada, yet the British strategy was excellent and the Spanish ignored the frequency of storms at that time of year. Religious people argue that God is in the details.

Historians maintain that luck and coincidence are reduced in importance as we mine the resources thoroughly. Nevertheless, much in history seems to occur contrary to the predictions of data.

8. Here the historian sometimes separates a personal belief system from his function as a professional historian. Most scientists make a similar distinction. The historian searches for empirical answers, for "natural" explanations, for secular causes. Of course the religious beliefs of people in the past are significant and must be considered and weighed as factors in events and developments. But contentment with arguments that a divine intervention took place is not acceptable or adequate. The historian may personally believe that the hand of God is at work in history, but his calling is to explore, in as much detail as possible, the nonsupernatural answers to the phenomena of history.

9. Parkman is ethnocentric and describes the exploration from a European perspective. Yet few people given the choice of a tribal/hunting style of life over a "civilized" agrarian or urban existence would choose the former. In North America, the Indian was not really introduced to the desirable elements of European civilization so much as to the less desirable elements—guns, alcohol, and materialism. Isolated incidents of Puritan and Quaker kindness do not offset the overall attitude and behavior of English settlers toward the Indians.

In many cases no reasonable compensation in land is available. One cannot hunt in Central Park. In other cases, Indian tribes argue among themselves about former landholdings. Conquest is a technique of acquiring land and conquest over time offers some "legitimacy" to later claims. Did one Indian group take land from another in the 1400s? Is this to be returned to the original group? Are the Ainu people of Hokkaido entitled to all Japan? And how does one apply principles or rules to the Middle East situation with the many waves of people invading and controlling land areas there? Yet the mistreatment and disregard of Indians and their rights seems so obvious and so great, perhaps compensation is called for in specific claims based on treaty violations.

The student must decide the issue of judgment in history. If moral principles are absolute and universal, then they should apply throughout history, in which case the Spanish behaved immorally in the sixteenth century. If moral ideas are relative and must fit accepted standards of the times, then the Spanish did what was normally expected of a soldier and missionary in the moral atmosphere of the times. Operating without *any* moral absolutes leaves one in a wilderness of situation ethics that could lead to a justification of horrible incidents in history. But applying absolutes leads to the charge of self-righteous arrogance.

10. The quote by St. Augustine implies that whatever evil or harmful developments that take place in history can be accepted as long as the goal (in his case the expansion of Christianity) is being achieved. In the end, the good will prevail and the overall outcome will be beneficial. The evil is justified by the ultimate good. Do you agree?

When people act or make decisions, they most often do so without using all of the relevant information and through a process involving emotion, personal consideration, bias, and ambition, and without careful consideration of the long-term consequences. Yet historians seek to place a pattern of rational behavior on these actions and decisions as if the economic, social, and political causes explain, in a logical fashion, the causes of the event or decision. The realm of unreasonable behavior is often anathema to the historian who attempts to explain the past. There *must* be a "good reason!"

CHAPTER

2

THE ENGLISH COLONIES IN AMERICA

"The happiest hours of mankind are recorded in the blank pages of history."

Thomas Carlyle

"It is the mark of a civilized man that he seeks to understand his traditions and to criticize them, not to swallow them whole."

M. I. Finley

PART I
Acquiring Essential Data

ESSENTIAL DATES

Determine the correct sequence and write the approximate date for each of the following events.

1. The Glorious Revolution in England; William I to throne _____
2. Large migration of Puritans to New England begins. _____
3. Witchcraft trials in Salem, Massachusetts _____
4. Beginning of the French and Indian War in America _____
5. First Navigation Act is passed by Parliament. _____
6. Harvard College founded. _____
7. Beginning of smallpox inoculation in Boston _____
8. Proprietary grant of Pennsylvania to William Penn _____
9. Slavery is legalized in the southern colonies. _____
10. Great Awakening religious revival _____

ESSENTIAL CONCEPTS

Examine each concept and write what contemporary relevance it might have.

1. *enlightenment*   An intellectual movement in Europe and America that encouraged the use of reason and science and anticipated human progress.

   _____

   _____

   _____

2. *Puritans*   Protestant religious group that advocated a theology similar to Calvinism in Europe and intended to purify the Church of England from Catholic influences.

   _____

   _____

   _____

3. *proprietary*   Colonies such as Maryland and Pennsylvania that were grants by the King to small groups or individuals—settlers had to pay the proprietor for the use of land.

   _____

   _____

   _____

4. *ethnic mix* Especially in the middle colonies, settlers arrived from many areas of Europe—England, Scotland, Wales, Ireland, Switzerland, Finland, Holland, and Germany.

_____

_____

_____

5. *gentry* Large landholders of Virginia and South Carolina who combined a commercial crop, slave labor, and political power to dominate society and set models of conduct.

_____

_____

_____

6. *staples* Market crops often prized by England, but dependent on English merchants for commercial transactions—sometimes encouraged by subsidies from England (called bounties).

_____

_____

_____

7. *acculturation* The process by which black slaves assimilated into American society creating a new Afro-American subculture of distinct characteristics.

_____

_____

_____

8. *gentlefolks* The upper class in the colonies, often deferred to by their "inferiors" and entitled to wear certain clothes; sometimes referred to as "betters."

_____

_____

_____

9. *"best poor man's country"* Reference to the colonies as being a place of opportunity devoid of serious social restraints on mobility and without an established legal aristocracy.

_____

_____

_____

10. *pluralism* The diversity of faiths prompting colonists to move away from the demands for "one state, one church" to the acceptance and toleration of several religious groups.

_____

_____

_____

ANSWERS

The correct sequence of events and their dates.

1. 2; 1620
2. 6; 1636
3. 9; 1640
4. 5; 1651
5. 8; 1681

6. 1; 1688
7. 3; 1692
8. 7; 1720
9. 10; 1720s
10. 4; 1754

PART II
Developing Thinking Skills

SKILL EXERCISE ONE: QUESTIONING

Asking questions is a key to learning. It is instinctive among children. Yet very few times in formal schooling is the skill of asking appropriate questions practiced or taught. Too often the student is required only to answer questions, in many cases to answer with a single word, a true or false, or a correct letter for a multiple-choice test. Productive questioning by the student can lead to a wealth of insight and to a much deeper and more thorough understanding of a topic or issue. The student needs practice and guidance in the skill of asking questions.

Some questions are productive. They lead to more questions, bring out useful and helpful information, and are thought-provoking. Other questions are nonproductive, a dead end as far as analytical thinking or the stimulation of new ideas and thoughts.

Of course questions are related to the purpose of the questioner. A question about the birth date of Thomas Jefferson is not productive, but it might well be important if the historian is writing a biography of Jefferson. A question on the most prevalent method of preparing corn as human food in colonial Delaware would not normally be important to the general historian, but for a study of health and diet in the eighteenth century, it would be essential.

Assume a group of average history students is attempting to understand the "Influence of the Quakers on Colonial Pennsylvania." Examine carefully the following questions and write under each whether it is productive or nonproductive. Then explain why you have made that decision. Finally, for those that are nonproductive, explain how they might become productive under special conditions related to the purposes of the questioner.

1. What was the height and weight of Quaker William Penn in the year 1692?

_____

_____

2. What external characteristics marked a Quaker from other colonial people in Philadelphia?

_____

_____

3. Were the Quakers correct in their religious beliefs?

_____

_____

4. Since Quakers were strong believers in equality, what were the features of government established by the Quakers in Pennsylvania?

_____

_____

5. Did William Penn become seasick on his voyages across the Atlantic Ocean?

_____

_____

6. How did the Quakers treat blacks and the poor in Philadelphia?

_____

_____

7. Since the Quakers believed in a simple, humble life-style, what effect did wealth and political leadership responsibility have on their behavior?

_____

_____

8. How long did it take William Penn to learn the language of the Delaware Indians?

_____

_____

FURTHER QUESTIONS

1. Decide which question is the most productive of each of the following pairs and explain your choice in each case.

    A. (1.) What were the Quaker beliefs?
        (2.) In what ways were the Quaker beliefs similar and in what ways different from the teachings of the Church of England?

_____

_____

    B. (1.) In what specific ways did the Quakers apply their pacifist beliefs to colonial Pennsylvania and with what consequences?
        (2.) Was the Quaker belief in pacifism (no participation in or support of war) beneficial or harmful?

_____

_____

2. To what extent is it necessary to already know some information about a topic in order to ask productive questions? Give examples from the list of the eight questions in Skill Exercise One.

_____

_____

_____

3. Construct two productive and one unproductive question about the Quakers.

Productive

(1.) _____

_____

(2.) _____

_____

Unproductive _____

_____

ANSWERS AND EXPLANATIONS

    1. Unproductive. The answer here is inconsequential to our purposes. Perhaps the information would be useful in a biography of Penn or in an effort to determine the size of people in seventeenth-century Europe.

    2. Productive. Not only is this a matter of interest, but it also may reveal observable manifestations of Quaker beliefs.

    3. Unproductive. Correct from whose viewpoint? What is meant by correct and what standards could be used to establish correctness? A "yes" or "no" answer would be rather meaningless.

4. Productive. Since most of the world espoused inequality at the time, it becomes significant that the Quakers had an opportunity to form a new government based on different principles.

5. Unproductive, except for a biography or for a specialized study on ocean voyages in the seventeenth century. Otherwise, what is the difference whether he did or not?

6. Productive. This question calls for significant information about a religious group that had strict standards of equality. It is important to learn the application of their standards in a community in the seventeenth and eighteenth centuries.

7. Productive. The arrival of success and prosperity for a group that, by doctrine, normally rejects money and power, is an interesting and thought-provoking social problem.

8. Unproductive. It really doesn't matter except as data for a biography of Penn or for a study of native American languages. The fact that he learned their language is significant. The reasons why he learned their language and the consequences—what he proceeded to do with his knowledge—are important.

ANSWERS AND EXPLANATIONS FOR FURTHER QUESTION 1

A. Number 2 is the preferable question. It encourages learning with a purpose, in this case a higher-level skill of comparing. Not only does the answer yield knowledge of Quaker beliefs, but it also compares these beliefs to another set of doctrines of a rival religious group.

B. Number 1 is the preferable question. The second question calls for a one-word answer that is meaningless. Who can define beneficial and harmless in this context? The first question demands an examination of the actual Quaker influence in a historical context. The historian is much more comfortable seeking an answer to the first question.

SKILL EXERCISE TWO: DETERMINING RELEVANCE OF EVIDENCE

The historian cannot present *all* the data on a major event or development. In that case the history student would be reading multivolume works on each historical period. The historian must condense, discriminate, and choose from among a multitude of data too plentiful for the average student to study in the time allotted. In the writing of history, the historian is obligated to pick what is to be included and excluded. The key to this process is *relevance*. Historians must determine whether a bit of information, an idea, or an insight is related in an important way to the understanding of the topic or thesis. They may have to drop information and ideas that are true and interesting, but are not relevant to an understanding of the topic or thesis. Sometimes this is a subjective choice, but in most cases historians can agree on the relevance or irrelevance of much of the data. Of course nearly all data could be relevant dependent on the purposes of the historian. Data on what Thomas Jefferson normally had for breakfast would not be important for a study of his contribution to the American Revolution, but it may be important for a study of food and diet in the eighteenth century. The determination of relevance is a vital skill not only for the historian and the history student, but also for anyone who presents a thesis or viewpoint and then offers evidence, arguments, and examples to support that viewpoint.

Examine carefully the following statements of data related to the given topic. Under each indicate whether the data is relevant or irrelevant to the topic. Then explain briefly your decision. Compare your choices with those offered after the questions.

TOPIC: WOMEN IN COLONIAL VIRGINIA

1. The average family in Virginia contained four to six children.

   _____

   _____

2. When a woman married in colonial America, she agreed to honor and obey her husband and to be in "reverend subjection" to him.

   _____

   _____

3. Men outnumbered women by as much as three to two in early New England.

   _____

   _____

4. The log cabin was introduced by early Swedish settlers along the Delaware River, but was not used on the frontier until the 1700s.

   _____

   _____

5. In Virginia the woman turned over to her husband whatever property she possessed before marriage.

   _____

   _____

6. At the age of sixteen, Eliza Lucas managed three plantations in South Carolina and aided in developing the growth of indigo (a blue dye).

   _____

   _____

7. Childbirth was painful for women in colonial Virginia.

   _____

   _____

8. Women in the colonies were employed as doctors, printers, painters, silversmiths, and shipwrights, and also served as tavern hostesses and shopkeepers.

   _____

   _____

List four other items of *relevant* data that you would like to have available in order to better understand the topic. Do not list the actual data, but ask for a *type* of information.

1. _____

2. _____

3. _____

4. _____

QUESTIONS

1. Would several historians be likely to choose most of the same information as relevant about any topic or thesis? Why or why not? Check this by comparing two United States history textbooks for data on the above topic. Note the similarities and differences. Is "relevance" obvious to any thinking person? Explain.

   _____

   _____

   _____

2. Would a male historian likely choose different items of information than a female historian on this topic? Why or why not? Would a textbook published in the 1980s likely have more data and ideas on this topic than one published in the 1950s? Why? Does "relevance" change over time?

   _____

   _____

   _____

3. Do you think that once a topic such as "Women in Colonial America" has been established as a viable and worthwhile topic, we tend to notice and "find" resources because the topic has become important? Explain.

   _____

   _____

   _____

4. Is *all* history potentially important, dependent on the purposes of the historian? For example: "A woman in Ephrata, Pennsylvania, baked corn bread on Saturday morning, 7 September, 1761." Can you conceive this fact being important for the historian in any research or writing? Explain.

   _____

   _____

   _____

ANSWERS AND EXPLANATIONS

1. Relevant. The woman bore and cared for the children. This statement reveals the extent of some of her work.

2. Relevant. This indicates the social relationship between husband and wife and the existing expectations of society. Of course reality might have been somewhat different.

3. Irrelevant. Although a ratio similar to this may have existed in Virginia also, the historian cannot transfer the data automatically to another colony.

4. Irrelevant. This was not in Virginia and does not indicate that the custom spread into Virginia.

5. Relevant. This shows the economic status of the woman as a dependent of the husband.

6. Irrelevant. It does reveal the responsibilities of women in the colonies, but not necessarily in Virginia. One might assume that if this happened in South Carolina then it probably did in Virginia, but this process of implication is dangerous. Opportunities might have been different in Virginia.

7. Irrelevant. Of course the fact that women brought forth children in pain is significant, but it is universal and not peculiar to Virginia. It is also a "common knowledge" statement that is probably not important to express.

8. Relevant. Although the statement does not specifically name Virginia, there is no reason to believe that Virginia was an exception, nor is data given to exclude Virginia. It is important to know that women were engaged in the professions and other diverse occupations.

PART III
Debating Historical, Social, and Moral Issues

QUESTIONS FOR THOUGHT

1. Puritans were very intolerant, sometimes harsh, and self-righteous in many ways. Yet they produced a stimulating cultural life, promoted education, and established churches and towns on a democratic basis. Can their narrowness be excused, considering the aura of the times and their positive contributions to American life? To what degree must the historian take into account the "accepted behavior of the times" in evaluation of the attitudes and behavior of people of the past? Explain.

_____

_____

_____

_____

_____

2. The Puritans tried to establish a closed religious community. When Quakers arrived in Massachusetts to preach Quakerism, the Puritans warned them, threw them out of Boston, and, when the Quakers persisted, hanged two of them. Do you blame the Quakers or the Puritans? Why?

_____

_____

_____

_____

_____

3. Early New England farmers lived together in towns. Their fields were held in scattered strips of land outside of town. Later arrivals built houses out in the fields and consolidated their land holdings around their separate houses. Which social structure of a farm area is most beneficial to a community and its inhabitants—the town community or the farmhouses scattered over a wide area? Why?

_____

_____

_____

_____

_____

4. Some slaves were captured in Africa by other Africans. They were sold at ports and then transported by sea captains (many from New England) across the Atlantic to the West Indies or to the southern colonies (through Sullivan's Island in Charleston Harbor). There they were sold by slave traders to planters who kept them and their children in perpetual servitude. Leaders in the northern and middle colonies (Quakers being a notable exception) acquiesced and even agreed to give legal recognition to the institution of slavery in the American Constitution. Which of the groups bear the most blame for the existence of slavery in North America—the Africans, the traders, the transporters, the slaveholders, or the northern leaders? Why? What problems arise in an effort to ascribe guilt in history? Are we better off declaring no one guilty or all equally guilty? Explain.

_____

_____

_____

_____

_____

5. Many religious groups came to America: Anglicans, Presbyterians, Puritans, Quakers, Dutch Reformers, Anabaptists, Lutherans, Jews, and so forth. After the Great Awakening of the 1730s and 1740s many of these groups split. Baptists soon appeared and later Methodists. Division and subdivision continued. Is

this division and multitude of religious groups a sign of strength or of weakness in American religion? Explain.

_____

_____

_____

_____

_____

6. Williamsburg, Virginia, has been restored to much as it was in the 1700s. Houses, shops, and government and old William and Mary College buildings are all arranged as they would have been in that period. Some people trained in the speech and history of the 1700s converse with visitors as if they were back in the eighteenth century. Of what value is all of this in really understanding the past? Of what importance is it to the historian? Is antiquarianism (an interest in material goods of the past, implying value and intrinsic worth) an important aspect of history? Explain.

_____

_____

_____

_____

_____

7. Mercantilism was an economic system designed to foster the wealth and commercial well-being of the European nations. It required a favorable balance of trade, and, in relation to the thirteen colonies, that colonial areas existed for England's benefit. Historians have debated the fairness of the system—was it a mechanism for oppression, or a smoothly functioning system to benefit all segments of the Empire? George Bancroft, a nineteenth-century historian, viewed the system as one designed to thwart initiative and to place unfair artificial controls on the colonial economy, restrictions that benefited only England. Lawrence Gipson judged mercantilism to be a logical system that had many benefits for colonists: protection of the British navy, supplying markets, credit, insurance, and middlemen, and so forth. The colonists in turn were selfish and shortsighted. The moderate taxation the British required was light and easy to pay. After you consider the elements of the mercantilist system, which of these views—Bancroft's or Gipson's—seems the accurate one? Why?

_____

_____

_____

_____

_____

8. Two strains of thought had spread through the colonies by the 1750s. One of these emphasized spiritual aspects of life, a revealed truth, a doctrinal certainty in religion, a submission of the mind to scriptures, and an emphasis on feeling and emotion in producing a viable life and society. The other emphasized the mind, reason, and the use of empirical evidence before settling on beliefs. Truth was to be discovered by investigation and thinking. This process would produce a better world, one structured to meet the needs of society, and a well-ordered, balanced life for the individual. To which of these approaches would you have gravitated? Explain.

_____

_____

_____

_____

_____

9. Quakers dominated politics in Pennsylvania down to the middle of the eighteenth century. Quakers were pacifists; they frowned on the appropriation of colonial funds for gunpowder or for military purposes. Meanwhile, on the Pennsylvania frontier, clashes took place between the settlers (many Scotch-Irish Presbyterians) and Indians. The settlers requested funds for military support and troops to help them against the Indians. Eventually the Quakers withdrew from politics. Was this a wise and proper decision on their part? Why or why not?

_____

_____

_____

_____

_____

10. Several people were hanged as witches in New England in 1692–1693. Before the trials, cows died mysteriously, young girls became hysterical, wounds appeared on bodies, and several of the accused admitted that they were, indeed, witches. Could we conclude that witchcraft was, as understood at that time, being practiced in Salem in 1692, and that the citizens of the town had a responsibility to protect themselves from witches? Explain.

_____

_____

_____

_____

11. The British looked at representative government in a different manner than colonists. To the British, a representative chosen by a few eligible voters in a district would represent the entire nation, not a particular constituency. Indeed,

elected representatives would not even have to reside in the district from which they were elected. The representative would not be bound by the narrow interests of a geographical area. This was called *virtual* representation. The colonists had developed, in the eighteenth century, a system whereby elected representatives reflected and promoted local interests and were required to reside among their constituents. They were spokespersons for their districts and reported back to their districts. Which of these systems do you believe best demonstrates the true meaning of representative government? Why?

_____

_____

_____

_____

_____

12. Consider the quotations at the beginning of the chapter. Explain their meaning and implication, and whether you agree or disagree with each quote.

_____

_____

_____

_____

_____

THOUGHTS FOR QUESTIONS

1. Puritans have acquired a bad name in history. As a frontier community faced with survival, they organized with strict rules and forced conformity to community values. They acted much as other societies did at that time. This defense is not to excuse harshness, oppression, and intolerance. Their remarkable accomplishments in education, science, and theological thought is unusual under the circumstances. Several historians have sought to "recover the reputation" of the Puritans and, to some extent, have done so.

2. We operate today under an ethic that urges acceptance of those who differ. Religious freedom sometimes reflects lack of religious commitment. Quakers, to some extent, had a martyr complex. Using the value of religious toleration, a present-day American value, we criticize the Puritans. Yet it may be deemed foolish or perhaps heroic to preach against the wishes of a community when there is a real threat of death.

3. Most agrarian structures throughout history have centered on a community of people who live together in a village. Often farm work was done in a cooperative manner. However, the abundance of land, an inclination for land speculation, and an emerging individualism prompted the separation of farmhouses. This pattern continued on the western frontier. It resulted in loneliness and a reluctance to seek community assistance in production and marketing. Yet, it provided social freedom and family-oriented behavior.

4. It is difficult to ascribe guilt by percentages or degrees; however, to indict everyone equally is irresponsible. Everyone certainly bears some guilt in the slave phenomena. Some groups spoke out in opposition—especially Quakers and Methodists. The economic gain that led to the demand for slaves centered on southern planters and Caribbean sugar growers. Without this demand there would have been no slave trade. Of course all of those involved gained financially. In some respects Africans who hunted down, captured, and enslaved other Africans bear primary guilt. One could argue that the Founding Fathers had little option if their higher goal was to form a viable nation. Each group had excuses and could point the finger at others. Historians must deal with this complexity in every social issue or moral question in history.

5. Division is to be expected of a society that is multiracial, multiethnic, and large in geographical spread. It is a way of meeting individual needs in a personal way. However, it does lead to much religious bickering and controversy and interferes with combining efforts toward accomplishing Christian goals. And, as diverse groups claim attachment to absolute truth, it raises doubts about the authenticity and accuracy of proclamations and creeds. They cannot all be right. The irony is that tightly structured, numerous denominations may have promoted diversification in politics and social structure as well as religion. It was impractical to insist on a unified belief system in the face of such diversity.

6. Professional historians encourage any interest in the past. But the mere collection and display of artifacts from the past is not a historian's aim. Material culture is becoming of increasing importance, but only if it is analyzed and scrutinized to reveal insights into significant issues regarding those who used the items. The arrangement of a colonial kitchen may be of interest to a tour group, but the historian would ask about the implications related to the woman's place in colonial society or to family organization and responsibility. Trained guides can give a sense of the past, and can raise issues that were important to people living in Williamsburg during the colonial period. Nearly all historians do see worth in artifacts, but usually attempt to move beyond the object to the significance of the object—an inquiry into how it fits in a scheme of the past.

7. For the period before 1763, one would have to favor Gipson's view. Although colonists, at times, lacked hard currency and were upset at restrictions on the processing of finished goods (iron products or beaver skins), the benefits seemed to outweigh the disadvantages. Some benefits were accepted without notice and only became evident after the Revolution for independence. However, the regulations and taxation that came after 1763 may not seem as beneficial. Enforcement of regulations that had been ignored previously was irritating. Inherent in mercantilism was political domination by England. This was exercised more and more in economic regulations and sanctions. The tie between economic freedom and political liberty was already accepted by the colonists. Gipson counted and produced economic statistics; and, in this realm, he may have been accurate. But the political implications were much more emotional and thus more likely to lead to violence. Colonists believed that many precedents were being set that could severely hamper the colonial economy. The most effective device to get the attention of Parliament was a boycott of English goods. This indicates the value of the colonies as a market, a value that the British should have recognized. What type of statistics do you think Gipson used to acquire data on the positive influences of the British mercantile system?

8. This is the student's choice. The democratic process and governmental institutions were probably based more on the latter than the former.

9. When saying that the Quakers withdrew from politics, one is assuming that they *could* have continued to hold power in Philadelphia. This is debatable. It does represent a withdrawal of principles of conduct from serious consideration in political debate. Should the pacifist view have a significant place in the dark reality of political turmoil? Most pacifist groups—Quaker, Mennonite, Brethren—have abstained from political involvement, at least until recent times. Is pacifism unrealistic or even dangerous if injected into politics and diplomacy? Or has that approach never really been tried? Or did the Quakers try it in the early eighteenth century and decide it would not work? (At least two presidents—Herbert Hoover and Richard Nixon—came from Quaker backgrounds).

10. It is difficult to argue on behalf of Puritans hanging witches. Recent studies have emphasized the social and economic turmoil, the arrival of outsiders, and even the influence of a young immigrant from the West Indies as factors in this unfortunate incident; but the community did feel threatened. Strange events took place, events traditionally associated with witchcraft. Could the community plead self-defense? Are we to judge the Salem community in 1692 by standards of the late twentieth century? Are people still ostracized and harassed because they do not meet community standards?

11. The Supreme Court has decided that the American principle is one of direct and actual representation. And the American tradition, especially in the House of Representatives, has formed around the habit of going back to the people, the grass roots, by consulting the constituency. One difficulty with virtual representation is that many groups may be unrepresented. Who decides what interests need representation? One advantage of the British idea is that representatives, being detached from local pressures, can vote conscience; that is, can support what they consider best for the entire nation. Some nations such as Peoples' Republic of China have devised a system of dual representation whereby the Peoples' Congress has representatives not only from geographical areas but also from interest groups—labor unions, youth groups, women's organizations, and so forth. Is that a helpful system?

12. Carlyle maintains that people's lives are peaceful and content when not much of traditional historical significance is happening. Historians tend to dwell on wars, revolutions, painful upheavals, the unusual, and the agitation of society. During these times people suffer physically and endure the uncertainty of unrest. A Chinese curse says "May you live in exciting times." Yet perhaps the mundane needs to be interspersed with conflict in order for people to be "happy." For those who survive conflict and continue normal lives, the excitement may have been worth the risk. Do blank pages mean blank lives? Are most pages of history blank or filled?

Finley argues that the traditions and myths of history need to be scrutinized before acceptance. This is what the good historian intends to do in analytical research—to question, to doubt, to criticize, and to ask for evidence. Even the most sacred story from the past becomes a subject for examination, not a pleasant thought for those who thrive on accepted traditions and unquestioned assumptions about the past.

CHAPTER

3

FROM PROTEST TO REVOLUTION

"The chief lesson to be derived from the study of the past, is that it holds no simple lessons, and . . . the historian's main responsibility is to prevent anyone from claiming that it does."

Martin Duberman

"This I regard as history's highest function, to let no worthy action be uncommemorated, and, to hold out the reprobation of posterity as a terror to evil words and deeds."

Tacitus

PART I
Acquiring Essential Data

ESSENTIAL DATES

Determine the correct sequence and write the approximate date for each of the following events.

1. First Continental Congress meets in Philadelphia. _____

2. The Tea Act followed by the Boston Tea Party _____

3. Battle of Yorktown, Virginia, ending the American Revolution _____

4. Articles of Confederation go into effect. _____

5. Treaty of Paris ending the French and Indian War _____

6. Washington and his troops winter at Valley Forge. _____

7. Proclamation of the Declaration of Independence _____

8. Treaty of Paris is signed ending the American Revolution. _____

9. Stamp Act and Quartering Act are passed by British Parliament. _____

10. Period of "salutary neglect"—loose British colonial control over the colonies _____

11. The colonies organize governments and become states of "these United States." _____

12. Boston Massacre—British troops fire into a Boston crowd. _____

13. The Franco-American alliance against the British is signed. _____

14. Pennsylvania abolishes slavery. _____

15. Thomas Paine publishes *Common Sense.* _____

ESSENTIAL CONCEPTS

Examine each concept and write what contemporary relevance it might have.

1. *self-determination* The right of people in a geographical area to declare independence from previous political attachments in order to form their own government.

_____

_____

2. *inalienable rights* The belief that certain rights and privileges are available not because of the decisions of existing governments or by the agreement of a majority of citizens, but are acquired by being born into the human race.

_____

_____

3. *natural law*   The argument that beyond traditions or particular circumstances surrounding a situation, a law of nature exists that can be attained by the use of reason and that applies universally.

_____

_____

4. *no taxation without representation*   The concept that only by a vote of elected representatives can a government apply taxes to an individual's private possessions.

_____

_____

5. *patriot*   A person loyal to a government and willing to take action on its behalf. In the American Revolution, patriots were defined as those who fought under the Continental Congress against the British.

_____

_____

6. *dominion theory*   The belief that the American colonies owed loyalty only to the British monarchy and not to Parliament, and that their local Assemblies served as their own "parliaments."

_____

_____

7. *mercenary*   A soldier hired to fight. The British hired thirty thousand soldiers, mostly from Hesse-Kessell in Germany, to fight in America.

_____

_____

8. *common sense*   This concept became the title of a book by Thomas Paine that argued that King George III had usurped power and misused the colonies and, therefore, should be rejected as monarch of America.

_____

_____

9. *militia*   Part-time "amateur" soldiers. George Washington criticized them, but they rushed in to take charge whenever the British moved out of an area, thus preventing British hegemony over large areas in America.

_____

_____

10. *separate peace*   The French, allies of the Americans during the Revolution, did not want the Americans to make peace with Britain without their consent. A separate peace was made.

_____

_____

ANSWERS

Correct sequence of events and their dates.

1. 10; 1721–48
2. 5; 1763
3. 9; 1763
4. 12; 1770
5. 2; 1773
6. 1; 1774
7. 15; 1776
8. 7; 1776
9. 11; 1776
10. 6; 1777
11. 13; 1778
12. 14; 1780
13. 4; 1781
14. 3; 1781
15. 8; 1783

PART II
Developing Thinking Skills

SKILL EXERCISE ONE: CATEGORIZING AND CLASSIFYING

In reading and examining resources, the historian encounters a mass of data. This variety of information must be organized and assembled in a rational, usable form. The process of organizing this diverse data is an essential and primary skill for the historian and, obviously, is important in other areas of thinking, both academic and nonacademic. The mind cannot function well in the chaos of unrelated and disconnected data. Making sense out of random information is an indispensable skill in thinking.

The historian organizes data in several ways. Two of the most-often-used techniques are arranging information by rank or in distinct categories. To some extent all data arrangement is arbitrary and, to varying degrees, subjective. The plan, the structure, the paradigm placed (or at times imposed) on random information emerges from the mind of the historian. This mind-set may be under the influence of ideologies, or of the historian's background experiences, or may be related to some intent that the historian has decided on beforehand. Yet the historian would argue that the data "demands" to be placed in a certain set of categories, that the arrangement of data is obvious and falls into place naturally, as if it were meant to be that way. For example, a historian examining the battles of the American Revolution might conclude that some chronological sequence is a logical approach. Yet the diverse factors that caused the Revolution—such as political, economic, social, diplomatic, and cultural—seem to be obvious categories of organization. Without categories, the historian is left afloat in a sea of disorganized facts and inferences. Intelligent communication among scholars dictates presentations and papers arranged according to some scheme.

Causes and their effects are especially convenient to categorize for evaluation. Causes of an event can be structured in several ways. One approach is to divide them into "underlying" and "immediate." Another technique is to rank causes in order of importance. This ranking inevitably leads to disagreement and argument, but at the same time has at least two benefits. First, it does offer a viable way of arranging data for careful examination with a common basis for understanding and debate. Second, it serves to stimulate argument and leads the historian to further research and to more insightful thinking in the defense of a selected ranking. It can do the same for the history student.

Still another method of categorizing causes is separating information into prearranged topics. This also stimulates critical thinking and provides an arrangement for rational communication and a common ground for gathering evidence. Categorizing by topics and by ranking is especially useful when studying the causes of war or revolution. In the following exercise the student will employ the skills of both ranking and placing data in topics.

Below is a random listing of factors that probably had some influence on the coming of the American Revolution. Examine each carefully. Read your textbook or another history book for a more thorough understanding of each factor. Then place the factor under the appropriate topic headings that follow the list. For example, "British restrictions on colonial trade" is primarily an economic factor and should be placed in that category. Remember that the selected structure is somewhat arbitrary and is offered only as a convenient way of arranging data. It is not to be considered *the* accurate arrangement or *the* correct way of examining information. The purpose is to enable the student to discuss related data on common ground and in an organized manner.

Factors Related to the Outbreak of the American Revolution

1. The British Parliament taxed the colonies without any direct colonial representation in the Parliament.

2. The British limited colonial manufacturing through the Wool Act, the Hat Act, and the Iron Act.

3. British troops were stationed in American cities, along with British insistence that the Americans help pay for their necessities.

4. Americans defied British trade regulations, smuggled goods in and out illegally, avoided taxes, and bribed British officers.

5. The British restricted the rights of Americans by conducting illegal searches and denying trial by jury in smuggling cases.

6. Many colonial leaders felt they were looked down on and poorly treated by British officials and their American supporters.

7. The British Parliament, three thousand miles away, did not have good communications with American leaders and was not aware of moods and attitudes in the colonies.

8. The French were eliminated by the British victory in the French and Indian War (1754–1763), and thus removed as a threat to the colonies.

9. Parliament granted a virtual monopoly for the sale of tea in the colonies by the British East India Company, a monopoly that threatened the tea merchants and, if extended, other merchants as well.

10. The lower-class workers of Boston resented the presence of arrogant British troops who took jobs from them and as a "standing army" seemed to threaten their liberties.

11. Some radical American leaders (Sam Adams, especially) disliked the British and made use of inflammatory situations and propaganda to excite colonial mobs.

12. The British would not give recognition to colonial legislators as lawmaking bodies, but considered them primarily as administrative units.

13. French agents operated in the colonies to encourage opposition to England.

14. British officials in the colonies acted arrogantly, entrapped merchants in minor aspects of complex laws, and demanded bribes and payoffs.

15. Rumors spread that the Church of England was going to be "established" (taxes collected for its support) in all of the colonies, and that a bishop would be sent to America.

16. The British merchants and aristocracy (along with the monarchy) dominated Parliament, while the colonies had middle- and some lower-class influence in their local assemblies.

17. American merchants and landowners objected to trade restrictions and sought a free market and a competitive economic structure (absent of special benefits and privileges).

18. The British restricted expansion and migration into areas west of the Appalachian mountains, thus upsetting frontier settlers and land speculation by Americans.

19. The British believed in *virtual* representation (interest groups rather than population as a basis for representation) and the Americans believed in *actual* representation (representation based on the population of geographical units).

20. After 150 years of settlement in America, the colonial people had developed a different set of values and a culture that had drifted away from the British values and culture.

21. Of the many non-English settlers in the colonies, some disliked English power and influence: Scotch-Irish, Irish, Scotch, French, German, and Dutch.

Place the above items under the proper category below (by number): (*Note:* some may fit under more than one category.)

Political factors _____

_____

_____

Social factors _____

_____

_____

Economic factors _____

_____

_____

Cultural factors _____

_____

_____

Factors that do not fit above categories _____

_____

_____

What are some of the problems in attempting to fit the factors in these categories?

_____

_____

_____

Is this process rather arbitrary and subjective?

Ranking is also a way of arranging data for study and debate. Look again at the twenty-one factors and choose the three that you judge to be the most important. Explain why for each.

1. _____

_____

2. _____

_____

3. _____

_____

Now examine the four categories in which you placed the factors (political, social, economic, cultural). Rank these four from most important to least important. Explain why you ranked the one at the top of the list.

1. _____

2. _____

3. _____

4. _____

Note: Your ranking will probably not correspond with the rankings of all other students. You may be in the majority or in one of several minority rankings. It is beneficial to debate and defend your rankings against those of other students. Scholarly articles and even books have been written defending one or more of the twenty-one factors, and especially defending one of the categories as being the primary cause of the American Revolution. Not all are equally important. But ranking does stimulate the mind to formulate evidence, arguments, and counter-arguments—skills worthy of development and refinement.

1. How can one explain the dilemma that competent, professional historians, having carefully studied and gained command of the resources related to the Revolution, have arrived at conflicting conclusions about the primary cause of the American Revolution?

_____

_____

_____

2. Is the concept of multiple causation (many different causes or factors) always valid? Is multiple causation only an excuse for those who do not want to study the sources carefully enough to reach a conclusion about *the* cause? Is multiple causation closer to the truth than single causation about most events in history and in life?

_____

_____

_____

3. Which factors (if any) of the twenty-one listed were indispensable to the occurrence of the American Revolution; that is, if they had not been present, would the Revolution have taken place? Explain why. Is there a *synergistic* effect (an interaction of two or more factors to achieve a greater impact than when considered individually) among the various causes? Explain.

_____

_____

_____

4. How can the historian distinguish between a factor that "caused" an event to take place and a factor that happened to take place chronologically before the event? (For example, is the restriction on western settlement, the Proclamation Line of 1763, a "cause" of the Revolution?) Is there a tendency to label the development that takes place *before* a major event as being a *cause* of the event? Explain.

_____

_____

_____

SKILL EXERCISE TWO: EVALUATING ARGUMENTS

In any effort to support or dispute the validity and accuracy of an inferential statement (a statement inferred from data), the advocates and the opponents of the statement approach it with arguments based on one or more criteria. (See Chapter 1.) The inferential statement is *not* one that is in itself presented as factual; that is, it is not inherently true or false (such as "George Washington died in 1799"). The inferential statement is one drawn out of facts—an interpretation, a conviction, or a conclusion, (such as "George Washington was the indispensable man in the American Revolution"). The appeals to encourage acceptance of an inferential statement can be classified into five categories.

The appeal to *authority*. Here the historian refers to an expert or an *a priori* argument (one based on theory). This authority may be a person, a respected book, or an ideology (organized set of doctrines and theory).

The appeal to *reason*. In this case the historian relies on common sense or logic—a deductive process, a transaction taking place in the mind (such as, if we know *that* is true then it follows that *this* is true)—to convince the reader.

The appeal to *empirical evidence*. This argument is based on data supplied by experiment and scientifically-structured observation. Accurate factual data is presented as evidence to support the inferential statement.

The appeal to *intuition*. This appeal to intuition or instinct implies that the historian does not have "hard" data to support an inferential statement, but that a thorough knowledge of the subject results in an impression or feeling that the statement is probably true.

The appeal to *example* or *anecdote*. Sometimes the historian will, in order to supply support for an argument, offer one or two examples or describe an incident related to the inferential statement. An anecdote, a brief insightful account of a relevant event, is presented as support for the statement.

Examine carefully each of the following *inferential* statements. Then read the sentence or sentences that follow each *inferential statement* and decide which of the five argument categories explained above are being used to support the inferential statement. Write your choices under each and explain them. (*Note:* The "Loyalists" were those who fought on the British side in the American Revolution.)

1. *Inferential statement:* A surprising number of Americans opposed the war against the British. *Argument:* Between thirty and fifty thousand Loyalists fought on a regular basis with the British side. At least one-fifth of the colonial population sympathized with the British.

   _____

   _____

2. The Loyalists were grossly mistreated by American patriots. One family, the Cartwrights, had their home outside Philadelphia plundered and burned by a patriot mob.

   _____

   _____

3. Loyalists deserved their poor treatment and loss of property. The revolutionary struggle of the patriots was a just one based on the natural right of self-rule and on the desire for freedom that inhabits every human heart.

   _____

   _____

4. Loyalists were tarred and feathered and punished without due legal process. The American Revolution was a bitter one filled with hatred between different peoples; therefore, one could expect that the Loyalists would be discriminated against, physically attacked, and sent into exile.

   _____

   _____

5. Although Loyalists came from all classes, there were large numbers from the wealthier class who had close connections with the British rule in America. They

were probably afraid that independence would bring anarchy and, for many, a loss of prestige and position enjoyed under the rule of Parliament.

_____

_____

6. Philadelphia was a hotbed of Loyalist sentiment for the British. One American couple, the Bards, attended many parties given by British officers during the British occupation of the city.

_____

_____

7. Colonists who had strong religious feelings had good justification for siding with the king. The Bible instructs the Christian "to submit to the powers that be . . . to the king . . ." and to obey the authorities that are provided by God.

_____

_____

8. The British had an army and navy superior to those of the patriots, so the outcome of the Revolution was always in doubt. Thus, many Americans either supported the British or attempted to remain quietly neutral.

_____

_____

QUESTIONS

1. In which of the items above did you have the most difficulty deciding the argument category? Why?

_____

_____

_____

2. Of the five categories explained earlier, which *type* of argument is the strongest? Why?

_____

_____

_____

3. Which *type* of argument is the weakest? Why?

_____

_____

_____

4. Should statements by a respected historian who has spent a lifetime researching the sources on the American Revolution be regarded as an appeal to authority? Why or why not?

_____

_____

_____

ANSWERS AND EXPLANATIONS

1. Empirical. This is an approach to facts: thirty to fifty thousand and one-fifth. If we assume that the numbers are accurate, a result of research (the historian's "experiment"), then the argument here is based on factual evidence.

2. Anecdote or example. The fact that the experience of one family does support the generalization is probably being offered as representative of a large number of other examples.

3. Authority. The appeal here is based on the truth and the value of the two principles. The principles are presented as the only evidence needed to support the inferential statement.

4. Reason. The word "therefore" is a key. The logical argument is that, given the nature of war, one can expect suffering by the Loyalists.

5. Intuition. No proof is offered that Loyalists did indeed feel this fear of anarchy or loss of position. This comes very close to being an argument based on reason, also.

6. Anecdote or example. Only one case is presented, but the aim is to make the example stand up as proof of Loyalist sentiment in Philadelphia.

7. Authority. The appeal here is to a book, the Bible. Since it teaches submission (by this interpretation), no more need be said about the proper response to a revolutionary upheaval against a king.

8. Reason. "Thus" is the key word to indicate an effort to explain the reluctance of many Americans to support the patriot cause. The basic appeal here is the logical position of those who supported the British or remained quiet.

PART III
Debating Historical, Social, and Moral Issues

QUESTIONS FOR THOUGHT

1. Consider the following "repetition of history":

In 1776, the poor, underdeveloped American colonies successfully revolted against the wealthy, powerful British Empire and gained independence.

In the 1950s and the 1960s many colonial areas of Africa and Asia successfully revolted against wealthy powerful European nations and gained their independence.

A. What are the *similarities* and the *differences* in these two developments separated by almost two hundred years? (Consider pride and patriotism, the nature of the population, military conditions, ideologies and cultures, transportation and communication, and so forth.)

_____

_____

B. Why have the various Asian and African nations not become as prosperous, progressive, and stable as the United States?

_____

_____

C. Is the above question a "loaded" one filled with cultural ethnocentrism and unproved notions of the universal appeal of U.S. goals? Explain.

_____

_____

2. In comparing the American Revolution to twentieth-century conflicts of colonial areas and European nations, do factors of ideology (Marxism, democracy, capitalism, imperialism) or religion (Islam, Hinduism) become more important in the twentieth century than in the 1770s? Why or why not? (Consider Protestant and Catholic beliefs, systems of representations, economic regulations and theory, aristocracy, and other factors in the 1770s).

_____

_____

_____

_____

_____

3. Would you judge the American Revolution as *inevitable*; that is, were "forces" at work for the separation of the colonies from Great Britain and could any efforts by individuals or small groups have changed the course of history? Was it as natural as "apples falling from a tree?" Why or why not?

_____

_____

_____

_____

4. Some historians have argued that the steps leading to the American Revolution should be viewed not from Philadelphia or Boston, but from London. The implication is that the British had to make decisions for an entire empire—the West Indies, Ireland, Canada, and even India. The further implication is that

in view of the overall situation (the protection provided by the British navy and army; the use of the British credit, insurance, and marketing systems; the costs of supervising an empire; and the relatively small degree of interference by the British in colonial affairs), the British were fair, just, and equitable in their policies and actions toward the colonies in the twenty years preceding the American Revolution. React to this viewpoint.

_____

_____

_____

_____

_____

5. The lower classes, the inarticulate, have been neglected in historical studies. Since they were "inarticulate"; that is, they left few written records, it is difficult for the historian to study their opinions, their contributions, and their influence on historical events. During the American Revolution, we know that the lower classes participated in the protest against the British government, clashed with the British soldiers in urban areas, and supplied the bulk of the American army and navy throughout the revolutionary war.

   A. Have historians given too much credit for a successful revolution to heroic leaders and to prominent men who wrote letters, diaries, journals, and articles (Washington, Adams, Jefferson, Hamilton)? Should more recognition and credit be given to the lower classes? Explain.

_____

_____

_____

   B. How might the historian go about this task of examining the role of the lower classes, the inarticulate, in the Revolution? What records or sources could be used?

_____

_____

_____

   C. Would the use of inference be an important way of determining the lower-class attitudes and contributions? Examine the following examples, then answer the questions.
      (1) Their willingness to put up with terrible conditions at Valley Forge indicates a strong motivation for independence.
      (2) They were outnumbered and faced an enemy that was better trained and equipped, yet had commitment to continue to risk their lives.
      (3) The desertion rate was high, especially as Washington's army moved from one location to another. Does this reveal a hesitancy to protect the entire United States?

(4) As many Americans fought on the British side as on the American side. Does this imply that a very large number of the lower classes disapproved of the Revolution?

_____

_____

_____

_____

_____

D. How does one balance the leadership qualities of George Washington with the common man's commitment to freedom and independence? Were the patriot soldiers so motivated to seek freedom that Washington's presence counted for little? Or, without Washington, would the army have disbanded and the Revolution failed? Explain.

_____

_____

_____

_____

_____

6. What parallels, if any, can you see between the American Revolution and the recent American involvement in Vietnam? (In Vietnam a revolutionary Viet Cong, with support from North Vietnam and the U.S.S.R., fought against a South Vietnamese government and army that was supported, with people and materiel, by the United States.) Consider ideology, influence of outside nations, methods of fighting, leadership, dissent, world opinion, and outcome.

_____

_____

_____

_____

_____

7. One of the principles of the American Revolution was self-determination—the right of a group of people in a geographical area, if they feel oppressed and misused by an existing government, to separate from that government and form their own nation. Do you accept that principle as valid? Explain. Should the Southern states have had this right in 1861? Should there be any limit on the geographical size and population amount before people are allowed to form their own nation? Why or why not? How does one define the degree of oppression or the inadequacy of the existing government? What percentage of the population

in this geographical area must be committed to a new government before it is "proper" to establish one?

_____

_____

_____

_____

_____

8. In all upheavals or events that bring conflict, historians differ in their interpretations. The American Revolution is no exception. Consider the following viewpoints and react to each in the space provided (reflect on accuracy and your agreement or disagreement).

   A. George Bancroft contended that the American Revolution was a step in human progress brought on by British efforts to trammel upon colonial liberties. The ideals stated in the Declaration of Independence were worthy ones and formed the basis for the rebellion. The patriots supported a righteous cause and were rewarded for their adherence to universal ideals. God's hand could be seen in these pure motives of heroic, sacrificing citizens.

   _____

   _____

   _____

   B. Herbert Osgood blamed the Americans for not supporting the British Empire, for not paying their fair portion for the groups that protected their interests. Colonial planters and merchants went their own way, pursued selfish interests, and resented legitimate interference. They took advantage of British protection of shipping, of bounties, and of credit facilities, and when they were unable to get their way, they resorted to illegal smuggling. The freest people in the world at that time demanded more freedom, without regard to the economic consequences on a large economic structure involving the entire empire.

   _____

   _____

   _____

   C. Carl Becker saw many different groups agitating for revolution, all with their own motives. Some attacked the British. Others objected to the power of the upper class within the colonies and were concerned about who would "rule at home." In some cases local issues reflected grievances against the British or against the patriots. The American Revolution was complex. Generalizations are difficult and all general statements have exceptions.

   _____

   _____

   _____

D. Clinton Rossiter did not perceive the revolutionaries as radicals. To the contrary, they were attempting to conserve rights that they already practiced. American colonies were middle-class democracies living in harmony and with widespread voting privileges. Thus there was no need for class conflict, nor for the acquisition of new rights. The struggle in the Revolution was a conservative movement to stop British government efforts to despotically suppress American liberties. It was not a struggle among colonists, nor was it an effort to establish radical innovations in politics.

_____

_____

_____

Which of these four views seem to be most accurate? Why?

_____

_____

Is the "truth" to be found in an integration of all four into a comprehensive whole? Explain.

_____

_____

What different types of sources might each of the four historians have used in coming up with their ideas? Use your imagination.

_____

_____

_____

9. At a time of revolution it is difficult to separate traitors and patriots. In the American Revolution the patriots (those loyal to the Continental Congress) labeled those loyal to the king "traitors" to the cause. On the other hand, those loyal to the king considered the revolutionaries traitors and, indeed, the king called them traitors. The patriots mistreated those loyal to the king (Loyalists), forced some out of their communities, confiscated their property, and threatened their lives. Loyalists argued that they had pledged their loyalty to the king and, in some cases, this loyalty emerged from serious religious convictions or matters of conscience. Was this persecution of Loyalists proper behavior on the part of the patriots or was it deplorable behavior involving prejudice and a refusal to understand their honest convictions? Explain.

_____

_____

_____

_____

_____

124 10. Here is a Soviet view of the American Revolution (*A Soviet View of the American Past*, O. Lawrence Burnett, Jr., and William Converse Haygood, eds. Scott, Foresman and Co. 1964, pp. 17, 18, 19):

"The War for Independence was a bourgeois revolution. Popular masses won the victory over England . . . The Negroes took an active part in the struggle against the English. As a result of the War for Independence the American people freed themselves from the colonial oppression hampering the development of productive powers . . . Also important to the colonial victory was the position of Russia, on whose initiative (Declaration of 1780) a number of European states declared an 'Armed Neutrality,' directed against England . . . With the transition of the plantations to the growing of cotton, slavery—as K. Marx pointed out—changed into a commercial system of exploitation . . . As a result of the War for Independence the bourgeoisie and the planters came into power in the country, turning the victory over England to their own class interests . . . The intensification of the class struggle manifested itself in the postwar period in the agitations in the Army (1783) and the uprisings of the poorer farmers . . . [This] reinforced the aim of the bourgeoisie towards the consolidation of their dictatorship and the centralization of power for the suppression of popular mass resistance."

125

What is your reaction to this Marxist interpretation of the American Revolution? Is it a biased, ideological viewpoint not worthy of serious consideration? Or is it a "fresh" perspective that offers insight and a new understanding of the Revolution? Explain.

_____

_____

_____

_____

_____

_____

Does the use of concepts such as "bourgeoisie," "masses," and "dictatorship" add to our understanding or cause confusion? Why?

_____

_____

_____

_____

_____

_____

11. Consider carefully the two quotes at the beginning of the chapter. What does each mean? (Try to consider them in relation to the American Revolution.) Do you agree or disagree with each? Explain.

_____

_____

_____

_____

_____

THOUGHTS FOR QUESTIONS

1. A. The more recent revolt took place against a weak Europe still recovering from a devastating war. The American colonies were wealthier and better prepared to "do it alone" than colonies of recent years. The American colonies had direct help from a foreign power (France). Several colonial areas in Africa and Asia revolted at the same time, which gave a certain legitimacy to the whole process, whereas the Americans were the first colony to revolt since European colonization began. Greater logistical problems existed for the British in 1776 than for European powers in the modern period. Racial overtones existed in the modern revolts against Europe.

On the other hand, in both cases the rebellion often took on characteristics of guerrilla warfare. Both proclaimed a desire for self-government and for a democratic system to replace authoritarianism. Leaders often had specific personal grievances against the ruling power. Nationalism was a factor in both developments.

B. Certainly climate, size, and resources are factors here. The clash of ideologies is evident in the modern period, with two superpowers conducting a duel over the underdeveloped world. The United States was relatively free from foreign threats. Also, the United States had leaders with much experience in government and whose religious and ethnic backgrounds were compatible. Of course "progressive" and "stable" are loaded words, given America's Indian wars, threats to secede, debates over slavery, expansionist tendencies, and, later, devastating Civil War.

C. It seems so, yet if advances in standard of living and technology, increased gross national product, development of basic freedoms, gains in health care, education, comforts, and leisure, and accomplishment of political cooperation are considered "progressive" and "stable," then the United States achieved these goals. Leaders of many emerging nations state that they seek many of these same objectives even though their techniques may differ. The ideals of basic human rights, representative government, and a decent standard of living seem universal—beyond ethnic or racial considerations. To state that the United States has "arrived" at these goals may involve ethnocentrism.

2. The American ideology of actual representation, limited influence of a monarch, universal adult-white-male voting rights, an egalitarian mood, an open economic system, and an absence of titled aristocracy was a radical agenda for the 1770s. In a sense American beliefs were dangerous to European rulers. The French government did not assist Americans because of sympathy for the American ideology. The

British worried about the spread of the American system into the West Indies and Ireland. American dissenters (Congregationalists and Presbyterians, especially) were fearful of an effort to establish the Church of England throughout the colonies with a resident American bishop. Freethinkers who supported the Revolution posed a danger to established religions of Europe. Unfettered capitalism posed a threat to the accepted mercantilist system. Perhaps the ideologies were not as sharply defined or as intensively held in the 1770s, but they existed.

3. Thomas Paine argues in *Common Sense* that it was unnatural for an island (England) to rule over a continent (America). Historians prefer to identify causes and factors rather than call them "forces." Perhaps an accumulation of factors might gain the momentum of a "force." One could argue that if not the Tea Party and Coercive Acts, other incidents would have fomented rebellion. But underlying causes still set the stage for an incident. Sometimes an incident then sets in motion events and decisions that gain momentum until the process seems inevitable. However, we view from hindsight and are sometimes blind to alternatives that were real at the time.

4. When viewed carefully and honestly from the "other side," many events in history take on a different perspective. In a study of American history, we naturally view events from the American side. A Soviet view of American history is interesting. So is a Chinese history of the United States.

The British have a strong case when viewed from London. Americans later discovered some of the economic problems of being outside the empire when the cord was cut in the 1780s. The British were afraid of a chain reaction in other colonial areas if the thirteen colonies gained independence. The thirteen colonies were not paying their way if one considers the bureaucratic and military expenditures beyond the costs associated with the British navy. The inhabitants of the American colonies were probably freer than any people in the world in 1770. To request payment for at least part of the empire's costs was not unreasonable when viewed from London. The method of obtaining financial aid brought on the debate and, ultimately, the Revolution.

5. A. Both roles are necessary for the success of the Revolution. Nevertheless, more thought and words have been given to each of the leading figures in the Revolution than to all the soldiers in Washington's army. The masses are listed as "people." These "people" become an inhuman statistical conglomerate. The soldiers who risked their lives on the field of battle facing British guns and bayonets deserve as much credit as the field commander. But how do we give a common soldier credit? He is one of many and has left records only in the form of group statistics.

B. Some letters, journals, and other writings exist. Records of units, commissary and supply accounts, military regulations (especially ones added during the Revolution), descriptions by those who could write, casualty records, enlistment information, and pay records all would help understand the soldier's life. Newspaper accounts about riots and attacks on Loyalists, letters, and articles written on behalf of the lower class appeared from time to time. The historian does not, for this period, have mounds of evidence to sift through. Artifacts often give insight. Detective work is necessary, sometimes with the use of only one or two clues.

C. This is one means available. Numbers 1 and 2 indicate a commitment to independence. Pay was low and uncertain. Punishment for treason often seemed more likely than rewards for victory. In number 3, desertion may be connected to the need to be near home to help with the farm and to the assumption that young men in other areas would protect their own territory. For number 4, information would be needed on the class background of those who fought for the British. A large number fought for neither side. Indifference or a fearful neutrality prevailed.

D. Washington has been called the indispensable man and stands out above all others in his individual contribution to the Revolution. No single common man could possibly have that much influence. Weighing contributions is fruitless. Washington depended on the two or three thousand men ready and willing to fight. Without them it was back to Mount Vernon. Yet no one else could have inspired men to remain in the army after losing battle after battle and retreating so often. Since Washington left a large number of papers as resources, historians write about Washington and he becomes, partly because of quantity of sources, larger than life.

6. The parallels are tempting. The North Vietnamese and Viet Cong espoused Marxism, an ideology that challenged American principles. American ideology in 1776 challenged the British political, social, and economic system. In Vietnam, one could consider Americans as hired Hessians assisting the Loyalists (South Vietnamese) in an effort to stop a revolution leading to dominance by the new ideology. American guerrilla warfare, seen as early as 1775 at Lexington and Concord, parallels the methods of the Viet Cong. The Americans in Vietnam and the British in the colonies both seemed to have total military superiority. There were dissenters to American policy in Congress, and objections were raised to British policy in Parliament in 1776. World opinion was against the United States in Vietnam and against the British in the American Revolution. In this scenario the Soviet Union performs as the French did in the American Revolution (except for the absence of Soviet troops in Vietnam). The Viet Cong outlasted the United States in Vietnam. The Americans outlasted the British in America. Of course the Viet Cong ideology was much different as seen by the aftermath of the Vietnam War. The Americans went on to produce a free society that protected the rights of individuals (with the exception of slaves and Indians) and formed a government responsive to the people. An authoritarian system still restricts freedom in Vietnam. History does not repeat itself—but as Mark Twain said, "it rhymes."

7. Most of us would agree with the principle. The crucial questions relate to the size limit and circumstances. The integration of a committed people into a society and government over a period of time without serious oppression or a denial of equal rights seems to forbid the "right" of self-determination. The South probably did not have as many grievances in 1861 as the American colonies did in 1775. This is debatable. It seems unreasonable that five or ten thousand people should be allowed to form a separate nation. Following the principle of self-determination to extremes invites chaos. The question of percentage is dangerous since a heavily armed but small minority can take control by force and attempt to withdraw from an established union. Fairness in the eyes of some may seem discriminatory and oppressive to others. Perhaps the ultimate test of this "right" is the long-term *success* of the revolutionaries, acquiescence by the existing government, and recognition from abroad—all achieved by the American revolutionaries.

8. Carl Becker's emphasis on a variety of factors at a local level and on the complexity of the Revolution is attractive. It seems closer to reality than the others. Bancroft paints a black-and-white picture that, knowing human motivation in history, is doubtful and simplistic. It is difficult to calculate the influence of "God's

hand." One guesses that the patriots were not quite that virtuous nor the British all that evil. Certainly Osgood is correct in his observation that Americans were reluctant to pay the empire's costs, but whether that was the primary reason for violent behavior is debatable. Rossiter's point is well-taken. Americans had grown detached from England and quite capable of caring for their own problems. Yet to downplay the struggle within is to ignore the numbers who flocked to the British side, the Loyalists who departed for Canada or England, and the many patriots who demanded a more egalitarian treatment after the Revolution.

For sources, Bancroft would likely use the public writings of the Founding Fathers, writings filled with lofty idealism and condemnation for the British. The Declaration of Independence would be a document supporting his interpretation. Osgood's emphasis on economics would require a study of trade, tax revenues, bureaucratic and military costs, and British taxation. Becker's position might be supported in local newspapers and debates of colonial assemblies (legislatures). Rossiter, no doubt, studied voting patterns that included eligibility and numbers who actually voted, as well as protest speeches in the colonies.

9. Every revolution produces extremism because of the intense emotions (such as fear) and confusion inherent in such an upheaval. Does one tolerate those who support or have sympathy for the enemy, an enemy who intends to destroy the effort of which you are a part? Perhaps those who chose the king should move to a place where the king prevails. It would be unreasonable to expect those who fight and risk their lives to tolerate any "traitors" who actually aid an enemy. The best solution to this dichotomy may have been movement or exile. And yet, what is considered "loyalty" and what is the legitimate authority that must be obeyed at a time of shifting fortunes for British armies and patriot militia?

10. Historians welcome new ways of viewing the past—fresh insights, innovative structures. But ideology sometimes interferes with accurate comprehension and especially with balance. Ideology fits everything into categories. The historian guards against placing each information item into a special constraining box with parameters fixed beforehand. History is diverse and unpredictable. The Soviet view may offer some arguments for the consideration of economic motivation and of a class basis for past events. However, the actual complexity of any major event refutes neat categorization.

A word such as "bourgeoisie" can be useful. Nevertheless, in the American Revolution we find some wealthy leaders supporting the Revolution while others opposed it. Some of the "masses" joined the patriots; many others were indifferent or aided the British. "Dictatorship" is hardly the word for the American system of government following the Revolution. The lack of participation by the masses in politics stemmed mostly from the fact that the government interfered only slightly with their lives. Except for the institution of slavery, no authoritarian "dictatorship" existed in the 1790s. To use terms such as these too frequently and inappropriately renders the terms innocuous. Perhaps the Soviet ideological version does force the historian to consider similar jargon—liberty, equality, natural law, human rights, and so forth. A slave-based society that cheats the Indians and offers little opportunity to women is not exactly one of liberty and equality.

11. To Duberman, the task of the historian is a defensive one—to guard against the misuse of history. The key word in this quote is "simple." We hope that there are some overall lessons from the past that might impart wisdom. But there is no

absolute rule, law, or generalization about history that can apply directly to a present situation and tell us exactly what to do. The historian must guard against an effort by leaders to make such binding associations.

Thinking especially of the American Revolution and the sacrifices and courage shown by patriots, Tacitus would conclude that making these acts known is the primary function of history. History gives inspiration from the deeds of the past. And the opposite is also true. The fact that historians will write about what is done should be a factor in molding behavior. Although several presidents have recently shown interest in this judgment of posterity, it is debatable as to how many leaders really think about their place in history. Certainly those who have suffered in the past at the hands of "evildoers" deserve a place in history to commemorate these sufferings and the actions of those who brought on the evil.

CHAPTER

4

A NEW NATION EMERGES

"When I want to understand what is happening today or try to decide what will happen tomorrow, I look back. A page of history is worth a volume of logic."

Oliver Wendell Holmes

"Seldom any splendid story is wholly true."

Samuel Johnson

PART I
Acquiring Essential Data

ESSENTIAL DATES

Determine the correct sequence and write the approximate date for each of the following events.

1. Thomas Jefferson takes office as president in a peaceful transition of power. ‾‾‾‾‾‾‾

2. The Alien and Sedition acts are passed. ‾‾‾‾‾‾‾

3. The Genet mission from France arrives to encourage American help for France against the British. ‾‾‾‾‾‾‾

4. George Washington is elected president. ‾‾‾‾‾‾‾

5. The Bill of Rights (first ten amendments) is approved. ‾‾‾‾‾‾‾

6. The Whiskey Rebellion in western Pennsylvania is put down by Washington. ‾‾‾‾‾‾‾

7. Washington, D.C., becomes the nation's capital. ‾‾‾‾‾‾‾

8. The Constitutional Convention is held in Philadelphia. ‾‾‾‾‾‾‾

9. Treasurer Alexander Hamilton's *First Report on the Public Credit* is submitted. ‾‾‾‾‾‾‾

10. The French Revolution begins in Paris. ‾‾‾‾‾‾‾

ESSENTIAL CONCEPTS

Examine each concept and write what contemporary relevance it might have.

1. *written frame of government* That the structures, responsibilities, processes, and limitations of government should be *written*—made known to all—and that the frame of government is distinct from laws passed by a representative body.

‾‾‾

‾‾‾

‾‾‾

2. *federalism* Over the same geographical area and populace, two governments function with separate powers and responsibilities, both governments elected by the people and operating independently and interdependently (states and "federal" or national government).

‾‾‾

‾‾‾

‾‾‾

3. *basic rights and liberties* Rights that adhere to the individual and come with being human. They cannot be infringed on by government or by a majority of the people (freedom of speech, press, religion, and so forth).

_____

_____

_____

4. *rebellion* The act of opposing by force the actions and policies of a government (Shay's Rebellion, Whiskey Rebellion).

_____

_____

_____

5. *mixed government* The balancing of elements of monarchy (president), aristocracy (a Senate and a Supreme Court), and democracy (House of Representatives) into a complex system of divided power and checks and balances.

_____

_____

_____

6. *impressment* British practice of stopping American ships on the high seas and searching for and then removing sailors whom they considered to be deserters from the British navy. These sailors were then impressed (forced) to serve in the British navy.

_____

_____

_____

7. *sedition* Conduct or language that incites citizens to hold the government in disrespect. A law in 1798 defined this to include statements that hold the government in "contempt or disrepute."

_____

_____

_____

8. *judicial review* The power of a Supreme Court to declare state and federal laws void and inoperable when they conflict with the Constitution.

_____

_____

_____

9. *economic interpretation* The viewpoint, held most notably by Charles Beard, that in almost every event, the people making decisions will be greatly influenced by prospects of financial gain. Beard applied this concept to the writing of the Constitution of 1787.

_____

_____

_____

10. *limited government* The concept that the possible actions of government are limited to the specific powers given in the Constitution. Other needs of society are to be met by state and local governments or belong to the people.

_____

_____

_____

ANSWERS

Correct sequence of events and their dates.

1.   8; 1787
2.   4; 1788
3. 10; 1789
4.   9; 1791
5.   5; 1791

6. 3; 1793
7. 6; 1794
8. 2; 1798
9. 7; 1800
10. 1; 1801

PART II
Developing Thinking Skills

SKILL EXERCISE ONE: EVALUATING AND APPLYING EVIDENCE

After a historian has decided on a thesis, the next step is to accumulate all of the relevant evidence related to this thesis. The evidence may consist of facts, statistics, rational arguments, and expert opinion. After this, the historian proceeds to divide the evidence into one of three categories. These categories normally would be evidence in *support* of the thesis, evidence that *challenges* the thesis or raises questions about the validity of the thesis, or evidence that can be called *neutral*; that is, it is appropriate to understand the thesis but not necessary to clearly support one side or the other. This skill of differentiation between data that supports and data that challenges a thesis is of utmost importance in the analyzing process. It requires evaluation, judgment, and application of data.

The following thesis relates to the American Revolution. Ten items of data are listed after the thesis. Under each of the items write whether the information is *supportive* of the thesis, a *challenge* to the thesis, or *neutral* data. Briefly explain each answer. Then check your judgment against the suggested answers.

The Thesis

"The American Revolution was caused more by *propaganda* (movement for the spread of certain ideas, doctrines, images, or beliefs) and *emotional* factors (anger, resentment, hatred) than by actual political or economic conditions."

Items of Data

1. Copies of the American version of the Battle of Lexington (a report depicting the British as cruel and merciless) were prepared quickly and sent to England by fast packet ship. They reached England two weeks before the arrival of official British army reports of the battle.

   _____

   _____

2. The British navy provided protection to American ships moving to and from the American colonies and the West Indies.

   _____

   _____

3. For the most part Americans had control of their local government. A higher proportion of Americans had the right to vote for representation to their legislatures than Englishmen had in voting for members of Parliament.

   _____

   _____

4. The British sought by several acts of Parliament to restrict American manufacturing and to force Americans to supply unfinished raw materials.

   _____

   _____

5. Governors of each colony, in most cases appointed by the king of England, could veto laws passed by the colonial legislatures. The king also could and did veto those laws.

   _____

   _____

6. Many southern planters were continually in debt to British factors (agents), who sold their tobacco for them (at what seemed to be very low prices) and purchased goods for them in England (at what seemed to be very high prices).

   _____

   _____

7. An engraving was made of British troops firing on a Boston crowd at the "Boston Massacre." Also, copies of "Massacre" drawings were sold to the public and the event was commemorated each year on March 5.

   _____

   _____

8. Americans were supposed to shelter (quarter) British soldiers and stories were spread that soldiers would be quartered in private homes, there to threaten American women.

   _____

   _____

9. The British Parliament gave agents of the East Indian Company, a London-based company in which many members of Parliament had financial interest, a virtual monopoly on the sale of tea in North America.

   _____

   _____

10. Although colonists complained about taxation by Parliament without representation in Parliament, when Parliament broached the possibility of such representation, the colonists refused to consider the idea.

    _____

    _____

QUESTIONS

1. It is feasible to separate the emotional aspects of economic issues. For example, item number 9 is economic in nature, but the issue probably raised emotional feelings of resentment and anger. If the British confiscated an American merchant's cargo, using a minor legal technicality in the customs law, would that be primarily an economic or an emotional factor? Explain.

   _____

   _____

   _____

2. Must propaganda be an exaggerated or "twisted" version of what happened? Can it be an accurate description of an unfortunate incident, couched in highly emotional words and spread in an inflammatory manner (gruesome pictures, vivid descriptions)? Explain.

   _____

   _____

   _____

3. In the Declaration of Independence only one side is presented—the "oppressive" acts of the British and their unjust treatment of Americans. No mention is made

of any benefits to being a part of the British Empire. In this case is the Declaration of Independence a propaganda document? Why or why not?

_____

_____

_____

ANSWERS AND EXPLANATIONS

1. Supports. The expeditious handling of the exaggerated American version indicates an effort of propaganda, in this case by Samuel Adams.

2. Supports. This describes a benefit to being part of the British Empire and thus would be evidence that Americans had real economic reasons for remaining *loyal* to England.

3. Supports. This points out that Americans should have had no complaint about the independent operation of their local governments.

4. Challenges. In as much as this brought hardships on Americans who were interested in manufacturing, it was a real economic issue.

5. Challenges. It is a political factor that reveals a thwarting of the intentions of members of the colonial legislatures.

6. Challenges. This debt, if somehow cancelled by a successful revolution, is obviously a real economic factor.

7. Supports. The "Massacre" was kept alive and used to stimulate the emotions of Americans.

8. Supports. Whether the soldiers actually were a threat or not, those who wanted to use this issue of propaganda and anti-British feeling could do so.

9. Challenges. The tea monopoly upset not only American tea merchants, who smuggled tea from the Dutch, but also other merchants who saw the possibilities of future monopolies. This was a real economic grievance.

10. Neutral. This indicates that the phrase "no taxation without representation" may have been partially a smoke screen covering other intentions. Representation in Parliament would have been available—thus taxation *with* representation—but was not acceptable or sufficient in the minds of colonists. This item may fit any of the categories. On the one hand, it casts doubt on a supposedly "real" factor (lack of colonial representation in Parliament), thus supporting the thesis. On the other hand, representation was a political issue and the colonists maintained that they *were* represented in their local assemblies and that these should have the sole power to tax.

SKILL EXERCISE TWO: ANALYZING QUANTIFIED DATA

Quantification—the use of numbers or statistics—is of growing importance in the field of history. This is, no doubt, partly due to the historian's increased use of sociology and economics to help explain history. It also represents an effort to be more precise in stating data that is inherently quantitative. Numbers and statistics often give insight into historical developments and situations, insight that cannot be acquired by words such as "a lot," "several," "many," "most," and "a sizeable group." Numbers, if they are clearly defined and accurate, are like some pictures—worth a thousand words. However, numbers need to be communicated and interpreted in words in order to make sense. We as readers need to determine exactly what the numbers tell us and what they do not tell us. Most numbers are presented with implications drawn from the numbers; meanings are attached and conclusions formed. In an increasingly computerized and quantification-oriented society, the student should become aware of how numbers are acquired, what numbers are included and what excluded, and what numbers mean, might possibly mean, and do not mean.

One danger is that a reliance on numbers might lead to too much emphasis on economics compared to other factors—political, social, ideological, emotional—in the interpretation of any period or event in history. As a matter of fact, numbers can be deceptively convincing. They seem so final and crucial to an argument. They are definite and, seemingly, free of the subjective elements of opinion and bias. We know this is not true, but researchers know it is often psychologically influential to throw in a statistic or two to bolster an argument or to support a thesis. Historians must gather and use statistics, but at the same time balance them with other relevant data. Appropriate skepticism and critical evaluation of materials are necessary skills for the historian. Examine the following two viewpoints on the Constitutional Convention.

An Economic Interpretation of the Constitution

Some historians—most notably Charles A. Beard in 1913—have offered an economic interpretation of the writing of the American Constitution. The Founding Fathers, they argue, were not so much interested in the high-sounding ideals of liberty and the rights of individuals as they were interested in securing their wealth, suppressing any sign of opposition to their political power, protecting their property, and reducing the influence of the common man. These historians maintain that the writing of the Constitution of 1787 was an undemocratic process whereby a wealthy elite, interested in their own economic security, forced a conservative Constitution on an unsuspecting and politically outnumbered majority. Furthermore, these historians have argued that the primary motive of the Founding Fathers was to acquire full payment for their depreciated government securities (papers of government indebtedness to the holder) and to produce a Constitution that would protect their financial interests. Convention delegates "captured" the new government and passed legislation to pay debts at full par value rather than at the depreciated value. Thus, the convention scene becomes one of *counter*-revolution of a small, wealthy group meeting in secret and producing a powerful central government not in keeping with the spirit and ideals of the Revolution.

Other historians, in response to this theory, have argued that the process of writing and ratifying the Constitution was an open one with plenty of opportunity for popular input and that the main interest of the Founding Fathers was to establish an effective, respected government that could provide order and stability while maintaining the basic rights of the people. The protection of property and the establishment of a government that could promote commerce and bring stability to the economic system was a goal of the vast majority of Americans in the 1780s. Thus the Founding Fathers spoke for the interests of most Americans.

Many statistics have been advanced to support each of these viewpoints. Some are given here. Examine these statistics related to the Constitutional Convention of

1787 and the ratifying process of 1787 and 1788. Then answer the questions at the end.

1. *Forty* of the *fifty-five* Convention delegates owned depreciated government "paper" (certificates indicating government debt to the holder or purchaser) that would rise in value if paid at par or face value. They expected to be in a position to assure full payment. The U.S. Treasury records of this debt are for the year 1791.

2. *Ninety-six* percent of the wealth of the delegates to the Convention was tied up in land.

3. *Thirty* of the *forty-three* living signers of the Declaration of Independence worked to obtain ratification of the Constitution. (Patrick Henry, Samuel Adams, and Thomas Jefferson did not work for ratification.)

4. The Constitution was ratified by individual state ratifying conventions with delegates elected by eligible voters. Voting was restricted to white male adults who met residency, and in some cases, tax-paying requirements. Research indicates a *large majority* of white males could have voted for convention delegates; however, about 75 percent of those eligible to vote did *not* vote for delegates.

5. The ratification vote by state:

STATE	VOTE	DATE
1. Delaware	unanimous	December 7, 1787
2. Pennsylvania[1]	46–23	December 12, 1787
3. New Jersey	unanimous	December 18, 1787
4. Georgia	unanimous	January 2, 1788
5. Connecticut	128–40	January 9, 1788
6. Massachusetts[2]	187–168	February 6, 1788
7. Maryland	63–11	April 26, 1788
8. South Carolina	149–73	May 23, 1788
9. New Hampshire[3]	57–47	June 21, 1788

The Constitution was approved with nine states ratifying.

10. Virginia[4]	89–79	June 25, 1788
11. New York[5]	30–27	July 26, 1788

The Articles of Confederation Congress expired on December 10, 1788. The new government was organized in the spring of 1789.

12. North Carolina	194–77	November 21, 1789
13. Rhode Island[6]	34–32	May 29, 1790

---

[1] Two opponents of the Constitution were physically forced to attend in order to obtain a quorum.

[2] Opponents had an early edge until a Bill of Rights was promised.

[3] The first convention session failed to approve.

[4] Promise of a Bill of Rights was crucial to approval.

[5] A fast courier arrived to report Virginia's approval.

[6] Rhode Island was considered the most "democratic" state.

6. Votes of the delegates to ratifying conventions in Pennsylvania, Connecticut, and New Hampshire:

SOCIO-ECONOMIC STANDING	FOR THE CONSTITUTION	AGAINST THE CONSTITUTION
Merchants, manufacturers, clergymen, large landholders, doctors, lawyers	84%	16%
Artisans, innkeepers, surveyors	64	36
Farmers, laborers	46	54

7. The three states that ratified early and *unanimously* were primarily noncommercial and agrarian: Delaware, New Jersey, and Georgia.

8. An overall tally of votes in the thirteen state ratifying conventions indicates a *two* to *one* vote in favor of the Constitution. One historian concludes that those who voted in favor represented 59.3 percent of the total population.

9. The Constitution, Article VI, states that "*all* debts contracted and Engagements entered into, before the Adoption of this Constitution, shall be as valid . . ." The Constitution gave Congress power "to coin Money, regulate the Value thereof, . . . To regulate Commerce . . . To borrow money . . ." and ". . . To lay and collect Taxes, . . ."

10. Of the *four* government branches created by the Constitution, only *one*, the House of Representatives, was to be elected by a direct vote of the eligible voters (white male adults). Senators were to be chosen by state legislatures, the executive to be picked by an electoral college, and federal judges were to be appointed for life terms by the executive.

QUESTIONS

1. Without looking at any of the specific questions that follow, what conclusions, inferences, and observations can you make from the ten statistical items given above?

_____

_____

_____

2. What *specific* items of numerical information offer the most support or tend to refute historians who argue that the process of writing and ratifying the Constitution was undemocratic and that the motivation was primarily economic?

Support	*Refute or Call into Question*
_____	_____
_____	_____
_____	_____

3. What other *types* of quantified data (statistics) would you consider helpful in understanding the issue?

_____

_____

_____

4. What questions should be asked about the data offered in item number 1? Consider the date, the phrase "if paid at par or face value," the exact holdings of those who supported or opposed the Constitution, and so forth.

_____

_____

_____

5. What implications might be drawn from the fact that 75 percent of the eligible voters did not vote for delegates to state ratifying conventions? Consider inconvenience, lack of interest, satisfaction with the Articles of Confederation, assumption that it would be ratified anyway, political manipulation by advocates of the Constitution, and other factors.

_____

_____

_____

6. If a few votes had been *reversed*—ten in Massachusetts, three each in New Hampshire and New York, and five in Virginia—a total of twenty-one votes out of 684 votes cast in those states, the Constitution would not have been ratified. In each of these states there were indications that, in the early stages, those opposed to the Constitution were in the majority. What might have taken place if this small reversal in voting had occurred?

_____

_____

_____

7. "Item number 6 proves an upper-class support against lower-class opposition to the Constitution." Do you accept this statement as accurate? What other factors must be considered? Think about the facts that the data are on only three states and are a total listing rather than of individual states, about whether the statement is the proper designation of classes, and about the percentage of the total population represented by each grouping.

_____

_____

_____

8. Could other factors besides economic ones have been involved in the quick, unanimous ratification by Delaware, New Jersey, and Georgia (see item number 7)? Consider size, location, and threats that called for national protection.

   _____

   _____

   _____

9. How does item number 8 relate to the democratic process of ratifying the Constitution? What questions should be raised about the statistic?

   _____

   _____

   _____

10. Does item number 10 indicate a fear of direct voting by the general population—a belief that the government is best controlled by those with wisdom, experience, and perhaps wealth? Why or why not?

    _____

    _____

    _____

11. Often a quantified item can appear accurate and clear to those who read it. However, the reaction to it; that is, the decision about what it means, about what attitude or action should be taken on the basis of the quantified item, is controversial. For example, item number 3 might generate at least two opposite reactions to its numbers. One side would question why *only* thirty worked for ratification and find it significant and disturbing that thirteen did not. Another would consider the thirty out of forty-three an indication of overwhelming support. Often statistics raise questions rather than solve problems. What is your reaction to this item—an impressive number in support of the Constitution or a sign that it was not very popular with the Declaration signers? Explain.

    _____

    _____

    _____

12. To what extent do you accept the economic interpretation of the Constitution of 1787 and the viewpoint that it was an undemocratic process of approval? Have the statistics clarified the issue or made it more confusing? Explain your answers.

    _____

    _____

    _____

PART III
Debating Historical, Social, and Moral Issues

QUESTIONS FOR THOUGHT

1. After examining many different revolutions in the twentieth century and earlier, some historians find recurring patterns in the process of a successful revolutionary upheaval. The patterns tend to follow these lines in chronological sequence.

   A. A period of protests and grievances against the old system. Emotion-packed incidents occur.

   B. Moderate reform—old government yields. Reformers bring about changes and satisfy some grievances. Symbolic statements are made and ideology is developed.

   C. Radical phase—a move to extremism. An effort, often puritanical in its devotion to the ideals of the revolution, is made to completely change the old system: violence, foreign involvement, expulsion or execution of old group, alteration of signs and symbols of the old order.

   D. Conservative reaction—a group of conservative leaders conclude that developments have gone too far and reformers have begun to gain control. Radical groups lose power.

   E. Emergence of a dominant individual—"man on horseback." The leader extends modified ideas of the revolution—often using revolutionary terms—but suppresses domestic uprisings, meets foreign challenges, and establishes a strong government.

   F. A restoration of modified ideals of the prerevolutionary past with many revolutionary reforms continued and integrated within the new system.

   In the period from about 1760 to 1800, in what ways did the American Revolution follow the above pattern? Consider these developments as they might relate to phases A through F: Stamp Act Congress (1765), Boston Tea Party (1773), the Battle of Lexington to the Battle of Yorktown (1775–1781), Shay's Rebellion (1786), Constitutional Convention (1787), Washington as president (1787–97), Whiskey Rebellion (1795), and Adams's presidency (1797–1801).

   _____

   _____

   _____

   _____

   _____

In what ways was the American Revolution different from this pattern? How is the American Revolution different from the French Revolution (1789–1815) and the Russian Revolution (1905–1925)?

_____

_____

_____

_____

_____

2. The *conspiracy* theory of history, sometimes called the *reality* technique, has been practiced by many historians and journalists. Historian Charles Beard applied this to the formation of the Constitution of 1787. This theory maintains that the reality of history lies underneath what is seen publicly. Real history—true motivation and action—is never hinted at publicly. Therefore, the historian must dig below the surface, look behind the scenes, and uncover the true past that has been purposely concealed from public view. The implication is that those in positions of power—political, economic, diplomatic—are constantly attempting to conceal their actions in order to keep and even expand their power and influence.

Do you agree with this conspiracy theory or reality technique? Why or why not? Could it be possible that a great man such as George Washington took part in a conspiracy? What evidence would you use to support or to disprove such a thesis? Consider the fact that ardent revolutionaries—Thomas Jefferson, Patrick Henry, Sam Adams—did not attend the Constitutional Convention of 1787 and that the convention meetings were conducted in secret.

_____

_____

_____

Should the historian, in most cases, take at face value the expressed intent and public statements of important people in history as a reflection of true belief and intent, as accurate and honest? Why or why not?

_____

_____

_____

3. Often the Confederation period—the 1780s, under the Articles of Confederation—is considered a period lacking in achievement or progress. Yet the passage of the Northwest Ordinance of July 1787 was a decision of enormous importance. It allowed new lands to the west to follow a process to statehood and gave these new states all the rights and privileges of the original thirteen states.

Why is this decision so important? What alternatives did Congress have regarding this huge area of unsettled land west of the Appalachian Mountains?

_____

_____

_____

_____

_____

4. Many have discussed ways to find the "original intent" of the Founding Fathers, so that judges can base constitutionally related decisions on the exact meaning delegates intended in the constitutional provision of the late summer of 1787. Do you think it proper to interpret present-day cases on the basis of a historical study on the intent of that 1787 group of Philadelphia delegates? If "yes," how will the historian find out the intent of the Founding Fathers? Will reading their letters, diaries or journals, and notes be sufficient? If "no," then what other criteria or standards should be used for contemporary constitutional interpretations—justices' reasoning, past precedents, needs of the times, or what else?

_____

_____

_____

_____

_____

Soon after the new government got under way, a debate arose over the government's right to establish a national bank. James Madison and Edmund Randolph, important convention members, argued that the government did not have that right. Alexander Hamilton and George Washington, also convention members, proceeded to establish a bank. In what way does this disagreement indicate how difficult it is to establish the "original intent" of the convention delegates?

_____

_____

_____

_____

_____

5. Historians have written about a possible career crisis among the members of the 1787 Constitutional Convention. Leaders among the delegates had reached their status because of their performance on a national level either in the Revolution or in the Continental Congress. Under the relatively weak Articles of Confederation, they felt the scope of their influence narrowed and their futures restricted. They faced a "career foreclosure," as one researcher put it. Local

politicians dominated state governments. Those who fought on a national scale for the glory of a powerful America—Washington, Madison, Hamilton, John Jay, John Marshall—could realize this dream only if, instead of revising the weak Articles of Confederation, they created a frame of government with authority over the states and the people. This would give them opportunity to continue their careers on a grand scale. Most of the convention leaders did go on to hold office under the new Constitution. What is your reaction to this theory? Is it possible? Probably not true? Probably accurate? Explain.

_____

_____

_____

_____

6. An examination of Madison's notes on the Constitutional Convention and of other evidence from letters and writings indicate that the Founding Fathers feared both a strong central government and a government directly influenced by the people. Their answer was the separation of powers, checks and balances, and the placement of intervening bodies between the people and high officials— election of senators by state legislatures, judges chosen by the executive, and an electoral college. This system is sometimes cumbersome and slow in accomplishing what seems to be the wishes of the people of a particular time. Has the government designed by the Founding Fathers worked both in avoiding the concentration of power nationally and in avoiding the potential for radical changes brought about by a precipitate swing in public opinion? Explain.

_____

_____

_____

_____

7. The Sedition Act of 1798 was an effort to restrict criticism of the government and its personnel, including the president. Those who support freedom of the press and freedom of speech have opposed such acts, including a similar one in 1918. Should limits be imposed on the right of the press to be critical of the government and elected representatives? If not, why not? If so, explain what type of restrictions.

_____

_____

_____

_____

8. Hamilton's program of funding the national debt involved the borrowing of money in the form of government bonds purchased from Americans and foreign investors. Interest would be paid through the sale of public land, a tariff, and other taxes. At the end of a specified period the principal would be paid by issuing new government bonds. Thus the nation might be continually in debt. Hamilton considered this a blessing since it attracted wealthy men as supporters of the government. Do you agree with Hamilton? Why or why not?

_____

_____

_____

_____

_____

9. Some have said that Madison and Jefferson, in the Virginia and Kentucky resolutions of 1798 that upheld states' rights, presented a more dangerous concept than the Sedition Act of 1798, the act that Madison and Jefferson opposed by their resolutions. Do you agree or disagree? Why?

_____

_____

_____

_____

_____

10. Two political parties emerged from the political and diplomatic turmoil of the 1790s—the Federalists and the Republicans (later the Democratic Party). Washington deplored factions and political parties. John Adams spoke against political division. No one admitted the desirability of political parties. Were political parties as an institution inevitable or an unfortunate innovation that could and should have been avoided? Explain.

_____

_____

_____

_____

_____

11. As he left office, Washington warned against permanent alliances with foreign nations. He suggested that American entanglements abroad be limited to temporary alliances for particular immediate purposes and commercial treaties. Other presidents repeated this advice. At present the United States has several long-term alliances with many other nations, one in particular with several non-Communist nations of Europe (NATO). What has taken place since 1796—

Washington's first warning—that has led to this policy change? Is Washington's advice obsolete? Why or why not?

_____

_____

_____

_____

_____

12. Examine the two quotations at the beginning of the chapter. Briefly explain the meaning of each. How might each be applied to the content of this chapter?

_____

_____

_____

_____

_____

THOUGHTS FOR QUESTIONS

1. One problem is dating a beginning to the process of revolution. The Stamp Act Congress and the Boston Tea Party would be part of the protest phase. The Boston Massacre provided an emotional incident. Parliament continued to back down in the face of protests, boycotts, and noncompliance. They repealed the Stamp Act and the Grenville program. They provided for external taxes only. This was moderate reform, although it was reform of a recently imposed program, not a long-standing tradition. Phase C is fulfilled by the battles at Lexington and Concord, the French assistance, the destruction of a statue of George III, the expulsion of the Loyalists, and finally by the war itself. Phase D: Washington and others, after hearing of Shay's Rebellion in Massachusetts, decided that threats to the colonies' stability and unity had gone too far, so they called for a convention to write a constitution that gave much authority to a central government. Several "radicals" who had brought about the Revolution stood in opposition—Sam Adams, Patrick Henry, Richard Henry Lee, and Jefferson, who was in France at the time. Phase E: General Washington, president of the Constitutional Convention and unanimous choice as the first president of the United States, put down the Whiskey Rebellion by leading a large number of troops against the rebels. Phase F: Jefferson's election restored some revolutionary ideals—equality, simplicity, a low budget, local government power—but retained part of the traditional government program—a tariff, expansion, a national bank, for example.

Perhaps the degree of conservative reaction, Phase D, in the American case could be questioned. The leaders of the Revolution followed it through to completion. Thus the American Revolution had more continuity than other revolutions. Also, the American Revolution was primarily an effort at independence from a colonial power. It was not an internal civil war such as in France and Russia. Probably the ideology of the other two revolutions was, for that time, more extreme than in the American case. The Americans were not seeking new values, but trying to retain their old ones. The American Revolution may resemble the independence movements in Nigeria or India more than the European revolutions. Fitting the American Revolution into this pattern may be squeezing events into an *unsuitable* mold.

2. Certainly the historian needs to probe and dig below the surface to discover what happened in the past. However, to assume that every public figure is constantly hiding thoughts, feelings, and intent is to operate with too much suspicion. Many statements contain a mixture of true feelings and hidden intent. Actions spring from multiple motivations. If the meeting of a group of people who aim to convince others of the need to change a form of government is a "conspiracy," then Washington was a conspirator. However, to assume that this means he intended to thwart the will of the American people in order to gain his own advantage is not necessarily correct. A person can join with others to seek what he or she thinks is best for society and the nation. This is at the heart of the "right to assembly." Washington's sacrifices, risks, and long hours of service tend to offset the charge of conspiracy for private advantage. Many of his public statements seem sincere and relate closely to his behavior.

Accepting public statements is the first step in the historian's quest for accuracy about the past. However, no true historian would stop there. Digging deeper, as any good detective might, should be an automatic procedure for a professional historian.

3. Individual states or Congress could have held the area west of the Appalachian Mountains as a colony, subservient to the East. Or Ohio, Kentucky, and Alabama could have become part of Pennsylvania, Virginia, and Georgia. The ideal of allowing large groups of people to make their own decisions about most aspects of their lives could only be preserved if something akin to statehood was devised. This equal participation was contradictory to the colonial experience under the British.

4. We live in a much different society than that of 1787. Yet some of the basic principles adhered to in 1787 are still important—representative government, limited government, regular elections, and so forth. These were the "original intent" and are the "current intent" for most Americans. Finding the original intent in many other matters is almost impossible. Convention issues settled by majority vote were compromises and often did not embody the exact wishes of any single delegate. Reading primary sources may help; however, few sources are preserved and those may not reflect the precise views of the authors. Delegates' minds may have changed upon later reflections. Meetings were in secret and there were no verbatim records. Interpreters of constitutional law try to balance the three criteria listed, and in most cases also attempt to consider the intent of the authors of the Constitution. Would it be better if we knew the exact intent of convention delegates?

Regarding the establishment of a national bank, if convention delegates could not agree on original intent at the time, how can we discover original intent two hundred years later? Of course, some delegates, knowing the original intent of the majority, may have spoken out against it at a later time. Or they may have disagreed during the convention and voted accordingly.

5. This seems reasonable, but it is difficult to prove. The ages of the delegates supports this contention; those who supported the Constitution were younger than those who opposed it. The supporters sought and obtained public office. Neverthe-

less, most of those who held public office had substantial sources of income in private endeavors. Several—Washington, Jefferson, and John Adams—preferred to retire to the plantation or farm rather than hold office. At least they expressed this sentiment in public.

6. It has accomplished this as well as any other arrangement could. Although many citizens maintain that the national government has too much power, the fifty state governments still retain important responsibilities. Radical and sudden change is difficult, if not impossible. The balance and tension continue.

7. The key is the type of restriction. Some media criticism is extreme and in bad taste. It is difficult to engender respect or admiration for the government and officials when so much negative, supercritical castigation of them appears on the daily menu. Yet taking steps toward restrictions is dangerous. Perhaps to err on the side of excesses in criticism is safer in a democracy than excessive censorship of criticism. Most Americans feel the press goes too far, but the parameters of "too far" are impossible to define.

8. Jefferson believed that a national debt was a badge of dishonor. He reduced the debt during his two terms in office. There is some evidence that a national debt enables the government to influence the economy. Those who have invested in government bonds do support the financial soundness of the government and may serve as watchdogs over excesses. Yet this debt may, at the same time, lead to the selfish influence of interest groups on government. Those who do not have money to invest and who pay part of their income to reduce the debt may have a different perspective. Excessive debt has caused catastrophe in many governments throughout history. How does one define what is excessive? Ironically, the soundness of American credit allowed Jefferson to make his Louisiana Purchase in 1803.

9. The Sedition Act was short-lived, applied to a handful of Republican newspaper editors and writers, and has been condemned as un-American since that time. On the other hand, the concept of states' rights, especially the right to oppose action by the central government, has caused controversy and problems throughout American history. It created crises in 1815, 1832, and 1954. And the concept was at the heart of the decision by the Southern states in 1860–1861 to secede. It still lingers in issues such as regulating speed limits, abortion, affirmative action, and law enforcement. One must be careful of arguments involving states' rights, even if the cause seems just.

10. It is difficult to imagine a nation functioning without some form of political groupings. This is true even if a monarchy or totalitarian system prevails. The American tradition began with two political groupings and has continued with two parties. For a pragmatic people not given to ideological struggles, this seems natural. Some of the behavior of political-party members must be deplored. The parties are the butt of much humor. But they do gather and focus public opinion on issues. They are, for the most part, responsive to the people, and despite ridicule and criticism, select reasonably competent candidates for office. Try to imagine the functioning of a democratic political system without political parties.

11. Obviously, changes in communication and transportation have put Washington, D.C., in more immediate contact with Bonn, Moscow, or Tokyo than the time it took in 1800 to travel merely from the White House to Congress. We no longer have two oceans serving as gigantic moats to defend the fortress of America. Economic interdependence draws the United States into interaction with *all* the world,

literally all the world. The threat of massive retaliation for any offense is as immediate as the prospect in 1796 of having a squadron of British or French warships at the mouth of the Potomac. The United States has replaced England as the leading nation in the world in both an economic sense and in the diplomatic arena. As such, it seems to have no alternative but to form diplomatic alliances with many other nations. The extent and conditions of obligations to foreign countries need to be examined carefully.

12. The roots of present-day problems and issues lie in the past. Using only reason and empirical evidence to solve a problem may not be sufficient unless that logic is based on what has developed in the past. The past reveals how people *actually* behaved, not how they *should* have behaved. Holmes's insight into actual behavior gives more enlightenment about present conduct than does any analysis of factors drawn only from the present.

The founding of this nation and the establishment of a representative government can be glorified and idealized. A generation of heroes emerged in 1787 to produce an ideal document and then to lay the benevolent foundations of a perfect government—a "splendid story"! Yet biased economic interests, the acceptance of slavery in the Constitution, the struggle for political power, the clash of Hamilton and Jefferson, the ridiculing of Washington by the Republican press, and other examples of less than ideal behavior mar the splendid story. A jaundiced eye on the past, at least an acceptance of the past as a mixture of selfishness and selflessness, is a more realistic attitude. It was still a splendid story, but with a panorama of vices as well as virtues.

Map Exercise One

Maps are very important to historians. It is difficult to proceed through any period of history without the use of a map. Many times the location is vital to an understanding of the development of historical events. Deeper insights into events emerge from knowing physical locations and relationships among locations. Placing Gettysburg somewhere on the East Coast, for example, is not the same as knowing that Gettysburg is located in southeastern Pennsylvania.

Study Map 1A and become acquainted with the important sites. Then, using Map 1B and the following list of sites with descriptions of their importance, practice locating these sites on Map 1B. The list of sites is in random order.

1. *St. Augustine* Oldest city in North America. It was an early Spanish settlement that gave them claim to Florida; in 1819 Florida was sold to the United States.

2. *New Orleans* A Spanish and French city that was sold to the United States along with the Louisiana Territory purchase. The city was captured by the North in the Civil War.

3. *New York* Settled first by the Dutch and then taken by the English in the seventeenth century. It was the first capital of the United States and later a commercial center for western trade. Immigrants from Europe were processed through Ellis Island in its harbor.

4. *Montreal* French-Canadian city captured by the British during the French and Indian War (1754–1763) and attacked by Americans in the War of 1812.

5. *Atlanta* A city in Georgia that was burned in 1864 during the Civil War by a Northern army under orders from General William Tecumseh Sherman.

6. *Washington, D.C.* Made the nation's capital during the administration of John Adams (1787–1801). It is located along the Potomac River between Virginia and Maryland.

7. *The Alamo* Site of the battle at which Mexican general Antonio López de Santa Anna and his army destroyed a small detachment of Americans during the struggle for Texas independence.

8. *Vicksburg* City along the Mississippi River that was successfully attacked by General Ulysses S. Grant in July 1863. The fall of the city and fort opened the Mississippi to Northern shipping and separated Texas from the Confederacy.

9. *Northwest Territory* Area acquired from England at the end of the Revolutionary War (1783). Later, under congressional supervision, several free states were formed from this territory.

10. *Pittsburgh* Formerly Fort Duquesne, under the French, and site of an English defeat in the French and Indian War. It became a center for the iron and steel industry in the later nineteenth century.

11. *St. Louis* French fur trading settlement and later gateway to the West. It was the departure site for Lewis and Clark on their scientific expedition and for many western settlers.

12. *Detroit* Site of a French and later an English fort. In the eighteenth century it was a center for the fur trade and later became the automobile capital of the world.

13. *Iroquois* Home of the largest Indian confederation in North America, centered in New York State.

14. *Jamestown* The site in 1607 of the first permanent English settlement in what is today the United States.

15. *Philadelphia* City in Pennsylvania established by William Penn and the Quakers. It was the eighteenth-century cultural center of the American colonies and port of entry for immigrants from many European nations.

16. *Boston* A Puritan city that became the shipping center for the thirteen colonies and the city where the American Revolution began. It was later a center for nineteenth-century reform and abolitionism.

17. *Richmond* The capital of the Confederacy during the Civil War—attacked by General Grant in 1865.

18. *Chesapeake Bay* Along this bay many important settlements were founded in the colonial period: Jamestown, Annapolis, Baltimore, and, up the Potomac River, Washington, D.C.

19. *San Salvador* Island where Columbus first landed at the end of his 1492 voyage across the Atlantic.

20. *Charleston* Cultural center of the South and entrepôt for the overseas transport of rice, indigo, and, later, cotton. Fort Sumpter, which drew the first shots of the Civil War, is located in the harbor.

CANADA

Montreal

Great
Lakes

NEW
HAMPSHIRE

NEW YORK
IROQUOIS

Boston

MASS.

RHODE ISLAND
CONNECTICUT

Detroit

PENNSYLVANIA

New York

Chicago

Philadelphia

NEW JERSEY

NORTHWEST TERRITORY

Gettysburg
Pittsburgh

DELAWARE

Ohio River

Washington, D.C.

MARYLAND

St. Louis

Richmond

Chesapeake Bay

Jamestown

MISSOURI

VIRGINIA

36°30′

NORTH
CAROLINA

Atlantic Ocean

Arkansas River

Mississippi River

SOUTH
CAROLINA

MEXICO
(TEXAS)

Red River

Atlanta

Charleston

Vicksburg

GEORGIA

N

W   E

S

St. Augustine

New Orleans

The Alamo

FLORIDA

BAHAMA
ISLANDS

Gulf of Mexico

San Salvador

CUBA

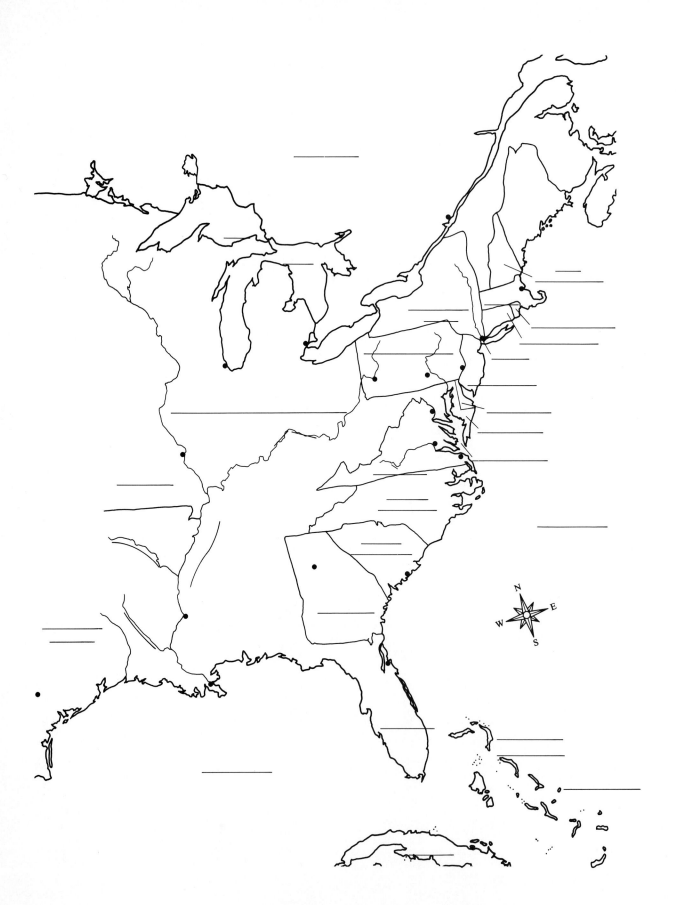

CHAPTER

5

THE NEW NATION MATURES

*"Any event of the past can be made to appear inevitable
by a competent historian."*

Dick Mumford

*"We have constantly to check ourselves in reading history with the remem-
brance that, to the actors in the drama, events appeared very different
from the way they appear to us. We know what they were doing far better
than they knew themselves."*

Randolph Bowne

PART I
Acquiring Essential Data

ESSENTIAL DATES

Determine the correct sequence and write the approximate date for each of the following events.

1. The British burn Washington, D.C. ⎯⎯⎯⎯

2. The Erie Canal across New York State is opened. ⎯⎯⎯⎯

3. President James Monroe presents his doctrine on the relations between America and Europe. ⎯⎯⎯⎯

4. Congress passes the Missouri Compromise bill. ⎯⎯⎯⎯

5. William Henry Harrison defeats the British at the Battle of the Thames. Tecumseh, a prominent Indian leader, is killed. ⎯⎯⎯⎯

6. Eli Whitney invents the cotton gin. ⎯⎯⎯⎯

7. In *Marbury* v. *Madison* the Supreme Court declares a law passed by Congress unconstitutional. ⎯⎯⎯⎯

8. The Rush-Bagot Agreement demilitarizes the Great Lakes. ⎯⎯⎯⎯

9. The United States fights a second war against the British. ⎯⎯⎯⎯

10. President Thomas Jefferson purchases the land west of the Mississippi from France. ⎯⎯⎯⎯

ESSENTIAL CONCEPTS

Examine each concept and write what contemporary relevance it might have.

1. *peaceful transition of power* The willingness to yield political power without violence or other obstruction, but on the basis of the election process. An example is the yielding by the Federalists and John Adams to Thomas Jefferson and the Republicans.

⎯⎯⎯⎯⎯⎯⎯⎯⎯⎯⎯⎯⎯⎯⎯⎯⎯⎯⎯⎯⎯⎯⎯⎯⎯⎯⎯⎯

⎯⎯⎯⎯⎯⎯⎯⎯⎯⎯⎯⎯⎯⎯⎯⎯⎯⎯⎯⎯⎯⎯⎯⎯⎯⎯⎯⎯

⎯⎯⎯⎯⎯⎯⎯⎯⎯⎯⎯⎯⎯⎯⎯⎯⎯⎯⎯⎯⎯⎯⎯⎯⎯⎯⎯⎯

2. *tribute* The demand for money by North African states for the safe passage of American merchant ships in the Mediterranean Sea.

⎯⎯⎯⎯⎯⎯⎯⎯⎯⎯⎯⎯⎯⎯⎯⎯⎯⎯⎯⎯⎯⎯⎯⎯⎯⎯⎯⎯

⎯⎯⎯⎯⎯⎯⎯⎯⎯⎯⎯⎯⎯⎯⎯⎯⎯⎯⎯⎯⎯⎯⎯⎯⎯⎯⎯⎯

⎯⎯⎯⎯⎯⎯⎯⎯⎯⎯⎯⎯⎯⎯⎯⎯⎯⎯⎯⎯⎯⎯⎯⎯⎯⎯⎯⎯

3. *"agrarian cupidity"* The demand by westerners for more land, especially Canada, to use for settlements or speculation.

_____

_____

_____

4. *American system* The program that allows the central (federal) government to finance and sponsor internal improvements with higher tariffs and land sales.

_____

_____

_____

5. *"factions"* Political groupings that organize to influence and obtain elective office—interest groups or, on a large scale, political parties.

_____

_____

_____

6. *steam power* The process of heating water to form steam in an enclosed space, and thereby producing pressure with power to drive machinery.

_____

_____

_____

7. *limited liability* Protection offered investors who thus are liable to lose only their actual investment in a corporation, not any personal possessions unrelated to the corporation.

_____

_____

_____

8. *common law* An unwritten law based on custom, habit, and previous judicial decisions.

_____

_____

_____

9. *laissez faire* The economic policy that allows private business to function on its own with a minimum of government involvement.

_____

_____

_____

10. *speculation* The economic process of purchasing land, usually large amounts, at a low price in the hope of selling it for a higher price in the future. It has been practiced by individual settlers and land companies throughout American history.

_____

_____

_____

ANSWERS

Correct sequence of events and their dates.

1. 6; 1793
2. 7; 1803
3. 10; 1803
4. 9; 1812–15
5. 5; 1813

6. 1; 1814
7. 8; 1817
8. 4; 1820
9. 3; 1823
10. 2; 1825

PART II
Developing Thinking Skills

SKILL EXERCISE ONE: FACT, INFERENCE, OR OPINION

Under each of the following statements, write whether it is a fact, an inference, or an opinion. Explain your choices and check them with those suggested.

1. President Jefferson chose to send a clerk to read his annual messages to Congress rather than appear in person and deliver the message.

   _____

   _____

2. The men in Jefferson's administration were capable, well-educated, and experienced, and had as much ability as the Federalists they replaced.

   _____

   _____

3. Jefferson was better than both presidents George Washington and John Adams and was an ideal president for any period of history.

   _____

   _____

4. Jefferson said in his first inaugural address that "this Government" was "the world's best hope" and "the strongest Government on earth."

   _____

   _____

5. Jefferson catered to banking, commercial, and manufacturing interests and sought to win their political support and even possibly attach them to his political party.

_____

_____

6. Jefferson's desire to destroy the Federalists controlled his policies and appointment choices.

_____

_____

7. The opponents of Jefferson were unscrupulous men seeking wealth and aristocratic powers.

_____

_____

8. Jefferson was informal at state dinners and, rather than rank each guest by position and honor, allowed each person to find a place at the table.

_____

_____

9. Jefferson studied and wrote on Neo-platonism, the pronunciation of Greek, the Anglo-Saxon language, the future of the steam engine, archaeology, and theology.

_____

_____

10. Jefferson was ignorant about economics and made several serious mistakes in that area, especially in regard to an embargo in 1807.

_____

_____

ANSWERS AND EXPLANATIONS

1. Fact. Any theory of why Jefferson did this would be an inference—lack of ability to speak well in public or, as he claimed, to avoid appearing as a monarch speaking from a throne—but that he did it is a fact.

2. Inference. This is probably true, but it is an inference from several facts about their backgrounds.

3. Opinion. What is meant by "better" and "ideal"? This statement is exaggerated and cannot be convincingly maintained.

4. Fact. He did say this. The words themselves are his inference or opinion.

5. Fact. He did this and evidence for it exists. Yet the word "cater" gives some pause since we also know of his interests in farmers and agrarian matters.

6. Inference. The words "destroy" and "controlled" are difficult to establish as facts. He followed many policies because they seemed desirable.

7. Opinion. This generalization about all opponents classifies them in the same way. Certainly their motives were mixed. It is an exaggerated statement of opinion.

8. Fact. This informality disturbed many diplomats, especially the British.

9. Fact. Very few subjects escaped this man's interest; he did, indeed, study these diverse topics.

10. Inference. This is the consensus of historians, but only by inference. It is not a factual-type statement to be proven beyond reasonable doubt.

Write a factual statement about Jefferson. Then write an inference statement related to the factual statement. Finally, write an opinion statement also related to the factual statement.

_____

_____

_____

Find and write below an inference statement from a textbook or another source about Jefferson. What makes the statement an inference rather than a fact? Explain.

_____

_____

SKILL EXERCISE TWO: EVALUATING ARGUMENTS

Examine the following arguments relating to the American decision to go to war with the British in 1812. In each, determine the primary type of appeal used and classify it in one of the following categories: *Reason, Intuition, Anecdotal, Empirical,* or *Authority.* Check your choices with those provided afterward.

1. When the Hartford Convention representatives, who had opposed the war and even contemplated secession, arrived in Washington in 1814, they found people celebrating Andrew Jackson's victory over the British at New Orleans.

_____

_____

2. President James Madison and a majority of Congress believed that the British had gone too far in insulting the United States.

_____

_____

3. The British stopped American ships at sea and removed five thousand sailors and some naturalized American citizens, and confiscated cargoes believed to be from the French West Indies.

_____

_____

4. Indians had guns and ammunition as well as encouragement from the British to attack American settlers; therefore, it seemed proper to make war on the source of the problem, the British in Canada.

_____

_____

5. The principle a nation must follow when harassed and humiliated by an enemy is to strike back at that enemy even if odds favor the enemy.

_____

_____

6. Many citizens instinctively felt that the nation had to stand up for its rights or it would lose its reputation and honor.

_____

_____

7. Despite their cry for war, most of the militia in Kentucky and Tennessee decided they would not march into Canada to acquire more land for the United States.

_____

_____

8. The Congress did not support the war with sufficient appropriations or measures to raise revenue; it merely authorized loans and levied some new taxes that were inadequate to offset the costs of war.

_____

_____

9. If the Americans had put into the field the number of troops necessary to defeat the British (and they did have this potential), then they could have easily captured Canada and even Florida.

_____

_____

10. During the debate over the addition of ten frigates to the navy a few months before the war, one of the militant "War Hawks" refused to support a stronger navy because it would mean "perpetual taxes and perpetually increasing public debt."

_____

_____

ANSWERS AND EXPLANATIONS

1. Anecdotal. This is an ironic incident that reveals how far the representatives were out of touch with popular opinion. It is an interesting and significant anecdote.

2. Authority. The appeal here is that persons of high authority should be aware of the total situation.

3. Empirical. The use of specific evidence to make a point is an empirical approach.

4. Reason. The logical movement goes from one statement to an inference from that statement. "Therefore" is a key signal to the use of reason.

5. Authority. The *principle* here becomes the authority; it is not evidence or reason. It may not be reasonable or prudent to fight, but the principle argues for a proper course of action.

6. Intuition. This is about a feeling and no proof or authority is cited. It may well be unreasonable and without support.

7. Anecdotal. This is a situation or story that is not presented as empirical evidence or as a process of reasoning.

8. Empirical. This is an effort to offer specific evidence that although Congress voted for the war, it was reluctant to actually support it.

9. Reason. The "if" and "then" gives this away as an effort to employ logic to prove the point.

10. Anecdotal. This is a small incident or a story that could be meant to give insight into the "War Hawks's" unrealistic attitude about not raising taxes in preparation for war. But from the viewpoint of the "War Hawks," the story might be construed as reasoning, and to some extent it presents evidence and, therefore, is empirical.

PART III
Debating Historical, Social, and Moral Issues

QUESTIONS FOR THOUGHT

After reading and reflecting, write your answers to these questions.

1. Thomas Jefferson's style as president differed from that of his predecessors. He kept a low profile. The key words to his approach were simplicity and economy. He was informal. He would not give speeches lest he appear as a monarch. No pomp and circumstance were allowed; no seats were assigned by prestige or honor at his table. He decided to walk rather than ride in a carriage after his inaugural. He did not let his birthday be known or celebrated. Is this style fitting for a president of a democratic society? Why or why not?

_____

_____

_____

_____

_____

2. Jefferson faced a major dilemma in 1803. French emperor Napoleon Bonaparte had offered him a bargain for the purchase of the Louisiana Territory. He had to act quickly to purchase this strategic area before Napoleon changed his mind. However, the Constitution did not grant specific powers for such a purpose. Jefferson always had been an advocate of a strict interpretation of the Constitution. He made the purchase anyway. Did Jefferson betray his principles? Explain. Should he have made the purchase? Imagine the course of American history without it.

_____

_____

_____

_____

_____

3. The Hartford Convention, meeting in 1814 during the War of 1812—which New England opposed—proposed several amendments to the Constitution. React to each of the following; do you agree or disagree with the amendment and why?

  A. Abolition of the three-fifths compromise (counting slaves for apportionment of representatives and taxation)

  _____

  _____

  B. Requirement of a two-thirds vote of both houses of Congress to declare war and to admit new states

  _____

  _____

  C. Exclusion of foreign-born residents from federal offices

  _____

  _____

  D. Limitation of the presidency to one term

  _____

  _____

  E. Prohibition of the election of two successive presidents from the same state

  _____

  _____

4. Below are three major interpretations of the causes of the War of 1812.

  A. The British mistreated Americans on the high seas. They impressed sailors and interrupted commercial shipping. They had no respect for the international rights of the United States. President Madison had little choice but to call for war.

B. The major reason for the war was the western hunger for land, especially Canada. Westerners also wanted to end the Indian threat, which they believed was instigated by and supported by the British. The South and West joined together to pressure Madison and then to vote for war. The South

C. The primary motivations for war were patriotism and honor. A country practicing Republicanism and self-government must be able to stand alone and not accept humiliation by foreign powers. A political idealism and devotion to the country brought on the war. This is especially true for the Middle Atlantic states that supported the war and yet had little commerce and no Indian threat.

Which of the three interpretations seems most reasonable to you? Why?

_____

_____

_____

What type of evidence could be gathered or sources consulted to support each of the three?

_____

_____

_____

Is determining the causes of the war an unsolvable historical problem or would sufficient research and study bring us to accept one view over the others? Explain.

_____

_____

5. The New England states voted against the war. During the war they met at the Hartford Convention to make plans to avoid similar situations in the future; they continued to trade with the British during the war; and some even gave signals to the British about the movement of American ships. Was this treason? How much dissent should be allowed in wartime? Did the Federalists of New England go too far in opposition to the War of 1812? Explain.

_____

_____

_____

_____

_____

6. Historians have long debated the Monroe Doctrine. Below are the three major viewpoints about the policy.

A. One group concludes that Monroe's statement was defensive in purpose and was aimed at preserving the security of the United States. The United

States intended to fight European, and especially Russian, imperialism and to maintain the concept of self-determination for all people. The doctrine was a statement of idealism mixed with practical diplomatic considerations.

B. Other historians, mostly writing in the 1960s, emphasize the economic motivation—the desire for commercial strength, for control of trade in Latin America. The exclusion of Europeans was an effort to monopolize the economic scene and to exploit Latin America, a plan that has been executed since that time in a harmful and dangerous fashion.

C. A third view relates the doctrine to politics at the time, especially the ambition of John Quincy Adams to be president. Not much was really at stake in diplomacy and the doctrine had little impact at the time or for the next twenty-five years. Economic factors were irrelevant and the protection of independent republics in Latin America was nice rhetoric, but impossible in any practical manner.

Which of these three views seems the most accurate interpretation of the Monroe Doctrine? Why?

_____

_____

_____

The Monroe Doctrine was issued in 1823 to meet the challenges of the time. It was unilateral, that is, not agreed to by any other nation. Should it be brought up today in consideration of problems in Latin America? Why or why not?

_____

_____

7. The laissez faire economic philosophy calls for a minimum of government intervention in business. The economist Adam Smith argued that entrepreneurs should be free to pursue profits and to gain wealth. The consequences of this action would be better and cheaper products for the consumer. Government interference, except in law enforcement and the maintenance of order, would be counterproductive and promote inefficiency. This philosophy was the accepted one in nineteenth-century America. Do you accept it as valid? What, if any, limitations or modifications would you place on a laissez faire system? Would business interests then have a right to demand government intervention *on behalf* of business? Consider government aid through a protective tariff, a national bank, government-financed roads and canals, limited liability, and low-cost public land.

_____

_____

_____

_____

8. The Missouri Compromise settled the slavery issue for about thirty years. Yet, later, the controversial subject entered politics again in the 1850s and led to the Civil War in 1861. Read about the controversy over slavery in 1820 and suggest

how the issue might have been settled in a more satisfactory manner at that time. Was the Missouri Compromise a failure? Was it actually more harmful than no compromise? Explain.

_____

_____

_____

_____

_____

9. Consider the quotations at the beginning of the chapter. Explain the meaning and implications of each and determine whether you agree or disagree with the quotation. How might each quotation apply to this period of history?

_____

_____

_____

_____

_____

THOUGHTS FOR QUESTIONS

1. Some people have argued that in order to obtain respect it is necessary for a president to be dignified and appear with some majesty. As a result, the people will respect the government and obey its laws. Americans have developed in recent times what is called the "Imperial Presidency." Some presidents have gone out of their way to show that they are "of the people." One has invited the press in to watch him cook breakfast (Ford); another decided to wear a sweater and walk to the inaugural parade (Carter). Perhaps respect is much deeper than appearances?

2. Principles sometimes have a way of interfering with "doing the right thing." By most standards of measurement the purchase of the Louisiana Territory was the right course of action in 1803. If the primary principle is to make the best decision in a given dilemma, then Jefferson followed this principle. However, since the United States is a nation that subscribes to favoring the law over individual choice, challenging the law could be harmful. In some cases the law prevents the achievement of justice. Yet it is dangerous to have leaders who decide to do what they think is "best for the country" even if it is illegal. History is filled with tyrants who were acting on behalf of "the people." No one would call Jefferson a tyrant (except perhaps some of his slaves), but to bypass the law for the apparent benefit of the nation can lead to tyranny.

3. These are the student's choices. The three-fifths compromise was eliminated later. The two-thirds war vote would not have affected world wars I and II. Foreign-born residents are excluded from the presidency, but this does not seem to have been an issue throughout most of American history. Item *D* is still being debated, although usually with a provision for a six-year term rather than the four-year term. After the Virginia dynasty, no state has dominated the office of the president.

4. Madison emphasized the first interpretation and dwelled on it in his speech calling for war. Item A no doubt influenced the degree of patriotism and honor described in item C. So did the belief that the British encouraged the Indians to raid white settlements in the West. Westerners talked about needing land, but seemed unwilling to fight for it once war was declared. Item A supplies the emotional spark for war.

It is especially difficult to find evidence for item C. What proves devotion to country or concern about honor? Perhaps political speeches or newspaper editorials would reveal some opinions on causes of the war. Actual cases of Indian attacks and statistics on the number of sailors impressed and cargoes confiscated would be helpful. The private writings of members of Congress and of President Madison should be consulted.

The problem of what caused the war is unsolvable because there is some evidence for each of the positions and no effective way to quantify the data and arrive at fractions or percentages. The historian usually resorts to combining the factors and may not choose to weigh each with any exactness. Perhaps the combined effect of all the factors was needed in order to bring war. Most historians would agree with the known causes but the primary one is still being debated.

5. This situation brings us to an age-old dilemma—the relationship between personal beliefs and needs and one's commitment to the nation. Once war is declared or fighting begins, is it a citizen's obligation to participate and support the country in all cases? Or is a belief that the war is immoral or the fighting unnecessary sufficient reason to speak and act in opposition? What are the limits of this opposition? The issue was clouded in 1812 because of the commercial interests of New Englanders. Profits more than principles brought on the pro-British stance.

6. Monroe's message did not seem all that important at the time; therefore, perhaps the third interpretation relates more to the motivation and intent of those participating at the time. Practical political considerations prevail many times over matters of policy and principle. The United States did indeed come to dominate the economies of Latin America, but it might be difficult to prove that this was anticipated in the 1820s. Most Americans sympathized with the ideal of self-determination, but throughout American history the Monroe Doctrine has been used to establish stability and diplomatic friendliness rather than to promote freedom.

No other nation or group is required to legally recognize and submit to the Monroe Doctrine. It is a traditional American "attitude" or statement of intent and represents sentiments that must be taken into consideration. It has no standing in international law. If it still represents the best interests of the United States in relations with Latin America, then it has validity. However, *it* does not give the United States the legal or moral *right* to act in Latin America.

7. One weakness of this philosophy appeared in the late nineteenth century. When left completely alone, corporations tend to move in the direction of monopolistic control over particular aspects of manufacturing or commerce. Thus competition is ended or severely blunted. Few chief executives today would conclude that profits are the only consideration in economic activity. Regulations for safety are widely accepted. The protection of labor brings limitations to the system. Perhaps the public interest is more important than profits, although this public interest is sometimes difficult to determine. The partial list of ways in which the government has *aided* business indicates that even the entrepreneur does not accept complete government

aloofness from the economy. To call for nonintervention in matters that might interfere with profits and then to request government protection and assistance in order to enhance profits seems illogical and inconsistent philosophically.

8. One way to look at the compromise is to note that war and violence among the states were avoided for forty years. To some extent, the postponement of violence is of itself a benefit. To argue that we eventually went through a horrible civil war does not mean that it would have been better to have the war in 1820 or to have split up as a nation then. Wars postponed are often wars avoided. Gradual manumission (emancipation) over the twenty years after the compromise would have been preferable. And restriction on slavery expansion beyond the states in which it existed might have been a more positive settlement. A strong stand against slavery in 1820 and forceful action to remove the institution from the United States would have avoided the immense suffering of slaves for the next forty-five years. Since the Missouri Compromise sanctioned slavery and allowed for its expansion, one might well argue that it had a negative impact on the problem.

9. Historians seek and find causes for events—the War of 1812 and the Louisiana Purchase, for example. The danger is that historians become so wrapped up in explaining why events occur that they do not envision alternatives. Thus each event takes on an air of inevitability. The event *had* to happen, and in the manner in which it did happen. Unfortunately, this eliminates the freedom of action decision-makers have. Did Madison really have a choice about war in 1812? One would like to think he did, but historians tend to surround his action with pressures and influences that make his action "inevitable."

In contrast to the above, when looking back at history we can see the consequences of what took place. We know the outcome. This means we can never actually put ourselves in the place of the actor at the scene who did not know the consequences. However, we can gain insight into the many factors that cause an event, many of which the decision-maker did not know. We know the results of the development of the steam engine, and thereby better understand the ramifications of Oliver Evans's work at the time. We know the ultimate outcome of the slave issue, so we understand the significance of the Missouri Compromise better than those who worked it out in 1820.

CHAPTER

6

MANIFEST DESTINY AND DEMOCRACY

"History is baroque. It smiles at all attempts to force its flow into theoretical patterns or logical grooves; it plays havoc with our generalizations, breaks all our rules."

Will Durant

"Men make their own history, but they do not know that they are making it."

Karl Marx

PART I
Acquiring Essential Data

ESSENTIAL DATES

Determine the correct sequence and write the approximate date for each of the following events.

1. The Cherokees are forced out of Georgia into Oklahoma, moving along a "Trail of Tears." _____

2. A severe depression and economic panic _____

3. The United States fights a war against Mexico for control of the Southwest. _____

4. The Mormons migrate to Utah. _____

5. The discovery of gold in California _____

6. A Franciscan mission is established in California. _____

7. South Carolina issues an Ordinance of Nullification declaring the tariff law to be "not in effect" in the state. _____

8. James K. Polk becomes president. _____

9. Texas declares its independence from Mexico. _____

10. Andrew Jackson's two terms as president of the "common man" _____

ESSENTIAL CONCEPTS

Examine each concept and write what contemporary relevance it might have.

1. *unassimilable* The charge that certain people were very much different from the average white citizen of the United States, and thus could never become an integral part of society. It especially was used against minorities such as the American Indian.

_____

_____

_____

2. *Manifest Destiny* The belief that it was the destiny of the United States to dominate this continent and to acquire land from sea to sea. This was either ordained by God or an aspect of natural development.

_____

_____

_____

3. *nullification* The argument that any law passed by the federal government and deemed by a state to be unconstitutional would not be applied in that state.

_____

_____

_____

4. *"Trail of Tears"* The inhumane twelve-hundred-mile journey the Cherokees and other tribes from the southern states took across the Mississippi River into what is today Oklahoma. A large percentage of the Indians died on this "trail."

_____

_____

_____

5. *"American blood on American soil"* A statement made by President James Polk indicating that the Mexicans had killed several American soldiers on American territory in Texas. They were killed in a disputed area along the Rio Grande river.

_____

_____

_____

6. *common man* In the 1830s this meant the average American who was not wealthy or well-educated, but who had common sense and practical experience and formed the "backbone" of the American republic.

_____

_____

_____

7. *property qualification* Residents in many states until the Jacksonian period were required to own a certain amount of taxable property in order to vote or to hold office. This gave potential voters a "stake in society" and made them more responsible in the area of taxation.

_____

_____

_____

8. *"corrupt bargain"* Said of the process by which John Quincy Adams was chosen president by the House of Representatives. It was widely believed that in return for Henry Clay's influence, Adams appointed Clay secretary of state and, as such, Clay became a prime candidate to succeed Adams as president.

_____

_____

_____

9. *spoils system* The process of rewarding with public office those supporters who have worked for the election of a president. "To the victor belongs the spoils."

_____

_____

_____

10. *preemption* People who settled on and improved a parcel of land had the first right of purchase at the minimum price when the government put up the land for sale.

_____

_____

_____

ANSWERS

Correct sequence of events and their dates.

1. 6; 1648
2. 10; 1829–37
3. 7; 1832
4. 9; 1836
5. 2; 1837–41

6. 1; 1838
7. 8; 1845–49
8. 4; 1846–47
9. 3; 1846–48
10. 5; 1848

PART II
Developing Thinking Skills

SKILL EXERCISE ONE: PERCEIVING SIMILARITIES AND DIFFERENCES

The following are the viewpoints of the adherents of Jacksonian and Jeffersonian democracies. Some of these political attitudes remain prominent and influential in the contemporary world. Read each carefully while looking for similarities and differences. List these in the questions at the end of the descriptions.

Democracy as Envisioned by a Jacksonian

Although supportive of public education, the Jacksonians rely heavily on the instinctive behavior of citizens who serve in public office. Common sense or "horse sense" is superior to higher learning, that is, to book learning. The average man from the street or farm can effectively carry out the duties of public office both in appointed positions and as elected officials. As a matter of fact, it is beneficial for all white male citizens to serve the government in some official capacity. The goal is to establish a government of the common man. This encourages civic virtue and responsible citizenship. For this reason public office should be rotated among those

eligible for office. The greatest fear should be ingrown bureaucrats rather than inex-
perienced but eager new officials. Party workers who have encouraged and stimulated
the common man to become engaged in the political process deserve to be rewarded
with positions in government.

Intellectuals make ineffective rulers; mediocrity in government is a virtue. Nearly
all public offices should be elective, and there should be no property qualifications
for voting or officeholding. The best method for choosing candidates for election is
through the party convention, followed by an exciting and vigorous campaign that
will help the common man make intelligent decisions. The people are the final
source of authority—all the people in cities, towns, and on farms. The people are
defined as white male adults who are not members of Indian tribes. Jacksonians must
attempt to increase the influence of the common man as a common man.

The majority of the people are usually correct in their decisions. They will never
knowingly do wrong. The people are the depository of moral virtue and common-
sense wisdom. Therefore, representatives must do the bidding of their constituents,
the people who elected them. The president is the direct representative of all the
people, the embodiment of national powers. The national government is superior to
the individual state governments, but must not infringe on their legitimate powers.
A small group of justices on the Supreme Court do not determine the constitutionality of laws; the president and Congress do. The president is bound to observe the
Constitution as he understands it. The president must be able to distill the collective
wisdom and will of the masses before making decisions.

In the end, self-government is better than "good" government. The best government governs least. The government serves as an umpire to see that the rules of
society are obeyed and that no person or group acquires special privileges or artificial
advantage. This is especially true regarding monopolistic economic privileges. Those
who expect the government to spend funds for local projects to gain unfair advantage
must be turned away. Frugality in government is to be encouraged.

Democracy as Envisioned by a Jeffersonian

Political parties are inimical to the best interests of a democratic government.
These factions ought to be eliminated because they are intrinsically evil and corrupt.
They also appeal to the emotions of the masses, lead to demagoguery, and promote
self-interest instead of the public good. When all those engaged in politics instead
search for the common welfare, reason will lead away from party conflict and toward
public virtue. Candidates should not seek office by campaigning or speech-making,
but should let the people select them by using wisdom untainted by emotion.

Although the majority will must prevail, minority rights must be protected by law,
even the right to propose the abolition of the democratic system. Any sign of demagoguery must be avoided, even speech-making as a means of asserting authority.
Rather, a republic demands simple manners. The farmer is the backbone of this
nation. Correspondingly, one must beware of the urban mob and its susceptibility to
unscrupulous politicians.

Society must be governed by a "natural aristocracy"—people of education and
experience—not by common men untrained and ill-prepared for carrying out government duties. Once elected, representatives must use their wisdom and judgment to
decide the best policy and not be swayed by the public's temporary inclinations.

According to Thomas Jefferson, the government must be "wise and frugal . . . [and] restrain men from injuring one another . . . [leaving] them otherwise free to regulate their own pursuits of industry and improvement."

It is proper to remove from office those who are guilty of misconduct or who have shown intense partisanship. Otherwise, those who carry out their duties in a competent manner, whatever the political party, should be left to serve the republic. The states are the bulwark against anti-republicanism and the final authorities on the constitutional conduct of those elected. A caucus (party meeting) of elected representatives knows the eligible citizens who aspire to office and should be responsible for choosing the candidates. The president must, as much as possible, remain in the background, allowing the people and their representatives to determine and act in their own best interests. Economy in government, avoidance of urban-class influence, and a policy of leaving manufacturing in the hands of Europeans is in the best interest of the people. Blacks and Indians cannot be expected to participate in the government as responsible citizens. However, Indians eventually may be assimilated into white society. It is not feasible to involve females in government.

QUESTIONS

1. What are the similarities in the two views of democracy?

2. What are the differences between the two views?

3. Which democracy best fits your understanding of the essence of democratic government? Why?

4. What specific points do you object to in each of these descriptions?

5. What three principle features of both views do you consider essential for a strong, effective democracy? Explain why for each.

A. _____

_____

_____

B. _____

_____

_____

C. _____

_____

_____

6. What other features of a democratic system used currently are not found in the above descriptions?

_____

_____

_____

SUGGESTED ANSWERS

1. Similarities
   A. Respect for the power of the people
   B. Opposition to an aristocracy of birth
   C. The common man's right to vote and to hold office
   D. Exclusion of women, blacks, and Indians from politics
   E. Approval of a passive, inactive government
   F. Dislike of the authority exercised by the Supreme Court
   G. Opposition to special privileges for selected groups
   H. Support of a frugal, simple government

2. Differences
   A. Educated, experienced elite in government / or common man in office
   B. Does not accept political parties / or accepts parties
   C. Caucus to select candidates / or convention
   D. Representatives follow their best judgments / or carry out wishes of constituency
   E. States determine constitutionality / or elected officials and the president
   F. The agrarian segment of society must rule / or urban as well as the rural
   G. President should remain in the background / or exert authority and rule
   H. Reason and education are the best guides / or instincts and common sense
   I. Campaigns for office are not necessary / or must be vigorous and active
   J. National government is supreme / or state governments have equal power

3. This is the student's choice.

4. Jacksonianism places the voice of the people in such an authoritarian position that demagoguery could lead to the suppression of the rights of minorities. A constant change in the bureaucracy could lead to chaos. Jefferson's caucus system reduces voter input into the selection of candidates. Certainly Jefferson's opposition to participation in politics and government by blacks, Indians, and women is not supported by a majority in contemporary times.

5. A. Jefferson's willingness to allow opponents to speak out and be free to work against the system.

B. Both advocate a democratic system based on majority rule and yet adhere to the Constitution and its safeguards for minority rights.

C. Both oppose any government support for the special privileges of a few individuals or groups.

6. Some modern democratic features: the secret ballot; primaries; disclosure of campaign contributions; vote of all citizens including women and all races; merit civil service; use of referendum, initiative, and recall; and widespread dissemination of information about candidates and issues through the media.

SKILL EXERCISE TWO: EVALUATING AND APPLYING EVIDENCE

The following thesis relates to the Mexican War and Manifest Destiny. Ten items of data are listed after the thesis. Under each of the items, write whether the information *supports* the thesis, *challenges* the thesis, or is *neutral* data. Briefly explain each answer. Then check your judgment against Answers and Explanations.

The Thesis

"American expansion into Mexican territory under the banner of Manifest Destiny was an unprovoked attack on innocent people in an effort to acquire land and to expand economically."

Items of Data

1. The Mexican government had refused several offers from President James Polk to purchase California, yet the Mexican ambassador in Washington was meeting with the Prussian ambassador about the possible sale of California to Prussia.

_____

_____

2. All the land south of the Rio Grande had been confirmed to Texas by an 1836 agreement with General López de Santa Anna, yet the Mexican government insisted that the Texas border was the Nueces River north of the Rio Grande.

_____

_____

3. Polk told his cabinet that he was preparing a war message—according to Senator Thomas Hart Benton, Polk wanted a small war "just large enough to acquire a

treaty of peace"—before news of the skirmish between American and Mexican troops reached his office.

_____

_____

4. Opponents of the war argued that American blood had not been shed by fighting Mexicans on American soil, but on disputed territory between the Nueces and Rio Grande where American troops should not have been sent.

_____

_____

5. Polk sent John Slidell as a special minister to Mexico to negotiate outstanding differences, but neither the old government nor the new government would talk to Slidell.

_____

_____

6. Despite the fact that the incident of bloodshed in 1846 took place near the Rio Grande border, Polk sent American troops into Santa Fe, throughout California, and finally deep into Mexico.

_____

_____

7. On September 14, 1847, General Winfield Scott led American troops into Mexico City and brought about Mexican surrender.

_____

_____

8. In the Treaty of Guadalupe Hidalgo, the United States acquired California, New Mexico, and the Rio Grande boundary for $15 million and the assumption of the claims of United States citizens against Mexico.

_____

_____

9. The Mexicans welcomed the war with more enthusiasm and support than the Americans and were confident that their larger regular army would easily defeat the United States.

_____

_____

10. Several senators called for rejection of the treaty with Mexico and insisted that all of Mexico be annexed to the United States.

_____

_____

QUESTIONS

1. From the evidence presented here, is the thesis valid or invalid? Why?

_____

_____

_____

2. What other types of evidence would be helpful in order to better evaluate the thesis?

_____

_____

_____

3. What problems might the word choice in a thesis statement generate? Consider, in the one given for this exercise, the words "banner," "unprovoked," and "innocent." Could the thesis have been stated in a more neutral manner? Explain. Is a thesis, by the very nature of the concept, controversial? (The dictionary definition of *thesis:* a proposition to be defended in argument.)

_____

_____

_____

4. What is the difference between supplying a narrative description of the Mexican War and offering a thesis about the Mexican War?

_____

_____

_____

ANSWERS AND EXPLANATIONS

1. Challenges. Not that the Mexicans were obligated to sell to Polk, but the fact that they seemed willing to sell to Prussia gave some reason for his apprehension. This related more to the security of the United States than to land and economic gain.

2. Challenges. Assuming Santa Anna's agreement was "legal"—it was arranged after his capture and perhaps under duress—the southern Texas border should have been the Rio Grande. The war began north of this disputed area.

3. Supports. Other evidence, especially Polk's diary, also indicates that Polk wanted war and was about to request it from Congress even without a provocation.

4. Supports. The proper approach would have been to await a negotiated settlement before sending in troops to disputed territory. Even many Americans saw this as a land grab rather than a protection of American rights.

5. Challenges. This makes a case for embarrassment and humiliation by the Mexican governments. Not in itself a justification for war, but certainly an "excuse" once shots were fired.

6. Supports. One could argue that in war a rival must attack the enemy's territory and army. Yet, there was no sizable Mexican army in Sante Fe or California and Mexico posed no real threat to the United States in 1846.

7. Neutral. This fact does not support or challenge the thesis, as seizing the enemy's capital is a legitimate goal in wartime. It merely describes a phase of the war.

8. Supports. This indicates that beyond an apology and reparations, the United States all along had as its goal the acquisition of territory.

9. Challenges. Mexico was far from innocent; it was Mexican soldiers who crossed the Rio Grande and attacked American troops, killing sixteen. Mexico welcomed war, perhaps hoping to gain back part of Texas. War was not exactly imposed on the United States, but a challenge went out from Mexico.

10. Supports. This indicates the land hunger of some elected leaders in the United States.

Suggested Answers to Questions

1. The evidence seems to support the thesis. Certainly Mexico bears some blame, but the impetus was American; the whole war was a carefully planned sequence of events unfolding just as Polk and the expansionists had contrived.

2. Evidence from the Mexican side as to whether the incident at the Rio Grande was deliberately provoked would help. So would excerpts from Polk's diary for the spring of 1846; sources relating to the southern expectation of an expansion of slavery in the new territories; and specific orders given on both sides to troops who moved into the disputed area.

3. Words are very important in giving a slant to any statement, including a thesis. The thesis could be reworded to state, "The United States should not have entered into the war against Mexico." Few nations are truly "innocent"; "banner" implies a patriotic conquest or heroic marches; hardly any event is "unprovoked" according to those involved. A thesis is intended to be argued. A statement not in thesis form is likely to be bland and would not stimulate thought.

4. Often narrative descriptions are entertaining and interesting, but do not lead one to some of the values and uses of history: to provoke critical thinking and to approach events in an analytical framework. Of course, one purpose of history is to entertain.

PART III
Debating Historical, Social, and Moral Issues

QUESTIONS FOR THOUGHT

After reading about each of the following issues, reflect on them, analyze possible answers, and write your own reflections. Compare your responses with Thoughts for Questions.

1. From the Jeffersonian period to about 1830, candidates for federal office were chosen through a caucus of congressional members from a particular political group. During Jackson's administration, parties began to hold conventions in which state delegates met to decide on candidates. In the present, the main presidential candidates are chosen usually by a system whereby voters affiliated with a party in each state select candidates in a primary election. Which system is preferable? Why? Is there another system that would work better than any of the above? Explain.

_____

_____

_____

_____

_____

2. Since he was chosen by a national election, Jackson felt that he was the true representative of *all* the people. Members of Congress, chosen on a state or regional basis, represented narrow, selfish, local interests. Therefore, presidential authority should be exerted in a much more active way than under previous presidents. The best interests and the *will* of all the people was best expressed in the presidency, not in Congress. Do you agree with Jackson? Why or why not?

_____

_____

_____

_____

_____

3. Historians have debated the source and effect of the Manifest Destiny concept. Consider the following views:

    A. Americans believed that they had developed the finest political and economic system ever created. They sought to spread this enlightened system across the continent and perhaps throughout the world. The idealism grew out of the American Revolution and was promoted with a missionary zeal. It was a natural process or perhaps even a divine mission. Those who stood in the way, such as Indians and Mexicans, had to be subdued by force, if necessary.

    B. Later, in the 1930s, some historians saw this expansionism as a politically motivated realism. France was a threat west of the Mississippi, Mexico posed a threat to Texas, and the British controlled the Northwest. Some Americans felt a need for land—or the political influence that went with the land—for the expansion of slavery. Thus internal politics and sometimes naked aggression were more important than idealism.

    C. In the 1950s, several historians began to emphasize the economic factors that prompted Manifest Destiny. The primary focus was the wealth of the Pacific: the lumber, furs, and fish, along with the excellent harbors along the coast. Manifest Destiny can be seen as a consistent, sequential process stretching from the end of the Revolution, with the acquisition of land up to the Mississippi River, to the Mexican War and the conquest of land to the Pacific. This expansionism was encouraged usually by a few who enriched themselves at majority expense. The majority accepted this forceful movement because it was couched in terms of the spread of democracy and patriotism, and of the creation of opportunity for the common man. It was really empire-building by an elite class who sought to impact American foreign involvements.

Which of these historical interpretations do you agree with most? Why?

---

4. While Jackson was president, Indians, mostly in the South and Gulf states, were forced to leave their ancient grounds and move to designated land west of the Mississippi. Jackson favored this expulsion on the grounds that, even though it was painful, it was the best solution because the Indians were threatened with extinction, would be in an "unhappy" relationship with white neighbors, and after the move eventually could see their true condition and convert to the white man's ways. Lewis Cass agreed and added that God intended the earth to be cultivated and that the Indian hunting economy was not a suitable use of the land.

On the opposite side, the Cherokees pointed out that they already had an advanced civilization—a written language, schools, and a constitutional government, for example—and the land on which they lived was legally their land. Chief Justice John Marshall agreed and decided that the state of Georgia had no jurisdiction over the Cherokees and no claim to their lands. Of course, the Indians and Marshall lost and Jackson won. With which argument do you agree? Why?

What would have been the sensible and humane solution to the problem of Indian tribes existing in sections of these states?

---

5. There is little doubt that President Polk brought about the Mexican War. He intended to acquire California and the Southwest for the United States. By current standards, this might be labeled aggression and even warmongering. Yet the United States acquired territory it developed for both farming and commerce—activities that brought wealth and opportunity to a large number of people, in-

cluding Mexicans. Is this a case of the ends justifying the means? Can short-term "immoral" strategies lead to long-term benefits? Explain.

_____

_____

_____

_____

_____

6. The issue of states rights arose again during the Jackson presidency. John C. Calhoun and others argued that the states were the fundamental political institution of the United States; the federal government was the agent of the states. Therefore, the states had a right to determine when the federal government exerted powers beyond those allowed by the Constitution. If a state decided that the federal government had exceeded its powers, the state could nullify an act of Congress and declare that the law was inoperative in that state. Jackson objected to this and threatened to lead a military force into South Carolina if it did not repeal an ordinance of nullification. Do you agree with Calhoun or with Jackson? Explain.

_____

_____

_____

_____

_____

7. Chancellor James Kent, a New York Federalist, argued in favor of property qualifications for holding office. He maintained that the "power to tax was the power to destroy." This meant that if those without property were allowed to vote, they would select candidates who would then tax property out of existence. "Those who own the country ought to govern it." Do you agree with Chancellor Kent? Why or why not? Since the common man—many without property—did acquire the right to vote in the 1820s and 1830s, why do you think this taxing of the wealthy did not take place?

_____

_____

_____

_____

_____

8. Consider the quotations at the beginning of the chapter. Explain the meaning and implications of each and determine whether you agree or disagree. How might each quotation apply to this period of history?

_____

_____

_____

_____

_____

THOUGHTS FOR QUESTIONS

1. The Founding Fathers intended to carry throughout the political system the principle that judicious men should be chosen by other judicious men. The electoral college, the choice of senators by state legislatures, and the appointment of the federal judiciary are examples of this. Thus, a caucus of legislators would use their wisdom and judgment to select worthy candidates. This system is not very democratic and, of course, has the danger of rule by an entrenched oligarchy. Conventions allow for the involvement of more people and primaries bring most of the electorate into choosing. Conventions encourage political "horse trading" and corrupt deals. Primaries are expensive and give advantage to name recognition. The Greeks chose rulers by lot. Do primaries create a democratic atmosphere and lead to the selection of the best men or women? Or might they involve exploiting connections to pressure groups and lead to demagoguery?

2. Congressmen were not required to refuse to consider the national interest. On many issues the members of Congress represented the entire nation and did so as a collective group. They had a double role when they represented the interests of their constituents. The president also might have spoken for various local interests or for groups who helped him get elected. Both Jefferson and Jackson had agrarian sentiments and tended to see issues from their point of view. John Adams was very much interested in the welfare of commercial cod fishing along the coast of New England; Jackson spoke for the frontier.

3. Once again we may avoid difficult choices by concluding that there is truth in all three views. But the historians, when joined in this debate on interpretations, propose that their particular viewpoint is the *primary* one. One must determine how much influence small interest groups had on government in the first half of the nineteenth century. Could southern planters and commercial interests who wanted to trade across the Pacific have so influenced political leaders that a policy of expansionism and war prevailed? Or did the pervasive ideals of a divine mission to spread democracy and liberty across the continent open up opportunities for commercial and slave interests?

Determining motivation is tricky. Key sources may contain arguments based on all three factors. Idealism may cover up real motives. Some believed that commercial expansion would be a vehicle to extend the American system and values into other areas. The evidence shows that during this period little could be accomplished in government without the approval of the South. American values did spread across the continent and commerce was extended across the Pacific. But slavery was stopped at Texas and Missouri.

4. It is easy using hindsight and current moral standards, to condemn Jackson's attitude. Our sympathies are with the Indians, and we clearly see the terrible injustices done to the Cherokees. Modern ecological concepts would give us pause in supporting soil cultivation over hunting. Yet, how does one deal with pockets of Indian groups living in the midst of white communities? Would their removal to a separate area be preferable to the discrimination and threats they would continually face? Would the ultimate welfare of the Indians have been better served if Jackson had insisted on their right to remain in Georgia? Moral indictment is easy. Solutions are difficult and require the wisdom of several Solomons.

5. One does not know how this region would have developed if it had *not* been acquired by the United States. Our ethnocentrism leads us to conclude that what has happened after its annexation to the United States has been better than leaving it in the hands of Mexico. Yet most historians can cite several cases in the past when unjust action seemed to result in long-range benefits. Americans currently enjoy the material benefits of an unjust labor system and a cruel exploitation of immigrants and minorities. Do we reject these benefits in an act of protest against this exploitation? Some philosophers argue that we live in the best of all possible worlds. Some theologians agree. Do you?

6. Nullification or state "interposition" is a practice that would lead to chaos. Who would know which laws apply in which states? Businesspersons could not conduct business on a national scale. Wealthy states that could function on their own could raise barriers that would discriminate against weaker, poorer states. National laws would be so modified or blunted as to be ineffective. Certainly Calhoun, an honorable man, did not intend to use nullification as a common policy. But its existence and recognition as a possibility would lead to misuse. One might as well go back to the Articles of Confederation and completely decentralize the American system.

7. This fear has not been realized. Possibly many of those who do not hold property hope to acquire property in the future. Or maybe those who hold large amounts of property have been able to remain in control of the American government and prevent the taxation of wealth. The values of free enterprise, private ownership of property, and the opportunity to make profits have so permeated the American system that to oppose this ideology seems unAmerican. And of course the income tax has, to some extent, led to a moderate taxation of wealth.

8. Durant disliked efforts to establish laws of history, that is, patterns that could predict the future and serve as an exact guide to decisions. As soon as the historian finds several developments that seem to repeat in a very similar fashion, an exception appears that refutes the rule. How might this quote apply to the Jacksonian period, considering the designation of the period as the "age of democracy" and yet blacks, women, and Indians were excluded from the political process? The unpredictable belongs to the past as well as to the future.

Marx emphasized forces in history, forces that inevitably move forward according to a pattern. Men do not understand this; but by their behavior, they support the forces and fulfill the pattern. The average man has no idea how history is moving, but the flow continues and men unconsciously contribute to this flow.

7

ECONOMIC, SOCIAL, AND CULTURAL CHANGE

"No past event has any intrinsic importance. The knowledge of it is valuable only as it leads us to form just calculations with respect to the future."

Thomas Babington Macaulay

"I shall be content [as one of] those who [seeks] to give a view of events as they really happened, and, as they are very likely, in accordance with human nature, to repeat themselves at some future time—if not exactly the same, yet very similar."

Thucydides

PART I
Acquiring Essential Data

ESSENTIAL DATES

Determine the correct sequence and write the approximate date for each of the following events.

1. First telegraph message is sent. _____

2. Women's Rights Convention meets in Seneca Falls, New York. _____

3. Large-scale immigration of Germans and Irish _____

4. National Trade Union is formed. _____

5. Ralph Waldo Emerson's *Nature* is published, marking the beginning of transcendentalism. _____

6. First temperance law is passed in Maine. _____

7. Cyrus Hall McCormick invents the reaper. _____

8. Nat Turner's slave rebellion _____

9. William Lloyd Garrison publishes the first copy of *The Liberator*, an abolitionist newspaper. _____

10. Thomas Cole begins the Hudson River school of painting. _____

ESSENTIAL CONCEPTS

Examine each concept and write what contemporary relevance it might have.

1. *nativism* An anti-foreign and anti-catholic movement of the 1850s that advocated an end to immigration.

_____

_____

_____

2. *transcendentalism* A loosely constructed philosophy that emphasized the goodness of humanity and a belief in the progress of mankind.

_____

_____

_____

3. *"Daniel Boone syndrome"* Extolling the virtues of individualism and of living independently away from civilization. James Fenimore Cooper made it popular with his character, Natty Bumpo.

_____

_____

_____

4. *multiplier effect* When one invention or technological development influences and leads to several others—discoveries demand other inventions.

_____

_____

_____

5. *psychic income* The slaveholder's income from slavery was substantial, but he also benefited from the prestige of owning a large number of slaves.

_____

_____

_____

6. *factory system* The decision to build a large center of production near a power source—water at first—so large machinery could be used and laborers could be required to work in one building and live nearby.

_____

_____

_____

7. *"Yankee" ingenuity* The ability of skilled craftsmen in the North to meet problems involving manufacturing and other practical needs by inventing tools, machines, and devices.

_____

_____

_____

8. *tenement houses* Apartment buildings built back to back, often without windows or plumbing, for housing factory workers in large numbers.

_____

_____

_____

9. *"hands"* Workers who previously had used their skills as craftsmen to manufacture goods later merely tended machines as "hands." All they needed to supply was the work of their "hands."

_____

_____

_____

10. *unitarianism* Organized religious group that denied the Trinity doctrine and believed that mankind was full of virtue and goodness rather than sin and evil.

_____

_____

_____

ANSWERS

Correct sequence of events and their dates.

1. 10; 1827
2. 7; 1831
3. 9; 1831
4. 8; 1831
5. 4; 1834

6. 5; 1836
7. 3; 1840s–1850s
8. 1; 1844
9. 2; 1848
10. 6; 1851

PART II
Developing Thinking Skills

SKILL EXERCISE ONE: ANALYZING QUANTIFIED DATA

Several items of quantified data are given below; eleven inferences follow the data. After each inference indicate whether it is a reasonably valid inference drawn from the data or whether it cannot be inferred from the data. Do not judge the inferences on the basis of whether or not you believe the statement to be true. Of course, few, if any, *absolutely* valid inferences can be made from statistics, but in most cases several *reasonably* valid implications are possible.

Quantified Data

A. Editor Horace Greeley in 1850 calculated that a family of five in New York City needed $10.37 a week for the bare necessities of shelter, food, and clothes; nothing was added for medicine or savings. Yet the average wage in manufacturing was less than $5.00 a week per worker.

B. In the depression of 1857, textile jobs dropped 68 percent and jobs in iron works dropped 43 percent in Rhode Island.

C. In the 1850s, approximately one-half of cotton textile workers were children under age sixteen or women.

D. The top 1 percent of the New York City population held 40 percent of the wealth and the top 4 percent held 75 percent of the wealth in the 1850s.

Under each inference indicate whether it is valid or invalid and why.

1. Wealth in New York City was unequally distributed in the 1850s.

_____

_____

2. The only fair solution to the economic hardships of the 1850s was a lower-class revolution.

   _____

   _____

3. In order to survive, working-class families involved in manufacturing—assuming they had no other source of income—would have to ensure that several family members were employed.

   _____

   _____

4. Many families starved in New York City in the 1850s.

   _____

   _____

5. Christianity's ethical values would dictate some action to alleviate such desperate conditions of the poor in the 1850s.

   _____

   _____

6. The upper class had too much wealth and should have shared it with the poor.

   _____

   _____

7. The prospect of losing their jobs at a time of recession or depression was a reality to a large number of laborers.

   _____

   _____

8. For some reason, manufacturers employed large numbers of women and children in the 1850s.

   _____

   _____

9. The worker and his family needed some type of help or protection in the 1850s.

   _____

   _____

10. A strong labor union movement, a minimum wage, and a graduated income tax may have alleviated some of the problems workers in manufacturing faced in the 1850s.

    _____

    _____

11. Karl Marx was correct in his evaluation of the plight of workers and what they should do about their condition.

_____

_____

ANSWERS AND EXPLANATIONS

1. Valid. The statistics indicate this beyond much doubt.

2. Invalid. One may believe this, but it is not inferred from the quantified data.

3. Valid. With such low weekly wages—even less for women and children—the labor of several family members was necessary to reach the $10.37 level.

4. Invalid. Some may have, but with several family members working and with charity, survival was possible. No doubt disease and malnutrition took its toll. The statistics do not indicate that people starved.

5. Valid. This is a difficult one since Christian morality has several interpretations. However, one cannot imagine reading the New Testament and not considering at least charitable help for poor families. Even Charles Dickins's Scrooge supported the poorhouse.

6. Invalid. This cannot reasonably be inferred from the data even though it seems to be a solution. If all the wealth of the top 4 percent had been taken away, its division and distribution to the poor may have been negligible.

7. Valid. This is obvious from the statistics.

8. Valid. This is obvious from the statistics; women and children were paid less.

9. Valid. Common sense would lead to this inference. Of course one could argue that families were receiving what they deserved and that to interfere would have upset the natural laws of economics!

10. Valid. From the problems presented in the quantified data, it seems reasonable that these efforts would help the situation. Whether they were advisable or not depends on one's economic philosophy.

11. Invalid. Karl Marx had his own answers and believed he understood the problems and their roots. But the statistics here do not validate his analysis or solutions. Many of the problems have been partially solved without the application of Marx's principles.

What other types of statistics might be requested in order to better understand the meaning of the data given? The following are some suggested inquiries:

1. What alternatives besides work were available to children from twelve to sixteen years old?

_____

_____

_____

2. What was the unemployment rate in years other than the depression years?

_____

_____

_____

3. If conditions were so bad, why did so many immigrants risk a voyage across the Atlantic and an uncertain life in a strange land during the 1840s and 1850s?

   _____

   _____

   _____

4. Was the wealth of the top 4 percent being used as capital to expand the economy and to create more jobs and wealth?

   _____

   _____

   _____

5. What were the comparable incomes for non-manufacturing jobs—farming, farm laborer, clerical, sailor, and so forth?

   _____

   _____

   _____

6. Student's questions:

   _____

   _____

   _____

   The student should examine the following numerical data carefully. Then try to write reasonably valid statements about the statistics. Debate the validity of the statements with your instructor and other students.

   In 1860 the richest 10 percent of the farmers owned 40 percent of the property in Wisconsin. In Jacksonville, Illinois, two-thirds of the inhabitants did not own real estate. The average Wisconsin state senator owned property worth $6,500, while the average adult male in the state owned property worth $425. In New York City in the 1850s, 95 percent of the wealthiest three hundred residents were the sons and daughters of wealthy parents. There were only three hundred public high schools in the United States in 1860, but there were six thousand private academies.

Student's statements of inference:

_____

_____

_____

_____

_____

QUESTIONS

1. Does a combination of statistical data give a better description of an event or situation than a paragraph of prose? Why or why not?

   _____

   _____

2. Are statistics so misleading that very simple prose statements that are often actual descriptions of the numerical figures become the only valid statements obtainable from the numerical data? That is, are *all* inferences questionable? Explain.

   _____

   _____

3. Give several examples from any of the numerical data given in this skill exercise of how false and misleading inferences can be drawn from statistics.

   _____

   _____

SKILL EXERCISE TWO: DETERMINING RELEVANCE OF EVIDENCE

Examine carefully the following statements of data related to the given topic. Under each indicate whether the data is relevant or irrelevant to the topic. Then explain briefly your decision. Compare your choices with those offered.

TOPIC: A STUDY OF WOMEN'S RIGHTS IN THE MID-NINETEENTH-CENTURY UNITED STATES

1. According to most women's magazines at the time, the proper place for women was in the home, not in public life where they would lose the expected traits of piety, purity, and obedience to men.

   _____

   _____

2. Divorce was not common in the nineteenth century and, when it did occur, the husband normally received custody of the children and most of the property.

   _____

   _____

3. In an age when much difficult physical work was required on farms and in factories, women could not do some of the tasks.

   _____

   _____

4. Tending children in an age when playgrounds, recreational facilities, and schools were scarce meant that women, who have a natural affinity in this area, should remain at home.

_____

_____

5. Women, being shy and reserved, were ineffective in most public arenas outside the home, especially in the areas of politics and social issues.

_____

_____

6. Several women, such as Elizabeth Cady Stanton and Lucretia Mott, went to the World Anti-Slavery Convention in London in 1840 but were not allowed to participate.

_____

_____

7. Women wore many layers of clothing from top to bottom, covering around the neck—scarves or high collars, and hair combed tightly against the head.

_____

_____

8. Women were not supposed to speak in public or to even offer prayers in church, so when the Grimke sisters of South Carolina spoke to audiences in the North about the evils of slavery, they were severely criticized.

_____

_____

9. Many Ivy League universities and small private colleges opened their doors to women after the Second World War.

_____

_____

10. Most men considered a woman who left home to participate in reform activity as "unsexed," and many ridiculed Mrs. Amelia Bloomer's pantalettes.

_____

_____

ANSWERS AND EXPLANATIONS

1. Relevant. This expectation, spread by most men and reinforced by magazines designed for women, made it very difficult to progress in women's rights.

2. Relevant. Like the strike in labor disputes, the threat of divorce was a poten-

tial weapon for women in establishing recognition. It was not effective if divorce meant social and financial disaster.

3. Irrelevant. Some men could not do the tasks that other men could do. Women made up more than half of the textile workers. They did as much work, if not more, than men did on farms.

4. Irrelevant. There was no reason some of these tasks could not be shared, as they are today. In the mid-nineteenth century, most of the educational opportunities went to men who thus should have been able to contribute to the education of their children.

5. Irrelevant. This is also not true, since women organized their conventions at Seneca Falls, New York; were leaders in reform—such as Dorthea Dix in bringing state aid to the insane, in the temperance movement, in newspaper reporting, and in abolitionism.

6. Relevant. In this case an effort to participate in a reform movement to free enslaved human beings was denied purely on the basis of sex. This indicates the extent to which male reformers, liberal men of the times, were actually sexist in outlook.

7. Irrelevant. The dress and appearance of women are not relevant to the topic of women's rights.

8. Relevant. Although some men would condone women giving speeches to an audience of women, this opposition to a basic freedom indicates the prejudice of men against "active" women.

9. Irrelevant. This is certainly important in relation to the overall women's rights movement, but not as important for the mid-nineteenth century since only Oberlin College was open to women as late as 1837. This does indirectly indicate that the best colleges were closed to women, but the main focus of the statement is on post-1945.

10. Relevant. This reveals prevalent attitudes and the tendency, when only feeble arguments are available, to latch onto an unimportant item such as clothing and hold it up as a symbol of where the trend would lead women.

PART III
Debating Historical, Social, and Moral Issues

QUESTIONS FOR THOUGHT

1. One of the significant and recurring debates among historians about this period involves the abolitionists. Were the abolitionists dangerous fanatics or stimulators of the American conscience? At least three interpretations have emerged.

A. Some historians consider these reformers to be irresponsible fanatics who brought upon the nation an unnecessary war. Their emotional arguments caused suspicion, fear, anger, and hysteria. By their exaggerated descriptions of the plight of the slave and the evil of the slave owners, they brought about the Civil War. Without them, outstanding issues might have been settled peacefully.

B. Other historians praise these agitators as far-sighted reformers who encouraged fair-minded citizens to follow their conscience and put an end to slavery. They made people aware of the horror of the institution. They were part of the best in the American tradition because they upheld the ideals of liberty and true democracy. They may have helped bring on the war; however, the war was necessary, a good cause, and fought for high moral issues.

C. Finally, a more recent study concludes that the abolitionists were not really very influential. They were a small force of people who might have agitated a few groups, but overall they had little impact. There were real reasons for the war and these were economic, political, and sectional.

Which of these views do you agree with most? Why?

_____

_____

Assuming the abolitionists had some impact on the coming of the Civil War, should small groups be allowed to exert a disproportionate influence on society—especially by the use of emotion and hatred? Why or why not?

_____

_____

What comparable groups are there in the nation or the world today? Are they also a threat to society's stability? Explain.

_____

_____

_____

2. The inequality and injustice of society during this period of industrial growth is obvious: Women doing needlework for twelve cents per day, many of them forced into prostitution to make a living; men unemployed or partially employed; families living in cramped one-room apartments; little opportunity for education; unsafe and unhealthy working conditions. The sad descriptions could continue. What could be done about these conditions? At least four answers emerged from the period.

A. There were calls for government action. The legal recognition of labor unions occurred during this period. Later in the century, the government began, ever so slowly, to regulate excesses and to control business enterprise for the common good.

B. Workers began to organize in the 1830s. Skilled workers especially had some influence using the threat not to work. A few achieved better pay and more congenial conditions. The strike was still not a legally accepted weapon, but the trend toward workers' organizations did supply one answer to the poor labor conditions.

C. Some who supported the capitalist system with strong faith and confidence argued for time to show the accomplishments of the free-enterprise system. Given the atmosphere and opportunity, the system would alleviate poverty and produce plenty for everyone. In the meantime, some suffering was an unfortunate but necessary part of progress. Charity was also necessary to comfort those who were casualties of the system. A transforming spirit, which altered Charles Dickens's Ebeneezer Scrooge, could soften the system. The work of volunteers who had religious or philosophical convictions, and who were financed by the rich, would suffice until a material paradise was produced through the energy of capitalism.

D. Karl Marx directly opposed all of the above ideas. He saw a need to radically change the entire system: An end to profits, to competition, and to the inequality of rewards in the production system! Capitalism should be replaced with socialism, the means of production owned and operated not by the wealthy elite, but by the workers themselves. The government, under the control of the workers and their representatives, would see to it that equality and justice were achieved. The capitalist system did not need modification or more time, it needed eradication.

Which of these views appeals to you most? Why?

_____

_____

_____

What are the strengths and weaknesses of each?

_____

_____

_____

_____

_____

For the next one hundred fifty years which of these answers did the United States follow? Was it the right choice? Why?

_____

_____

_____

3. Assume you were opposed to the institution of slavery and were living in the 1850s. Consider the following tactics, programs, and efforts to end the institution. Under each, indicate whether or not you would have supported it and why.

A. Colonization of blacks into selected areas of Africa

_____

_____

B. Support of abolitionists such as William Lloyd Garrison through financial contributions and printing pamphlets

_____

_____

C. Aid slaves in their efforts to escape by participating in an underground railroad or secret movement of slaves from the South to the North and Canada

_____

_____

D. Make speeches against slavery, distribute pamphlets in the North, and send anti-slavery pamphlets into the South

_____

_____

E. Support a government program to pay slave owners for the freeing of slaves and a constitutional amendment to end slavery

_____

_____

F. Suggest and support the use of violence by slaves and on behalf of slaves, such as John Brown did at Harper's Ferry

_____

_____

G. Sign a petition and attend an anti-slavery rally

_____

_____

H. March in a southern city carrying a sign protesting slavery

_____

_____

Would you consider people morally reprehensible if they refused to get involved in the struggle against slavery? Why or why not?

_____

_____

_____

4. Those who supported slavery argued not only for its necessity, but many considered it a positive institution. Consider the arguments below and offer an answer to each.

A. There seems no other way to have people of two races and two cultures live together in the same area than with one as slaves and the other free.

_____

_____

B. The Bible supports slavery, the Jews allowed it, and Jesus did not condemn it and even advised a slave to return to his master Philemon.

_____

_____

C. All great civilizations have consisted of two groups: those who work with their hands—slaves, serfs, workers, and those of superior talent who, living off the work of this first group, have the time to produce the higher forms of civilization.

_____

_____

D. One race is superior and the other inferior—nature dictates the dominance of one over the other.

_____

_____

E. The Constitution of the United States sanctions and supports slavery and five of the first seven presidents owned slaves.

_____

_____

F. Slaves are better off and are treated more kindly than northern factory workers. They are happy and sing a lot.

_____

_____

G. Slaves are absolutely essential to the country's economy and especially important to the northern economy since they produce cotton for northern textile mills.

_____

_____

Which is the strongest argument for slavery? Why?

_____

_____

Which is the worst argument, the one that seems to have the least validity? Why?

_____

_____

5. What factors lead to industrial growth? This question has been studied again and again by economists, historians, and political scientists. It is vitally important to underdeveloped nations that are attempting to industrialize. A list of most of the ingredients that encouraged the industrial growth of the United States follows. These features formed the foundation for growth the first half of the nineteenth century. Examine them carefully. Then rank them from most important to least important using your own analytical thinking processes. They are listed in random order.

A. *strong agricultural base* Plenty of low-cost food; export of food for foreign exchange; profits assist capital formation.

B. *entrepreneurship* The encouragement and willingness of individuals and groups to launch out and establish enterprises, spending time and effort to manage successfully; risk-taking.

C. *plentiful resources* Abundance of the exact resources needed for industrial growth—oil, iron, timber, coal, cotton, and many minerals; navigable rivers and water power.

D. *security* Two large oceans for defense; no rival political threat—therefore, little expenditure on defense; a standing army was unnecessary.

E. *trait of inventiveness* Americans were tinkerers, resourceful, and always interested in a new device; patent laws were enforced.

F. *abundance of workers* Labor-saving machinery on farms meant less need for sons to remain on the farm; migration to cities to work; open doors to immigration; Americans were prolific—had large families; health and diet meant that more children lived longer; this increase in numbers supplied more consumers.

G. *friendly government* Pro-business; aid for the infrastructure—roads, railroads, canals, education; legal protection for corporations and property; stable banking system; protective tariff (at times); economic activity free of stringent government control or regulation.

H. *ease of social and geographical mobility* No barriers to movement; opportunity to move up the social ladder, except for blacks and Indians; no legally established aristocracy.

I. *a federal governmental structure* Allowed free play to cultural differences yet maintained a national market for business; government was not a priority because of its small range of activities, and universal voting rights for white males helped avoid serious political turmoil (until the Civil War); the diverse religious and ethnic groups developed a toleration that avoided serious clashes.

J. *free trade* Foreign countries were receptive to American products, both manufactured and agricultural; capital investments by foreign banks and businesses, especially the British; American cotton dominated the world market.

K. *a Protestant ethic prevailed* Hard work, frugality, saving, devotion to the job as a religious calling; an energy to progress, to succeed, to use individual effort for personal advancement.

Student ranking of the above eleven:

_____

Explain the reasons for the three you ranked as the most important:

_____

_____

_____

For the two you listed at the end, explain why.

_____

_____

Compare these factors in American industrial development to the current situations in areas of the underdeveloped world. Which features are missing? Which are present? Was American development rather unique in the opportunity provided by the combination of circumstances, or should other nations be able to duplicate that experience? Explain.

_____

_____

_____

_____

_____

6. With such a large number of blacks concentrated in the South, the question has been raised as to why there were not many slave revolts. Of course, "many" is a key word here. Research in the 1960s revealed many more revolts than were documented earlier. But slaves were restrained by the easy identification of skin color, by not having a safe haven for escape, by family connections on the plantation, by the severe punishment in failure, by serious discrimination in the North, and by the armed preparation of whites against conspiracies and revolts. Some historians argue that widespread protest did actually occur in the form of blacks breaking machinery, of not "understanding" instructions, of refusal to work hard, and even of songs that voiced protest—obvious to slaves, but not understood by whites. React to this form of protest.

_____

_____

_____

_____

_____

7. A collection of pithy sayings by Ralph Waldo Emerson and Henry Thoreau, two leaders in the movement known as transcendentalism, follows. After each, write your reaction and explain to what extent you agree or disagree with the thought.

A. "Under a government which imprisons any unjustly, the true place for a just man is also a prison." *Thoreau*

_____

_____

B. "There is no strong performance without a little fanaticism in the performer." *Emerson*

_____

_____

C. "Great men are they who see that spiritual is stronger than any material force; that thought rules the world." *Emerson*

_____

_____

D. "If a man does not keep pace with his companions, perhaps it is because he hears a different drummer. Let him step to the music he hears, however measured or far away." *Thoreau*

_____

_____

E. "Do not be too moral. You may cheat yourself out of much life so. Aim above morality. Be not simply good; be good for something." *Thoreau*

_____

_____

F. "I heartily accept the motto, 'That government is best which governs least' . . . Carried out, it finally amounts to this, which I also believe: 'That government is best which governs not at all'; and when men are prepared for it, that will be the kind of government which they will have." *Thoreau*

_____

_____

G. "Every burned book enlightens the world." *Emerson*

_____

_____

8. Consider the quotations at the beginning of the chapter. Explain their meaning and whether you agree or disagree with each.

_____

_____

_____

_____

_____

Thoughts for Questions

1. The degree of abolitionists' influence is difficult to judge. They may have been a catalyst, a last step without which the war would not have taken place. Perhaps a strong emotional feeling is necessary for war. If so, abolitionists may have supplied it, though there were obvious causes for the war beyond "emotion." Slavery was

morally wrong, and the abolitionists were willing to not only state this, but to encourage others to join the effort to end it. This entitles them to respect. However, when methods are considered, one wonders if there was a less bloody way of ending it. The evaluation of impact involves scrutiny of the total situation, the costs, and the results in the lives of people.

Allowing groups to organize and agitate for change is essential for a free society. Those who brought off the American Revolution were such a group. To muzzle the right to assembly, freedom of speech, and the right to petition the government would be to thwart the process of democratic change. However, some would even now question the right to actually promote hatred, prejudice, and unsubstantiated fear.

Terrorists, especially in the Middle East, come to mind; however, the comparison would probably not include most abolitionists, many of whom were also pacifists and most of whom were non-violent. Those who demonstrate on environmental issues, abortion, and women's rights reveal parallels to the abolitionists.

2. The solution is the student's choice. Answer *D* calls for such a massive change that it seems impossible to accomplish. Also, the actual results of such a drastic change remain unknown. The ideas may look reasonable on paper, but when put into practice in socialist nations, the beneficial results are questionable. Answer *C*: In times of depression, charity was never sufficient. Uncontrolled capitalism leads to a greater gap between rich and poor, and at the end of the century, led to a reduction of competition as whole industries consolidated into giant trusts. The American solution combined *A* and *B*. Perfection has not been reached; however, these answers join the energy of free enterprise with organizations that look after the public interest and the needs of the commonwealth.

3. This is the student's choice. How does the historian judge the actions or non-actions of those in the past? Slavery seems such a reprehensible institution that one cannot imagine not participating in an effort to end it. However, attitudes toward races, respect for states' rights, the inertia of overturning such a widespread system, and a questioning about ultimate solutions to the side-by-side existence of two races gave pause to many who agreed that the system of slavery was "unfortunate."

4. Item *A* is unrealistic in that ways to coexist have been discovered. Although they are not perfect, they represent the beginning of what may be a successful coalition of races. Item *B*: The Bible does not condone slavery either. The slave in Jewish society was not racially different nor was it a perpetual condition. It seems incompatible with the Christian teachings of the New Testament. Item *C*: The powerful machinery of the Industrial Revolution promised an end to serfdom and the need for a servile class. Many societies in history have shown more progress without slavery than with it. As a matter of fact, slavery and serfdom may be a sign of the decline of a civilization. Item *D*: We have, one hopes, rejected notions of racial inequality. The facts stated in item *E* do not mean that slavery is, therefore, a beneficial institution; merely that, in the context of time, the writers of the Constitution decided that it was feasible to sanction slavery. Many at the convention resisted and even those who owned slaves hoped and expected the system to gradually disappear. Item *G*: The economic argument is a valid one, but an immoral one. It is unjust and unethical to retain a harmful institution in order to gain economically. Could this final argument be the "real" argument, the one that kept the institution alive in the South and caused hesitation on the part of northerners whose consciences told them that it was wrong?

5. Suggested ranking: C, B, A, I, K, F, H, G, J, E, D. Resources were essential for industrial growth. Not only were there resources, but a variety of just the right kind. Farm land should be included in the resources, which means item A comes into play. The activities of businessmen with incentive and managerial skills (B) is a factor ignored by the socialist system. But it is vital, and combined with an atmosphere of free economic activity, creates that extra energy so necessary for economic change. No society has industrialized without a revolution in agriculture. The abundance of cheap food either within the nation or by import allows workers to function with low pay and with sufficient energy to work hard.

Expenditures for armies and weapons do pull resources and capital from the non-military sector. However, to some extent, military expenditures can stimulate production, and an enemy nearby can result in patriotic endeavor on the part of workers. But fear and national survival replace profits and higher pay as prime motivators. Many societies produce inventors and innovators. The Chinese have a long history of inventions. But the inventions must become "technology," must be applied in an imaginative way; hence, the importance of the entrepreneur.

So many underdeveloped nations are lacking at least half of these eleven ingredients. A variety of resources, an ethic of production, abundant food, security, and mobility are noticeably absent. The single resource of an abundance of workers, and a friendly government are normally available.

6. This type of protest seems likely to have occurred and is still to be found on the part of discontented workers or those who are not involved in the mainstream of the successful middle class. The songs of protest are a fact; the other signs of protest and resistance are more difficult to document. A fire in a cotton shed could have been caused by lightning, or by a protesting slave. A broken wagon might have been caused by wear and tear, or the result of a field hand running it over rocks. That form of protest seemed the only option in most cases.

7. These are the student's reactions. Are these pithy sayings "profound" or are they common sense? Are they idealistic or realistic? Why?

8. Macaulay implies that history teaches us about the future. It may, indeed, but do we know what to look for? The abolitionists protested slavery and the institution disappeared. Is this some sort of guarantee that protest gets results? A protective tariff allowed infant industries to get a start in the early nineteenth century. Should, therefore, underdeveloped nations raise tariffs to a protective level? How does one know what wisdom or lessons to draw from an event? Yet we hope history can be "instructive" about decisions for the future.

Thucydides's use of "very similar" is a key. Are new variables that appear in the future vital enough to change outcomes? Dare we conduct diplomacy currently as we did in the 1840s? Does the existence of nuclear missiles bring about a "whole new ball game"? Human nature is presented as a constant throughout history. Is it? Does the medieval serf behave with the same urges and feelings as the Midwest farmer of the twentieth century? Did Charles I have the same motivations and goals as Richard Nixon? However, we can observe very similar behavior patterns in past and present—the behavior of mobs, the struggle for political power, the desire for profits, the need for security, and so forth.

CHAPTER
8

THE CIVIL WAR

"Statesmen think they make history; but history makes itself and drags the statesmen along."

Will Rogers

"It is the true office of history to represent the events themselves, together with the counsels, and to leave the observations and conclusions thereupon to the liberty and faculty of everyman's judgment."

Sir Francis Bacon

PART I
Acquiring Essential Data

ESSENTIAL DATES

Determine the correct sequence and write the approximate date for each of the following events.

1. Battle of Gettysburg, Pennsylvania _____

2. Emancipation Proclamation is issued by President Abraham Lincoln. _____

3. General Robert E. Lee surrenders to General Ulysses S. Grant at Appomattox Court House in Virginia. _____

4. John Brown's raid on Harper's Ferry _____

5. The North adopts conscription of soldiers. _____

6. The Dred Scott decision is handed down by the Supreme Court. _____

7. Seven states secede from the Union. _____

8. Publication of *Uncle Tom's Cabin* _____

9. The Homestead Act granting free land to settlers is passed. _____

10. Confederate forces fire on Fort Sumter in South Carolina. _____

ESSENTIAL CONCEPTS

Examine each concept and write what contemporary relevance it might have.

1. *"King Cotton"* The concept that cotton was so essential for European and northern textile mills that the North could not fight a lengthy war and Europe would have to intervene for the South.

_____
_____
_____

2. *colonial South* The South functioned as a colonial area in its relationship to the North—the North controlled credit, shipping, insurance, and marketing of cotton and supplied manufactured goods to the South.

_____
_____
_____

3. *peculiar institution* Due to the reluctance to call slavery by its name, it was labeled the South's "peculiar" institution—southerners also referred to slaves

as "servants." Slavery in the South was considered different from slavery elsewhere.

_____

_____

_____

4. *popular sovereignty* Stephen A. Douglas's proposal that in western territories the people should decide by their votes and their constitution whether or not they want slavery as a legal institution.

_____

_____

_____

5. *"down the river"* The selling and transporting of slaves from the old South (eastern seaboard) to the Gulf States and the new cotton lands. Between 1800 and 1860 about one million slaves were sent "down the river."

_____

_____

_____

6. *secession* The withdrawal of the southern states from the federal Union in 1860 and 1861. These states assumed that this was a legal and constitutional process.

_____

_____

_____

7. *Union* The concept that a nation is more than just a legal arrangement of groups of people in several states combined under one government; it is a vital entity that is so mystically integrated that it is impossible to separate into parts.

_____

_____

_____

8. *total war* The transformation of the nature of warfare during the Civil War, whereby Northern armies began to destroy civilian property rather than maintain only military objectives. The order went out in April 1863 to "forage and destroy" property in the confederacy. It is associated mostly with General William T. Sherman.

_____

_____

_____

9. *copperheads* Groups in the North who spoke in opposition to the Civil War and in some cases attempted to interfere with the war effort. Many were northern Democrats; some were imprisoned by President Lincoln.

_____

_____

_____

10. *"puttin' on ole massa"* The protective mask put on by slaves, whereby they seemed to be dependent and childlike in their attachment to their owners, but were really protesting their enslavement in many small ways. It was a false appearance of submission.

_____

_____

_____

ANSWERS

Correct sequence of events and their dates.

1. 8; 1852
2. 6; 1857
3. 4; 1859
4. 7; 1860–61
5. 10; 1861

6. 9; 1862
7. 2; 1863
8. 5; 1863
9. 1; 1863
10. 3; 1865

PART II
Developing Thinking Skills

SKILL EXERCISE ONE: QUESTIONING

Assume you are attempting to gain a deeper understanding of "The Debate Over Slavery: Apologists and Abolitionists." Examine carefully the following questions and write under each whether it is productive or unproductive. Explain your choice.

1. What were the main arguments in favor of slavery offered by apologists for the institution?

_____

_____

2. Did slaves behave better after beatings?

_____

_____

3. In their speeches, what points did abolitionists make in expressing their opposition to slavery?

_____

_____

4. Are all races equal?

_____

_____

5. Were slaves content serving under a kind master who cared for their needs?

_____

_____

6. What techniques besides speeches and pamphlets did abolitionists use in their attack on slavery?

_____

_____

7. How would an abolitionist answer each of the specific arguments that an apologist might make in favor of slavery?

_____

_____

8. Who won the debate over slavery—the apologists or the abolitionists?

_____

_____

9. What information is available on the background of abolitionist leaders, and what evidence exists about their overall motives for participating in this reform?

_____

_____

10. What does the Bible say about slavery and how was it used in the debate by both sides?

_____

_____

ANSWERS AND EXPLANATIONS

1. Productive. These arguments are essential to an understanding of the debate.

2. Unproductive. Whether they did or did not makes no difference as far as the debate is concerned. The question is also vague.

3. Productive. It is important to know what they said publicly about the institution—what was their particular appeal to audiences.

4. Unproductive. This is an important question, but not relevant to the issue itself, which is the enslavement of one race by another. Also, "equal" in what way?

5. Unproductive. This is impossible to determine when considering four million slaves under various living conditions. It calls for an unexplained "yes" or "no" answer that leads nowhere.

6. Productive. This will yield important data, but a better question would call for some analysis of the techniques, their successes and failures.

7. Productive. This will pull in viewpoints beyond the criticisms of the institution that the abolitionists would normally make.

8. Unproductive. How can this ever be determined? Of course, slaves were freed, but it took a Civil War, not merely the words of abolitionists, to accomplish it.

9. Productive. It is important for the historian to know the other related factors when studying any issue and to analyze a broad range of causes and influences.

10. Productive. Since the Bible was used in the debate, its statements related to slavery and the use of those statements are significant.

SKILL EXERCISE TWO: CATEGORIZING AND CLASSIFYING

One way of categorizing history data is to place them into related groups and then analyze similar data in each particular group. The historian often groups diverse items into five categories: political, economic, social, diplomatic, and cultural (including religious and intellectual cultures). This categorizing seems to work well in the analysis of many events and developments.

Assume you are investigating the coming of the Civil War. Listed below are information items related to this topic. In the space under each item, write in the appropriate category—*political, economic, social, diplomatic,* or *cultural.* Check your selection with the suggested answers.

1. Southern society was much more violent than northern or western societies; the southerner quickly resorted to force and the use of a gun to settle disputes.

2. Even if slaves were freed, no one, including Lincoln, could understand how blacks and whites could live side by side together in harmony.

3. Lincoln's election meant that not only was the Senate in the hands of the North, but that now the executive branch was occupied by a person who opposed slavery.

4. The South considered itself in many respects a "colony" of the North—dependent on the North for manufactured goods; for transportation, insurance, and storage of cotton; and for financial arrangements of the cotton trade.

5. The Supreme Court's Dred Scott decision cast doubt on the possibility that Congress could influence the spread of slavery to the territories because slaves were property and property could not be taken from individuals without "due process of law." _____

6. Racist attitudes existed in both the North and South and segregation was probably more severe in the North than in the South.

_____

7. The South assumed that England could not do without cotton; thus, if war came, England would offer assistance and, perhaps, recognize the South as an independent political entity. _____

8. John Brown's efforts to encourage a slave revolt was praised in the North by writers and intellectuals, and he was considered a martyr to the abolitionist cause. _____

9. The newly-developed system of a large number of elective offices and frequent elections meant that candidates spoke about slavery often before large crowds, since the slavery issue was a vote winner. _____

10. *Uncle Tom's Cabin* was read by a large number of people and performed as a drama before thousands. It offered an emotional picture of some of the worst features of slavery. _____

11. The French and British aristocracy, although not favoring the institution of slavery, felt a kinship with southern plantation owners and would likely sympathize with their views. _____

12. Southerners believed that they had developed a unique and viable way of life, a system by which the arrangement of classes and groups worked in harmony for the benefit of the whole. _____

13. The northern capitalists had acquired fish and merchant-marine bounties from the government, financing of a vast railroad network, and a protective tariff, while the South struggled to defend its economically essential institution.

_____

14. Lincoln would not stand for the extension of slavery in the territories, nor would he accept the right to secede from the Union.

_____

15. Southern states insisted that the national government was an agent of the states— an agent created by the states and not independent of them—and, furthermore, that they should have a negative (veto power) on acts of this agent that were not in keeping with the powers surrendered to the agent.

_____

ANSWERS AND EXPLANATIONS

1. Cultural. This factor relates to the mind-set and behavior of people in the society.

2. Social. The adjustment problem of two races is a social issue.

3. Political. This statement relates to government and political affairs.

4. Economic. Obviously trade, manufactured goods, and insurance relate to economic affairs.

5. Political. A Supreme Court decision related to the powers of Congress is definitely political.

6. Social/Cultural. Racism is both social and cultural, but segregation is in the social category.

7. Diplomatic. Despite the word "political" and the political considerations, this is a diplomatic factor between two separate political units.

8. Cultural. This involves intellectuals and a cultural attitude.

9. Political/Cultural. The campaigning makes this a political factor, but that a society would be influenced in this process means cultural attributes are also at work.

10. Cultural. The impact was political, but the play was a cultural event.

11. Diplomatic. This involves two nations, although in some respects it is a cultural relationship.

12. Social. The arranging of groups is a social factor.

13. Economic. Certainly there are political factors here as well, but the essence is economic.

14. Political. That an executive opposes two points of vital importance to southern politicians is a political factor.

15. Political. This deals with political theory, a view of the nature of the Constitution.

PART III
Debating Historical, Social, and Moral Issues

QUESTIONS FOR THOUGHT

1. One alternative for Lincoln before the Civil War had been practiced by President James Buchanan from December 1860 to March 1861, and had been suggested by many leaders in the North. It was to "let the erring sisters go"; that is, settle property differences and other smaller matters and allow the confederacy to go its own way. Given the six hundred thousand dead, the devastation of the South, the monetary and material costs, and the intense bitterness and hatred generated, should that have been Lincoln's decision? Why or why not?

_____

_____

_____

_____

_____

2. It is easy to be critical of slaveholders in the South and of Lincoln for allowing the split of the Union to develop into a bitter and bloody war. Yet what were

the alternatives—how might the slavery problems have been solved? Consider the following alternatives and react to each. Then suggest your own.

A. Federal appropriation to pay for the freeing of slaves with a program of gradual transition from slavery to restricted farm workers to complete freedom.

_____

_____

B. A federal tax on slaves to force their gradual emancipation.

_____

_____

C. A lump-sum settlement to slave owners, with provisions for the transportation of slaves to selected areas in the West and northern Mexico.

_____

_____

D. A program of gradual emancipation for a forty-year period with federal government compensation. Newly freed slaves would be given the choice, with financial aid, of movement to Africa, the West, the North, or the West Indies.

_____

_____

E. Let the confederacy separate from the United States; let the slavery problem alone, to be solved gradually by southerners.

_____

_____

F. Student's solution:

_____

_____

Is it likely that any of the above solutions would have worked? Why or why not?

_____

_____

_____

_____

_____

_____

3. John Brown assumed that slavery was such an evil that it should be abolished in any way possible, even by the use of force, of a violent revolt. He took a step in this direction by seizing the armory at Harper's Ferry. He was captured and hanged. Should Brown be considered, as some said then, a "martyr in a righteous cause" who aroused the conscience of the nation to finally settle the moral issue of slavery or should he be considered a "misled fanatic," dangerous to the republic, who caused the slaughter of thousands in a terrible Civil War? Explain.

_____

_____

_____

_____

4. In December of 1860, Senator John J. Crittenden of Kentucky introduced resolutions into the Senate that would have:

   A. Protected slavery in the territories south of the old Missouri Compromise (36° 30′) westward to the Pacific.
   B. Provided a constitutional amendment for a federal slave code and a repeal of personal liberty laws—northern laws that impeded the enforcement of the fugitive slave law.
   C. Provided an amendment that, in itself, could not be amended and would guarantee slavery forever.

   Should these proposals have been the basis for discussion by the Republicans and the Confederates? Why or why not?

_____

_____

_____

_____

5. The Federal Fugitive Slave Act allowed the recovery of runaway slaves in the North and required that citizens aid federal marshals in capturing runaways. Individual northern states passed personal liberty laws giving alleged slaves the right of legal defense and forbidding the use of local police and jails to detain them. Should citizens and states in the North have obeyed the federal law or the personal liberty laws? Explain.

_____

_____

_____

_____

6. The novel *Uncle Tom's Cabin* was read by three hundred thousand Americans in 1852. It was performed many times on stage and described the terrible conditions of slavery in dramatic form. When Lincoln met the author, Harriet Beecher Stowe, he referred to her as the little woman who started a war. To what extent was Lincoln exaggerating?

_____

_____

_____

_____

_____

7. The issue in the 1850s was not slavery in the South, but slavery in the territories of the West. Which of the following would have been your choice in solving this problem? Why? Suggest your own solution.

   A. Restrict slavery to the South where it then existed.
   B. Popular sovereignty: let the people in a territory decide whether or not laws should be passed supporting slavery.
   C. Since slaves are legal property, the property can be taken anywhere.
   D. The line of the Missouri Compromise should be revived (36° 30′)—slavery allowed below, disallowed above.

_____

_____

_____

_____

_____

8. How would you have answered the following southern arguments in 1860? A state has a right to an independent existence. This is based on the absolute right of self-government central to the Declaration of Independence. The process of secession was legal since it was conducted through conventions elected by the people. The states existed first (1776–78) and created the national government later (1787). The national government receives limited powers from the states and the states have the right to judge when these powers have been exceeded. Since the states voluntarily joined the Union, they have the right to voluntarily leave the Union in peace.

_____

_____

_____

_____

_____

9. Several factors have been advanced as contributing to the coming of the Civil War. Examine and, if necessary, seek more information about the following factors listed in random order. Then rank them in order of importance.

   A. Excessive fanaticism on both sides, fomenting emotions of fear and hatred by uncompromising radicals.
   B. Southern belief in the right to secede legitimately and Lincoln's firm belief that the Union was indissoluble.
   C. Northern and western moral indignation against slavery combined with a reforming spirit to set things right.
   D. An adherence to principles by both sides, with a refusal to compromise or negotiate these principles.
   E. Northern capitalists wrested control over the American government from the feudal, agrarian South in order to impose a system of high tariffs and other economic measures beneficial to the North's own interests.
   F. The democratic political system, based on frequent elections, promoted demagoguery—emotional speeches based on pro-slavery and anti-slavery themes.
   G. A breakdown in communication—each side manufactured false images of the other and misread intent.
   H. The way of life for two large geographical areas, larger than most European nations, had developed so differently that a firm basis for a Union no longer existed.

   _____

   Explain why you chose the factor you consider most important.

   _____

   _____

   In what ways are several of these factors interrelated?

   _____

   _____

   _____

   Which of these might be considered lessons for the avoidance of violent conflict in a democracy? Why?

   _____

   _____

   _____

10. General William Tecumseh Sherman marched through Georgia and cut a swath of destruction all the way to the sea. On the way he burned the city of Atlanta. In a letter to the people of that city, Sherman explained why it was necessary to burn it. He maintained that his goal was to end the war quickly in order to save lives and prevent further destruction. The people of Atlanta, he wrote,

must know that they are defeated and that there is no use to continue. Do you agree with Sherman's reasoning? Why or why not?

_____

_____

_____

_____

_____

11. Some people advised Lincoln to let the South depart in peace. Lincoln and others in his administration argued otherwise. Some of the arguments are listed below. Which do you consider valid and which questionable? Comment after each.

   A. If the South is allowed to leave the Union, other regions will follow—the West, the Southwest, New England—creating a Europeanization of America.

   _____

   _____

   B. The Union is sacred, a mystical entity that cannot be dissolved by a political act.

   _____

   _____

   C. The division will indicate that republican government has failed, that democracy is an absurdity since a democratically elected government is ignored and humiliated.

   _____

   _____

   D. The federal property in the South—forts, post offices, and so on—belongs to all the American people and must be controlled by the federal government.

   _____

   _____

   E. Constant border clashes will occur, especially over the disposition of the western territories.

   _____

   _____

F. Slavery will be even more entrenched in the southern way of life and will never end.

_____

_____

G. The national market will be shattered and western trade down the Mississippi River will be curtailed.

_____

_____

H. The price of cotton will be inflated with export duties, and tariffs of the confederacy will keep out northern goods.

_____

_____

I. Europeans will become involved in American affairs and a single strong nation will not exist to challenge such diplomatic tampering.

_____

_____

Which are the two most convincing arguments? Why?

_____

_____

Are these nine points sufficient to support Lincoln's decision to call for seventy-five thousand volunteers to put down the Southern rebellion? Why or why not?

_____

_____

_____

How might have the confederacy answered some of these arguments?

_____

_____

_____

_____

12. Consider carefully the two quotes at the beginning of the chapter. What does each mean? Do you agree or disagree with them? Explain.

_____

_____

_____

_____

_____

THOUGHTS FOR QUESTIONS

1. This is the student's choice. What price is to be paid for the Union? What price for emancipation? Knowing the ultimate costs and results, both sides might have preferred a negotiated settlement in 1861 of the controversy over slavery in the territories. Would the South have returned to the Union before the end of the nineteenth century without war? Would freedom for the slaves have occurred without a war? Unlike scientists, historians cannot redo the experiment with a change of variables.

2. The appropriation would have been unprecedented, but not as costly as the war itself. Delaware was offered a program of compensation, but refused. Of course southern slaveholders would have had to support this, a very unlikely step. Item B: The tax may have been unconstitutional and may have, in the 1860s, led to rebellion. Item C: The transportation to another location of freed slaves would have solved the dilemma that concerned Lincoln—the adjustment after freedom of two different races living side by side. However, western settlers would have objected and blacks might have suffered the same fate as the Native Americans in these areas. Would black states have been admitted to the Union? Would blacks, like the Cherokees of the Andrew Jackson era, have been *forced* to move west? Item D: The gradual emancipation idea has promise, but the movement of blacks to another location is a problem not only for blacks but for the labor needs of the South. Perhaps you have some insights. Is the problem beyond reasonable solution?

3. This is for the student to judge. Brown was a hero in New England and to many abolitionists. He became a hero again in the 1960s during the civil rights movement. Those who follow a principle or moral ideal in an uncompromising fashion normally have an impact. But is the American way ordinarily a gradual process of negotiation and compromise, leading to a temporary solution that can be extended or modified later? Brown was certainly an influence on the coming of the war, but perhaps not the determining factor.

4. Lincoln was adamantly opposed to any extension of the evil system of slavery (A), and he hoped for the ultimate extinction of slavery, not the opposite (C). The leaders of the Republican party agreed, more or less, with him on this. Northerners were unlikely to cooperate with the federal slave code or the fugitive slave law (B). So, from personal conviction and political reality, Lincoln and the Republicans would not seriously consider such arrangements. All of these favored the South and were designed to bring those states back into the Union. However, the price seems too high. The question calls for these arrangements as a *basis for discussion;* if they had

been modified, and if Lincoln's goal was to preserve the Union, who knows what compromises and assurances might have been worked out.

5. One hesitates to advocate a defiance of law. Of course the North had always maintained that federal law was superior to state law. Ironically, the South was arguing that federal law superseded state law in the area of police power while the northern states argued states' rights! You must determine if a higher ethical law or philosophical principle prevails, in this case, over a law made by a representative body.

6. Certainly no single event or book "caused" the war, and to that extent, Lincoln exaggerated. Nevertheless, the influence of a publication and its derivative in drama is difficult to evaluate. No one can penetrate the minds of people to discover if the book's ideas and representations formed attitudes that led to decisions. Economic data is easier to measure. Political information is evident by actual decisions and voting. But intellectual or cultural influences are not easily measured, especially in *extent* of impact.

7. Lincoln opted for A and the result was the Civil War. Stephen A. Douglas preferred B and took the nation into bloodshed in Kansas and to a collapse of previous compromises. The constitutional solution was C, which favored the southern position. Solution D was not acceptable to Lincoln and would restrict slave territory severely. Democracy seemed to dictate B. Yet the rights of property, if the slave is considered property, are upheld by C. Morally, A seems to be the proper position, especially if the goal is the eventual abolition of slavery.

8. This is the position held by John C. Calhoun and supported with many variations by most southern politicians. Similar views appeared in Thomas Jefferson's and James Madison's Kentucky and Virginia resolutions (1798) and at the Hartford Convention in New England in 1814. The Constitution begins, "We the people," not "We the states." The opposing view is that the states formed a woven fabric or an organic body so intertwined and interdependent that no part can be separated from the whole. Of course, parts were added on in the form of new states. Later, in 1918, President Woodrow Wilson spoke of the self-determination of all people, but we have not yet defined exactly what that means in practice. The southern states were not in the same relationship to Washington, D.C., in 1860 as the thirteen colonies were to London in 1776. The South had representation, political influence, and functioned as an integral part of a government to which it had sworn loyalty. Nothing in the Constitution gave the South the right to secede or implied that states could thwart the will of a national congress. The original thirteen colonies appealed not to a legal right to secede from the British Empire, but to a philosophical principle or a natural right.

9. Suggested ranking: B, D, A, E, F, C, G, H. Item B is chosen first because this is a stated belief of both sides and the basis of each side's arguments. The historian has no reason to doubt the sincerity of these beliefs, and they are inherently contradictory.

The other factors were influential, but to see them as more important assumes that each side was not honest in their public statements. Factor B is based on the attitude reflected in D, the refusal to negotiate. The emotion generated by A and F fed the arguments of B. Fanaticism by some in the North and moderate attitudes by many other northerners were based on C. Factor G was part of the problem due to A and F.

Lessons from history are easy to extract with hindsight. Do not be unduly swayed by extremists. Inflexible principles can be troublesome in a democracy. They may be maintained, but their advocates should still allow for compromise on specific issues. Talking and negotiating often enhance accurate communication. Vociferous moral indignation at the behavior of others can be hypocritical, given the treatment of free blacks in the North and the conditions of the factory laborer. Possibly the North and the South each underestimated the strength of beliefs and the degree of adherence to principles by the other.

10. Without Sherman's march through Georgia to the sea, the South might have continued to fight after 1865. Would the South have yielded if it were still intact from New Orleans to Virginia? Would the Confederates have been encouraged to fight on since no Yankees were in sight and the South had not been militarily conquered by the North? Sherman saved lives on both sides by shortening the war. He destroyed property, but did not harm civilians. Lee's surrender was not followed by charges of political betrayal of the Southern cause or by continued guerrilla warfare in the South.

11. Arguments C, E, G, and I seem to have the most validity. Some negotiated arrangements might have solved D since public buildings existed in the North, and the South also had paid taxes to build these. Item A: It seems unlikely that other regions planned to leave the Union; however, the South's precedent would have offered encouragement to other dissatisfied regions. Argument B evokes a comparison to mystical ties with England and the King in 1776. Item F: A division would not have changed the institution of slavery. Item H: The South normally opposed tariffs and the need to sell cotton would have kept duties low. The North might have lost some advantages it had over the British in purchasing cotton and in the hidden expenses of insurance, loans, and storage. Middlemen agents might have ended up in British hands rather than in the hands of New England merchants.

Arguments C and E are the most convincing. The great experiment in an effective republican government would begin to crumble. The western problem had already resulted in bloodshed in Kansas. This would continue in other western areas, especially since the Supreme Court had ruled that slaves could legally be taken into the territories.

The cumulative evidence would give Lincoln very convincing arguments to put down a rebellion. They relate to politics, economics, diplomacy, and moral ideals— something for everyone. Taking military action is serious and sometimes beyond the severity of the situation. But Lincoln had cognate arguments for military action, given an imperfect world and an arrogant, belligerent enemy.

The South would have, at least theoretically, supported A, F, G, and H. For C they may have maintained that the process of secession was an example of democracy in action, of the self-determination of a people and a way of life. The South would not fear Europeans (I) and would attempt to resolve western problems by negotiation (E). They would reject the "sacred Union" concept (B), but probably would apply the sentiment to a "sacred state." The simple solution to D would be to have both nations maintain the federal property within the borders of each.

12. Rogers implies that the forces of history are beyond the control of leaders and their choices. There are times when this seems true. One could argue that when the steps leading to the Civil War occurred, little could have been done to avoid the inevitable forces that prevailed. However, this leaves us with a sense of profound

helplessness. Should we, as the Chinese Taoists advise, "do nothing so that all will be accomplished?" Our western tradition has supported the concept of individual freedom of choice. On that basis, the freedom of choice of those in leadership positions, if they are encouraged, persuaded, and convinced by evidence and argument, could lead to decisions that are not merely dictated by the "blind forces" of history. Individuals and groups do make choices from several alternatives. The choices relate to the circumstances as well as to the assumptions, experiences, values, and we hope, reasonable decisions of leaders. Lincoln could have called for a high-level session of negotiations in Richmond, Virginia, rather than for seventy-five thousand volunteers in April 1861. Do you agree?

The old "Dragnet" radio program left us with the phrase, "give us the facts, lady, just the facts." This seems desirable and feasible. But in most cases, the facts are numerous, the historian must choose from among them, and these choices, of themselves, lead to "observations and conclusions." To present only the facts is to produce a chronology or encyclopedia of history. No one reads these and they have no value beyond their reference use. As soon as one chooses details from the large amount of information available and puts these facts in a coherent prose form, "observation and conclusion" has begun. Is the recorder and compiler of history different from the historian? Explain.

CHAPTER

9

RECONSTRUCTION AND NINETEENTH-CENTURY POLITICS

"What is excluded from a historical account reflects as strong a bias as the slanting of what is included."

Dick Mumford

"The historian must have some conception of how men who are not historians behave."

E. M. Forster

PART I
Acquiring Essential Data

ESSENTIAL DATES

Determine the correct sequence and write the approximate date for each of the following events.

1. In the *Plessy* v. *Ferguson* case, the Supreme Court determines that "separate but equal" facilities for different races are constitutional. _____

2. The Fourteenth Amendment is ratified, defining citizenship and offering citizens equal protection of the law. _____

3. The Populist party is organized to express farmers' discontent. _____

4. The Pendleton Act (civil-service reform) establishes a Civil Service Commission. _____

5. Grover Cleveland is elected president for the second time. _____

6. The first Military Reconstruction Act provides for the military occupation of the South. _____

7. Abraham Lincoln dies and Andrew Johnson becomes president. _____

8. North Dakota, South Dakota, Montana, Washington, Idaho, and Wyoming become states. _____

9. Severe depressions occur at two different times. _____

10. The Specie Resumption Act establishes the gold standard in the United States. _____

ESSENTIAL CONCEPTS

Examine each concept and write what contemporary relevance it might have.

1. *"conquered territories"* The southern states that seceded from the Union were considered to have reverted back to territories controlled by Congress.

_____

_____

_____

2. *redemption* The efforts to bring the South back under the control of white southerners and away from northern domination.

_____

_____

_____

3. *pork barrel* Bills passed, usually at the end of a congressional session and attached to the appropriation bill, that financed public works (paid for by the federal government) in local districts. Congressmen could gain support for reelection by getting such projects for their districts.

_____

_____

_____

4. *swing state* A state that could "swing" to either political party in an election. Voters were evenly divided and often presidential candidates were chosen from these states.

_____

_____

_____

5. *patronage* The act of rewarding political party or candidate workers with a government job or project.

_____

_____

_____

6. *protective tariff* A high tariff that was supposed to offer American manufacturers protection from lower-priced imports.

_____

_____

_____

7. *hard money* Circulating currency actually made of gold or silver coin or redeemable in gold from the government. Paper money, not redeemable in gold, was called greenbacks in this period.

_____

_____

_____

8. *political machine* A political organization in which a boss controlled political workers—ward heelers in cities—who made sure their district delivered the vote for the candidate advanced by the "machine."

_____

_____

_____

9. *"wave the bloody shirt"* The use of descriptions of Civil War horrors and bloodshed as a constant reminder of what the Democratic South had done by its secession.

_____

_____

_____

10. *"due process of law"* The Fourteenth Amendment guaranteed equal rights for all citizens and established that a citizen could not be deprived of life, liberty, or property "without due process of law."

_____

_____

_____

ANSWERS

Correct sequence of events and their dates.

1. 7; 1865
2. 6; 1867
3. 2; 1868
4. 10; 1875
5. 4; 1883
6. 9; 1884–85

7. 8; 1889–90
8. 3; 1892
9. 5; 1892
10. 9 again; 1893–97
11. 1; 1896

PART II
Developing Thinking Skills

SKILL EXERCISE ONE: EVALUATING AND APPLYING EVIDENCE

The following thesis relates to Reconstruction. Ten items of data are listed after the thesis. Under each of them, write whether the information *supports* the thesis, *challenges* the thesis, or is *neutral* data. Briefly explain each classification. Then check your decisions with the suggested answers.

The Thesis

"Southern Reconstruction state governments, because of corruption and huge expenditures, were examples of the inability of those untrained in democracy—blacks newly freed from slavery, in this case—to operate an effective democratic government."

Items of Data

1. Both Abraham Lincoln and Andrew Johnson believed that the reconstruction of the South was the responsibility of the executive branch of government rather than the legislature.

_____

_____

2. One reconstruction governor, a Republican from Louisiana on a salary of $8,000, put more than $100,000 in his bank account in one year.

_____

_____

3. The vote was given to freedmen who did not have homes, money, education, or economic and physical security, as if the vote alone would overcome the other problems.

_____

_____

4. A black politician from South Carolina explained that, although blacks were not prepared for voting, ". . . we can learn. Give a man tools and let him commence to use them, and in time he will learn a trade. So it is with voting."

_____

_____

5. Only a few blacks served in positions of power during Reconstruction. There were no black governors, few judges, and only in South Carolina—for two years—did blacks make up a majority in a state legislature.

_____

_____

6. Black legislators in control of the lower house in South Carolina voted an appropriation of $1,000 to a legislator who had lost money on a horse-race bet.

_____

_____

7. In Louisiana, public funds during Reconstruction were squandered on liquor, expensive furniture, jewelry, and other luxuries for legislators.

_____

_____

8. Reconstruction state governments founded statewide public school systems and provided, in many cases for the first time, aid for the poor and handicapped.

_____

_____

9. The level of corruption in Reconstruction state governments in the South was probably less than that of the national government and certainly less than that of northern city governments in the same period.

_____

_____

10. The Fourteenth Amendment declared that if a state refused the vote to any male inhabitant older than age twenty-one who was a citizen, the number of representatives for that state would be reduced.

_____

_____

ANSWERS AND EXPLANATIONS

1. Neutral. The determination of whether Congress or the president has power over Reconstruction is not relevant to the thesis.

2. Supports. Of course the governor was white and had functioned in a democracy for many years. Yet the fact that he could get away with this indicates a lack of control.

3. Challenges. The failure of the blacks to continue to have influence was due as much to these other factors as it was to practicing democracy poorly.

4. Challenges. To learn democracy one must practice democracy and little time was given to blacks to learn from this limited practice.

5. Challenges. Blacks, then, did not really control state governments during Reconstruction and thus could be held responsible only for their own voting habits.

6. Supports. This silly appropriation indicates a lack of concern about the responsibilities of elected representatives in a democracy.

7. Supports. Despite the fact that the government was dominated by whites and that previous legislatures in Louisiana had done the same thing, black voters, white carpetbaggers, and the large number of black legislators bear much responsibility.

8. Challenges. The legislature passed significant legislation for the benefit of citizens. Even though untrained in democracy, the Reconstruction legislature was able to perform well in several cases.

9. Challenges. Although this does not excuse cases of corruption and incompetence, it does indicate that the shortcomings of democracy were nationwide and not confined to the freedmen and their political influence in the South.

10. Neutral. This very important amendment does not directly pertain to the thesis.

QUESTIONS

1. What other data would be useful to know in order to adequately evaluate this thesis?

_____

_____

_____

2. Considering the evidence presented in the ten items, is the thesis validated or refuted? Explain.

_____

_____

_____

3. Can it be argued that this thesis will never be proven or disproven beyond a reasonable doubt? Why or why not?

_____

_____

_____

SKILL EXERCISE TWO: DETERMINING RELEVANCE OF EVIDENCE

Examine carefully the following statements of data related to the given topic. Under each indicate whether the data is *relevant* or *irrelevant* to the topic. Then briefly explain your decision. Compare your choices with those offered.

TOPIC: THE POWER OF THE PRESIDENCY IN THE LATE NINETEENTH CENTURY

1. Mrs. Rutherford B. Hayes served only lemonade at White House receptions; no alcohol was allowed.

_____

_____

2. The House of Representatives brought impeachment proceedings against Andrew Johnson, but the Senate failed to convict him by one vote.

_____

_____

3. Ulysses S. Grant was an inefficient administrator and lacked initiative in matters of government.

_____

_____

4. The United States was isolationist in the late nineteenth century and did not engage in any significant foreign involvements until 1898.

_____

_____

5. Many liberal Republicans, known as "Mugwumps," wanted business separated from politics and a restoration of integrity to government.

_____

_____

6. The most popular interpretation of the Constitution in this period held that it was up to Congress to make the laws and the president to merely carry them out.

_____

_____

7. On July 2, 1881, Charles J. Guiteau shot President James Garfield as he waited for a train in a Washington station.

_____

_____

8. No president during this period had the luxury of political party control over both houses of Congress for a lengthy duration.

_____

_____

9. The election of 1884 was one of the dirtiest in American history and centered on the personal morality of the two candidates.

_____

_____

10. The election of 1888 was influenced by high-tariff supporters who contributed four million dollars, enabling the Republican party to buy a large number of votes for Benjamin Harrison.

_____

_____

ANSWERS AND EXPLANATIONS

1. Irrelevant. This bears no relationship to the power of the presidency.

2. Relevant. This tended to weaken the presidency and put future presidents on guard as to what Congress might ultimately do.

3. Relevant. The beginning of decline in power is when, after a previous president is impeached, the next one appears weak and allows an aggressive Congress to take charge.

4. Relevant. Presidents increase their influence and assume a greater leadership role when foreign affairs grow in importance. Since none took place, presidents had no opportunity to gain prestige and recognition.

5. Irrelevant. This is a political topic and may relate to the presidency, but not directly to the power issue.

6. Relevant. The president, thereby, is to follow the lead of Congress and not take part in a cooperative legislative function with Congress. This is a decline in power, especially compared to presidents Abraham Lincoln, James Polk, and Andrew Jackson.

7. Irrelevant. It could be argued that assassination creates an aura of weakness, but this did not directly influence the power of the presidency.

8. Relevant. Party control might have been translated into effective legislation as part of a cohesive program. Successes here would embolden presidents to attempt to lead.

9. Irrelevant. Dirty elections are endemic and some strong presidents have emerged from mud-slinging, corrupt campaigns. Personal morality is also a recurring issue in nearly every election.

10. Irrevelant. Money has helped elect many presidents and has not usually been related to the power and influence exerted by that particular president.

PART III
Debating Historical, Social, and Moral Issues

QUESTIONS FOR THOUGHT

1. The southern states left the Union in 1860–61. Congress argued that these states had indeed severed ties with the rest of the United States and should be treated as territories. As such, it was necessary for them to petition to reenter the Union. Lincoln maintained that the southern states had never left the Union since to secede was unconstitutional and not legally possible. Therefore, as *states* in rebellion, they had only to end the rebellion, pledge loyalty, and continue their interrupted connection with the other states and the federal government. Do you agree with Lincoln or with Congress? Why?

_____

_____

_____

_____

_____

2. The Black Codes were state laws that restricted the freedom of blacks and required them to find jobs or be hired out to work by the authorities. They were restricted in voting rights, in holding office, in testifying in court, and could not bear arms. Was this an effort to restore the conditions and relationships characteristic of slavery or merely an effort to provide an orderly transition from

slavery to a stable social arrangement that would be acceptable to whites and would give direction to the recently freed blacks? Explain.

_____

_____

_____

_____

_____

3. Some historians argue that if Andrew Johnson's impeachment case would have resulted in a guilty verdict the United States government might have evolved into a parliamentary system—members of the executive branch serving at the pleasure of the legislature and responsible to it. Future presidents would be impeached or threatened with impeachment. The president's duties would have been reduced to merely administering the laws passed by Congress. Would this have been a helpful step for the American government, increasing its efficiency and making it more responsive to elected representatives? Why or why not?

_____

_____

_____

_____

_____

4. Several explanations have been given for the failure of Reconstruction. Examine the following five offered here and rank them in order of importance.

   A. Blacks were given political rights, but no economic base, no land or other property, no stake in society.
   B. Northerners lost interest in the high ideals of the war; their enthusiasm flagged; they surrendered their goals.
   C. The Ku Klux Klan frightened blacks from the polls and from officeholding—the use of and threat of violence prevented blacks from continuing to gain political strength without help from the federal government.
   D. White southern leaders mounted a white supremacy movement to restore their control, to "redeem" the South—even moderate whites were not willing to incorporate blacks into southern society on an equal basis.
   E. Widespread racism pervaded the North and only a minority believed in racial equality, so no groundswell of public support emerged there.

Explain your ranking.

_____

_____

_____

Given the social structure of slavery before the war, given the hatred generated by the war, and given the racial attitudes in the North, could one *predict* the social and political outcome in the decades after the war? Why or why not?

_____

_____

_____

5. Although the Pendleton Act of 1883 established a civil-service merit system for the government bureaucracy, it led political parties to turn to big business for financial contributions that had formerly been acquired by assessment of office-holders and patronage. It also tended to guarantee jobs and make it difficult to dismiss incompetent officeholders. Was a civil-service system based on merit beneficial? Explain.

_____

_____

_____

_____

6. In the presidential election of 1884, one candidate, James G. Blaine, was accused of corrupt stock deals while the other, Grover Cleveland, admitted that he had fathered an illegitimate child. Which would be a more significant issue to raise in a presidential campaign? If the candidates' abilities and programs were similar, for which candidate would you have voted? Why?

_____

_____

_____

_____

7. Two important issues of the period were tariffs and currency. Many conservatives argued that a high tariff was necessary both for the protection of "infant industry" and of jobs for workers. They also supported gold as the basis of currency, calling it "nature's money" or even "God's currency." Opponents maintained that the free-enterprise system should support free competition and trade and that both gold and silver should be coined in order to increase the supply of money. Which sides of these issues do you support? Explain.

_____

_____

_____

_____

8. City "bosses" often provided coal, turkeys, jobs, gifts, and emergency help to voters in cities—a type of "social security" program for those in need. Yet they overcharged the city and received kickbacks and payoffs. Reformers attempted to end this corruption but, in the name of frugality and efficiency, provided none of these social services to the needy. One could argue that the "bosses" benefited the people more than the reformers. React to this last statement.

_____

_____

_____

_____

9. Political parties in the United States in the late nineteenth century, and throughout most of American history, represented community interests and organization loyalties rather than espousing a system of ideological beliefs. Thus American politics tend to be issue-oriented rather than philosophically or ideologically centered. Is this system preferable to the adherence to a set of coherent and consistent beliefs as the basis of political parties? Explain. What are the advantages and disadvantages of each?

_____

_____

_____

_____

_____

10. Historians have offered several interpretations of the Reconstruction period.

   A. Early interpretations placed the South in an exploited position. Devastated by war, willing to accept emancipation, and eager to get on with their lives, southerners were harassed by federal troops and forced to resist the corrupt and self-serving efforts by northerners to acquire wealth and political power at the expense of the South. This experience serves as a lesson on the misuse of federal power over the states and is a warning to future generations on the abuses of power.

   B. Historians in the 1930s added greedy capitalists to the list of those who exploited the South in a time of weakness and humiliation. Business groups used the Radical Republicans to prevent southern competition and to keep the South as a "colony" of the north. The culprit was not so much the government as it was those business interests who controlled the government for their own gain.

   C. Later historians, beginning in the 1960s, argued that the actual leaders in Congress, the moderate Republicans, had real concern about the well-being of the freed slaves and sought primarily to secure their rights as citizens. It was the South that resisted, that attempted to impose slave-like conditions on blacks, and that resorted to violence to undo the logical outcome of the northern victory in the war. Programs introduced by state legislatures in the South were long overdue efforts to provide education and social services to those in need. Corruption existed, but not on the scale of corruption in other sections of the United States. The federal government acted in good conscience in a noble experiment to reshape a society for the benefit of all of its citizens.

Which view do you agree with most? Why?

_____

_____

_____

Should the federal government have even tried to restructure southern society? Why or why not?

Would a black historian from Chicago and a southern historian from Mississippi view the issue differently? Why or why not? If both are competent professional historians seeking truth in a nonobjective manner, should they reach the same conclusions? Why or why not?

_____

_____

_____

11. React to the two quotes at the beginning of the chapter and briefly explain their meaning. Do you agree or disagree? Why? How might each apply to the content of this chapter?

_____

_____

_____

_____

_____

THOUGHTS FOR QUESTIONS

1. Lincoln's program seemed more consistent and smoother. It might have avoided some racial tensions. However, it left the structures of society intact except for the legal abolition of slavery. Does treason on the part of a state forfeit its existence as a state? The southern states were hardly territories. The war was fought on the assumption that it was illegal or not possible to secede. Lincoln wanted to settle the major political issue and then deal with racial adjustment and "reconstruction." Congress chose to mix the political issue with the process of Reconstruction and to use reentry as a lever for social change and political power.

2. Certainly the codes were intended to "control" the newly freed slaves and to assure a reliable labor supply for southern planters. They were also an attempt to restore some of the features of an unequal class system politically, socially, and economically. However, given the situation and considering the lack of federal prece-

dent at that point, some decisions were necessary. A large number of confused people, without land or jobs, illiterate, and lacking marketable skills needed some direction. Some directions may have been necessary, but the actual codes were harsh and smacked of the restoration of involuntary servitude.

3. It would still have taken quite an effort on the part of Congress to continually seek impeachment of a president. Most members of Congress probably recognized and supported the separation-of-powers system. The anger of Congress was directed at Johnson, not at the institution of the presidency. Furthermore, the parliamentary system provides for the executive to be chosen out of the legislature. The American president is elected separately. Efficiency was not a goal of the Founding Fathers.

4. Suggested ranking: E, D, A, B, C. Attitudes play a significant role in a situation such as this. The moderate white attitude in the South and the prevailing outlook in the North worked against the success of an effort to restructure southern society. If this attitude had been congenial and favorable to a remolding of the South, then ways would have been found to carry out the changes.

With hindsight it is easy to conclude that the mission of the Radical Republicans was an impossible one. But at the time a victorious group with power, prestige, and money could hope to achieve its goals. Perhaps the mission was not completely impossible if one examines the success of the American occupation of Japan after World War II.

5. Few people would seek to abolish a merit basis for selecting government officials. Yet, a president needs to have many people in key positions who support his outlook and program. Otherwise, the president cannot really be held responsible. Many presidents have complained that an entrenched bureaucracy can become a force unto itself, can reinterpret laws as they are applied and thwart the will of both Congress and the president. Compared to the bureaucracies in other nations, however, the American bureaucracy has been remarkably honest and efficient.

6. The people chose Cleveland. Moral indiscretions occur in the lives of many people. Cleveland acknowledged the child, cared for it, and continued to concentrate on the issues of government. But corruption in office reflects an attitude that is dangerous and can impact the future. The media exploits both types of behavior. Is past behavior a prologue—or are unfortunate incidents to be acknowledged and forgotten?

7. In theory, the opponents seem to have a stronger case. Those who advocate a free-enterprise system must be consistent and not demand protective tariffs to protect manufacturing, which in this period was no longer an "infant industry". Where is it written that gold should be the only basis for money? An effective currency is currency that is accepted by people who use it. Of course, both tariffs and the gold standard helped wealthy businessmen who produced manufactured goods for profits and had the scarce money.

8. More money might have been made available for social services without excessive charges and corruption. Millions were stolen from taxpayers and indirectly from citizens in the cities. The "bosses" made a travesty of democracy with their vote-buying and their use of government for their own gain. Yet reformers seemed unconcerned about the plight of the poor and had little to offer them. Their reforms produced a frugal government that lowered taxes. The poor had to wait for the Progressives to acquire true reform that effectively promoted honesty in government and sought to relieve their needs. As a poor tenement dweller, would you have

supported the reformer who promised honesty and sought to get rid of the political boss who had found a job for your son and provided coal for your family the previous winter?

9. Giving ideological commitment priority often results in several political parties rather than only two. This confuses the political process. It alienates many voters and, in a pragmatic democracy of checks and balances, makes it difficult to practice the politics of the possible. The American system, on the other hand, with its umbrella collections of a variety of beliefs and their resultant programs, sacrifices strong convictions based on justice or political principles to the need for victory in an upcoming election. Parties tend to stand for whatever wins votes; they follow rather than lead; and they yield to constituents rather than present, and argue the merits of, a coherent program.

10. Certainly the effort to reconstruct the South was not without ill-advised programs and unworkable principles. Evidence indicates that northern capitalists did hope to exploit the South and dominate it economically. The Republican party sought to gain politically from the vote of blacks and to use that vote to retain control of the national government. But these do not deny the efforts of many well-meaning people to create a viable social arrangement in the South, one that reflected American ideals and that would integrate freed slaves into the mainstream of American political, social, and economic life. Precedents in education and social services were established under the reconstruction governments. It is sometimes easy to indict those who make an effort to bring about beneficial change while others resist and interfere with these honest efforts. The noble experiment view is that the effort was worth the risk. Not to have tried reconstruction would have been a betrayal of all the sacrifices made during the war and would have meant a denial of the American democratic ideals.

Theoretically, the Chicago historian's views should correspond with those of the Mississippi historian. In many cases, historians are able to conquer regionalism and personal sympathies. But historians suffer, as do others, with perceptions that betray the influence of environment. Some become defensive, consciously or unconsciously. Perhaps different perspectives are necessary in a free society and eventually lead to a balanced view closer to the truth.

11. This quote deals with the problem of condensing a massive amount of data into a limited form for presentation. Someone must choose what to include and what to exclude. On what basis? On the basis of importance—but who decides what is important? Even two standard textbooks on Reconstruction would contain different material. Historians make personal choices of what is important enough to include. The history student must recognize bias in the selection of data.

Forster has hit at a weakness of historians. Most historians write from a desk in an academic institution and may have grown up in an academic setting. Yet they attempt to understand the feelings and attitudes of a white southerner, a newly freed black, a poor voter in a city, or a politician hoping to win the next election. Maybe a tour of duty in the "real world" should be required of all historians. But who is so experienced as to be able to "cast the first stone"?

CHAPTER

10

ECONOMIC GROWTH,
EAST AND WEST

*"If you would understand anything, observe its beginning and
its development."*

Aristotle

*"The history of the world is the record of man in quest of his daily bread
and butter."*

H. W. Van Loon

PART I
Acquiring Essential Data

ESSENTIAL DATES

Determine the correct sequence and write the approximate date for each of the following events.

1. Massacre at Wounded Knee—Indian men, women, and children are killed after Ghost Dance ceremony. _____

2. Comstock Lode of large amounts of gold and silver is discovered in western Nevada. _____

3. Interstate Commerce Act is passed, representing the first efforts at government regulation of business. _____

4. Edwin L. Drake drills the first successful oil well in Pennsylvania. _____

5. Thomas A. Edison develops the electric light bulb. _____

6. Indian chiefs accept the reservation system after their defeat in the Sioux wars. _____

7. Barbed wire for fences is first manufactured. _____

8. The Homestead Act opens up free land in the West to settlers. _____

9. The Bessemer process for steel manufacturing is first used in the United States. _____

10. Alexander Graham Bell introduces the telephone. _____

11. Custer and his troops are defeated by the Indians at Little Big Horn in Montana. _____

ESSENTIAL CONCEPTS

Examine each concept and write what contemporary relevance it might have.

1. *frontier thesis* Frederick Jackson Turner's thesis that the American frontier promoted democracy, individualism, and other characteristics and behavior patterns as the most significant part of American character and way of life.

_____

_____

_____

2. *assimilation* Beginning in 1876, the effort to break up the Indian tribes and make Indians live like whites in small family units on farms. It was abandoned in 1934.

_____

_____

_____

3. *Californios* Mexican and mixed Spanish and Indian residents of California who were made citizens in 1848, but were not guaranteed land titles and were discriminated against.

_____

_____

_____

4. *massacres* The attacks, sometimes by Indians, sometimes by soldiers, in which men, women, and children were killed, often without specific provocation or warning.

_____

_____

_____

5. *"boom towns"* Towns that arose overnight to supply miners with necessities and pleasures. Saloons, gambling, and prostitutes were common features of these western settlements.

_____

_____

_____

6. *telephone* The transmission of the voice over wire with the aid of electricity. Developed in 1876 and commonly used by the 1890s, it opened employment opportunities for women.

_____

_____

_____

7. *soldier societies* Part of the Indian culture. Some warrior groups skilled in the use of weapons and horses would raid villages and start skirmishes against other Indian groups, usually over buffalo or territory.

_____

_____

_____

8. *entrepreneurs* Individuals who, with great determination, pursue a business enterprise by taking risks and applying creativity, management skills, and vision to make it successful.

_____

_____

_____

9. *"stock watering"* The process of issuing more stock for sale than the company is worth according to its assets and earning power. It is associated especially with Jay Gould and the Erie Railroad in the 1860s.

_____

_____

_____

10. *vertical integration* A monopolistic practice of corporations in the later nineteenth century. It is an effort to gain control over an entire business process, from the ownership of resources to the transportation, manufacturing, and marketing of a single product, thus reducing middleman costs at each point.

_____

_____

_____

ANSWERS

Correct sequence of events and their dates.

1. 2; 1859
2. 4; 1859
3. 8; 1862
4. 9; 1864
5. 6; 1867–68
6. 7; 1874

7. 10; 1876
8. 11; 1876
9. 5; 1879
10. 3; 1887
11. 1; 1890

PART II
Developing Thinking Skills

SKILL EXERCISE ONE: FACT, INFERENCE, OR OPINION

Under each of the following statements, write whether it is a fact, an inference, or an opinion. Explain your choices and check them with those suggested. Remember that you are determining the *type* of statement, not whether or not it is true.

1. Much of the Great Plains area was treeless, so settlers had to construct sod houses until they could purchase lumber from the East.

_____

_____

2. The changes that bring the greatest social and cultural adjustments in history are technological, such as the introduction of the plow and barbed wire.

_____

_____

3. The Indians conducted a dastardly sneak attack on General George Custer's innocent and peaceful troops and brutally destroyed the helpless soldiers.

   _____

   _____

4. The Bureau of Indian Affairs was rent with corruption and, although assigned the task of protecting and caring for the Native American, cared little about their welfare.

   _____

   _____

5. Only 80 million of the 430 million acres available in the West were settled by actual family farmers (homesteaders), and two-thirds of these farmers failed within thirty years.

   _____

   _____

6. The 225,000 savage Indians fought continual bloodthirsty wars among themselves as they carelessly slaughtered the fifteen million bison spread across the Great Plains.

   _____

   _____

7. Much of the process of settlement of the West could be categorized as exploitation—of the Indians, of the bison, of the water supply, of the minerals, and even of many of the settlers who moved there.

   _____

   _____

8. The white man had no business in the West and should have left the land in the hands of the rightful owners, the Indians, whose rights over the land stemmed from their burial and spiritual traditions.

   _____

   _____

9. It would have been easier to set each Indian family up on a large farm with a house, tools, and seed, and to educate the parents and children than to have pursued and killed them or driven them onto a reservation.

   _____

   _____

10. Research has shown that the typical cowboy of the West was not used to a pistol, had a boring, difficult job following the cattle to market, and was generally not the free spirit depicted in romantic fiction.

    _____

    _____

ANSWERS AND EXPLANATIONS

1. Fact. "Much" is vague, but this is still a factual-type statement.

2. Inference. Perhaps this is an accurate observation, but the use of the word "greatest" and the overall nature of the statement is an inference from the facts. It might be argued that religious change brings major adjustment.

3. Opinion. Too many loaded words are here—"dastardly, sneak, innocent, brutally". The troops, being soldiers, were prepared to fight back and did.

4. Inference. Some parts like corruption may be documented, but the words "little" and "rent with" make this interpretive.

5. Fact. Some insightful inferences could be drawn from this fact. The statement is precise and without interpretive phrases.

6. Opinion. There are two accurate statistics here—the Native Americans did fight among themselves as well as kill bison for food. But the use of words like "savage," "bloodthirsty," and "carelessly" place this out of the factual classification and beyond the reasonable inference level.

7. Inference. This statement could draw out an opposite viewpoint based on the abundance produced on sparsely settled lands. It is a respectable, reasonable interpretation based on evidence and thus not merely an opinion.

8. Opinion. The words "no business" and "rightful owners" place this in the opinion category. The burial and spiritual traditions, although significant to the Indian, do not mean the white man should be excluded.

9. Inference. Full evidence for this might be given in statistical form; however, since the statement is comparative, it is one of judgment.

10. Inference. Some facts support this, but the gun *was* used and many would still see the cowboy as working out in the open—hence a "free spirit." Boring is a relative term. This is not an exaggerated opinion, but it is not a factual-type statement either.

SKILL EXERCISE TWO: ANALYZING QUANTIFIED DATA

Consider each of the following quantified data (first sentence) and the inference (second sentence) drawn from it. Indicate whether or not the inference is an accurate one and explain your answer.

1. From 1870 to 1900, the population of the United States increased from 40 to 76 million, and the Gross National Product rose from 9 billion to 37 billion.
   Inference: The United States was increasing its wealth faster than its population growth.

   _____

   _____

2. The United States patent office registered 276 inventions in the decade of the 1790s, but 234,956 inventions in the decade of the 1890s.
   Inference: Inventions increased and were the key factor in the industrial growth of the United States.

   _____

   _____

3. By 1900, foreigners had invested $3.4 billion in the United States.
   Inference: A significant amount of capital for industrial growth came from abroad, so American economic growth was dependent on foreign investment.

---

4. The overall prices of goods dropped by 50 percent in the period from 1865 to 1900.
   Inference: Americans had a much better life, materially speaking, in 1900 than in 1865.

---

5. Two of three farms acquired from the government under the Homestead Act (1862) failed by 1900.
   Inference: The Homestead Act was a colossal failure.

---

6. Farm tenancy—farmers working on land they did not own and paying rent to the owner—increased from 26 percent of farmers in 1880 to 35 percent in 1900.
   Inference: Farmers became poorer in the late nineteenth century with a reduced standard of living.

---

7. In 1900, 98 percent of the nation's physical assets were owned by 50 percent of the people and the top 10 percent of Americans owned 75 percent of those physical assets.
   Inference: Physical assets were unequally distributed among the American people in 1900.

---

8. It is estimated that in the 1890s corporate profits were 40 percent higher or $400 million more than they would have been under free competitive conditions.
   Inference: Free competition reduces profits for corporations, and thus the American people would have been better off without the various trusts and monopolies that dominated the economy in the 1890s.

---

9. Expenses on education increased from $60 million per year in 1870 to $500 million in 1900, and the expenditure per child went up from $5.33 to $20.53 in the same period.

Inference: American young people received a better education in 1900 than in 1870.

_____

_____

10. In the depression of 1893–94, 4.5 million workers, one-sixth of the work force, were unemployed and only 50 to 60 percent of the labor force worked a full twelve months a year.
    Inference: Job security was not high in 1893–94 and many who did work during the year could not expect to receive a full year's wages.

_____

_____

ANSWERS AND EXPLANATIONS

1. Accurate. This seems obvious from the numbers presented. Of course, the statement is not a profound one and the addition of related data might yield more insightful generalizations.

2. Questionable. Inventions did increase, but the numbers do not substantiate inventions as the "key" factor. They may have been, but the numbers are not proof.

3. Questionable. The $3.4 billion is "significant," but whether or not this was a leading growth factor requires more information—for example, the total capital invested from *all* sources in 1900.

4. Questionable. If life is measured by the amount of cheaper material goods available, perhaps the statement has some accuracy. Of course, the distribution of these goods is a factor to be considered.

5. Questionable. One-third of the farmers established and maintained farms. The "failure" of the rest may have allowed others to purchase the farms and achieve success. "Colossal" is too strong a word.

6. Questionable. The statistic does not prove farmers generally became poorer. Many farmers may have prospered in the period—65 percent in 1900 farmed their own land. However, the data tends to lean in the direction of the inference.

7. Accurate. The distribution was not only unequal, but from the quantified data it seems that the inequality was widespread or "gross." Of course, if the nation's total wealth increased substantially, then the living standards may have risen for a majority.

8. Questionable. The statistic does imply increased profits from the avoidance of competition. But the inference that the American people would have been better off in competition is not proven, especially if the assumption is that the $400 million would have gone to the workers or consumers.

9. Questionable. "Better" education is difficult to define. With more money being spent both per child and overall, one would *expect* better education.

10. Accurate. This inference follows from the data. If five-sixths of the work force was permanently employed the full twelve months of a year, then the inference is questionable. In the use of quantified data, one has to be careful that the same group is not being counted twice. Does the 50 percent include the one-sixth unemployed?

Which two of the items of quantified data do you consider most significant? Explain why.

_____

_____

_____

If, for item number 9, we add the data that the illiteracy rate dropped from 20 percent in 1870 to 11 percent in 1900 and that high school graduates had increased from 2 percent of seventeen-year-olds to 6.4 percent in the same period, would this make the inference accurate? Explain.

_____

_____

_____

What inferences, if any, can be drawn from the following fact: From 1870 to 1900 the circulation of daily newspapers increased sevenfold?

_____

_____

_____

Would the following numerical data be more impressive than the data offered in item number 7? Many high-society parties in the 1890s cost more than $100,000 and a typical costume cost the wearer $10,000. The average wage of manufacturing workers was $435 per year and of unskilled workers was $270 per year. Explain.

_____

_____

_____

In 1888 Edward Bellamy's book, *Looking Backward, 2000–1887,* sold two hundred thousand copies—equivalent to one or two million currently. The book advocated a socialist America with government ownership and management of the means of production. What inferences can be drawn from this statistic?

_____

_____

_____

PART III
Debating Historical, Social, and Moral Issues

QUESTIONS FOR THOUGHT

1. The causes of American economic development and progress in the late nineteenth century are numerous. Scholars debate the relative importance of the various factors. They also argue over the "credit" that should be attributed to two possible climates for this development—the good fortune and opportunity presented by the circumstances in the United States, not easily duplicated elsewhere, versus the ideological system used to promote this economic growth, free-enterprise capitalism. Examine the following factors related to the economic growth of the United States in the second half of the nineteenth century. For each, explain whether the factor is primarily one of *circumstances* or of *ideology*, the system of free enterprise.

   A. Existence of natural resources: iron ore, coal, oil, wood, water, gold, silver, and more.

   _____

   _____

   B. Population growth—prolific birth rate and immigration.

   _____

   _____

   C. Abundant rich farm land with ample water supply.

   _____

   _____

   D. A knack for invention and technological development, a patent system to protect inventions, and the application of science.

   _____

   _____

   E. Sufficient capital from profits, foreign loans, agricultural surplus, and the sale of stocks and bonds.

   _____

   _____

   F. A strong infrastructure: good roads, railroads, educational system, bridges, harbors and docks, and so forth.

   _____

   _____

   G. A friendly and supportive government that allowed individual initiative and profits without taxes and provided tariff protection, court support to business, protection of private property, grants to railroads, and other benefits.

_____

_____

H. Acceptance of Social Darwinism in modified forms—no pressure to care for worker's needs, no unions, no workman's compensation, no social security—so social costs were minimal.

_____

_____

I. Entrepreneurs were praised and idolized; the concept of self-made men pervaded the culture; the spirit of free enterprise and the value of business success were accepted in society.

_____

_____

J. A strong cultural value of hard work, the "work ethic"—rewards were earned through drive and determination; leisure was under suspicion; the religious "calling" was to work and save.

_____

_____

K. Temperate climate—conducive to hard work and good health; no debilitating heat and plenty of rainfall; "vigorous."

_____

_____

L. A national market under one stable government—no internal tariffs or fees; similar language and religion nationwide; geographic mobility; ethnic toleration (if not approval).

_____

_____

M. Strategic location protected by two oceans, with weak neighbors north and south; no need for expensive military, so a concentration on production of consumer goods.

_____

_____

N. Democratic governmental system—allowed social mobility and opportunity for nonviolent protest; problems were solved through the political process.

_____

_____

O. Timing—made use of many inventions and developments in Europe, especially England; competed early enough not to be overwhelmed; open markets overseas (England, China, Latin America, Europe).

Overall, should we give great credit to the ideological system of free-enterprise capitalism or are other factors equally important? Explain.

_____

_____

_____

Which three of the above fifteen do you consider most important? Explain why.

_____

_____

_____

Should the economic development of the United States be considered a model for other nations? Why or why not?

_____

_____

_____

Which of the fifteen factors are still with us in our contemporary economic system and which have been lost or severely modified? Explain why.

_____

_____

_____

_____

Can you discover other factors that are not in the list, but were important in economic development? Explain these.

_____

_____

_____

2. The "locomotive god," as some referred to the railroad system, had an impact on many aspects of society. Obviously, the transportation of people and goods efficiently and cheaply was basic. See how many you can list of other influences the railroad had on the economic, social, and cultural life of the nation. One ex-

ample is the mail catalogue business of Sears and Roebuck. Compare your list with the suggested one.

_____

_____

_____

_____

_____

3. Obviously economic growth led to glaring examples of the inequality of wealth—huge fortunes and abject poverty. Several solutions were offered in the nineteenth century. Which of the following four solutions to or attitudes toward this inequality do you prefer? Explain.

   A. Social Darwinism—competition produces competent leaders who reach the top. The fit survive; some will fail and drop out of competition. The government is to merely police and not interfere with legitimate business enterprise. This is a process of nature, like evolution in the animal world, and is to be expected as "normal." (Herbert Spenser and William Graham Sumner)
   B. Capitalism is the best system; competition and the striving for profits will, in the long run, be beneficial for all society, will raise everyone's standard of living, and will supply goods and services that are cheap, plentiful, and of good quality. However, it is the responsibility of those who acquire wealth to use it for charitable and philanthropic purposes. The wealthy are stewards of their wealth and have a social obligation to society. (Charles Dickens and many wealthy businessmen of the period)
   C. An entirely different structure is needed. Workers must, either as small groups or through their control of governments, own and control the production and distribution of goods. The workers' government should promote equality of wealth, within reason; eliminate social and economic class distinctions; and supervise and plan economic development. Workers are not receiving their share of the value of their contribution to production. This change may take place in a violent or a nonviolent manner. (Karl Marx and Edward Bellamy)
   D. Both state and federal governments need to carefully regulate business for the common welfare. Free enterprise may continue to supply the energy for production, but only with supervision by various government bureaus and commissions. Taxation should restrict the accumulation of great wealth and tax income must be used to assist those on the lower end of the economic structure. Workers' unions must be protected and economic security must be provided for each citizen. (Henry George, William Ward, and later the Progressives and New Dealers)

_____

_____

_____

_____

_____

4. Do you agree or disagree with the landmark Supreme Court decision of *Munn* v. *Illinois* in 1877 that when private property affects public interest and welfare, its owners must submit to public control for the common good? Why or why not?

_____

_____

_____

_____

5. How would you have attempted to solve the problem of nomadic and seminomadic Indians roaming the West, threatened by the advance of white man's civilization? Consider these four possibilities:

   A. Leave them alone to survive or not survive as settlers move into the West. They would either become farmers, gather into groups to continue on their own, or retreat into areas not wanted by settlers and miners.
   B. Concentrate tribes in several large areas designated as Indian areas with the possibility of becoming states of the United States in the future.
   C. Place tribes on small reservations out of the way of settlers, there to be protected and helped by the federal government.
   D. Require that each Indian family move from their campsites to small homesteads where they will be encouraged to abandon their culture—at least the parts that might interfere with their adjustment to the "normal" American farm life—and to accept, like the immigrants from Europe, the American way of living.

_____

_____

_____

_____

6. The unjust and inhumane treatment of the Indian prevailed more than a century ago. Is it now the responsibility of the American government to make amends for the broken treaties and promises by returning ancestral lands and/or by compensation for the injustice and suffering of the past? Why or why not?

_____

_____

_____

_____

7. Frederick Jackson Turner in 1893 presented his thesis on the role of the West in the development of the United States. Some of his ideas follow:

   A. The United States developed differently from other nations due to the existence of a vast frontier. Americans had "rooms" in which to expand and were not hemmed in like other people.

B. This frontier experience produced an American character that was dominated by coarseness and strength, inquisitiveness, a practical and inventive turn of mind, materialism, individualism, a sense of equality, a strong belief in democracy, anti-intellectualism, optimism, and a boastful arrogance.

C. The frontier also served as a safety valve in that it tempered the class struggle, allowing the discontented in the East to move west and acquire farms. These settlers became self-sufficient voters not influenced by city bosses or corrupt political machines.

D. The roots of American democracy lie not in racial or Germanic traditions, nor in a legal and political inheritance from Europe, but in the environment of the frontier, the geographic, economic, and psychological experiences of those who went west.

Do you agree or disagree with these ideas of the frontier thesis? Criticize them.

_____

_____

_____

_____

_____

8. The historian must often rely on the archaeologist in order to gather data on the life of people who did not leave written records. The Native American fits that category, especially in the period prior to 1890. One way to discover information about the Native American culture is to uncover graves in sacred burial grounds. The artifacts buried with the body yield information about life-styles and the skeleton itself can offer data about the society—diseases, cause of death, diet, size, and so forth. Recently, Native Americans have objected to this "invasion" of their burial grounds and to the display of artifacts, even skulls, in museums. Should these objects be returned to the Indians to be buried with full rites? Should archaeologists refrain from digging in burial grounds in the future? Explain.

_____

_____

_____

_____

_____

9. React to the two quotes at the beginning of the chapter—their meaning and relevance. Do you agree or disagree?

_____

_____

_____

_____

_____

THOUGHTS FOR QUESTIONS

1. Suggested classification: Circumstances—A, B, C, K, M, O; Ideology—D, E, H, I, J, L, N; and Mixed—F and G.

Perhaps neither force will work without the other? Would the ideology, if the work ethic is included, of free enterprise bring industrial development and high productivity without resources? Consider Japan with its few resources yet high productivity. Japan does have fertile soil and much rainfall. A nation without any resources might not prosper under any system. And population growth is many times a hindrance. On the other hand, several nations with both vast resources and a large population have not prospered to the extent of the United States. Could ideology be a factor in those nations? Would a socialist economic system and ideology applied to the United States in 1870 have brought as much economic advance by 1970 as a capitalist system did?

The three that seem the most important: L, C, and J. These three seem to be at the root of American success. Others may stem from or be stimulated by these three.

It would be difficult to find another nation in the world that has items A, B, and C on the scale of the United States. Item M was unique for that period of history since there seem to be threats and dangers throughout the world today. One major difference to note is the current pressure on governments to encourage production—not at any cost, but only while providing decent conditions of employment, adequate wages, and the social services that are common goals of advanced nations. Also the new awareness of ecology constrains unlimited economic activity.

Possibly a sense of nationalism and patriotism in the late nineteenth century provided some incentive—the determination that the United States would be number one in the world.

2. Some influences of the railroad were:

A. Development of a management system based on merit.

B. Use of large amounts of steel, coal, and wood.

C. Establishment of standard time zones.

D. Settlement of the West; transportation of immigrants to and shipment of products from the West.

E. Huge financial deals and bank control of railroad management.

F. Involvement of the federal government in corporate business through loans and land grants.

G. Development of refrigerator cars for meat and vegetables.

H. Development of the "diner" concept for serving food.

I. Laying the basis for an urban transportation system.

J. Linking the nation together by yielding a nationalistic feeling.

K. Encouraging an efficient national postal system and telegraph network.

L. Leading to political corruption at the state and national level and large-scale influence of business in government.

M. Stimulating the first efforts by state and national governments to regulate corporations.

N. Redirecting the location of industry along railroad lines.

O. Stimulating pleasurable travel and tourism.

P. Leading to the organization of the first effective black labor organization—the Red Caps.

3. Some questions to consider follow:

A. Would Marx's structural changes bring about equality or destroy initiative and create a new upper class—the necessarily large bureaucracy?

B. Would the wealthy share large amounts of their wealth with the poor, or only a small portion, and that grudgingly?

C. Do species, as Spenser maintains, compete, or do they actually cooperate and prey upon *other* species? Are humans to be considered merely animals struggling to survive?

D. Are regulations and progressive taxation debilitating and stifling to the free-enterprise system? Do they restore competition or make it easier to establish monopolies with political influence and tax loopholes?

E. Are charitable gifts and philanthropic programs what the public needs or just the pet projects of individuals?

F. Do corporations gain control of regulatory agencies and blunt their efforts?

4. One of the decision's problems is how to determine which private property affects the public good and which does not. Are railroad rates; the price of corn, coal, or kerosene; telegraph lines; a new railroad spur for the common good? Without regulations, would private interests act to do harm to the public interest, to the environment, and to the economy? Or would public awareness and opinion force restraint?

5. The first solution is a nonsolution and heartless. It is an application of the survival of the fittest from the animal world to the human world. The Indian probably would have been overrun, but with much more savage fighting. Both B and C were tried. The first led to encroachments by white settlers and miners on Indian lands. Solution C emerged as the "final solution." Suggestion D was also employed in the Dawes act of 1877. While considered humane at the time, it embodied an effort to destroy a culture and to force conformity of behavior. Could large areas with known resources, perhaps what is now one or two large western states or parts of states, have been reserved for the Native Americans? Could they have been developed into states of the United States with Native American leadership and the maintenance of their culture? Was this realistic given the conditions and attitudes at the time? Hawaii became a state even though inhabited by large numbers of Orientals. Were politicians and government leaders shortsighted and immoral in their refusal to consider the rights and the welfare of Native Americans?

6. Does time cover a thousand wrongs? Does the process of history, especially over a hundred-year period, mean that the clock cannot and should not be turned back? What about conflicting claims among Native American groups? What about the farmers and ranchers who have lived on former Native American lands for generations? No other nation has attempted to care for the needs of its aboriginal inhabitants as the United States has in the last twenty years. Most aborigines are written off as unfortunate sacrifices for progress. Nomadic groups who formerly spread terror and havoc on settled communities—Germanic tribes, Huns, Vikings, Mongols, for example—have now gradually lost power and have surrendered culture and religion to "advanced civilizations." Of course, many recent acts by the United States also have been detrimental to Native American welfare.

7. A. Many areas of the world had a frontier at one time or another. Consider the Chinese movement south and west, the spread of various groups to populate

Europe, the Africans migrating into South Africa, the Russian migration across the Urals, and Brazil's penetration of the Amazon. But Turner is probably accurate in considering the size of and sparse population of the American West. Even driving across the West today imbues one with a sense of independence and freedom.

B. It is difficult to prove that these features are distinctly western. Individualism is American from the beginning and is encouraged by many Protestant religious groups. Most inventions came out of cities, by those closely connected to the problems of industry, not by the frontier farmer. Are coarseness and inquisitiveness found only in the West?

C. This is the most suspect of the thesis elements. To move to a Nebraska farm, the settler needed a wagon, horses, tools, seeds, and money to buy lumber and to sustain his family at least a year. The subsistence wage-earner in the city could hardly accumulate that much capital. Also, farming is a skill, one that the factory worker may not have had. The people who did move west were eastern farmers or the sons of farmers. The crowding in of immigrants and the largest migration of the period—from farm to urban area—produced a large proletariat anyway.

D. Trying to trace the sources of democracy is an inexact endeavor. Most of the western states actually modeled and even copied their constitutions from those of the eastern states, especially the original thirteen. One could argue that people who went West took democracy with them. Congress required that a representative system be established before statehood. Yet one wonders about the democratic, egalitarian spirit when one considers the treatment of Indians and the poverty of farm workers and migrant laborers. Many westerners accumulated wealth—ranchers, owners of large mines, and land speculators.

8. The unearthing of burial grounds is an "invasion" of privacy. Information must be acquired in other ways or not acquired at all. Perhaps there are accidental findings of burial remains in the preparation of construction sites, but even here the materials must be available for reburial if claimed by a legitimate party.

9. Aristotle states a simple idea. Yet it is many times ignored. Efforts are made to understand contemporary events—the Middle East situation, for example—without looking into their origins and development over time. History offers insight, perhaps not answers or solutions, but data that can help frame solutions. To live only in contemporary times is to suffer from amnesia.

Karl Marx might agree with Van Loon in his materialistic orientation. Actually the historian discovers a multitude of human motivations, many of which seem unconnected to "daily bread and butter." Van Loon might contend, as did Marx, that these other motivations are actually "covers" for the underlying drives to acquire and secure the necessities of life, but that is an *a priori* assumption. Multimillionaire John D. Rockefeller was not interested in "bread and butter" in 1900. The whole emphasis of productive energy during the industrial revolution shows consideration beyond only "bread and butter." For many in the industrialized world, life has gone beyond obtaining necessities.

11

RESPONDING TO INDUSTRIAL GROWTH

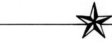

"Study the recorder and the historian before you begin to study the recorded facts and the written history."

Dick Mumford

"Our ignorance of history causes us to slander our own times."

Gustave Flaubert

PART I
Acquiring Essential Data

ESSENTIAL DATES

Determine the correct sequence and write the approximate date for each of the following events.

1. The game of basketball is invented. _____

2. Jane Addams establishes a settlement house—Hull House—to help the poor in Chicago. _____

3. Massive railroad strikes occur in many areas. _____

4. The first United States subway line is completed in Boston. _____

5. Chautauqua movement of summer education and lectures begins for adults. _____

6. The novel, *The Adventures of Huckleberry Finn*, by Mark Twain is published. _____

7. The Chinese are excluded from immigration into the United States. _____

8. The Knights of Labor union is established. _____

9. The National League of Professional Baseball Clubs is founded. _____

10. The first skyscraper is erected in Chicago, designed by William Le Baron Jenney. _____

11. The phonograph is invented by Thomas Edison. _____

ESSENTIAL CONCEPTS

Examine each concept and write what contemporary relevance it might have.

1. *Social Darwinism*   Belief that among humans, if left to natural tendencies, the strong will prevail over the weak, and a better society will emerge.

   _____

   _____

   _____

2. *"yellow dog" contract*   A one-sided contract to be signed by a worker that essentially forbids the worker from joining a labor union.

   _____

   _____

   _____

3. *poor relief*   The concept of charity as an answer to problems suffered by the poor. It is seldom available and never adequate.

_____

_____

_____

4. *success myth*   Belief that anyone can rise from humble beginnings to wealth by diligence and hard work, and any effort not to do so is the individual's fault.

_____

_____

_____

5. *Social Gospel*   A movement to apply the compassion of Christianity to reform of the inhumane conditions produced by industrialization—by offering aid and opportunity to the poor instead of doctrines.

_____

_____

_____

6. *pragmatism*   A philosophy that applied to ideas the criteria of whether or not a valued event had been produced rather than whether it was theoretically true or not. Ideas should be put into practice to determine their validity and value.

_____

_____

_____

7. *conspicuous consumption*   The very rich justifying their existence, not by work, but by living a life of leisure while purchasing items that reveal wealth.

_____

_____

_____

8. *sociological jurisprudence*   Legal principles are not fixed and absolute, but should be adjusted to meet needs at a given time. The important agenda is justice and fairness, not precedent or principles.

_____

_____

_____

9. *progressive education* Children learn by doing instead of memorizing. They should be trained to become good citizens and learn the techniques to changing society and how to think and analyze for themselves.

_____

_____

_____

10. *elective system* The college system, begun at Harvard, that allows students to select courses rather than having to follow the same curriculum prescribed for all.

_____

_____

_____

ANSWERS

Correct sequence of events and their dates.

1.	8; 1869	7.	6; 1884
2.	5; 1874	8.	10; 1885
3.	9; 1876	9.	2; 1889
4.	11; 1877	10.	1; 1891
5.	3; 1877	11.	4; 1897
6.	7; 1884		

PART II
Developing Thinking Skills

SKILL EXERCISE ONE: QUESTIONING

Examine carefully the following questions on *immigration* and write under each whether it is productive or nonproductive. Then explain your decision. Finally, for those that are nonproductive, explain how they might become productive if modified or if related to the questioner's special purposes.

1. Were the new immigrants from southern and eastern Europe unfit to function in a democratic society?

_____

_____

2. What did the various immigrant aid societies offer in the period from 1880 to 1910?

_____

_____

3. What were the problems of assimilation faced by immigrants and how did they attempt to cope with them?

_____

_____

4. What were the attitudes and reactions of Irish Catholics and Sephardic and German Jews to the arrival of Catholics and Jews from other areas and backgrounds?

_____

_____

5. How many immigrants came from Russia in 1892?

_____

_____

6. Did immigrants have fun on the voyage over and through the processing at Ellis Island in Upper New York Bay?

_____

_____

7. What were some of the specific difficulties encountered by immigrants in their journey from their home village or city to Ellis Island?

_____

_____

8. Who was the most famous immigrant to arrive in America in the 1890s?

_____

_____

9. Were the immigrants from Poland better people than the immigrants from Russia?

_____

_____

10. What impact did the departure of immigrants to America have on the sections of Europe from which they came?

_____

_____

ANSWERS AND EXPLANATIONS

1. Nonproductive. It is very difficult to define "unfit" and to make a general statement that covers so many individual situations. The questioner would do better concentrating on specific characteristics of small groups.

2. Productive. Knowledge of these services helps in our understanding of the aid available to immigrants.

3. Productive. The question is specific and calls for information useful in understanding the immigrant experience.

4. Productive. It is both interesting and instructive to investigate the reaction of earlier immigrants (1850s) to the new immigrants (1890s), even if both groups are of the same cultural background.

5. Nonproductive. Standing alone, the answer to this question is rather meaningless. If we know it is 52,000 or 9,000 or 180,000, it does not matter unless we connect it with numbers from other years or other groups to form insightful relationships.

6. Nonproductive. "Have fun" or "enjoy" is vague and cannot be applied to so many experiences. Besides, probably no large group of sources exists to reveal immigrant joy or misery. The answer called for seems to be "yes" or "no," which doesn't lead anywhere.

7. Productive. In contrast to the previous question, here we have a call for some of the actual problems encountered by many immigrants. Sources are probably available and an image of the immigrants' difficulties can be constructed.

8. Nonproductive. What is meant by "famous?" Several immigrants might be candidates. Of course, after we have a name, why is it important to know this? Perhaps if we sought the achievements of ten or twenty successful immigrants, that data begins to take on meaning in the immigrant experience.

9. Nonproductive. There is no way to decide this question because adequate criteria for judgment is unavailable. What is meant by "better?" It is a very vague word.

10. Productive. Were some areas economically depressed after the population loss, or were the immigrants "surplus" people? This is a good topic to study and the question opens the way.

SKILL EXERCISE TWO: CATEGORIZING AND CLASSIFYING

Assume the student is investigating *late-nineteenth-century America*. Data and ideas related to this topic follow. In the space below each item, write in the appropriate category: *political, economic, social, diplomatic,* or *cultural*. Check your selection with those suggested.

1. Industrial production drew large numbers of people into cities and forced them to congregate in crowded areas of substandard tenement housing.

_____

2. By 1900 the United States was the leading nation in the world in goods produced and in gross national product.

_____

3. Poets and artists used a concept of the "machine in the garden" in the 1890s to complain that industrialization had defiled the natural beauty of America.

_____

4. The Interstate Commerce Act was an effort, through a regulatory commission, to end rate discrimination by railroads and to put a stop to the pooling techniques of monopolistic control.

_____

5. Officials carefully examined immigrants at the port of departure before they were allowed to board ship for the United States.

_____

6. Frank Norris, in a novel, characterized the activities of industrial leaders as a gigantic octopus that threatened control of all aspects of society.

_____

7. The Sherman Anti-Trust Act was an attempt to dissolve illegal trusts that interfered with free competitive trade, but it was not vigorously applied by either a pro-business Justice Department or by a former corporation lawyer who was attorney general.

_____

8. Corporations in need of capital in the 1890s found profits slim and the sales of stock to the public inadequate, so they turned to investment banks to buy stocks and to operate as sales agents for stocks.

_____

9. In *The Rise of Silas Lapham*, William Dean Howells has a wealthy businessman discomforted by his wealth. Eventually the character loses his wealth and returns to the satisfaction of hard work.

_____

10. Thorstein Veblen coined the phrase "conspicuous consumption" to indicate the wasteful, show-off expenditures of the rich on yachts, jewelry, and homes.

_____

11. In 1900 about 20 percent of factory workers were women who were paid half as much as men; more than two million women worked as servants in domestic service.

_____

12. The Chinese made up 17 percent of the population of California in 1877. Because of protests that they were taking jobs from other Americans, they were excluded from immigrating in 1882.

_____

ANSWERS AND EXPLANATIONS

1. Social. This relates to the conditions of workers in urban areas, a social issue. Of course, economic factors caused the social problem.

2. Economic. Goods produced and gross national product are certainly economic factors.

3. Cultural. Although directly related to the economy, this concept is an idea, thus cultural.

4. Political. This act did regulate business, but it was primarily a governmental action with political involvement.

5. Diplomatic. This involves United States relations with other nations in mutual agreement, which saved the foreign nation the expense of shipping back immigrants who failed the physical examination at Ellis Island.

6. Cultural. The novel relates to business, but is a cultural expression.

7. Political. This was another effort by political forces to control economic developments.

8. Economic. Purely about an economic development, this statement does not directly involve any of the other categories.

9. Cultural. This is an insight into the life and feelings of a fictional businessman.

10. Social. Although in the realm of ideas and placed in a book, the concept involves an insight into the social behavior of people with wealth.

11. Social. Certainly related to the economy, this statement is not concerned so much with productivity or profits, but with a social group and its status in the economy.

12. Social. The conditions of an immigrant group that is difficult to assimilate belongs with the social issues. Although the anger at them may have stemmed from economic factors (low wages), and the restricting law was political, the emphasis here is on a social situation.

QUESTIONS

1. Which of the items above did you have the most difficulty categorizing? Why?

_____

_____

2. For which of the above did you have a different category than the one suggested? Justify your choice.

_____

_____

PART III
Debating Historical, Social, and Moral Issues

QUESTIONS FOR THOUGHT

After reading about each of the following issues, reflect on them, analyze possible answers, and write your own reflections. Compare your responses with Thoughts for Questions.

1. Karl Marx predicted that as industrial growth, a concentration of wealth in the hands of a few, and a consolidation of business proceeded, the mass of workers functioning on subsistence wages with no economic rights, living in slums and working long hours, would rise up in revolt against factory owners and eventually against the capitalist-controlled government. Conditions seemed to be ripe for this in the 1890s. Speculate as to why such an uprising to overthrow the capitalist system did *not* take place.

_____

_____

_____

_____

_____

2. After working a sixty-hour week, five and one-half or six days each week for fifty-two weeks at low wages and often under threatening working conditions, the worker was disappointed, frustrated, and despondent. They found ways to protest beyond street meetings or strikes. Some expressed discontent by chronic absenteeism (especially missing Mondays), by quitting for another job, or by sabotage. The sabotage could be direct—damaging machinery—or indirect, slowing down the pace of work. Given the conditions of the time, would you condone these expressions of discontent? Explain.

_____

_____

_____

_____

_____

3. Samuel Gompers organized and directed the American Federation of Labor into a strong, effective union. He opted for immediate "bread and butter" rewards rather than ideological or long-term goals of structural change in the system. Yet Gompers was prejudiced against immigrants and would not allow blacks or women into the union. He also rejected unskilled workers. Is Gompers to be admired and commended as a labor hero or condemned as a bigot who placed a roadblock in organizing *all* labor into an effective working-class force? Explain.

_____

_____

_____

_____

4. The skyscraper, made possible by the I-shaped steel girder and the elevator, and the suspension bridge were two architectural features of the 1880s and the 1890s. What is your reaction to these two structures—admiration for their size, func-

tional effectiveness, symmetry, and beauty, or disdain for the heavy, bulky, regularity of these practical structures being passed off as good architecture? Explain. Can they be compared at all to the cathedrals of Europe? Why or why not?

_____

_____

_____

_____

_____

5. Farmers faced many agrarian problems in the late nineteenth century. Some of these follow:

   A. Worldwide decline in prices due to surpluses.
   B. Tariff protection for industry, but not for farm products.
   C. Rise in farm foreclosures and tenancy arrangement—the landlord receives one-third of produce.
   D. Isolation, loneliness, drudgery of hard work all year.
   E. Railroad control of transportation rates and influence in state legislature.
   F. Droughts, grasshoppers, plant disease.
   G. Increase of middlemen to absorb profits and control markets.
   H. Difficulty in obtaining credit for the increased cost of farm machinery so necessary to new commercial farming.

   Explain what might have been done to alleviate some of these problems, to modify their effect. Would such efforts require political action by farmers and a larger involvement of government in agriculture? Explain.

_____

_____

_____

_____

_____

   On reflection about these problems, would you now question the advisability of the government giving away large tracts of land to farmers (Homestead Act of 1862) and thus enticing so many into the business of farming? Explain.

_____

_____

_____

6. In the case of *Plessy* v. *Ferguson* of 1896, the Supreme Court decided that separate-but-equal facilities were acceptable under the Constitution. This led to segregated schools, drinking fountains, bus seating, waiting rooms, restaurants, beaches, living areas, and more. What is your reaction to this ruling? Was the

Supreme Court reflecting the Constitution accurately or was the decision in 1954 ending segregation a more accurate reflection of the Constitution? Explain.

_____

_____

_____

_____

_____

7. Although the American tradition upholds both liberty and equality, a conflict exists between the two. Consider, if liberty is supported in an absolute sense, then often inequality results. On the other hand, if equality is emphasized as a primary value, then restrictions on liberty appear. Must a tension exist between the two—a certain amount of equality guaranteed, but a degree of liberty also allowed? React to this dilemma.

_____

_____

_____

_____

_____

8. React to the first stanza of the following poem written by Edwin Markham in 1899, entitled "The Man with the Hoe."

> *Bowed by the weight of centuries he leans*
> *Upon his hoe and gazes on the ground,*
> *The emptiness of ages in his face,*
> *And on his back the burden of the world.*
> *Who made him dead to rapture and despair,*
> *A thing that grieves not and that never hopes,*
> *Stolid and stunned, a brother to the ox?*
> *Who loosened and let down this brutal jaw?*
> *Whose was the hand that slanted back this brow?*
> *Whose breath blew out the light within this brain?*

A. Is this an accurate description of the American farmer in the late nineteenth century? Explain.

_____

_____

_____

B. Does the poem have political and ideological overtones (consider *"Who made him . . ."*)? An industrialist offered $700 for the best poetic rebuttal to the poem. Why do you think the offer was made?

_____

_____

C. Is the poem, written at the turn of the century, obsolete in regard to contemporary farmer-laborers? Why or why not?

_____

_____

9. An important issue for historians who write about this period is immigration. Was America the land of opportunity that opened up new horizons for immigrants? Or were they enticed here under false advertising and then oppressed and exploited without being offered that golden opportunity? Some historians argue that immigrants were abused by greedy landlords and harsh employers, were reduced to second-class citizens, and that the whole episode made a mockery out of the American dream. Others insist that opportunities existed, especially for the second generation, and that a large number of immigrants acquired a home and secured education for their children. The first generations had problems, but ultimately the dream came true for most of them. Some historians see capitalist exploitation, but others conclude that the immigrants lacked skills and were actually treated as other white Americans; that is, capitalism did not discriminate.

What is your reaction to this controversy? Would it have been better for most immigrants to remain in Europe or Asia, or perhaps to immigrate to another area, say Latin America? Explain.

_____

_____

_____

_____

_____

10. William James's pragmatism, presented at the close of the nineteenth century, emphasized the individual's freedom to make choices. He opposed Charles Darwin's deterministic science. James rejected eternal value and accepted the relativism of truth. Truth was something that "happened"; what "worked" was true; truth had to be placed in a context of action rather than existing as an entity divorced from reality. Moral truth was dependent on the conduct it dictated or inspired. If a religious belief gives meaning to a person's life, then that religious belief is "true."

Do you accept James's conclusions? Explain. What might be some of the outcomes of pragmatic assumptions?

_____

_____

_____

_____

_____

11. John Dewey, founder of an experimental school at the University of Chicago, produced ideas about education that eventually formed the basis of the progres-

sive education movement. Evaluate Dewey's ideas and explain, under each, why you agree or disagree with them.

A. Schools must inculcate values, especially good citizenship, since the parents or the community no longer teach them.

_____

_____

B. Knowledge must be kept flexible, with tentative acceptance of answers to important questions, since children must be prepared for a rapidly changing world.

_____

_____

C. Students do not need to memorize data as much as they need to develop a critical, analytical approach to deal with a complicated world.

_____

_____

D. Ideas are "instruments" for dealing with social issues, not reflections of some eternal reality.

_____

_____

E. Children learn by doing rather than by rote memorization.

_____

_____

F. Society can and should be reformed through the proper education of children in public schools.

_____

_____

G. Practical subjects such as homemaking, mechanical arts, and citizenship are as important, or more important, than the traditional curriculum.

_____

_____

12. Oliver Wendell Holmes, Jr., who served on the Supreme Court for thirty years, applied pragmatic concepts to the law. He argued that the old assumption that legal theory was a fixed body of logical rules was in error. Laws must be related to changing contemporary circumstances. Legal decisions must reflect practical needs, the conditions surrounding the case. Social and psychological evidence can be admitted. Although judges must consider laws and precedents, they also

must examine the special conditions of a particular case in order to apply justice. Do you agree with these ideas? Why or why not?

_____

_____

_____

_____

_____

13. Consider the quotations at the beginning of the chapter. Explain their meaning, implications, and whether you agree or disagree with each.

_____

_____

_____

_____

_____

THOUGHTS FOR QUESTIONS

1. Some explanations might include the emergence of labor unions both as an outlet for protest and as an organization that got some results in wage increases and shorter hours; the diversity of workers—many immigrants from different foreign lands made unified action difficult; the prevalent stories of some who made it and achieved the "dream"; the alliance between government and business, both willing to use force in the form of hired strike-breakers or soldiers; the rising standard of living overall, despite hardship; that 50 percent of American workers still lived on farms and were antagonistic toward unions and foreign workers; the prevailing American ideal of individualism; and, after 1900, reforms that relieved some of the abuses within the system.

2. Although sabotage might harm others and close down a section of a factory for a time (perhaps no pay was given during this shutdown?), the other forms of protest—being absent and finding another job—seem legitimate, given the severity of working conditions. Of course they may not have been helpful to the worker needing increased income. We often apply current standards of a forty-hour week, adequate pay, and benefits as judgment criteria.

3. For historians this issue is a difficult one because they cannot return to the time for context. Perhaps Gompers was a realist and understood that these limitations were necessary in the face of wealthy employers who had a friendly government for support. On the other hand, it could be that a larger union of all workers, or several large unions, might have brought immediate gains for workers—gains they did not begin to receive until the 1930s. The historian must deal with complex individuals who deserve both praise and censure—humans not unlike those of the present.

4. The gentle sweep and contrasting horizontal and curved lines give the suspen-

sion bridge great beauty. Its symmetry is pleasing and the lines tend to expand and contract at just the right places. Form your own judgment on skyscrapers, although the lights of Manhattan seen from a plane are impressive and alluring.

5. Programs to counteract these problems—regulation of railroad rates by state governments; establishment of farmer's banks or federal loan programs; a reduced tariff on manufactured goods; cooperative marketing and production control; irrigation systems; scientific research into plant disease; bringing culture to isolated communities (Grangers, and later federal programs during the New Deal; of course automobiles, televisions, radios, and films all helped alleviate this problem later)—were all tried. Yet still the farm problem exists. Foreclosures, the middleperson's influence, and large surpluses remain as serious problems.

It does seem that the government's encouragement of more farmers and more production was counter-productive. Yet the tremendous surpluses were not on the horizon in the 1870s. Efforts to control the number of farmers and the amount of production in the late nineteenth century would have been unthinkable.

6. First of all, the fact is that the separate-but-equal facilities were hardly ever equal—the blacks received poorer and less desirable facilities than the whites, and sometimes no facilities at all. The Supreme Court, in 1954, finally decided that segregated facilities were inherently unequal.

The Constitution is silent on the subject in any direct sense. However, the spirit of American tradition at its best would run counter to this 1896 case. Does one follow this spirit or look for precedents or the "intent" of the Founding Fathers?

7. Liberty is always restricted to some extent by laws that order society and provide harmony in social relations. Equality in some areas can never be attained. Perhaps this tension is inherent in the conflict. Society must determine in what cases equality can be encouraged and in what cases liberty is to be promoted—and set limits on each.

8. A. Farm life was regarded as monotonous and dirty, and absorbed most of one's waking hours. It dulled the cultural and intellectual growth of farmers and their families. The image of them as yokels and hayseeds became prominent. Ironically, at the same time a heroic, idealized vision of the virtues of those who worked close to the soil continued. Perhaps fear of this dubious fate drove many young women and men to the city. Certainly the opportunity for a variety of dissimilar experiences was not available in rural areas to the degree it was in cities.

B. The political overtones are strong. Is this poem an indictment of the banker, the railroads, the industrialist, or all three? Or does it leave the "who" as an unknown entity or as fate? The award offered by the industrialist indicates how many interpreted it at the time. No one is specifically indicted in the remainder of the poem, although the implied "someone" is guilty.

C. Radio, television, films, and *USA Today* have penetrated nearly every farm home since that time. The pickup truck provides mobility. Few farmers still use the hoe. Farms require attention and hard work; however, it is not unusual to find a farm couple touring Europe or camping out in Yellowstone. Many farmers have a college education, and many make use of modern science and technology, including computers.

9. Opportunity is difficult to define. There were no legal or political hindrances to getting ahead. Crucial to this question are statistical data that might reveal percentages of who, in their lifetime, owned homes and opened bank savings accounts.

What percentage of the sons and daughters of immigrants from 1890 to 1910 completed high school? How many took over their father's job in the same factory or mill (even in these cases, they may have had higher wages and better conditions than their father)? The level of general prosperity since World War II indicates a higher standard of living for the descendants of immigrants. Both sides of the issue carry truth; the situation is probably a good example of how the interpreter's background and outlook determines perception.

10. It is difficult to arrive at truth if it can constantly change by altered circumstances that yield different results. How does one determine whether or not those results are beneficial, and if so, for whom? Usually, when action is taken, it yields results that benefit some but are upsetting to others. Which results prevail? Are we back to the "greatest good for the greatest number?" Certainly philosophical truth concluded without thought of actual situations is rather useless truth. Most religions normally hold to absolutes, to moral codes that are eternal and unchanging. James's relativism of truth and morality would be disturbing to most of those who adhere to religious principles. Pragmatism does encourage people to believe that they can shape their own lives and work for change in society. But how can Americans speak of natural rights and support the principles found in the Bill of Rights unless there are *some* unchanging values?

11. Dewey's ideas were, and are, very controversial. His assumptions may be questioned. Items A, C, D, E, G, and F: Was it true that values were not being taught at home or in the church and community? Is it not necessary to have memorized *some* data in order to think critically about any subject? If ideas are relative, how does one distinguish good ideas from bad ideas? One advantage of formal education is that one can learn *without* doing, rather than using the trial-and-error process. Who determines what is practical? Are "nonpractical" subjects useful indirectly? Is the function of the school to change society or to educate children about heritage and to prepare them to *enter* society?

12. Varied circumstances make it difficult for judges to reach a consistency of justice if they decide each case separately, not according to legal principles but by the particular circumstances. The admission of nonlegal evidence sometimes confuses the case. The jury must search for answers from imprecise factors such as motivation, the condition of people's minds, the disagreement of professional experts, and the particular pressures on the people involved in the case. On the other hand, one might argue that legal principles, effective and applicable in an agrarian society, do not remain suitable for an urban, industrialized society. Laws have changed in the past, although not as quickly as Holmes intended them to change at the turn of the century. Justice is always difficult to find and render. One definition of justice is the consistent and equal application of the law in each case. Would Holmes agree with that definition? Why or why not?

13. The first quote implies that a slant in history is inevitable once it is reduced to words. Not only must one watch carefully what the person who researches and writes history says, but also one must consider the conditions under which an event is recorded. What background, attitudes, and degree of understanding did the person who created the historical documents have that might have influenced his or her perceptions. The written document is from a verbal rendition of what happened. The event is filled with thousands of detailed "facts." Only a portion is recorded. Why are some facts recorded and others left out?

Flaubert reflects on the habit of degrading our own times as inferior to the virtues and happiness found in the past. People seem to selectively forget some aspects when considering earlier times. For example, morality functioned on a much higher level, there was no pollution, people were kinder and more cooperative, and life was simpler and enjoyable. The only thing worse about the past was the weather. But what is true about an *individual's* past is also true when one looks at history. The Founding Fathers become superhuman men, all of whom would make excellent presidents now. Why don't we produce George Washingtons and Thomas Jeffersons today? Maybe we do, if we consider more the *total* lives of these two "great" men!

CHAPTER
12

THE WORLD SCENE

"To take no sides in history would be as false as to take no sides in life."

Barbara Tuchman

"Mankind are so much the same in all times and places that history informs us of nothing new or strange in this particular . . ."

David Hume

PART I
Acquiring Essential Data

ESSENTIAL DATES

Determine the correct sequence and write the approximate date for each of the following events.

1. The Philippines becomes independent from the United States. _____

2. The Open Door notes are sent out by Secretary of State John Hay, calling for open trade with an independent China. _____

3. Filipino rebels fight for independence against American troops. _____

4. The *U.S.S. Maine* American battleship is sunk in Cuba's Havana Harbor. _____

5. A congressional resolution calls for the American army and navy to oust Spain from Cuba. _____

6. The Hawaiian Islands are annexed to the United States. _____

7. Secretary of State William H. Seward purchases Alaska from Russia for $7.2 million. _____

8. The Wilson-Gorman Tariff brings a depression to Cuba. _____

9. Publication of *The Influence of Sea Power Upon History, 1660–1783,* by Alfred Thayer Mahan _____

10. The Panama area becomes independent from Colombia and the United States signs an agreement for the canal zone. _____

11. Commodore George Dewey defeats a Spanish fleet in Manila Bay. _____

ESSENTIAL CONCEPTS

Examine each concept and write what contemporary relevance it might have.

1. *"Cross of Gold"*   Phrase used by William Cullen Bryant to indicate the severity of the gold standard and the unwillingness of the government to coin large amounts of silver and thus expand the money supply.

_____

_____

_____

2. *sea power and history*   Concept from a book in 1890 by Alfred Mahan that maintains all great nations had strong navies, which usually meant they launched colonies and seaports in foreign lands.

_____

_____

_____

3. *Roosevelt Corollary* This supplement to the Monroe Doctrine contained the idea that the United States had the right to function as an international police force in Latin America, especially in the Caribbean.

_____

_____

_____

4. *reconcentrado* The Spanish effort to put Cuban peasants into detention camps in order to isolate rebels. The result was the spread of disease and thousands of deaths.

_____

_____

_____

5. *yellow press* Newspapers that wrote exaggerated and sensational stories, and sometimes even false reports, that inflamed events—all in order to sell more papers.

_____

_____

_____

6. *insular cases* The court decisions that determined that the American Constitution does not follow the flag; that is, an annexed area does not automatically obtain rights under the Constitution unless Congress so designates.

_____

_____

_____

7. *free security* The isolation that the United States enjoyed prior to 1898—protected by two oceans, it had weak neighbors and no holdings overseas.

_____

_____

_____

8. *"splendid little war"* John Hay's name for the Spanish-American War that seemed to develop in all ways to the benefit of the United States without too much expense or effort.

_____

_____

_____

9. *dollar diplomacy* American bankers were encouraged to invest in foreign areas of strategic importance. The government assured the bankers that their invest-

ments would be protected. Thus the United States could influence strategic areas without committing troops.

_____

_____

_____

10. *Open Door policy*   John Hay's policy statement applying to China at that time (and to other areas later), which received tacit agreement from other nations not to divide China into colonies and to allow open trade there for all nations.

_____

_____

_____

ANSWERS

Correct sequence of events and their dates.

1. 7; 1867
2. 9; 1890
3. 8; 1893
4. 4; February 1898
5. 5; April 1898
6. 11; May 1898

7. 6; August 1898
8. 3; 1899
9. 2; 1899–1900
10. 10; 1903
11. 1; 1946

PART II
Developing Thinking Skills

SKILL EXERCISE ONE: PERCEIVING SIMILARITIES AND DIFFERENCES

Two viewpoints—the imperialist and the anti-imperialist—of American foreign relations at the turn of the century follow. Read each carefully, then afterward write the similarities and differences. Compare your findings with those offered.

Imperialists, 1898–99

The United States has an obligation not to forsake the peoples of the Philippines and Puerto Rico. For one hundred years we have been training for this mission to bring peace, order, and organization to the rest of the world. It is part of the White Man's Burden to spread democratic institutions and high civilization to backward peoples in other lands. To teach them democracy will take years of guidance and, of course, protection from foreign threats while they learn civilization. They are a distinct people and will not become American citizens; but in the future, they will be proud and happy as citizens of their progressive governments.

Without our help chaos will reign. The Philippines, especially, will be grabbed up by foreign powers—Japan or Germany—unless we provide a military presence. Should we only declare our protection, war is possible with one of these nations, a war that would be costly in lives and dollars. It is better to take control and avoid conflict.

The two areas will provide markets for our manufactured products and places for investments. They also may have resources that we need. This will increase employment in the United States and relieve working class distress.

The British, French, and even the Japanese have empires and, as a great nation, we must shoulder our responsibility. We will introduce the Filipinos to Christianity and to civilized manners. With American control, missionaries can move about freely throughout the islands. The people of these lands have suffered long under the autocratic government of Spain and will likely revert back to autocracy if we now leave them on their own. The profits from our trade and the return on our investments will more than cover the cost of administering the empire.

All great nations have been sea powers. As a great nation and a trading power, we need bases overseas. Manila will be an excellent harbor for the China trade and a place for storage and shipment of goods, as well as a naval base for trade protection.

It is our responsibility to spread the ideals and principles of the Declaration of Independence. Once the Philippines are mature in their organization of society and democratic government, we will grant them their freedom. Our Monroe Doctrine speaks of our need to protect weaker peoples from European colonialism. Perhaps the Democrats are hoping to use the issue in an effort to win the election in 1900, but the American people will see the wisdom in our action.

Anti-Imperialists, 1898–99

Imperialism is in opposition to the American tradition. Our nation was born in a colonial revolt against an imperialist power—the British. We have a statement in our Declaration of Independence that calls for all nations to rule themselves, to establish a "separate and equal Station to which the Laws of Nature and of Nature's God entitle them." Thus we cannot rule over the Filipinos and Puerto Ricans, but must give them their chance to be free. We have an anticolonial heritage to uphold. Besides, they are a weaker people and cannot be assimilated into our predominately Anglo-Saxon culture. They would not have the ability to function as citizens in our democratic society.

Also, imperialism would involve us with foreign nations and might require us to establish a standing army—a threat to our freedom. These people do need our help and we might be able to establish trade relations and send out missionaries to improve their lives, but all of this must be done without political dominance. Trade is much more likely to be profitable if we have relations with a government chosen by its own people rather than one imposed from outside. We want them to establish democratic institutions, to adopt civilized ways, and to accept the true faith of Christianity, but these goals will not be achieved except by allowing them to be free and independent in their choice.

Although some people may welcome us, it is possible others may resist. Then the United States army and navy would have to be placed in control and then would be in a position much like that of the Spanish, the very group we fought in order to free these people. Our responsibility is to warn other nations to stay away, but to allow both the Philippines and Puerto Rico to develop their own institutions, just as we have opted for Cuba with the enlightened Teller Amendment.

While so many of our people are poor and in need, it is wrong to spend money on military and civilian programs for people in distant areas and of a different race. The United States will be required to raise taxes, which are already a burden on the middle class. We always have been proud of the fact that we are different from the European powers, from the "old world." If we acquire an empire, then we will ape their habits and lose that distinction. Our Monroe Doctrine speaks against any nation attempting to establish colonies in areas to our south, and yet we are now planning to do just that in Puerto Rico and far across the ocean in the Philippines. Perhaps the Republicans are intent on manufacturing a victory in the 1900 election by yielding to popular jingoism. Let us hope that they are wrong.

List the similarities in the two views:

_____

_____

_____

List the differences between the two views:

_____

_____

_____

QUESTIONS

1. Which, in your judgment, is the better argument—that of the imperialists or the anti-imperialists? Why?

_____

_____

_____

2. Which interpretations of the Declaration of Independence and of the Monroe Doctrine are most accurate? Why?

_____

_____

_____

3. What is the strongest argument on each side? Why?

_____

_____

_____

4. What is the weakest argument on each side? Why?

_____

_____

_____

5. Would you have voted on the side of the imperialists or the anti-imperialists when the question of annexation of the Philippines came up in 1899? Why?

_____

_____

_____

6. What arguments and attitudes, with a change in locations, might still be heard in debates over current foreign affairs?

_____

_____

_____

SUGGESTED ANSWERS

Similarities:

    A. Envisioning a Christian influence in the Philippines, ignoring the fact that Filipinos were already 90 percent Catholic
    B. Considering the Filipinos and Puerto Ricans inferior and in need of order and civilization
    C. Seeking democratic governments
    D. Wishing to avoid new taxes
    E. Seeing imperialism as a political issue
    F. Feeling an obligation to other people
    G. Appealing to the Declaration of Independence
    H. Having no intent of assimilating these people
    I. Seeing opportunity for trade and investment
    J. Hoping to keep other foreign powers out of the area
    K. Expecting the areas to be independent in the future

Differences:

    A. One believes that Christianity is better spread in a free atmosphere, while the other sees more opportunity with control.
    B. The Declaration of Independence supports or does not support imperialism.
    C. The anti-imperialists see a threat to American freedom.
    D. The anti-imperialists believe that the use of force is not the proper way to spread democracy.
    E. The anti-imperialists argue that we are replacing the Spanish as imperialists.
    F. They differ on the application of the Monroe Doctrine.
    G. The imperialists have a stronger sense of duty.
    H. The imperialists argue that only with control can the goals be realized.
    I. The imperialists believe that it is more dangerous to declare protection of areas than to actually annex them.
    J. The imperialists envision for the United States a deeper involvement in world affairs.

SKILL EXERCISE TWO: EVALUATING ARGUMENTS

Examine the following arguments relating to the *election of 1896.* Write under each the type of argument being used: *Reason, Intuition, Anecdotal, Empirical,* or *Authority.*

1. William Jennings Bryan captured the spirit of America, and I feel he epitomized the American tradition.

   _____

   _____

2. William McKinley sat on his front porch during the campaign and spoke a few words to visiting groups and indicated that he was an average American.

   _____

   _____

3. The gold standard is a creation of God and forms the basis for money according to the laws of nature.

   _____

   _____

4. Bryan was certainly not a spokesperson for the common man, since fourteen of fifteen big cities, crowded with "common men," voted for McKinley.

   _____

   _____

5. Bryan was a dangerous and fanatic radical who might have turned the nation backward, and I know he would have destroyed the foundations of an industrialized nation.

   _____

   _____

6. To workers in the big city, the Republicans' high tariff seemed to offer more than the promise of free coinage of silver, since it would protect home markets and increase jobs.

   _____

   _____

7. The election had unfair aspects: for example, Jones and McLaughlin Steel of Wilmington, Delaware, told their workers that if Bryan won they would close the plant.

   _____

   _____

8. The Republicans collected much money and printed and distributed five pamphlets for every voter in the country.

_____

_____

9. The philosophical principle of the 1896 election was that money and organization will always win out over oratory and emotion.

_____

_____

10. The Populist party in 1896 supported the Democratic candidate, Bryan, and thereby lost their program since Bryan did not approve of any part of the Populist platform except the silver plank.

_____

_____

ANSWERS AND EXPLANATIONS

1. Intuition. This cannot be proven except by appealing to intuition and feeling; no evidence or rational argument is offered.

2. Anecdotal. This evidence may have been significant, but it is only one small part of the total Republican campaign.

3. Authority. The appeal here is to two authorities: God and nature.

4. Empirical. Specific evidence is presented to support the statement about Bryan.

5. Intuition. No evidence or authority is cited.

6. Reason. This statement does not contain empirical evidence, but neither is it merely intuition; it represents the use of logic.

7. Anecdotal. This one case does not mean that the practice was widespread and it is not broad enough to be considered significant empirical evidence.

8. Empirical. The statement is based on hard evidence, beyond the anecdotal, and is not merely reason or intuition.

9. Authority. The appeal is to a principle as providing answers (a principle that, in this case, may or may not be true).

10. Reason. The use of "since" indicates reason. It gives enough evidence to remove it from intuition, but not enough evidence to make it empirical.

PART III
Debating Historical, Social, and Moral Issues

QUESTIONS FOR THOUGHT

1. President Theodore Roosevelt's corollary (1904 extension) to the Monroe Doctrine was applied to Latin American republics and led to numerous military interventions. The corollary explained American policy—to exercise international police power to correct chronic wrongdoing by these republics and to

prevent intervention by foreign powers. Do you agree with the corollary and the right of the United States to intervene? Why or why not? What are the differences between intervention in the early 1900s and currently?

_____

_____

_____

_____

_____

2. President Roosevelt claims that he "took" the Panama Canal area and initiated the building of the canal, implying that, if he had not, there would have been no canal. Certainly he used questionable procedures, given his support of a Panamanian revolution against Colombia and his immediate recognition of Panama as an independent republic. Is this a case of improper, perhaps illegal, action in the short run for a long-term gain—a canal for ships from all nations to use, a vital water link for trade and defense? Should Americans condemn Roosevelt's methods, or does the end sometimes justify the means in history? Explain.

_____

_____

_____

_____

_____

3. Should limits have been placed on the Pulitzer newspapers in 1897 and 1898 because of their inflammatory, exaggerated, and often inaccurate coverage of the revolution in Cuba? Why or why not?

_____

_____

_____

_____

4. Does American entry into the Spanish-American War indicate that democracies can be induced into a war as easily as dictatorships or totalitarian systems of government? Explain.

_____

_____

_____

_____

5. Varied reasons are offered for the expansion of American interest overseas in the 1890s and early 1900s. Examine the following "causes" and write under each whether you consider it to be of "great importance" or of "less importance."

A. Economic growth and exports—the need to find markets for goods and new lucrative investment opportunities.

_____

B. Intellectual currents—feelings of "manifest destiny," of Social Darwinism applied to a national reputation as one of the "fit" nations, of the Anglo-Saxon responsibility to "uplift backward peoples."

_____

C. Worldwide trend—the examples of the British, French, and Dutch, a need not to be left out; all "great nations" have empires with colonies overseas.

_____

D. Military and strategic needs—an emphasis on sea power as a key to greatness both in trade and world power; overseas bases help meet the strategic needs of the United States.

_____

E. Political pressures—the need to win elections and enhance the prestige of a political party; efforts to divert the attention of the American people from the economic problems at home (depression, labor strife, inequality of wealth, and others).

_____

F. Journalistic influences—a free press that needs to sell papers and is controlled by those who want expansionism, exploiting emotional situations by arousing public interest and feelings.

_____

G. Missionary impulse—a desire to spread Christianity to other lands.

_____

H. End of frontier—no more room to expand on the North American continent (the trend since 1607 had been to expand); thus, the interest overseas.

_____

I. Patriotism—a growing national pride that appears in all large nations as they thrive and progress; an internal energy that naturally seeks to exert influence abroad.

_____

J. Marxist-Leninist theory—a capitalist nation produces a surplus of goods and money and, to avoid depression and economic problems at home, seeks control abroad to secure markets and resources and to provide investment opportunities; imperialism is the final stage of capitalism, the temporary salvation of the capitalist system.

_____

Choose the two that you consider most important and explain your reasons.

_____

_____

_____

Are the intellectual and psychological factors *more* or *less* important than the "hard" factors of economics, diplomacy, and politics? Explain.

_____

_____

_____

Offer a critical evaluation of item J. If it has some validity, does it remain a factor in current diplomacy? Why or why not?

_____

_____

_____

Which factors would be the most upsetting and insulting to underdeveloped areas that became colonies? Why?

_____

_____

_____

Would one of these factors alone have been sufficient to cause expansion or does it take several factors interacting together? Explain.

_____

_____

_____

The term "moralistic aggression" has been used to represent the urge to reform the world, to set things right, to "uplift." Is this attitude central to American expansion or a window-dressing for an underlying desire for power and material gain? Explain.

_____

_____

_____

6. The attitude of the United States (and of European nations) in the 1890s was that much of the world was uncivilized, in need of the advanced civilization of the Christian Western world. What exactly is meant by the word "civilized"? Various "signs" of civilization have been offered. Below is a list of some of these. Examine them carefully and answer the questions that follow.

A. A high standard of living for the majority of the population.
B. Conveniences that offer leisure time to many citizens.
C. Scientific knowledge instead of superstition and demonology.
D. Conquest over the "relics of barbarism"—polygamy, infanticide, legalized prostitution, capricious divorce, immoral games, torture, caste social structure, slavery, harsh laws and penal code, and so forth.
E. Low death rate and long life expectancy.
F. Good sanitation, hygiene, and medical care, and low infant mortality rate.
G. High literacy rate and free public education.
H. Disciplined, hard-working labor force with high productivity.
I. Maintenance of the infrastructure.
J. Ability to negotiate, compromise, cooperate, and solve problems in a peaceful manner.
K. Compassion—philanthropy, charities, mutual aid and care for all groups in society.
L. Widespread enjoyment of "culture"—art, literature, and music—and the creative production of this culture.
M. Ability to reform, to constantly improve and adapt, and to correct abuses; a willingness to do so.
N. Guaranteed basic freedoms to speak, publish, move about, worship, and to be protected by the law.
O. Control over birth rate, population growth, and size of families.
P. Rule of law over the whims of rulers.
Q. A government responsive to the people and their outlook and decisions.
R. Respect for private property, enforcement of contracts, and freedom of business enterprise.
S. Care and respect for the environment and the conservation of resources.

Which three of the above do you consider the most important elements of a civilized nation? Explain your choices.

_____

_____

_____

Which two do you consider to be the least important signs of a civilized society? Explain.

_____

_____

_____

What other factors not on the list do you consider necessary in order to call a society "civilized"?

_____

_____

_____

Is the war-making propensity of a nation a factor that should be included—that a nation seldom, if ever, goes to war? Why or why not?

_____

_____

_____

From what you have read about the United States in that period, to what degree, considering the above list, was it a "civilized" society? Explain.

_____

_____

_____

Would *non*-Western societies agree to most of the items on the list?

_____

_____

_____

7. A cartoon appeared in *Punch*, an English magazine, that showed Uncle Sam trying to control a kicking, punching boy labeled "Cuba." The Spaniard standing nearby says to Uncle Sam, "Well, you wanted him! You've got him! And, I wish you joy of him!" What is the implication of this cartoon? Do you agree with its observation? Explain.

_____

_____

_____

_____

8. Historians have debated the Open Door policy in China and come to different conclusions about its intent.

   A. One view is that the policy represents imperialist greed. The United States wanted to dominate the world economy and could best do so by opening the markets of the world to make the American system function better. It was a ploy of industrial capitalism and led to unfortunate intervention by

the United States, ranging from the escapade in the Philippines in 1899 to Vietnam in 1965.
  B. The other view is that Americans felt a genuine sympathy for China and its territorial integrity. The United States was, except for the aberration in 1898, consistently in opposition to acquiring colonial areas. The policy reflects this and also upholds the ideals of a free and open market for trade throughout the world for all nations. The policy may have prevented a war over China at that time and has delayed and modified wars since that time.

Which of these views do you agree with most? Why?

_____

_____

_____

Should this policy be a part of the current diplomatic outlook of the United States? Why or why not?

_____

_____

_____

9. During the war in Vietnam, comparisons were made between the American effort to annex and control the Philippines and the involvement in Vietnam. What are the similarities in and differences between these two involvements?

_____

_____

_____

_____

_____

10. Consider the two quotations at the beginning of the chapter. Explain their meanings and implications and whether you agree or disagree with each.

_____

_____

_____

_____

_____

Thoughts for Questions

1. Latin Americans seldom agree with the need of others to intervene. This time it was mostly intervention to collect revenues to pay debts owed European nations

or to protect American citizens. What about the rights of self-government, self-determination, and sovereignty for each nation? Yet "chronic wrongdoing" may invite other nations to act; should the United States have stood aside and allowed this to happen? In contemporary times, the prospect of another ideology and of a "Cold War" foe gaining influence in Latin America is always present. The worldwide publicity about such intervention is much greater.

2. Is the proper duty of the historian to describe and not judge? The right to build the canal might have been approved after a payment of $25 million to Colombia. Therefore, if Roosevelt had been patient, he could have avoided exposing the United States to a military threat and other high-handed techniques. But this remains an "if" in history, a product of hindsight. The benefits of Roosevelt's actions are obvious. The techniques used are at least questionable, if not deplorable. The ends may not justify the means in a philosophical or moral sense, but often the results of an illegal or immoral action can be beneficial to a large number of people. Could other techniques have worked as well?

3. Much of your answer depends on your view of the extent of press freedom, a dilemma that is always with us. Certainly some limits must be set on what can be printed. All news is censored at its source. It has been said that freedom of the press belongs to those who own a press. Americans have been reluctant to interfere with this freedom (except in wartime), even to the extent of putting up with biased and inflammatory reporting. At what point do the courts draw the line? Who decides? A reliance on other "presses" to print opposing viewpoints is not always successful. A fundamental belief has been that with freedom to print, the truth will usually win out. Is this true?

4. This seems true for the past two hundred years. Perhaps democracies are more easily tempted. Dictatorships can control the press and public opinion so as to fight only in the wars that the dictators choose. McKinley seems to have been drawn into the Spanish-American War against his better judgment. Public pressure was brought to bear on the president and Congress. Of course, the public can also voice opposition to military involvement and perhaps influence that involvement, as in the Vietnam War.

5. While the student must make individual choices here, it is worth considering the basis for these choices. Did you choose on the basis of searching in history books for evidence and data for support *or* did your background, intuition, and experiences prevail over the "evidence"? Items *F* and *B* seem the most important. These choices obviously emphasize the American mood, attitudes, and public opinion pressures as molded by the press.

In regard to the "hard" factor of economics, businessmen did not support the Spanish-American War. They later did become involved in efforts at increasing trade by controlling or influencing foreign areas. American trade with Cuba already exceeded the Spanish trade with Cuba. The China market, with a port of exchange at Manila, was attractive. But the amount of trade remained small—less than 5 percent of total trade—and China had no essential resources. The capitalist system has continued to function with success, despite the end to imperialism, since World War II. One might argue that "control abroad" still exists as a primary goal of capitalism. Does the success of capitalism depend on the control of underdeveloped nations by capitalist nations?

Of all the factors, the most insulting is the attitude that these areas are inferior and need religion or culture. Most of the other factors are understandable in the competition among nations, even though they are not acceptable as a pretext for foreign influence.

The historian instinctively opposes single causation as an explanation for any event. Possibly *all* of the factors given must be considered as influencing imperialism. Perhaps *H* is the most questionable since it dwells on some vague forces of history.

This moralistic outlook is nearly always the excuse given by governments. Perhaps there is some truth to this motive, especially at the turn of the century. Only Genghis Khan revealed that his purpose for expansion was to kill, rape, destroy, and pillage. All other leaders and nations state that they actually intend "to do good." The historian instinctively searches below surface statements of altruism and benign goals. Yet it would be wrong to dismiss all such statements as only covers for the "real" motives.

6. The most important seem to be *N, M,* and *P.* The assumption is that if these three are assured, then the others can be obtained. Without these, all efforts may be lost. Both *B* and *O* are probably the least important although perhaps desirable.

Would the willingness to refrain from intervention in the affairs of other nations be a worthy addition to the list? Toleration of people and groups who depart from the cultural mainstream might be added as a sign of civilization.

If a reluctance to make war could be applied to all nations, it would be among the most important items on the list, perhaps *the* most important. Yet one assumes that a nation must protect itself and that at times this involves armed resistance.

All items on the list are present in American civilization; however, each is only partially developed. This brings up the issue of to what degree each of these elements must be developed. Do we place a 60 percent, 80 percent, or 95 percent requirement for each? Despite the anti-Americanism voiced in many areas of the world, few societies would object to having most of these features. Some might add particular religious characteristics (the Moslem world, especially). The influence of family and tribe could alter some. Communist societies would emphasize a spirit of community, of collective behavior, and of concern for the welfare of the State.

7. The United States, represented by Uncle Sam, had the problem after ousting Spain of controlling the "punching boy." Cubans were belligerent and resisted control. The Spaniard was taking some pleasure in the predicament that so resembled the difficulties Spain encountered before American intervention. Revolutionaries normally believe in high ideals and fight for freedom or justice. But they are men and women like all others. It is sometimes easier to fight a revolution for justice, equality, and freedom than, after winning, to establish a system of justice, equality, and freedom. Revolutionaries are in trouble when they must turn followers into bureaucrats and withstand the inevitable breakdown of idealism. Even the United States had its troubles after the Revolution.

8. Was this policy another case of mixed motives? A pattern of efforts to obtain the rights to trade in as many areas as possible can be found in American foreign policy, from the Monroe Doctrine to contemporary struggles. Yet at the same time episodes exist where aid seems to go beyond economic gain and reveals a genuine interest in the advancement and well-being of other people. Until the victory of Mao Tse-tung in 1949, the United States had a strong sympathy for the people of China—some say a sympathy that actually interfered with the best interests of the

United States. Noting China's poverty, one can doubt that the primary reason for the policy was trade and investment.

9. Both wars involved American troops intervening to establish a friendly government. In both cases, the American military found themselves fighting a guerrilla war against a civilian militia in a jungle area. The ostensible purposes in each case were to extend freedom and democracy. The Americans won in the Philippines. The Philippines had no outside influences, nor ideological enemies. Of course, American involvement in Vietnam was on a much more massive scale. In both wars, atrocities were committed, racism and cultural misunderstanding occurred, and a rival took possession (Japan took the Philippines from 1942 to 1945). Both incidents were opposed by many members of Congress and by many leaders in the United States.

10. In a sense, it is impossible not to take sides. Humans seem to lean instinctually in one direction or the other if two or more sides are available. Even in sporting events, people tend to take sides in every contest. Tuchman probably means something much deeper here, something involving a commitment based on a philosophical or moral principle. This is acceptable as long as historians realize the side they are taking and let the readers know about it, also.

The uniformity of human nature, especially in the past, is debatable. Are the impulses, motivations, and patterns of behavior of the Chinese peasant in the T'ang Dynasty similar to those of the Midwest farmer in 1900? Psychologists are reluctant to define human nature or even to acknowledge its existence. The historian can observe many similarities of behavior in the past with that of recent years. Uncanny parallels often appear, especially in the area of ideas and wisdom regarding life. The Chinese sage of twenty-five hundred years ago may have apt advice for the twentieth-century suburbanite. We cannot know if past individuals looked at the world with the same orientation as current individuals. Yet often historians assume a continuity of human desires and modes of behavior.

CHAPTER

13

PROGRESSIVE REFORM

"I hold the view that the greatest changes in human history are to be traced back to internal caused conditions, and that they are found upon internal psychological necessity. For it seems that external conditions serve merely as occasions on which a new attitude long in preparation becomes manifest."

Carl Jung

"To me it is comforting rather than otherwise to feel that history is determined by the illogical human record and not by large immutable scientific laws beyond our power to deflect."

Barbara Tuchman

PART I
Acquiring Essential Data

ESSENTIAL DATES

Determine the correct sequence and write the approximate date for each of the following events.

1. Ratification of the nineteenth Amendment, giving women the right to vote _____

2. Ratification of the seventeenth Amendment, allowing for a graduated income tax _____

3. Assassination of President William McKinley—Vice President Theodore Roosevelt becomes president. _____

4. Woodrow Wilson is elected president, defeating Theodore Roosevelt and William Howard Taft. _____

5. The secret ballot is used in an American election for the first time. _____

6. Passage of the Pure Food and Drug Act _____

7. Establishment of the National Association for the Advancement of Colored People (NAACP) _____

8. Federal Reserve Act is passed, creating the Federal Reserve Board. _____

9. United States troops occupy Haiti, remaining until 1934. _____

10. The Women's Christian Temperance Union (WCTU) is founded. _____

11. President Roosevelt decides to intervene in the coal strike. _____

12. Roosevelt decides to bring an antitrust suit against J. P. Morgan's Northern Securities Company. _____

ESSENTIAL CONCEPTS

Examine each concept and write what contemporary relevance it might have.

1. *direct democracy*   A democratic technique of using direct primaries, initiatives, referendums, and recall elections to involve the people in their government.

_____

_____

_____

2. *social surveys*   The efforts to map slums and to describe the lives of their inhabitants—an early form of sociological research.

_____

_____

_____

3. *"rule of reason"*   To be allied with business organizations through the antitrust department. A business was to be indicted only if "undue influence" was used to restrain trade.

_____

_____

_____

4. *statism*   The belief of many progressives that the government was the institution that should establish justice and promote the welfare of society.

_____

_____

_____

5. *muckrakers*   Probing reporters and writers who searched for injustice and improper behavior in society, especially in big business. Some were careful, others sensationalists.

_____

_____

_____

6. *Wisconsin idea*   Robert M. La Follette's plan of calling in experts and advisory commissions to provide research, advice, and help in the drafting of legislation.

_____

_____

_____

7. *"bread and butter" unionism*   The emphasis by labor organizations on wages, hours, and working conditions rather than on structural changes or ideological systems.

_____

_____

_____

8. *New Nationalism*   President Roosevelt's program that assumed business consolidation was inevitable and even beneficial, but federal regulation was necessary to protect the public.

_____

_____

_____

9. *anti-trust* The attitude that it is harmful for large corporations to merge and dominate the manufacturing or marketing of a product; therefore, action must be taken to break up and limit consolidation.

_____

_____

_____

10. *"cooling off" period* William Jennings Bryan's plan to require that nations involved in disputes wait for at least one year before they take any military action.

_____

_____

_____

ANSWERS

Correct sequence of events and their dates.

1. 10; 1874
2. 5; 1888
3. 3; 1901
4. 11; 1902
5. 12; 1904
6. 6; 1906

7. 7; 1910
8. 4; 1912
9. 8; 1913
10. 2; 1913
11. 9; 1915
12. 1; 1920

PART II
Developing Thinking Skills

SKILL EXERCISE ONE: PERCEIVING SIMILARITIES AND DIFFERENCES

Two attitudes toward the relationship among the government, business, and society follow. Read each carefully, then answer the questions about the similarities and differences. Compare your findings with those suggested.

Social Darwinists

Social Darwinists began with an assumption of the truth of Charles Darwin's theory of evolution and then applied it beyond the physical development of humans to their social development. In this sense, it was an application of science to society. Humans are in a natural state when they are in a "dog eat dog" world. The fittest are tough and hard-headed; they follow the law of the jungle. This is inevitable.

They survive and prosper; those unfit drop by the wayside. This is natural. The process, for the good of humanity and the progress of the race, does not warrant interference by the government or any other institution or group.

There should be no tariffs, no restrictions on business enterprise, no handouts to the poor, and no government interference in labor disputes. Prices, wages, and quality of merchandise are best determined by the free marketplace. Buyers are responsible for their choice of products and must be cautious and selective. Workers must be free to bargain individually for their jobs and pay. Those who are successful in this struggle acquire wealth.

This theory is just since wealth usually is an index of virtue and worth, the result of skill and performance in the struggle—hard work, frugality, insight into opportunities, timing, vision, and efficiency. If people fail, it's their own fault for not having the strength, courage, intelligence, drive, and determination to succeed. This scientific truth applies within a society, among nations, and among races.

In a religious sense, money is a gift from God to those who deserve it, who are responsible stewards in the use of money. Wealth is a sign of God's approval. This wealth is private property that cannot be taken from the holder. Strong nations emerge from the struggles among nations, and superior races survive and progress while weaker nations and races decline and disappear or remain to serve the stronger.

Progressives

The progressives were middle-class lawyers, physicians, ministers, teachers, and the wives and daughters of middle-class men. Their ideas and attitudes arose out of the Christian ethic, the Social Gospel movement of the 1890s, the organizing for women's rights, and the social workers' experiences of the 1890s. Some political influence probably came from the Populist movement, also. To some extent they made use of the pragmatic thought of William James, especially his emphasis on the freedom of the individual to act and to bring about change.

They revealed nonmaterialistic humanitarian motives. They sought to arouse the conscience of the people, to purify American life, and their instrument was the government—a government responsive to the people, that would act on behalf of the poor and defenseless. They also accepted a government that could even interfere with personal choices, such as the consumption of alcoholic beverages. The government must establish equal opportunity and universal justice.

They assumed that their personal values were the true ones, good for all of society. Their enemy was monopolistic big business and its influence on government. The government must protect consumers and workers from huge, impersonal corporations. They called for organization and cooperation, for attention to middle-class moral codes of honesty, self-sacrifice, and human concern about the good for society. Middle-class values of hard work and thrift also include human sympathy for those who need protection.

The government must restrict business activity and see that workers receive an adequate wage. It must set maximum charges for services provided by public utilities. Big business tipped the scales in favor of a lucky unscrupulous few who care nothing for their fellow humans. Races and nations should be dealt with equally, as should men and women.

What are the similarities in the attitudes and outlook of Social Darwinism and progressivism?

_____

_____

_____

_____

What are the differences between the attitudes and outlook of Social Darwinism and progressivism?

_____

_____

_____

_____

Overall, with which outlook do you agree? Why?

_____

_____

_____

SUGGESTED ANSWERS

Similarities:

    A. Both were interested in society's progress.
    B. Progress was expected to have a secular basis, even though references were made to God.
    C. Both supported the competitive, free-enterprise system; progressives had less enthusiasm for that system.
    D. Both supported the virtues of hard work and thrift.
    E. Both supported the free democratic system.

Differences:

    A. One was middle class, the other was primarily the business class.
    B. An orderly, humanitarian concern versus "law of the jungle."
    C. One emphasized reason and morality, the other science.
    D. They differed widely on the role of government.
    E. One spoke of equality, the other expected great inequality.
    F. One had an eclectic program, the other an organized philosophy.
    G. One was suspicious of big business, the other praised it.

H. One urged help for the poor, the other considered the poor unfit people who should be allowed to "fall by the wayside."

I. One chose a caring government as the dispenser of justice and the conscience of reformers as the energy for righteousness; the other praised the marketplace as the source of justice and the abilities and willpower of capable businesspersons as the source of energy.

SKILL EXERCISE TWO: EVALUATING AND APPLYING EVIDENCE

The following thesis relates to the progressives. Ten items of data are listed after the thesis. Under each of the items, write whether the information *supports* the thesis, *challenges* the thesis, or is *neutral* data. Briefly explain each answer. Then check your judgment against the suggested answers.

The Thesis

"The progressives were a successful reform group that was able to accomplish its goals and to dramatically improve the lives of the American people, especially the disadvantaged and the lower classes."

Items of Data

1. Many progressives argued that since 45 percent of blacks were illiterate, they may not deserve full citizenship and, therefore, the progressives continued to support the denial of the black vote.

   _____

   _____

2. Because a progressive exposed the filth and danger of meat processing, Congress passed regulation to monitor the sanitary conditions of meat processing.

   _____

   _____

3. Many progressive reformers were lukewarm on woman suffrage and argued that if women voted they would lose their moral influence in the home.

   _____

   _____

4. The Native Americans and their plight were ignored by nearly all progressives.

   _____

   _____

5. President Theodore Roosevelt, a progressive president, intervened in the anthracite coal strike in 1902 with the result that miners received a 10 percent pay increase and a nine-hour workday.

   _____

   _____

6. Conservative President William Howard Taft brought ninety antitrust suits against corporations and business monopolies, twice as many as the progressive Theodore Roosevelt.

_____

_____

7. In 1907 Congress passed and President Roosevelt signed into law a bill that forbade the president to reserve any more national forests in six western states.

_____

_____

8. Many progressives had prejudices against immigrants and tended to look to honest and efficient governments rather than to the needs of the "huddled masses" in city slums.

_____

_____

9. In 1916, Woodrow Wilson signed into law the Keating-Owen Act, which restricted the employment of children in most jobs.

_____

_____

10. A corporate and personal income tax was passed into law in 1913; it graduated from no payment at incomes of $4,000 and below up to 7 percent on incomes above $500,000.

_____

_____

ANSWERS AND EXPLANATIONS

1. Challenges. Even though the word "many" is used and some progressives did oppose racism and segregation and even helped organize the NAACP, this statement probably reflects a general attitude of progressives.

2. Supports. This statement leaves no room for doubt, although the law did not cover meat processing within a state, and the number of actual inspectors was small.

3. Challenges. Women were disadvantaged and the denial of the vote was one reason. The reformers' lack of all-out support for woman suffrage probably caused its delay until 1920. This is ironic, since women were such a vital part of the progressive reform effort.

4. Challenges. The Native Americans were not a large number, but certainly disadvantaged. They tended to be ignored after 1890 in history textbooks, also.

5. Supports. Certainly it was a help to miners that Roosevelt did not intervene to force workers back to work, as previous presidents had done.

6. Supports. Not all cases were won. Perhaps many more cases were needed. But

this effort to reduce the concentration and power of wealth was a progressive goal, even under a conservative president.

7. Challenges. Conservation was a goal of progressives, especially Roosevelt, but the private interests of large lumber companies prevailed in this case.

8. Challenges. Progressives favored white middle-class Americans from traditional stock (English, Germanic, northern European), and although progressives provided some efficient and honest services in cities, they were not (with notable exceptions) especially interested in aiding the newly arrived immigrant in adjusting to American life.

9. Supports. Child labor abuses were a prime target for progressive reformers, and after several confrontations with the courts, an effective law was passed. Wilson still had concerns about the child's individual freedom.

10. Supports. A graduated income tax tends to take from wealthy industrialists—both individuals and corporations—and provide tax moneys for general welfare purposes.

PART III
Debating Historical, Social, and Moral Issues

QUESTIONS FOR THOUGHT

1. Some social scientists and historians, in analyzing the progressive reformers, argue that they may *not* have had a genuine concern over the plight of the disadvantaged so much as a desire to seek personal fulfillment and to bring down or control those very wealthy individuals who seemed to wield so much influence over their lives. They were psychologically uneasy. Reflect on this possibility. What sort of evidence might be sought to support or to refute this contention? How does one separate genuine interest from one's effort to fulfill personal psychological needs? Is this "psychological" interpretation out of the realm of a historian's competency? Why or why not?

_____

_____

_____

_____

_____

2. Historians have offered several views of the progressives:

   A. The traditional view of the progressive movement is that it was a popular, democratic movement to reduce the influence of powerful financial interests and urban bosses on American government and society, an attempt to restore power to the people. The "people" opposed the "special interests."

Some historians have recently reaffirmed this traditional view and pointed out the impact on and support of the working class and even of immigrants to bring about a system devoted to the public good rather than to the private agendas of monopolies. It was a democratic movement "from the bottom up."

B. Another view characterized the progressives as middle-class men and women who were alarmed by the growing power of a new group of leaders and sought to regain their traditional position and influence in society. They suffered from "status anxiety," a personal urge to reassert leadership, rather than responding to economic conditions or injustice in society.

C. Another recent interpretation challenges the assumption that either the lower classes or the middle class had as much impact on progressive reform as big business did. The argument is that businesspersons promoted government regulation in an effort to avoid competition from small entrepreneurs who were making inroads against their control of the market. Small firms thus would be forced out of business because of the expense of meeting the new government regulations. The progressive movement therefore becomes a conservative big-business movement to acquire government assistance in maintaining dominance. The antitrust suits had little effect on big business, but the regulation of meat processing could wipe out small competitors and leave the market open to giant companies. The movement was one encouraged by business to bring order and stability to a confused system. Government helped bring this stability.

Which of the above views do you agree with most? Why?

_____

_____

_____

What sources should be sought out and what type of evidence might be collected to support or refute the above viewpoints? Use your imagination.

_____

_____

_____

Some historians argue that it is impossible to encompass the progressive movement and explain it through generalizations and overall interpretations. It was too complex and multifaceted. It was an inconsistent effort by people from diverse backgrounds—wealthy, professional, middle-class, and labor—who sought many goals, some immediate and practical, some far-reaching and idealistic, often working at cross purposes and many times attempting to fulfill personal needs. Thus it is counter-productive to reduce this activity to generalizations, to draw out overall interpretations, and to classify and label such a complicated movement. Do you agree? Why or why not? Is one purpose of historians to accom-

226 ★ *Progressive Reform*

plish this difficult task of generalization, interpretation, and classification? Must historians not only describe the past, but "make sense" out of it? Explain.

_____

_____

_____

_____

_____

3. Progressive reform ended with the American involvement in World War I. The reforms of the 1830s to the 1850s culminated in the Civil War. The Populist reform movement was blunted by the Spanish-American War. World War II brought New Deal reform to a close. The Kennedy-Johnson reforms of the 1960s subsided with the Vietnam War. Do these developments support a thesis that the reforming spirit tends to become so zealous and radical that it results in violence on behalf of the reform ideals, violence either at home (Civil War) or abroad—perhaps in an effort to extend the reforms to other areas, to "make the world safe for democracy," to remold Europe and Japan, and produce a "Great Society" in Vietnam? Or are these incidents merely a coincidence such that no pattern can be established? Explain your reaction to this "theory" that active and intense reform effort leads to war.

_____

_____

_____

_____

_____

4. In the midst of a major reform movement, an attempt to better the lives of the American people, how can we account for the little interest shown in the plight of blacks? Lynchings, strict segregation (Jim Crow laws), and racism, along with economic, social, and political discrimination continued throughout the United States. Were the reformers insincere and selective in their ideals? Did racist notions prevail over reform expectations? Was the problem just too great to attempt a solution? React to this neglect of a large segment of American society, perhaps the most oppressed and downtrodden group of the period.

_____

_____

_____

_____

_____

5. Thorstein Veblen presented the concept of "conspicuous consumption," the purchase of goods merely to impress others. Is this activity a benefit to society

since it tends to encourage people to purchase luxuries and thus add to the demand for goods, which in turn creates jobs and profits, *or* is it detrimental in that it ignores the scarcity elsewhere of some of the basic necessities of society— decent housing and proper sanitation, for example—and diverts production for the many toward luxuries for the few? Explain.

_____

_____

_____

_____

_____

6. In the 1908 case of *Mueller v. Oregon*, which involved a law restricting the work of women factory workers to ten hours a day, the Court upheld the law. The Court majority explained, "The two sexes differ in structure of body, in the functions to be performed by each, in the amount of physical strength, in the capacity for long continued labor . . . This difference justifies a difference in legislation . . ." Is this ruling sexist? Why or why not?

_____

_____

_____

_____

_____

7. Booker T. Washington accepted second-class political status for blacks and argued that they must first seek economic security through self-help, manual labor, vocational education, subsistence farming, and other ways before they would be prepared to exercise their full responsibility as citizens. Until then, they should accept a subordinate role in American society. W. E. B. Du Bois complained that Washington was too agriculture-oriented and that blacks should seek full citizenship rights immediately. The talented 10 percent of blacks must enter the professions. Blacks ought to seek equality in all areas of life, especially in the political arena. They must be active, must organize, and use all legitimate means to attain first-class citizenship. Do you agree with Washington or with Du Bois? Why?

_____

_____

_____

_____

_____

8. After examining their programs and capabilities, for which candidate would you have voted in the 1912 election—Wilson, Taft, Roosevelt, or Eugene V. Debs? Support your choice with specific arguments.

_____

_____

_____

_____

_____

9. Robert La Follette argued that "the people will do the right thing if properly informed and inspired," and that what society needed was more democracy, more influence and control by the people. To what extent do you agree or disagree with La Follette?

_____

_____

_____

_____

_____

10. Many progressives called for a direct primary to choose *candidates* for office, as well as for the initiative (people can initiate legislation), recall (removal of elected officials before their terms are up), and referendum (submission of bills to the people for a direct vote). With which, if any, of these do you agree? Explain.

_____

_____

_____

_____

_____

11. President Theodore Roosevelt was conservative in 1901, but became more liberal as he continued in office for seven years and even more liberal, at least reform-minded, in his 1912 campaign. Woodrow Wilson had strong conservative instincts, but ended up supporting a liberal agenda during his administration. This same pattern can be seen in the presidencies of Franklin Roosevelt, Harry Truman, and Lyndon Johnson, among others. Why do many presidents become more liberal in outlook once they enter the White House and very few, if any, become more conservative?

_____

_____

_____

_____

12. Are excesses such as those committed by some muckrakers in the progressive period the price that must be paid for a free press that seeks to uncover abuses and dangers in American society? What should be the limits, if any, to "investigative reporting"? Should a national censorship committee be established to review stories about alleged wrongdoing in government and business and determine whether or not they can be published? Why or why not?

_____

_____

_____

_____

_____

13. Consider the two questions at the beginning of the chapter. Explain their meanings and implications and whether you agree or disagree with each.

_____

_____

_____

_____

_____

THOUGHTS FOR QUESTIONS

1. Genuine concern is difficult to detect. Perhaps a look at letters, diaries, and other private writings of leading progressives would reveal their motivations. Many of the movement's outcomes—laws, regulations, and court decisions—aided the disadvantaged. Perhaps the effort to obtain such outcomes and their success is the most important indication of motivation. Can one find personal fulfillment *in* aid to those who are oppressed and need help? Many Progressive leaders did seem to fear the urban masses. To some extent, their reform operations took place without close contact with the masses.

2. Students can find evidence and arguments for each of the three interpretations. Much depends on the historian's vantage point, initial approach, or expectations of what constituted success. The most interesting interpretation is that the reforms aimed against big business actually aided big business (C). Certainly this was not the intent of the reformers. Data on reform leaders and on votes for reformers at the grass-roots level may be useful. The fact that reformers gained political office and influence indicates support by the common man. Leadership was drawn from the middle class, but they would have had little success without the votes of the common man.

It is meaningless to say that all three views are partly true; but in the end, a combination or synthesis of them may be closer to the truth than any one standing alone. To say that no cohesive explanation exists is to avoid the historian's need to structure a topic or period and leaves one with a conglomerate of unrelated facts, events, ideas, and attitudes that cannot be ordered in any rational format. Historians must make sense out of the past and establish relationships, even if these are not totally convincing. Besides, interpretations with supporting evidence make history interesting and stimulate both imagination and thinking. Disorganized data leads nowhere except to trivia games and answers for crossword puzzles.

3. History is filled with coincidences. It is hazardous to predict what might happen in the future if reformers agitate intensively for change in society. Yet the pattern seems convincing for the four examples offered. Of course, wars have occurred without any connection to reform—War of 1812 and the Mexican War. But all reform periods in American history culminated with a war. This fact still does not, however, establish a causal relationship between the two. Possibly most reform efforts had nothing to do with the war that followed, although a more direct connection can be made between abolitionism and the Civil War. When do several similar coincidences emerge as a legitimate generalization?

4. Certainly racist sentiments still had a hold on American society. Reformers were not immune to racist stereotypes and many still had not accepted blacks as equal citizens. All reformers have to be selective; it is impossible to activate all reforms at once. However, one might feel more comfortable if black rights were at least on the progressive agenda. For most they were not. Perhaps efforts to aid blacks had failed in Reconstruction and reformers saw little prospect for success in attacking segregation and racism. Theodore Roosevelt did invite Booker T. Washington to dinner in the White House, but only him and only once. Woodrow Wilson exhibited racist attitudes on several occasions. Some white reformers were involved in the founding of the NAACP in 1910. To support suffrage for blacks may have jeopardized other reform efforts, because southerners had significant political influence in Congress.

5. The early 1900s gave us scenes of women and children working long hours in unsafe factories while the wealthy built homes in Newport, Rhode Island, and vacation sites in Palm Beach, and traveled to Europe on huge yachts. One could argue the need for decent housing, adequate medical care, and parks for play and relaxation. But would the confiscated wealth of all millionaires have added much to the standard of living of the millions of poor in the slums? Was the continuation of and acceleration in mass production more important than the confiscation of a few fortunes?

6. It probably would be considered sexist based on current understanding of the rights of citizens of both sexes. The irony is that this was considered an enlightened ruling at the time, one sought by women reformers and applauded by the progressives. Can one argue for equal rights for both sexes and then support this ruling? Would this Court majority explanation apply to some men also—and perhaps not apply to some women?

7. Washington preferred to accept what he considered to be the reality of the times. Many immigrants made their way up the social and economic ladder in the manner Washington suggested. One difference is that blacks had been Americans for two hundred years and had already served their time at hard labor on farms. *When* would they have the opportunity to move into the mainstream of American society? Du Bois proposed a path that has been followed in recent years. For whatever reason, it seems to have worked better than the submission suggested by Washington. For the next fifty years, no matter how hard blacks worked, they were not able to obtain first-class citizenship.

8. This is the student's choice. Three candidates would be considered "liberals" who favored reform. Even Taft began ninety antitrust cases in four years, twice as many as Roosevelt in eight years. Debs received nearly a million votes.

9. The key words here are "properly informed and inspired." What does this mean and who does the informing and inspiring? What is "properly"? Of course the statement represents a cardinal principle of democracy—the voice of the people is to be obeyed. How does one determine the wishes of the people? Without a referendum, the exact nature of a mandate at election time is uncertain. So many different viewpoints on a particular issue may exist that it is impossible to achieve a consensus. How, then, is it possible to listen to the voice of the people, even assuming they are "properly informed"? The practice of democracy is often uncertain and wrought with difficult decisions. This is better than certainty and only one choice.

10. The implication of these democratic features is that the people must have a direct voice in each important decision. The principle of a republic is that the people have a choice in who will represent their interests, but do not make direct decisions on each issue. The acceptance of these "advanced" forms of democracy in state and national governments implies a change in the United States government from a republic to a direct democracy. This is a radical change and not in keeping with the wishes of the Founding Fathers. You may argue their merits, but you must recognize that they represent a change in the traditional methods of the American *republic*.

11. This gradual change in outlook can be documented. One could argue that once a president perceives and understands the total situation from the inside, the logical solution to many domestic problems seems closer to the liberal agenda than the conservative one. On the other hand, it could be that presidents opt for what seems to be the most humane solution (at least on the surface), either because they want votes or approval or because they begin to consider their records as they will be viewed by historians.

Conservatives argue, in many cases, that nothing should be done to change the status quo. A conservative president will thus be remembered for having done "nothing." In predicaments that reveal hardship and injustice, often the easiest action to take is government intervention on behalf of those who suffer. This is normally a liberal solution.

12. Responsible journalism should have accurate data and offer honest, balanced reports and comments. Often, the cries of press sensationalism or of interference in private lives are objections to a probing reporter seeking to acquire information necessary for the safety of an open democracy. Unfortunately, a few irresponsible journalists dig for incidents that will attract readers, regardless of the consequences or of the need for the information. It is difficult to imagine regulations on the latter journalists that would not seriously hamper the former. The censorship committee is unthinkable in a democracy. Thomas Jefferson said it was better to have newspapers without government than to have government without newspapers.

13. Jung's quote may be appropriately applied to reformers. Were psychologically necessary drives encouraging the reformers to act in a way that corresponded to the new attitude that was "long in preparation"? The mind, spirit, and internal feelings and attitudes of people really change history. The outward manifestations are mere reflections of this internal change. This makes it difficult for the historian to attempt to identify the internal necessities. Did Karl Marx's material necessities yield to Jung's psychological necessities?

History, then, is illogical and somewhat chaotic? There seems to be little cause for comfort in an illogical world that proceeds without direction or explanation. Tuchman has produced books that attempt to get at rational explanations of the past. The explanation of the past and the past itself differ. The historian may offer logical understanding of an illogical development of events. "Immutable scientific laws" about history, which few historians support, impose a finality about life to which it is difficult to adjust.

CHAPTER

14

THE GREAT WAR

"Even the best history is not much better than a mist through which we see shapes dimly moving."

Bruce Catton

"The artistic representation of history is a more scientific and serious pursuit than the exact writing of history. For the art of letters goes to the heart of things, whereas the factual report merely collates details."

Aristotle

PART I
Acquiring Essential Data

ESSENTIAL DATES

Determine the correct sequence and write the approximate date for each of the following events. Note the importance of the month for some; just knowing the year may be inadequate.

1. Germany issues the Sussex Pledge to spare all lives in future U-boat attacks on merchant ships. _____

2. The Zimmerman telegram is made public, calling for a German alliance with Mexico in case of war against the United States. _____

3. An armistice ends the war in Europe. _____

4. The United States declares war on Germany. _____

5. The Sedition Act is passed, making disloyal statements about the government and the war effort a crime. _____

6. The Senate rejects the Treaty of Versailles, including the League of Nations. _____

7. The passenger ship, *Lusitania,* is sunk by a German submarine off the Irish coast with the loss of 128 Americans. _____

8. President Woodrow Wilson proclaims American neutrality in thought and action. _____

9. Germany announces the beginning of unrestricted submarine warfare for the second time. _____

10. The First World War (the Great War) breaks out in Europe. _____

11. The Bolsheviks (Communists) are successful in a revolution to control the government of Russia. _____

12. The Selective Service Act is passed, providing for the drafting of men between the ages of 21 and 45. _____

ESSENTIAL CONCEPTS

Examine each concept and write what contemporary relevance it might have.

1. *"teach them to elect good men"* A reflection of the attitude of President Woodrow Wilson that the United States would refuse to recognize an undemocratic government in Mexico and would apply pressure on the Mexicans until they chose "good men" by the democratic process.

_____

_____

_____

2. *"dollar a year man"*   The name for businessmen and managers who came to Washington, D.C., during the war and volunteered to work for nothing in order to assist in the war effort. Of course, their companies made profits in war contracts.

_____

_____

_____

3. *hyphenates*   A stigma attached to Americans whose families came from the nations (Germany and Austria) opposed to the Allied powers or that were in sympathy with them (Irish). Suspicions about loyalty were aroused regarding them—German (hyphen) Americans.

_____

_____

_____

4. *peace without victory*   Wilson's dream that the war in Europe could end in a negotiated settlement without either side claiming victory, in the sense that the loser offered no reparations and no degree of guilt was applied.

_____

_____

_____

5. *Hooverized*   The effort by Food Administrator Herbert Hoover to get Americans to save and recycle during the First World War, to go without products needed in the war, to do so in the name of patriotism—"gospel of the clean plates."

_____

_____

_____

6. *autocracy*   The popular word in 1917 for the Central Powers, indicating their contrast with the democracies. The word implies authoritarian control and refers to the militarism of Germany and Austria, of government without popular consent. The United States made war against autocratic governments, not against the people of these nations.

_____

_____

_____

7. *Four-Minute Men*   The propagandists hired by George Creel, head of the Committee on Public Information, to make thousands of speeches to the public in support of the war effort. A brief four-minute speech in a theater is an example.

_____

_____

_____

8. *"liberty cabbage"*   The process of renaming items that had a German name. Thus German measles became "liberty measles" and sauerkraut became "liberty cabbage."

_____

_____

_____

9. *self-determination*   The term used by Wilson to indicate that all people with separate languages and cultures have the right to their own government. This concept was applied in Eastern and Southern Europe after the war, but not in colonial areas.

_____

_____

_____

10. *general association of nations*   Wilson's belief that a government body made up of representatives of all nations of the world could settle conflicts among nations and avoid wars. The League of Nations was an outgrowth of this concept.

_____

_____

_____

ANSWERS

Correct sequence of events and their dates.

1. 10; July 1914
2. 8; August 1914
3. 7; May 1915
4. 1; May 1916
5. 9; January 1917
6. 2; March 1917
7. 4; April 1917
8. 12; May 1917
9. 11; November 1917
10. 5; May 1918
11. 3; November 1918
12. 6; March 1920

PART II
Developing Thinking Skills

SKILL EXERCISE ONE: FACT, INFERENCE, OR OPINION

Under each of the following statements, write whether it is a fact, an inference, or an opinion. Explain your choices and check them with those suggested.

1. The Germans had every right to sink the *Lusitania* since it was carrying small-arms ammunition.

   _____

   _____

2. The French channel steamer, *Sussex,* was sunk by a German submarine in March 1916.

   _____

   _____

3. After Wilson's protest of the *Sussex* incident, the Germans promised to stop sinking passenger and merchant ships without warning.

   _____

   _____

4. The Germans were brutal and immoral, while the British were fair and considerate in the Great War.

   _____

   _____

5. Wilson's "strict accountability" doctrine toward German submarine warfare was unfair, considering the British mines in the North Sea that prevented trade with Germany.

   _____

   _____

6. The fatal move that cost the Germans the war was the decision for unrestricted submarine warfare against all vessels heading for allied ports.

   _____

   _____

7. If German submarines surfaced to inspect cargoes and if they allowed crews to seek safety, they could be easily rammed or blown up by the deck guns of the merchant ship.

   _____

   _____

8. Wilson should have ordered American ships into the North Sea to be blown up by British mines and then held the British "strictly accountable."

   _____

   _____

9. The British defined contraband as anything helpful to the enemy, including food.

_____

_____

10. Secretary of State William Jennings Bryan disagreed with Wilson on the "strict accountability" issue and resigned from office in protest, which indicates that Wilson's approach was unfair.

_____

_____

ANSWERS AND EXPLANATIONS

1. Inference. A very small amount of ammunition was aboard, and the ship was primarily a passenger ship. The words "right to" makes this an inference.

2. Fact. The event is provable by use of resources.

3. Fact. Whether they kept the promise or not, the statement can be verified.

4. Opinion. Too many loaded words are used to make this a reasonable inference.

5. Inference. You may not agree, but the statement is a reasoned argument and not a fact.

6. Inference. This is not a fact since we can't prove this cost the Germans the war. Yet it is a reasonable contention that could be defended with data and arguments.

7. Fact. This is a factual-type statement even though it presents a hypothetical situation.

8. Opinion. One might have approached Wilson with this suggestion in order to reveal his bias for England, but the belief that he really should have "sent ships to be blown up" is not reasonable.

9. Fact. It may not have been "legal" or proper, but it is factual.

10. Inference. Bryan disagreed and resigned. Wilson probably was biased toward the British, but Bryan's resignation does not "prove" the bias.

SKILL EXERCISE II: EVALUATING ARGUMENTS

Examine the following arguments relating to the proposition that the United States should have entered the First World War in 1917 on the side of the Allied Nations. In each, determine the primary type of appeal used and classify it in one of the following categories: *Reason, Intuition, Anecdotal, Empirical,* or *Authority.* Consider how the writer is trying to convince the reader. Check your choices with those provided afterward.

1. Before the United States entered the war, a munitions plant was blown up in New Jersey, and German diplomats with American documents were found in the area.

_____

_____

2. Most historians consider German behavior in early 1917 to be antagonistic, belligerent, and provocative, offering Wilson ample justification for calling for war.

   _____

   _____

3. It seems that Wilson did everything he could to keep the United States out of the war and, of course, he always was a man of peace.

   _____

   _____

4. If the United States had not entered the war and supported the Allies, then the Germans, with Russia out of the war, might have overrun France and England and placed an autocratic system in Europe.

   _____

   _____

5. German submarines sank ships carrying civilian passengers without warning, encouraged the Mexicans to attack the United States if the United States declared war against Germany (Zimmerman note), and treated the Belgians harshly.

   _____

   _____

6. The president of the United States stated in his war message that, because of German behavior, he saw no alternative to a declaration of war.

   _____

   _____

7. The French channel steamer *Sussex* was sunk by a German submarine in 1916, without warning and with some loss of American life.

   _____

   _____

8. It seems that the Germans, by 1917, really didn't care if the United States entered the war or not.

   _____

   _____

9. Both the British and French had democratic governments, the French had helped the United States during the American Revolution, and the British shared a common language and culture with the United States.

   _____

   _____

10. By 1917, the United States had to enter the war on the side of the Allies, because if the Germans won, American bankers and corporations would not have received payments of their loans and for the food and other goods delivered to the Allies.

_____

_____

ANSWERS AND EXPLANATIONS

1. Anecdotal. These two incidents are of a circumstantial nature—anecdotes.

2. Authority. The appeal here is to the historians as authorities on the developments of the period.

3. Intuition. No evidence is offered, nor is it an appeal to reason or authority. The statement is the writer's impression.

4. Reason. "If" is a key word here to classify this as an appeal to logic.

5. Empirical. Here three facts are offered as evidence to support the thesis. They may not be sufficient to bring a declaration of war, but the attempt is to supply convincing evidence.

6. Authority. The appeal in this argument is to the person in command, who as president is expected to know.

7. Anecdotal. This is a description of one incident and thus primarily anecdotal.

8. Intuition. The statement is a feeling or impression that may be based on some evidence, but no evidence is given.

9. Empirical. This is a presentation of factual evidence in favor of American entry into the war on the side of the Allies.

10. Reason. Although some empirical evidence is given here—the loans and sales, the main thrust is reasoning. The words "because" and "if" indicate reason.

A Skill Activity

In the space below, write five statements about the United States's entry into the First World War, illustrating each category of argument.

_____

_____

_____

_____

_____

_____

_____

_____

_____

PART III
Debating Historical, Social, and Moral Issues

QUESTIONS FOR THOUGHT

1. President Wilson criticized Theodore Roosevelt for "gunboat diplomacy" and objected to William Taft's "dollar diplomacy." He expected nations to discuss problems and solve them peacefully without resorting to violence. He appealed to law and morality. His secretary of state, William Jennings Bryan, went even further and leaned toward pacifism. Christian principles must prevail over self-interest. Is it reasonable to expect that moral principles will be employed in the conduct of foreign policy? Is a nation stronger if it employs moral principles or is it in a weaker position because of the ruthless and immoral approach of other nations? Explain.

_____

_____

_____

_____

_____

2. Twenty-four million young men registered for the draft, three million were inducted through the draft, and two million volunteered (many because of the threat of being drafted) in 1917 and 1918. Some argue that if a war is necessary and "worthwhile," young men should be eager to volunteer to fight for the righteous cause. Is conscription, a forced draft of citizens for military service, an affront to democracy and should it be unnecessary? Explain.

_____

_____

_____

_____

_____

3. Many history books have been written about the reasons America entered into the First World War. Examine carefully the following factors arranged in random order. Consult a textbook or other history book for more information about each. Then rank them in order of importance.

   A. American loans of billions of dollars to the Allies, along with extensive and profitable trade with them, compared to meager loans and trade with the Central Powers.
   B. The exposure of the Zimmerman note, which encouraged Mexico to attack the United States if the United States went to war with Germany (with the promise of land in the Southwest as a reward).
   C. The unrestricted submarine warfare conducted by Germany in the Atlantic.

D. The propaganda images, especially promoted by the British, of the auto-cratic, militaristic, brutal "Hun" of Germany, and the consequent threat to the United States and to free people everywhere.

E. The pro-British leanings of President Wilson and the English background of American leaders in all areas of life.

F. A desire by Wilson to end the bloody war, to spread democracy throughout the world, and to establish a world organization to prevent future conflicts.

G. A drift into war, an inertia or lack of effort to try to avoid war, a mind-set leaning toward considering war as inevitable.

H. Fear of saboteurs and a concern about the security of the United States should England and France fall to Germany.

Student ranking:

_____

Explain why you considered the first two so important.

_____

_____

_____

Explain why you ranked the last one as least important.

_____

_____

What other factors may have influenced President Wilson, Congress, and the American people to bring them to the point of entering the war?

_____

_____

_____

Do you consider the "hard" reasons (A, B, C, H) more important than the "soft" reasons (D, E, F, G)? Why or why not?

_____

_____

_____

Speculate as to what sort of evidence the historian should compile in order to support or refute these factors. Would any compilation of evidence be convincing to a group of intelligent people from a variety of backgrounds—German, British, French, Soviet, American? Why or why not?

_____

_____

4. Historians are reluctant to state lessons from history and to defend their validity. The problem is that they deal so much with special exceptions and see the uniqueness of each event; it becomes difficult to establish repetitious patterns

that yield advice on how to act, or what to avoid, or when a certain step will be successful in contemporary times. An effort to draw three lessons from the First World War follows. React to each lesson—is it valid, is it significant, will it apply as an insight into future choices?

A. Military predictions and expectations are highly uncertain and often the plans fail when put into practice. Usually an unforeseen development intervenes to thwart carefully laid plans: German plans to defeat France first failed due to the unexpected resistance of Belgium; the German expectation that submarine warfare would starve out the British was thwarted by the convoy system.

_____

_____

_____

B. A major nation finds it difficult not to take sides and becomes involved in a war with other major powers no matter how earnestly it attempts to remain neutral: the United States gradually drifted to the side of England and into the war.

_____

_____

_____

C. A patriotic war effort soon permeates society so that, even in a democratic society, those who oppose the war or have some connection with the enemy are discriminated against and have their freedoms reduced: the mistreatment of conscientious objectors and anti-German feeling in the United States in 1917 and 1918.

_____

_____

_____

5. Wilson's foreign-policy pattern was to take a stance usually on moralistic grounds, and then to challenge the opponent to "step over the line." He did this in the controversy with Mexico and again on the submarine issue. At one point he admitted that a single submarine commander could bring the United States into the war. Is this an ineffective and dangerous manner of conducting foreign policy? Had Wilson, by 1917, lost control of his own foreign affairs? Explain.

6. In 1916, Wilson's campaign used the slogan "He kept us out of war." In 1940, President Franklin Roosevelt explained to the American people that he did not intend to get us into the war in Europe. In 1964, President Lyndon Johnson said he "would not send American boys to fight in Vietnam." Is this a pattern of deceit by governments and leaders or an argument that the "forces of history" are stronger than the honest intent of a nation and its leader?

_____

_____

_____

_____

_____

7. In the case *Schenck* v. *the United States,* the Supreme Court in 1919 supported the Sedition Act of 1918. Justice Oliver Wendell Holmes, Jr., argued that certain actions and statements that were acceptable in normal times might in wartime present a "clear and present danger" of sedition. Charles Schenck had circulated 15,000 pamphlets against the war and against the draft and was prosecuted under the act. Do you agree with Holmes? Why or why not?

_____

_____

_____

_____

_____

8. Article X of the League of Nations Covenant pledged member nations to "preserve against external aggression the territorial integrity and . . . political independence of all members." Senator Henry Cabot Lodge and several other Republicans objected that this clause would commit the United States to war without going through the constitutional procedures for declaring war. Wilson argued that it was only a "moral obligation." Would you have voted for the League Covenant with Article X unchanged? Explain.

_____

_____

_____

_____

_____

9. Historians debate the motives for the entry of the United States into the war. Consider the following:

   A. Historians writing shortly after the war and in the 1930s charge Wilson with pro-British prejudices. They conclude that loans, trade, and especially that British propaganda went unchallenged shows this bias. The submarine incidents were really only an excuse. There was some public opinion pressure; however, Wilson did not keep faith with the voters and brought the United States into the war unnecessarily.

B. A later interpretation argues that Wilson did not want war. He was pressured by Germany and made an effort to protect the rights of a neutral nation. Germany misbehaved and Wilson merely responded to that country's action, albeit with lofty idealistic and legal principles.

C. A more recent interpretation is that Wilson was supporting capitalism and its need for free trade. He did want a League of Nations, international stability, and the rule of law, but this was motivated primarily by trade benefits and an expansion of capitalism. His intervention in the war aimed at destroying imperialism and communism, which would enhance the capitalist ability to trade freely. Wilson's real motives were economic and his actions reflect an ultimate goal of an "open door" policy worldwide.

Which of these three views do you agree with most? Why?

_____

_____

_____

How does one separate "ultimate goals" like economic gain from those stated as immediate goals—to end the war and create a concert of nations? Might it now also be argued that the ultimate goal was a peaceful and law-abiding national arrangement and that an end to imperialism and communism is a step to *that* goal? Explain.

_____

_____

_____

_____

_____

10. Consider the quotations at the beginning of the chapter. Explain their meanings and implications and determine whether you agree or disagree with them. How might each quote apply to this period of history?

_____

_____

_____

_____

_____

THOUGHTS FOR QUESTIONS

1. Perhaps nations do not really make the effort to discuss issues rather than fight. They seemed quick to go to war in 1914 when negotiation and calm discussion may

have made it possible to avoid war. History is filled with failures at talking and with premature decisions to fight. War is endemic to history and has entered the popular mind as an inevitability. If we look carefully at history, we might find that many times violence has been avoided by discussion and negotiation. But the avoidance of war when it seemed to be inevitable has not been studied as thoroughly as breakdowns in negotiations and subsequent wars. To what extent is the belief in the inevitability of war a self-fulfilling prophecy? Sometimes the morally proper course of action is confusing—a choice between several evils. Also, a leader behaving so as to follow high principles may prove to be detrimental to the national interest. In this period, secret treaties and spying were frowned on by the American State Department. Are these activities morally acceptable? How does a leader get all nations to act in a responsible manner at the same time? Does one behave in an upright manner even at some risk to the national interest? Is diplomatic activity *amoral?*

2. One would think that if war is justified and necessary for a nation, then its citizens would rise up in support. It is true of most wars that a euphoria at the beginning translates into a rush of volunteers. But, later, a draft forces participation, and many of those who volunteer do so to avoid the draft. Is it too idealistic to assume that enough young men will volunteer if the cause is just? Nearly every war in modern times has required conscription or the use of mercenaries.

3. Items A and E seem the most important and item H the least important. The combination of an administration's sympathy backed by support from financial interests is a potent challenge to neutrality. The mind and the pocketbook are both affected in this case.

The economic factors may have been more diverse than just loans and trade. Europe was the most important trading area in the world. Placing this under the control of Germany, which had been opposed to free trade, may have been a concern. Are personality factors in the character makeup of President Wilson—an idealistic, self-righteous puritan facing a world that seems chaotic—important to consider?

In most cases the "hard" reasons are easier to document than the "soft" reasons. The Zimmerman note actually existed, we have statistics on loans and trade, and the submarine attacks are well-documented. But how does a researcher factor in an equation Wilson's attitude or the actual impact of negative images of the Germans or inertia?

The following can be used for evidence: newspaper editorials, diaries and journals of leaders, letters, confidential memos between government departments (telephones were not widely used yet), banking reports, diplomatic correspondence, trade statistics—perhaps a lifetime of research.

4. A. The plan that went wrong is a recurring theme in military history, and all historians can cite many examples. Of course, these often get the attention. Plans that run smoothly go by unnoticed as if they are normal and almost arbitrary. The British mining of the North Sea, with only a mild protest from the United States, worked. The convoy system, initially opposed by naval leadership in England, transported millions of troops safely to Europe. The key word here is "often." The lesson is that one really should be cautious because "often" plans do *not* work out.

B. Certainly the United States serves as an example here in both world wars. Other nations did not become involved in the Civil War, but that was internal. The Spanish-American war involved only two nations, but that war was very brief. Other nations were not drawn directly into the Vietnam War. France was brought into the

American Revolution and the United States entered the Napoleonic Wars, but did not fight on the continent of Europe.

C. This may be so accurate as to make it obvious, and perhaps insignificant. In World War II the Japanese-Americans were placed in concentration camps. Even the unpopular Vietnam War induced some mistreatment of dissenters. British Parliament members spoke out in opposition to that government's policy toward rivals during the American Revolution. But there are probably few other exceptions to this generalization.

5. A prudent foreign policy keeps several options open. However, in this case the opposition did not know how the United States might behave and, therefore, the president took chances. President Kennedy let it be known that the United States would not tolerate the Soviet missiles in Cuba. An uncertain stand might have had different consequences. If Wilson had equivocated, the Germans would have launched unrestricted submarine warfare. Of course they did just that anyway. But Wilson did seem to put himself into a corner. When the U-boat crisis came in 1917, he had little alternative but to ask Congress for a declaration of war. It seems prudent to always have alternatives short of war; the reasons for war may dissolve before the first step is taken.

6. In fairness to Wilson, he never openly promised not to bring the United States into the war, and he was personally disturbed by the slogan. The attack on Pearl Harbor brought us into World War II. In Johnson's case, it was a campaign promise broken six months later. In each case the candidates during the campaign were less than candid. And several other events transpired between the election and the entry into the war. A majority of the people followed (or led) Wilson in the direction of war, although they were divided with several large and significant groups still in opposition to war in 1917. Germany changed its policy in February 1917; Wilson responded to this.

7. Students should note that the very vague wording of the Sedition Act allows for broad interpretations. No one was allowed to "utter . . . any disloyal . . . language about the government . . ." This gives wide leeway to enforcement and many government officers took liberties with the law. Holmes said no one was allowed to yell "fire" in a crowded theater, but is distributing pamphlets against the war to a nation of patriotic citizens the equivalent of yelling "fire"?

8. The government of any nation that does not want to go to war on behalf of another will certainly not be forced to participate on the basis of a provision in a covenant of nations. Furthermore, the League was never able to require nations to take military action on behalf of other nations (that was one of the League's weaknesses). Ironically, it was the United States that, in the United Nations in 1950, sought the assistance of other nations to help out in Korea. Perhaps a dozen actually did. Yet the United States has been faithful to most of its treaties, with the notable exception of those treaties with the Native Americans. Also, with the territorial settlements arranged at Versailles, it was likely that there would be future squabbles over boundaries. One could well argue that American international behavior would not have changed developments in Europe whether or not the reservations about the Covenant were included.

9. To Wilson the misbehavior of Germany was a serious problem. If he was biased, it was a bias based on what he considered to be concrete action by Germany. The United States has always pursued an international situation open to trade and in-

vestment. Perhaps the words of Wilson, an honorable man who tried to speak the truth as he saw it, should be accepted. If his attitude reflects unfairness on his part, it was an unconscious discrimination. The Allied powers were fighting a just war. Germany was wrong. The submarine warfare proved the flawed characters of Germany's leaders. The United States had no alternative but to go to war on the side of the Allies. This was the reasoning of Wilson. One might conclude that he was wrong, but the evidence seems to indicate that he was clear about his motives and goals.

10. The events and decisions surrounding the First World War, especially as they are explained in the previous question, indicate the clouded issues and uncertainty as to what actually took place. We cannot observe firsthand and even if we could, we might not see everything clearly. Wilson moved dimly behind the scenes. Catton's "mist" rose over Europe and the United States. We guess and we search for "indicators," but we come only to temporary solutions that often create still more problems.

The novelist has a freedom that the historian does not have. The historian is bound to follow the data as it is uncovered. As Aristotle wrote, the spirit of the times can be captured and related better by the novelist or the artist. But historians might ask, are the fiction accounts and drawings accurate? How much does the novelist know? What is sacrificed for the artist's style and liberty to follow aesthetics instead of truth? The artist captures a personal truth. The historian seeks, as much as possible, an objective truth that can be confirmed by other historians.

Map Exercise Two

The first map identifies many of the locations that have become important to the United States in the past century. Students should know at least these locations in order to understand United States history.

A list of some of the locations from Map 2A, along with their historical importance, follows. Study the map and then practice placing the locations on Map 2B. The list is in random order.

1. *Nicaragua*   A Central American nation, often occupied by American troops in the early twentieth century. In the 1980s this nation has been in economic and diplomatic conflict with the United States.

2. *Philippines*   An island-nation annexed by the United States in 1899 and given its independence in 1946. The Japanese took possession of the Philippines from the United States in 1942 until 1945.

3. *South Africa*   An area settled by the Dutch in the seventeenth century. In the twentieth century, the struggle for racial equality and political rights by black Africans has caused turmoil and has placed the United States in a diplomatic quandary.

4. *Persian Gulf*   The body of water at the heart of the richest oil deposits in the world. Bordered by Iran, Iraq, Saudi Arabia, and Kuwait, it is considered vital to American interests.

5. *Korea*   A peninsular nation and site of the war, or "police action," that lasted from 1950 to 1953. The war resulted in the division of Korea at the thirty-eighth parallel with a Communist North and a non-Communist South.

6. *San Francisco*   A city bordering a large harbor on the Pacific Ocean that became the main center for trade with East Asia. It was taken from Mexico during the Mexican War (1846–48).

7. *Cuba*   Intertwined with United States history—the United States freed Cuba from Spain in 1898 and then supported an abortive invasion of Cuba in 1961. The crisis over Soviet missiles in Cuba occurred in 1962.

8. *Hiroshima*   A city in central Japan on which the United States dropped the first atomic bomb on August 6, 1945.

9. *Iran*   Oil-rich Moslem nation in the Middle East that, since the overthrow of the Shah in the 1970s, has been anti-American.

10. *Panama*   A small nation in Central American that contains the canal connecting the Caribbean Sea and the Pacific Ocean. The United States supported Panama's separation from Colombia in 1902 and built the canal over the next ten years.

11. *British Isles*   The source of a large number of American immigrants and an American ally in World War I and World War II—England, Wales, Scotland, and Ireland.

12. *Guadalcanal*   An island in the Solomon group on which the Japanese were stopped in their efforts to expand toward Australia in 1942.

13. *France*   An ally of the United States in both World War I and World War II, as well as during the American Revolution. France is a member of the NATO alliance system in Europe.

14. *Egypt*   A North African nation that controls the Suez Canal and has been friendly with the United States and with the USSR. It was the first Moslem nation to offer diplomatic recognition to Israel.

15. *Bikini*   The test site in the Pacific for the hydrogen bombs in the 1950s. Tests were conducted in the atmosphere and yielded large amounts of radioactive fallout.

16. *Pearl Harbor*   The American naval base in the Pacific that was attacked by surprise by the Japanese on December 7, 1941. This brought the United States into the Second World War.

17. *Mexico City*   A city captured by the United States in the Mexican War (1848). This ended the war and yielded the United States land in the Southwest, including California.

18. *Alaska*   The forty-ninth state, purchased by the United States from Russia in 1867. Although a bargain, it was considered a foolish waste of money at the time.

19. *Germany*   The source of a large number of American immigrants. An enemy of the United States in both world wars, it later became an ally in the NATO alliance.

20. *Spain*   This country fought against the United States in 1898 and lost the war, surrendering control over Cuba, Puerto Rico, and the Philippines.

21. *Iwo Jima*   An island south of Japan and the site of a bloody battle between American marines and Japanese defenders in 1945.

22. *Vietnam*   The Southeast Asian nation in which American military forces supported the south in a war against the Communist North from 1965 to 1973. The North eventually won control over all of Vietnam.

23. *Moscow*   The capital of the USSR and nuclear rival of the United States. It was an ally of the United States in World War II and site of a heroic resistance to the German advance into Russia.

24. *Manchuria*   An area in northern China occupied by Japan in 1931 over the protests of the United States. It also was the launching area for Chinese troops who fought against the United Nations forces in the Korean War.

25. *Italy*   The source of many immigrants to the United States. Attacked by the United States in World War II in 1943, it was the birthplace of Christopher Columbus.

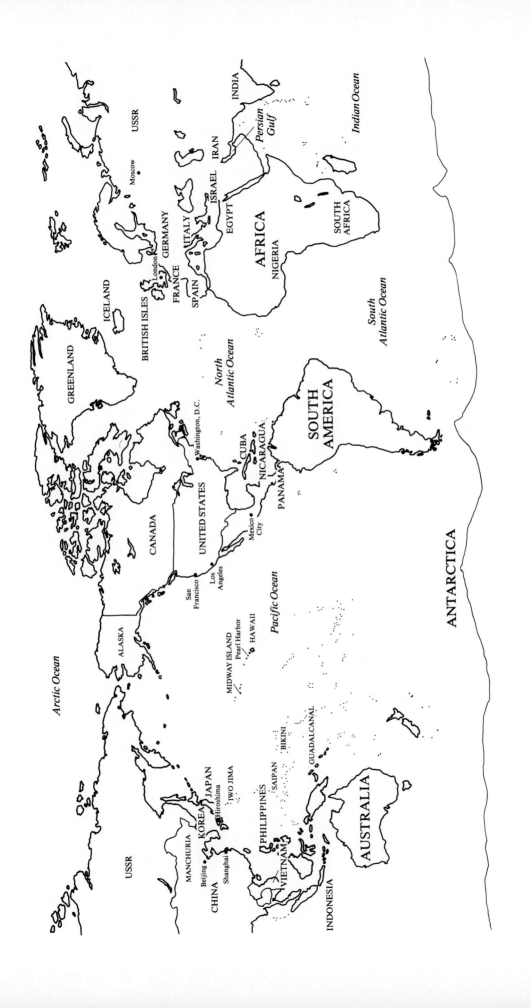

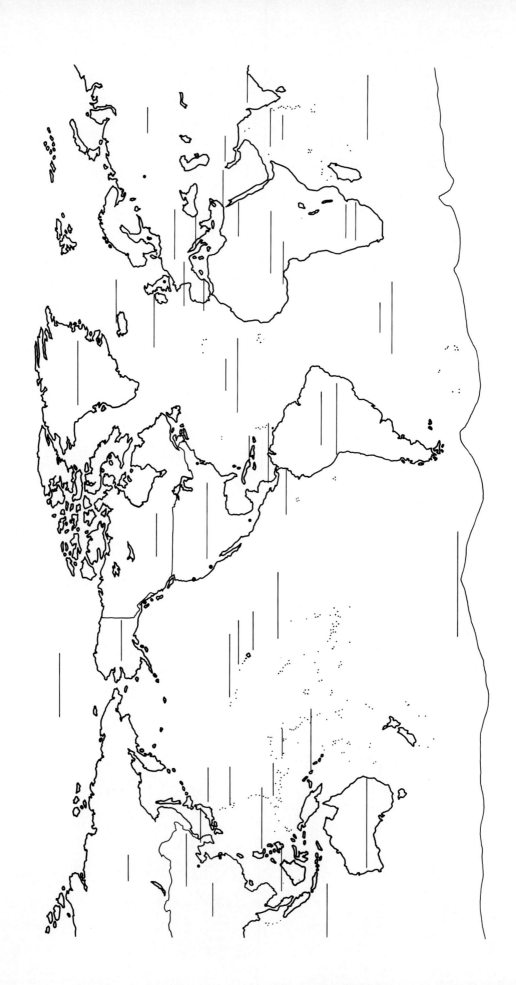

CHAPTER

15

THE TWENTIES: YEARS OF RAPID CHANGE

"The real history does not get written, because it is not in people's brains, but in their nerves and vitals."

Alfred North Whitehead

"Myths are often more potent than facts in the making of history."

Thomas Bailey

PART I
Acquiring Essential Data

ESSENTIAL DATES

Determine the correct sequence and write the approximate date for each of the following events.

1. The National Origins Act is passed, restricting immigration on the percentage basis of the population's national origins. _____

2. Beginning of the Harlem Renaissance of black literature and music _____

3. Publication of *The Sun Also Rises* by Ernest Hemingway _____

4. Charles Lindbergh flies solo and nonstop across the Atlantic to Paris, France. _____

5. Al Jolson stars in *The Jazz Singer,* the first talking motion picture. _____

6. Henry Ford begins using the moving assembly line and interchangeable parts for automobile production. _____

7. A radio station in Pittsburgh begins the first commercial broadcast. _____

8. The Eighteenth Amendment establishing prohibition is ratified. _____

9. Marcus Garvey founds the Universal Negro Improvement Association. _____

10. The Wright brothers make the first heavier-than-air flight from Kitty Hawk, North Carolina. _____

ESSENTIAL CONCEPTS

Examine each concept and write what contemporary relevance it might have.

1. *"trickle down"*   The theory that if government expenditures or private income are infused at the top to corporations or the wealthy, then as they spend the money, it will eventually reach the middle and lower classes.

_____

_____

_____

2. *Lost Generation*   The name used for writers and artists of the 1920s who felt a sense of alienation from the values of their society and were in despair at the horror of the First World War.

_____

_____

_____

3. *Nordics*   The word used to describe a "superior class" of whites who immigrated from the British Isles and Northern Europe and who must be preserved from intermarriage with "inferiors."

_____

_____

_____

4. *the unconscious*   The thoughts, impulses, and drives of which the individual is unaware, but that influence his or her behavior. Sigmund Freud related many of these impulses to sex.

_____

_____

_____

5. *installment buying*   The purchase of items with an amount paid down, followed by a series of subsequent payments made usually on a monthly basis.

_____

_____

_____

6. *anti-scientism*   An opposition to truth discovered through science and a reliance on revelation or common sense as superior to science as a method of obtaining truth.

_____

_____

_____

7. *invisible poor*   Poor people such as farm workers and marginal farmers who are hidden from public view and awareness in shacks and cabins on back roads.

_____

_____

_____

8. *image ads*   Advertisements that do not merely extol the virtues of a product, but associate the product with a positive image or an attractive personality.

_____

_____

_____

9. *Harlem Renaissance*   The revival of black culture in the arts and music in New York City in the 1920s.

_____

_____

_____

10. *buying on margin*   The purchase of stocks by paying only a small part of the price and borrowing the remainder from a broker or bank. The margin was usually 10 percent.

_____

_____

_____

ANSWERS

Correct sequence of events and their dates.

1. 10; 1903
2.   6; 1911
3.   9; 1914
4.   8; 1919
5.   2; 1920

6. 7; 1920
7. 1; 1924
8. 3; 1926
9. 4; 1927
10. 5; 1927

PART II
Developing Thinking Skills

SKILL EXERCISE ONE: CATEGORIZING AND CLASSIFYING

Assume you are investigating the 1920s. Items of information related to this topic follow. In the space below each item, write in the appropriate category—*political, economic, social, diplomatic,* or *cultural.* Check your selection with those suggested. Remember, select the *primary* category into which the statement fits.

1. In some areas the prohibition law was vigorously enforced, but in other areas drinking was "winked at" and ignored.

_____

_____

2. The government, to an unprecedented degree, cooperated with, supported, and favored the business community in the 1920s through tax benefits and encouragement of trade associations, and by suppression of those who opposed or wanted to limit capitalism.

_____

_____

3. The Red Scare offered the image of a fanatical, bearded foreigner who sought to violently overthrow the capitalist system and to force a repressive Communist structure on America.

_____

_____

4. Fundamentalists supported prohibition, opposed the teaching of evolution, and, especially in the South, many of them joined or condoned the views expressed by the Ku Klux Klan.

_____

_____

5. Writers of the 1920s—T. S. Eliot, Ernest Hemingway, William Faulkner—wrote poems and novels protesting and expressing alienation toward traditional American values and society.

_____

_____

6. President Calvin Coolidge felt that a factory builder was a temple builder and espoused the belief that material success was the mark of a superior person who deserved special praise and consideration.

_____

_____

7. The 1920s was a period of hero worship with widespread publicity for and even adulation of Babe Ruth, Charles Lindbergh, Henry Ford, Rudolph Valentino, and Jack Dempsey.

_____

_____

8. On New Year's Day in 1920, Attorney General A. Mitchell Palmer had six thousand people rounded up and imprisoned as dangerous radicals, even though none were charged with any crimes and many were innocent bystanders.

_____

_____

9. The Jazz Age youth were cynical about reform, chose to live for the present, and praised self-expression without much inhibition.

_____

_____

10. There was much catalogue (Sears Roebuck and Montgomery Ward) as well as installment buying in the 1920s.

_____

_____

ANSWERS AND EXPLANATIONS

1. Political. The emphasis here is on government enforcement, although certainly the issue of prohibition is also social and cultural.

2. Economic. Did you choose political? It is debatable, but one could argue that the relationship affected business more than government. A good case also could be made for *political.*

3. Political. Both the focus of the threat and the character image are political.

4. Social. Even though government was involved in prohibition and teaching, this religious persuasion operated primarily in the social arena.

5. Cultural. Although the subject of their writings was mostly social, literature is a cultural aspect of society.

6. Cultural. Of course Coolidge was a politician and his remarks were about economics, but his attitude reflects the culture of the time.

7. Cultural. This was an expression of the culture even though the heroes came from various walks of life.

8. Political. This also reflects a social attitude.

9. Cultural. This category leaves little room for doubt.

10. Economics. This was a social phenomenon as well, but the primary impact was economic.

SKILL EXERCISE TWO: QUESTIONING

Assume that you are interviewing several elderly people who were born between 1905 and 1910. You are attempting to discover what life was like in the 1920s. Determine if the following questions are *productive* or *nonproductive* and write your choice under each.

1. What was the month and day of your birth?

   _____

2. What memories do you have of popular writings of the times in newspapers and magazines?

   _____

3. Who were your heroes of the 1920s, and why did you consider them heroes?

   _____

4. What were your religious practices and beliefs in the 1920s?

   _____

5. Did you approve of Babe Ruth's $60,000 salary in 1927?

   _____

6. What was your reaction to and evaluation of the presidents of the 1920s—Warren G. Harding, Calvin Coolidge, and Herbert Hoover?

   _____

7. In what ways did you participate in, observe, or talk about some of the controversies of the 1920s—prohibition, the debate over evolution (Scopes trial), and the Ku Klux Klan?

_____

8. What things did you or your family order by catalogue or buy on credit in the 1920s?

_____

9. Did you ever get in trouble when you were young?

_____

10. What were some of your travel experiences in the 1920s—transportation by automobile or train, places visited, overnight lodging?

_____

What two productive questions would you ask about the 1920s?

11. _____

_____

12. _____

_____

ANSWERS AND EXPLANATIONS

1. Nonproductive. Unless you need the exact date or just want each of the participants to feel comfortable, the date is not essential.

2. Productive. This question might generate not only the types of literature being read then, but with the word "memories" it might elicit information about particular articles or impressions.

3. Productive. Asking someone to describe rather than just to name draws out more information.

4. Productive. However, these may be mixed up with later beliefs—more so than other more specific items.

5. Nonproductive. This is more likely to reflect attitudes to high salaries of current sports stars. It does not give much insight into life in the 1920s.

6. Productive. The presidents must be named to stimulate memories.

7. Productive. Perhaps this should be more than one question, but grouping controversies together may draw out overall attitudes in the 1920s.

8. Productive. The list of items would be important. This question might well be followed by one related to values about borrowing, frugality, and shopping.

9. Nonproductive. The answers might be interesting, but may not be related specifically to life in the 1920s. Everyone, in every decade, has disobeyed parents or pulled off pranks—often similar ones from decade to decade.

10. Productive. Much information about life in the 1920s should emerge from this question, especially about the impact of the automobile.

Students might find it interesting to actually interview a person who lived through the 1920s, a person who was old enough at that time to be aware, a great-grandparent or a friend in the community. Many people are "living sources" of information that take the history student beyond the textbook and sometimes into unchartered territory.

Is the person being interviewed likely to reflect his or her present attitudes rather than to remember attitudes felt in the 1920s? Explain. If so, are there any ways to overcome this?

Would the use of artifacts help—old magazines or physical objects out of the twenties? Give some suggestions of artifacts that might be useful.

PART III
Debating Historical, Social, and Moral Issues

QUESTIONS FOR THOUGHT

1. Change and continuity are difficult to perceive in the interpretation of history. The 1920s were especially a time when both change and continuity occurred. Examine three of the ways historians have interpreted the 1920s.

    A. The First World War impacted society, upsetting traditional values and changing the behavior and outlook of millions of Americans. Youth rebellion, loose sexual mores, and a rejection of the progressive optimism about reform—all of these features illustrate the changed outlook of a fun-loving, jazz-oriented society. A new society was being born, one alien to the traditional social order. Struggling workers were turned into installment-buying consumers. This sudden upheaval marked the arrival of the modern age in America.

    B. The changes in the first quarter of the twentieth century developed over three decades and were gradual, not related to the First World War. Automobiles appeared and were in widespread use before 1920. The move to the city for jobs, along with the excitement and variety of new life-styles, began in the 1890s. Ragtime music appeared at the beginning of the century. The attack on traditional values was a year-by-year transition from 1900 to 1930. Continuity with gradual change characterizes the period.

    C. The 1920s did see change. But it was a change back to more traditional values; a conservative aura dominated the period. The outer surface of society revealed innovation—flappers, bathtub gin, new literature and music, an open moral code, and an eagerness for the new. But all of this was superficial. Most people were seeking stability and security. They listened to traditional tunes and to John Philip Sousa's band music. They read nineteenth-century novels or new westerns that depicted the triumph of traditional good over traditional evil. The Klan was revived, legislation appeared against evolution, and prohibition continued throughout the decade. Fundamentalism, a return to traditional religion, found many new adherents. The government withdrew from involvement in society. Racism and nativism continued unabated. The change in values was conservative, a turn to the nineteenth century, not a domination of new values.

Which of these views do you agree with most? Explain why.

_____

_____

_____

What types of evidence would you look for in order to make a strong case for one or the other of these views?

_____

_____

_____

View B implies that what we consider as major events (World War I in this case) really do not have very much impact on change, but that change is gradual over time. Do you agree? Why or why not? If this is true, then why do historians gravitate to wars and revolutions as focal points for change in society?

_____

_____

_____

2. The Ku Klux Klan was revived in the 1920s and claimed a membership of more than four million. The Klan was anti-black, and also anti-Jew, anti-Catholic, and anti-immigrant. A large group of Klan members marched down the streets of Washington in 1925. Should this prejudiced group, who has often attempted to intimidate voters, be allowed to march within sight of the dome of the nation's capitol? Why or why not? Should an organization that preaches racial supremacy and inequality be allowed to function as any other group in American society? Why or why not?

_____

_____

_____

_____

3. Prohibition resulted in less consumption of alcohol (by most estimates), fewer arrests for drunkenness, and a reduction in deaths through alcoholism. Countless people were not tempted to drink because it was against the law. President Hoover called it a "noble experiment." It probably saved many marriages and made others more pleasant. Should the prohibition law have been continued throughout the 1930s in order to give the experiment a real chance to succeed? Explain. What is the difference in prohibiting alcohol consumption and prohibiting the use of other drugs? Explain.

_____

_____

_____

_____

_____

4. In the 1921 and 1924 Immigration acts, severe limits were placed on immigration, quotas were established for each nation, Orientals were excluded, and favoritism was given to people from Northern Europe over those of Southern and Eastern Europe. Do you approve of these acts to limit immigration? Why or why not? What should be the limitations on immigration, if any? Explain.

_____

_____

_____

_____

_____

5. Marcus Garvey, a black leader of the 1920s, preached segregation and black racial pride. He wanted to organize blacks and encourage black nationalism. Garvey created the Universal Negro Improvement Association, which had five hundred thousand members by 1923. The organization exalted blackness and served as an avenue for cultural expression. Garvey even hoped for a Negro republic in Africa as an escape from a society that denied blacks dignity and opportunity. Do these ideas have merit? Were they a necessary and helpful stage in the development of equal rights for blacks? Explain.

_____

_____

_____

_____

_____

6. Of course, the automobile provided an efficient, fast, relatively cheap, and reliable means of transportation. However, the automobile affected many other aspects of American society. Use your imagination to make a list of all the influences—social, economic, and cultural—the automobile had on society in

the 1920s. For example, young men and women moved from courting on the porch swing to the seats of a Model T. Compare your list with the one provided.

_____

_____

_____

_____

_____

7. The controversy over evolution reached a high point (or low point) with the Scopes trial in 1925. William Jennings Bryan dueled with Clarence Darrow over the issue of creationism versus evolution. John Scopes, who had deliberately taught evolution in a public school in Tennessee, thus breaking a state law, was found guilty and fined. Was the state law forbidding the teaching of evolution in public schools constitutional? Should it have been obeyed by a science teacher who believed in evolution? Why or why not?

_____

_____

_____

_____

_____

8. The "trickle down" concept in economics maintains that if money is infused into the economy at the top—profits for corporations, government assistance for big-business expansion, and tax reduction for the wealthy—then those who benefit will spend the money, with most of it trickling down to the middle and lower classes. It is argued that this is preferable to assisting the lower classes at their level with government programs that would infuse money at the bottom. Do you agree with this theory? Why or why not?

_____

_____

_____

_____

9. The Red Scare was an attack on socialists, Communists, anarchists, and other groups that were considered un-American or a danger to American society. The government attacked and broke up lawful assemblies, jailed suspects without charges, and even shipped some aliens back to Europe. People greatly feared that an alien system might try to take over the United States government. Those who supported these actions argued that a government must protect itself from destruction and from potential enemies. Thomas Jefferson once said "Eternal vigilance is the price of liberty." But in his first inaugural address, he maintained that those who opposed the government and sought to change it should be left free to try. Jefferson had confidence that in a free society truth would

always win out over error. Do you agree with the proponents of the Red Scare or with Jefferson? Why?

_____

_____

_____

_____

_____

10. A study of magazine biographies of prominent people of the period from 1900 to 1920 reveals that the biographers chose scientists, political leaders, reformers, writers, professors, and other professionals as their subjects. A similar study of the 1920s indicates a flood of biographies of sports stars (Babe Ruth, Jack Dempsey, Jim Thorpe), movie stars (Charlie Chaplin, Mary Pickford), adventurers (Charles Lindbergh, Admiral Richard Byrd), and bank robbers. Analyze the meaning of these research results.

_____

_____

_____

_____

_____

11. Fundamentalism, the adherence to traditional Protestant doctrines and to the Bible as sources of truth, increased in influence in the 1920s. Fundamentalists supported rural values, opposed evolution, encouraged prohibition, supported limitations on immigration, and were suspicious of cities. Fundamentalists were pessimistic about secular reform and progress, believed in absolutes, had clearly defined moral values, and maintained that they had discovered the "Truth." Were these attitudes and beliefs in the mainstream of American tradition or were they in conflict with much of American traditional values? Explain.

_____

_____

_____

_____

_____

12. Consider carefully the two quotations at the beginning of the chapter. What does each mean? Do you agree or disagree with them? Explain.

_____

_____

_____

_____

_____

THOUGHTS FOR QUESTIONS

1. Perhaps the interpretation is a matter of emphasis. Can truth be found in all three? Change certainly took place in the 1920s. Some of these adjustments in life-style originated as far back as the 1890s. New, innovative patterns of behavior, several created or enhanced by new technology—radios, films, automobiles, and other more subtle changes, such as additional leisure time for the middle and lower classes, occurred. It is probably impossible to provide a convincing answer along the lines of any of the three views. Item A seems the best. Changes in values and toward a new life-style did speed up in the 1920s. They did not permeate all of society, but set the tone for ensuing decades.

Change is gradual over time. However, major events (World War I) that impact all of society for a period of time speed up some gradual tendencies and create opportunities for developments that otherwise might disappear. The First World War did encourage women to move into the work force and favored the increased power of unions. Maybe most historians notice the *speed* of historical change and examine the causes of acceleration rather than the slow process of almost undetectable alterations in society.

Is anecdotal evidence all that is really applicable to research on this question? Do we count the number of people listening to jazz and compare it to the number attending a Sousa concert? Are Sousa marches actually traditional? We have reached a time period in our study of history when witnesses to the decade still live. Interviews of people born between 1900 and 1915 could be helpful. An analytical study of letters, diaries, and other private writings of the time could be used to determine the mind-set and aura of the times.

Many historians attempt to observe and detect gradual changes in behavioral patterns of masses of people over time. They study child-rearing, family relationships, burial customs, and a myriad of other developments. Historians are suspicious of arguments that change is sudden and happens in a single decade. Yet in textbooks, lectures, and popular histories "crucial" events such as World War I are emphasized over long-range, gradual changes. Politicians, for example, judge every year to be a crisis year in which the course of a nation is set. The excitement of events often clouds minds from seeing underlying, subtle changes.

2. The freedom to speak, to assemble, and to march is part of a free society, even for those who do not accept or abide by other principles that are at the heart of the best in the American tradition. As long as there is no threat to overthrow the government by force or no anticipated move in the direction of violence, even those with attitudes and goals distasteful to a majority of Americans must retain these freedoms.

3. Prohibition lasted for thirteen years on a national scale and for a longer period at the state level. Government interference in the private lives of individual citizens is a serious issue. Should all Americans be required to diet, to cut back on consumption of salt and sugar, and to eat salads for lunch? Although total alcohol consumption dropped, what was consumed was often dangerous. Prohibition encouraged people to break the law and to condone illegal activities. Gangsters became rich and influential. Students must form personal opinions on this delicate and controversial issue of government control.

4. The renowned historian Arnold Toynbee considered this legislation a turning point in American history. It did alter a practice and attitude that had existed

throughout American history. Maybe immigration needed more control and an orderly approach. But this policy produced both ethnic and racial discrimination. Should immigration be ended, except for the reunion of families or refugees fleeing from political oppression? In this latter case, the number may be in the millions.

5. The ideas are similar to those of the "black power" movement of the 1960s and involve a positive approach to identifying and promoting the achievements of blacks and to explaining the depth and beauty of black culture. No doubt pride in culture is very necessary for self-confidence and self-identity—note the importance of the continuation of ethnic pride of many immigrant groups. The idea of a Negro republic in Africa established by black Americans is unrealistic both in regard to the Africans' receptivity and to the American black's willingness to resettle there. Problems may arise when a group withdraws from the mainstream of society, and yet intends to have a voice in the economic and political developments of the commonwealth.

6. Consider the following list: the automobile brought the construction of roads that required labor, right-of-ways, cement or macadam, and the accompanying machinery; the use of steel, oil, rubber, paint, glass, and textiles for its manufacture; the construction of new businesses along the roads, such as gas stations, restaurants, and motels; the passage of new laws regarding speed and traffic control; a new bureaucracy to handle car registration and court cases; a special insurance and credit system; a new sport; an increase in medical care and lawsuits; suburbia, shopping centers; more tourism; jobs and businesses such as mechanics and car dealerships; international problems regarding imported cars and oil sources; air pollution; and more.

7. Laws against the teaching of evolution have been judged unconstitutional by the Supreme Court. A teacher's right to teach what the teacher believes has not been explored in any depth by the courts. Teaching a religious viewpoint in public school seems questionable, but the term "religion" covers so many areas that it creates a maze of problems and unsolvable dilemmas. Certain principles must be taught, for instance those found in the Bill of Rights; specific behavior, like rules of orderly conduct in a classroom, can be taught. But controversial issues, states one current interpretation, should be presented in the form of "value clarification," with the teacher presenting all sides and allowing the student to reach personal decisions. Does the teaching of evolution fall into this latter category?

8. Those in the lower class are suspicious that not much "trickles down." Indirectly, in the form of jobs and in the overall expansion of the economy, a case could be made for this theory. But do profits go into the acquisition of more companies for the conglomerate or into increased dividends and salaries for the upper class? It is difficult to follow the course of funds infused at the top. But the government aid programs for those in need seem in many cases to impact directly on that need. The expenditure of these funds also places them in the economy to be circulated and recycled.

9. Once again, the actual threat to society must be considered. Voicing opposition to the system and even advocating its demise is currently not considered a threat. Collecting weapons and actively planning an attack on the government is a threat. The courts must decide about the gray area in-between. Jefferson was willing to take risks in the direction of freedom. A move in the direction of the Red Scare, or the McCarthyism of the 1950s, risks destruction of the freedom their advocates

intended to preserve. Do we have to restrict freedom in order to guarantee its preservation?

10. This is an interesting comparison. Heroes, or the absence of heroes, may indicate something about the values of an era. One must consider the magazine readership in the two periods. Were magazines containing biographies more of the "popular" variety in the 1920s, and did a higher literacy rate, combined with more leisure time for reading and attending sports events and films, result in a new and different audience?

11. Fundamentalists were both in the mainstream and in conflict with some traditional values—note the Puritans and the revival tradition in America. America was born on the wave of the Enlightenment, which promoted the concept of secular progress. The Constitution emerged as a negotiated document to be interpreted not by a system of absolutes, except perhaps in the Bill of Rights, but as a practical structure to promote progress. It could be amended. The Founding Fathers did not assume that they had arrived at a document of absolute "Truth." Under a system of toleration, American leaders assumed that disagreement would exist, especially in regard to moral values. The process of frequent elections, of court decisions, and of private choices on moral issues would achieve an acceptance of differences without the requirements of dogmatic conformity. Certainly the Christian outlook has had great influence on American society and on the attitudes and decisions of leaders. But this influence impacts the voters and the elected representatives and not the formal policy of government as Christian laws or Christian principles written in a constitution.

12. Whitehead implies that history records contain a vague reflection of reason, but that hidden behind this mental state is a deeper feeling that goes unrecorded. Speeches, programs, written position papers, and even laws may reflect only surface intentions. Emotions and attitudes must be deciphered in some other way. What is this other way? Assuming Whitehead is accurate, how does the historian dig into these inner recesses to discover the "nerves and vitals"? By studying actual behavior? By searching for anecdotes that reflect inner inclinations?

Bailey distinguishes between the understanding of history and the "making" of history. Facts should lead to an understanding of the past. However, when leaders act, they often do so with myths about the past uppermost in their minds. A recent president seemed to base policy decisions on anecdotes, some of them of questionable accuracy. For some reasons, myths tend to prevail over facts. Is this because myths represent the view of the past that most people would like to believe? Or have unscrupulous leaders promoted myths for self-serving motives? Or do myths contain a germ of truth, a truth much deeper than the compilation of relevant facts?

CHAPTER

16

A NEW DEAL IS MADE

"Imagination plays too important a role in the writing of history, and what is imagination but the projection of the author's personality."

Pieter Geyl

"History has become more important than ever because of the unprecedented ability of the historical sciences to take in man's life on earth as a whole."

Alfred Kazin

PART I
Acquiring Essential Data

ESSENTIAL DATES

Determine the correct sequence and write the approximate date for each of the following events.

1. The Congress of Industrial Organizations, a large conglomerate of unskilled workers, is formed. _____

2. The Works Progress Administration, a work-relief program to supply jobs for the unemployed, is established. _____

3. The Tennessee Valley Authority, the development of the Tennessee river valley with dams for electricity and flood control, is established. _____

4. The Federal Deposit Insurance Corporation is approved, providing insurance on bank accounts up to $10,000 (at that time). _____

5. The Hawley-Smoot Tariff Act raises rates to the highest level in history, which drastically curtails foreign trade. _____

6. The Agricultural Adjustment Act (AAA) is passed, giving aid to farmers. _____

7. Franklin Roosevelt is elected president of the United States. _____

8. The stock-market crash of October _____

9. The Social Security Act is passed into law. _____

10. The Reconstruction Finance Corporation is set up to loan government funds for business expansion. _____

11. President Roosevelt's efforts to pack the Supreme Court fail. _____

ESSENTIAL CONCEPTS

Examine each concept and write what contemporary relevance it might have.

1. *New Deal* The name given to Roosevelt's programs. Although eclectic and lacking overall guiding principles, the programs called for an active government that intervened in the economy for the common good.

_____

_____

_____

2. *"Hoover blanket"* Newspapers used to stuff into clothing as protection against the cold, symbolic of the conditions of the poor during Herbert Hoover's presidency.

_____

_____

_____

3. *business cycle* The belief that historically a free economy moves from times of growth and prosperity to brief periods of stagnation and economic depression, and that this is a natural process.

_____

_____

_____

4. *socialist* A political group that calls for government and/or worker ownership of the means for production and distribution of goods. A variety of specific, often conflicting, socialist programs exist.

_____

_____

_____

5. *"fireside chat"* Roosevelt's process of communication to the American people. It consisted of speaking over the radio in an informal manner while supposedly seated near a fireplace.

_____

_____

_____

6. *Civilian Conservation Corps* A New Deal program that employed young men to engage in useful work as a group. Usually the work involved conserving natural resources; part of their pay was sent to their parents.

_____

_____

_____

7. *parity* The establishment of a model year or group of years that serves as the criteria for determining a reasonable price for goods at a future time. It is used most often in relation to farm prices.

_____

_____

_____

8. *deficit spending* The economic theory associated with the economist John Maynard Keynes that encouraged the government to stimulate the economy even if this created budget deficits. Economic growth would produce additional revenues through taxes.

_____

_____

_____

9. *"rugged individualism"* The principle of President Herbert Hoover and others encouraging a system that would give opportunities to individuals to excel, and demanding that people take care of themselves without government support.

_____

_____

_____

10. *work relief* The system at the heart of the New Deal. It maintained that although citizens had a right to receive help from their government, they also had an obligation to work in order to obtain these benefits.

_____

_____

_____

ANSWERS

Correct sequence of events and their dates.

1. 8; 1929
2. 5; 1930
3. 10; 1932
4. 7; 1932
5. 3; 1933
6. 4; 1933

7. 6; 1933
8. 9; 1935
9. 2; 1935
10. 11; 1937
11. 1; 1938

PART II
Developing Thinking Skills

SKILL EXERCISE ONE: DETERMINING RELEVANCE OF EVIDENCE

Examine carefully the following statements of data related to the given topic. Under each indicate whether the data is relevant or irrelevant to the topic. Then briefly explain your decision and compare your choices with those offered.

TOPIC: AN EXAMINATION OF THE NEW DEAL RELIEF PROGRAMS—AID FOR THE UNEMPLOYED AND NEEDY—FROM 1933–39.

1. The Social Security program of 1935 collected money from workers and employers and began paying out benefits in 1940.

_____

_____

2. The workers under the Works Progress Administration built 12,888 playgrounds; fifty-nine hundred schools; and planted millions of trees.

_____

_____

3. Senator Huey Long of Louisiana considered Roosevelt too conservative and promoted a "Share Our Wealth" campaign to build schools, roads, and hospitals in his state.

_____

_____

4. The Supreme Court considered parts of the National Recovery Administration (NRA) program to set quality standards for business an interference in intrastate commerce.

_____

_____

5. Each week one hundred thousand people lost their jobs in 1931.

_____

_____

6. The Tennessee Valley Authority put people to work building dams and constructing recreational areas near the newly formed lakes.

_____

_____

7. The Works Progress Administration hired artists to paint murals, writers to write state histories, and actors to perform in traveling troupes.

_____

_____

8. The Federal Emergency Relief Administration spent $11 billion and the Public Works Administration spent $3.3 billion in the 1930s.

_____

_____

9. The Wealth Tax Act of 1935 placed a higher tax on incomes more than $50,000 and raised estate and gift taxes.

_____

_____

10. Dr. Francis Townsend called for old-age pensions of $200 a month for those sixty years old and older if they agreed not to work and to spend the full pension amount each month.

_____

_____

ANSWERS AND EXPLANATIONS

1. Irrelevant. This was not a relief measure, but an insurance arrangement that did not help anyone until 1940.

2. Relevant. These are statistics on work done by people employed by the government during the New Deal.

3. Relevant. Although not part of Roosevelt's New Deal, this was a relief effort on a state level.

4. Irrelevant. The decision was a blow to the New Deal, but aimed at the effort to control business, not relief.

5. Irrelevant. This created the *need* for relief, but the statement says nothing about programs for actual help.

6. Relevant. Employment and other benefits—cheap electric power, fertilizer, and flood control—were derived from this program.

7. Relevant. This directly relates to the topic—relief for persons not of the "working" class, and aesthetic benefits for millions.

8. Relevant. It is important to know the amounts spent for relief.

9. Irrelevant. Indirectly the tax may have resulted in slightly more federal income, but it was not directly related to relief.

10. Relevant. Even though the plan was not put into effect, it was a relief program offered in this time period and perhaps encouraged a social-security law.

SKILL EXERCISE TWO: ANALYZING QUANTIFIED DATA

Examine the following numbered statistical items and then react to the inferences drawn from each. State whether you *agree* or *disagree* with the inference, based on whether or not the inference is accurate or can be drawn from the statistics given.

1. In the 1932 election, nearly 40 million people voted. The Communist party received 103,000 votes, up from 49,000 in 1928, and the Socialist party received 882,000 votes, up from 267,000 in 1928. Roosevelt won 104 of the nation's 106 largest cities.
   Inferences:

   A. The 1932 election revealed a remarkable voter turn to the leftist radicals for a solution to the depression.

   _____

   B. Although gaining in votes, the Marxist political groups did not prove attractive to a large number of Americans despite the depths of the depression.

   _____

   C. The voting trend from 1928 to 1932 indicated an increasing interest in radical solutions to economic problems and probably foreshadowed a further leaning to the left unless economic conditions changed.

   _____

2. In 1929, 83 percent of corporate dividends went to the richest 5 percent of the population. The richest 5 percent received 33 percent of the nation's income,

and 1 percent of the population owned 59 percent of its wealth (property and money). Those with incomes more than $1 million numbered 513, more than in 1960.
Inferences:

A. American wealth and income was unevenly distributed in 1929.

_____

B. The wealth and income of Americans were unjustly distributed, with the rich receiving more than they deserved and the poor, as usual, left to divide the smaller leftover amount.

_____

C. There was greater inequity in wealth than in income and probably greater inequity in 1929 than in 1960.

_____

3. Roosevelt's 1937 budget deficit was less than Hoover's 1932 deficit. A 1937 poll indicated that four-fifths of the American people did not believe in deficit financing. In his 1932 campaign, Roosevelt promised to cut government expenditures by 25 percent.
Inferences:

A. In the 1930s opposition to creating budget deficits in an effort to end the depression was widespread.

_____

B. Roosevelt was not afraid to spend large sums in an effort to end the depression.

_____

C. Hoover was more willing than Roosevelt to spend government funds to end the depression.

_____

4. Shirley Temple made $300,000 in 1935, and Sally Rand danced in the 1933 Chicago World's Fair for $6,000 a week. From 1929 to 1932, the average weekly wage for an industrial worker dropped from $25 to $17. The New York Welfare Council reported that twenty-nine people starved in one month in 1929.
Inferences:

A. It was time for a revolution to share the wealth, to take from the rich and to give to the poor.

_____

B. Something is wrong in a society that pays so much to a movie star and a fan dancer and so little to other workers.

_____

C. Shirley Temple and Sally Rand were in such demand in their occupations that they could command high salaries, whereas other employers could get away with paying a small wage to industrial workers.

ANSWERS AND EXPLANATIONS

1. A. Disagree. The total vote for the two Marxist-oriented parties was less than one million out of forty million. The American people rejected Marxism at a time when many might have had reason to be attracted to it. Urban areas tended to be more socialist, but Roosevelt won these areas.

B. Agree. The opportunity to make a free choice indicated a loyalty to the traditional political parties.

C. Agree. This does not mean dominance by a Marxist party. But without Roosevelt's program and assuming a deepening of the depression, one could anticipate a continued increase in votes for the Socialist and Communist parties.

2. A. Agree. The statistics clearly indicate this.

B. Disagree. Students may believe this to be true, but it is not a valid inference from the statistics. The terms "unjustly" and "more than they deserved" offer a value interpretation of personal standards of justice and morality not inherent in the statistics.

C. Agree. The first part of the sentence is clearly a true inference; the second part is not clearly implied, but the word "probably" conditions the statement.

3. A. Agree. This seems evident at the popular level as well as in the White House.

B. Disagree. Roosevelt did spend large sums, but no amounts are given here.

C. Disagree. This is not proven by the numbers. All we have are Hoover's deficit for one year and Roosevelt's for one year. We need to know the other years' budgets and also how much of the budget was spent for relief.

4. A. Disagree. You may react in favor of this sentiment, but the statistics here do not infer such a solution.

B. Disagree. Once again, this may be your conclusion based on your values, but it is not dictated by the numbers.

C. Agree. This is not a very profound statement, but it emerges from the statistics offered.

Considering all of the statistics in the four items, what other inferences can you draw?

PART III
Debating Historical, Social, and Moral Issues

QUESTIONS FOR THOUGHT

After reading about each of the following issues, reflect on them, analyze possible answers, and write your own reflections. Compare your responses with Thoughts for Questions.

1. Once again historians have, after viewing the same resources and data, arrived at different interpretations of a historical development—the New Deal, in this case. Three such interpretations follow:

   A. In the view of many liberals, the New Deal represents a sharp contrast to the 1920s, although it fits into the cycle of reform in American history. Roosevelt rejected the dogmatism and absolutes of communism and fascism for the energetic and pragmatic traditional American solutions. The New Deal saved the free-enterprise system and the American way of life. It was in the liberal tradition and an important phase of the struggle against monopolies, privilege, and special interests. It actually increased individual independence and confirmed the truth that individual freedom can be enhanced through government intervention on behalf of the underprivileged and defenseless.

   B. Critics argue that the New Deal regimented life and injected too much government into the economy and the private lives of Americans. It threatened the American values of self-reliance and individualism. It had no set goals and thus moved from crisis to crisis without planning or proper management. Too much power was granted to the president. A staggering federal debt was imposed on citizens and a habit of seeking help from government crept into American society. The unfortunate result was a move from equal rights for all to equal privileges for all.

   C. Later, critics of the 1960s judged that the New Deal was a failure despite its noble efforts. It disregarded racial segregation. Its efforts at redistributing income fell far short as wealth remained in the hands of a few. It did not end the depression. The NRA and the AAA sacrificed the small business person for those with great economic power. The main thrust of the New Deal was to avoid more radical legislation. New Dealers functioned in a paternalistic manner without considering true justice. The top 1 percent of the population actually increased their wealth, while the poor accepted their continued low income and poor living and working conditions as a way of life.

   Which of these views do you agree with most? Why?

   _____

   _____

   _____

Would the presentation of hard evidence—statistics and specific facts—likely convince those who hold one of the viewpoints that they are wrong? Why or why not?

_____

_____

_____

View *A* argues that the New Deal was just right and within the American tradition. View *B* concludes that it went too far, and view *C* judges that the reforms did not go far enough. Is this a common breakdown of any effort to bring about change—just right, too much, not enough? Does truth therefore lie in the middle, in moderation, between those who clamor for "more" or for "less"? Explain.

_____

_____

_____

2. Critics of Roosevelt and the New Deal argue that according to employment, gross national product, and other economic statistics, Americans were not much better off at the end of 1938 than they had been at the end of 1932. The Second World War got the country out of the depression. Therefore, increased government expenditures do not lead to economic progress nor to a better life for citizens. Some efforts to answer these critics follow:

A. Many statistics do show significant improvement and even those cited by critics show some improvement.

B. At least the depression did not worsen. Conditions could have worsened after 1932 without Roosevelt's program.

C. Violence and revolution were avoided. People had a sense of better times ahead and of hope within the existing system. This does not register in economic statistics.

D. Many millions of people were directly helped *during* the depression—prevented from starvation and serious malnutrition, helped with jobs.

E. Several new, long-lasting programs were initiated: social security, legal protection to unions, insurance on savings.

F. The benefits from constructed bridges, schools, parks, hospitals, and so on, were enormous. One could argue that these could have been built more cheaply by private enterprise, but would they have been built at all without government initiative?

G. Although economic statistics indicate that the Second World War brought full employment, a higher real income, full factory productivity and opportunity for minorities, it must be remembered that these were generated by government expenditure of huge sums, by deficit financing, and by more than ten million new government employees—the armed forces. Thus the government's vast involvement in the economy through expenditures, planning, and regulation brought the nation out of the depression.

Should these "answers" to the criticism of the New Deal be sufficient to silence critics? Why or why not?

_____

_____

_____

Which one of the seven is the most effective argument? Why? Which is the least effective? Why?

_____

_____

_____

3. The following list of "causes" of the depression are taken from the research and writings of several historians and economists. They are in random order. Rank these, using your judgment, in significance from the most important to the least important.

   A. Stock speculation, resulting in over-inflated stock prices. Many of the stocks were purchased on a 10 percent margin.
   B. Overproduction and underconsumption. Mass production had outdistanced the consumer's buying power, leaving large inventories.
   C. Monopolistic concentration of industry to an extent that prices could be kept artificially high, not reflecting the market.
   D. A noninterventionist government that refused to take action at the initial stages of economic crisis.
   E. Exceptionally high tariffs that reduced American exports and accentuated the large inventories.
   F. Profits and dividends were high while wages remained relatively low. This reduced the purchasing power of consumers.
   G. The farm surplus took the farmer out of the marketplace; he could not buy or reinvest.
   H. The psychology of decline. Many businesspersons referred to the business cycle as a purgative to clean out the system: few new investments, consumers saved instead of purchasing goods and tightened their belts instead of buying food.

Which two causes do you consider the most important? Why?

_____

_____

_____

Which one do you consider the least important? Why?

_____

_____

Is the depression a case in which history can be "useful" or teach "lessons"? That is, if we examine these causes carefully, can we avoid future depressions? Why or why not?

_____

_____

_____

A recent scholarly study concluded that the depression was caused by "some unexplained event." Is that more likely than any of the above causes? Explain.

_____

_____

_____

4. Former president Herbert Hoover objected to the New Deal. Examine these elements of his approach to the depression.

   A. American cultural vitality depends on rugged individualism, and massive handouts will destroy the American spirit.
   B. State and local governments must care for problems of social welfare—true federalism in the American tradition.
   C. The budget must be balanced and the currency remain attached to the gold standard.
   D. If the country waits it out, the business cycle will turn upward. This is natural and has happened in the past.
   E. Business assistance (like the Reconstruction Finance Corporation), in the form of loans to large financial institutions, will "trickle down" to the common people in the form of business expansion and more jobs.
   F. It is best to encourage and persuade people rather than to pass laws, better to restore confidence than to expand programs.
   G. The United States must not take any action that seems unconstitutional or departs from the wisdom of our traditions.

Which of these statements (if any) do you agree with most? Explain why.

_____

_____

_____

Which of these statements do you disagree with most? Why?

_____

_____

_____

To what extent, if any, can the seriousness of the depression and the suffering of many citizens be blamed on Hoover? Explain.

_____

_____

_____

5. President Franklin Roosevelt presented, in his annual message in 1944, a "second" Bill of Rights related to the social and economic order. A list of the rights follows:

A. The right to a useful and remunerative job.
B. The right to earn enough to provide adequate food, clothing, and recreation.
C. The right of every family to decent housing.
D. The right to adequate medical care.
E. The right to receive help in old age, for illness, accidents, and unemployment.
F. The right to a good education.

Do you agree that these are rights of citizens? Why or why not?

_____

_____

_____

If these are rights, then must the government become the "supplier of last resort," that is, guarantee these rights? Explain.

_____

_____

_____

Should any other social and economic rights be added to Roosevelt's list? Suggest these, if any.

_____

_____

_____

6. The Civilian Conservation Corps employed 450,000 youth and 50,000 World War I veterans to reforest land and work in parks. The Corps was run with a military-like discipline and required that workers send part of their paychecks home. Many city youth were put to work out in the countryside. Would you have approved this program in 1933? Would you recommend a similar program

for present-day youth? What problems might arise if there was an effort to establish such a program currently?

_____

_____

_____

_____

_____

7. The United States began to emerge from the depression just before war broke out in Europe and orders for exports flowed in from abroad. The war production created prosperity. After 1945, the United States retained a large expensive military. An observer has said that the United States has not yet proven that modern capitalism can flourish without the stimuli of massive military expenditures. React to this last statement.

_____

_____

_____

_____

_____

8. Many have said that Franklin Roosevelt was the perfect president for the American people, the model president. He was pragmatic and optimistic, with a sunny, magnetic personality. He had experience in government as a governor and as Assistant Secretary of the Navy. He radiated confidence. Although not especially brilliant, he surrounded himself with experts and soaked up information and ideas that he could use. Roosevelt was an effective speaker to small groups and to the nation through radio. He was willing to accept responsibility and to act. A very flexible man, Roosevelt would experiment, try out programs; if they failed, he would try another.
Do you agree that Roosevelt, in personality and habits, made an ideal president? What do you like or dislike about the above characteristics? What would you add or subtract for your ideal president?

_____

_____

_____

_____

_____

9. Historians make use of anecdotal materials—stories, small incidents, or trivial items—to highlight or give emotional impact to the "hard" data of facts, statistics, and the statements of experts. Consider the following trivia or historical anecdotes about the 1930s:

A. Agricultural prices in America in the 1930s had not been so low since the reign of England's Queen Elizabeth I in the sixteenth century.
B. Hospitals required patients to pay the costs before delivering their babies.
C. Mississippi paid $1.50 a week welfare for a family of four.
D. The Soviet trade agency, Amtorg, received 350 applications each day to emigrate to the Soviet Union.
E. Common customs were roll-your-own cigarettes, resharpened razor blades, catsup in hot water to make tomato soup, and sorted and reused Christmas cards.
F. Elevator men had Bachelor of Arts degrees, 20 percent of New York students suffered from malnutrition, and garbage was fought over in alleys.
G. The pacifist Henry Ford began carrying a gun.

Does this type of evidence add much to our understanding of the depression? Explain.

_____

_____

_____

Which situation is most disturbing to you? Why?

_____

_____

_____

Should historians spend time compiling these anecdotes to include in their histories or leave such trivial data to the popular press and novelists? Explain.

_____

_____

10. Many people during the depression blamed themselves for their condition. They did not point a finger at the government or the wealthy. A man might return home and say, "I failed. I didn't find a job." Psychologists tell us that people then seemed to feel a personal responsibility for their dilemma and for the plight of the nation. Use your imagination to offer explanations as to why people felt it was their fault, that *they* were responsible.

_____

_____

_____

_____

11. Consider carefully the two quotations at the beginning of the chapter. What does each mean? Do you agree or disagree with them? Explain.

_____

_____

_____

_____

_____

THOUGHTS FOR QUESTIONS

1. This is the student's choice. Each includes accurate observations. Views A and B tend toward the New Deal's theoretical or psychological aspects, the effects on character that are difficult to prove. View C is more specific in its criticism, but it is also philosophical.

It is unlikely statistics would help. The historians who put together these interpretations are competent and well-versed in resources and data. Their differences perhaps lie beyond the specific data. They see information from a certain vantage point appropriate to their own mental structures. They have different ideals and images, different visions of what society and America should be like.

This pattern often appears when change is attempted. However, it is false to think that the best solution is always the moderate one. Moderation is difficult to define in practice. The United States has moved well beyond the New Deal programs in social legislation and economic control. What is normal or "moderate" in the present would have been considered radical and extreme in the 1930s. Even Roosevelt may not have approved of present programs.

2. Critics probably would not be silenced in any case. But these arguments do provide evidence that the tendency to cite certain specific statistics is not always sufficient for complete evaluation of any event, including the New Deal. Such events are far too complex for simple generalizations and history students should be learning that nearly every development in history contains so many variables that it is difficult to make any accurate, broad generalizations without being plagued by exceptions.

Perhaps the last argument, G, is the most telling. It attacks the criticism on a philosophical plane and refutes the heart of the criticism—that government expenditures do not stimulate the economy. Response B is the least convincing. History indicates that business "ups and downs" run in cycles, so the likelihood is great that the economy would have improved instead of the depression deepening.

3. The most important causes seem to be B and F. Other factors may have caused the crash and deepened the depression, but the fact is, people no longer bought what was being produced. This meant cutbacks in production, higher unemployment, and less purchasing power. The supply began to exceed demand in automobiles, textiles, tires, and housing as early as 1927. Cause D seems least important. The marketplace is not doctrinal but practical, although the government might have acted earlier in the 1920s to avoid so severe a depression. The United States has

avoided a severe depression since the 1930s, and it seems that many of these causes have been acknowledged and hence conditions modified.

It seems prudent to stay with what are obviously related causes rather than search for an unexplained event.

4. Items A, B, C, and G are unrelated to research or the reality of the situation. Since they are based on tradition and philosophical beliefs, it is difficult to evaluate their truth. Only if Hoover had been reelected in 1932 and had continued to apply (or not apply) these approaches would we have a good practical "read" on their validity. Students must personally judge these ideas. Although democracy is based on certain principles, in practice it allows for different approaches to new circumstances. That is a strength of the democratic system.

"To what extent" Hoover can be blamed is the student's judgment. Seldom is one person, even an influential one, either the cause of an event or responsible for an event. However, the person in charge usually accepts responsibility. And historians normally comply with this acceptance.

5. These seem to be goals more than rights. No conditions, such as the willingness to work at any job and the acceptance of the opportunity for an education, are required. However, it seems that most of these "rights" would find wide acceptance among the American people. Crucial questions arise as to how the system can accommodate these "rights." Determining at what cost and at whose cost are vital to the transfer of the acknowledged rights into reality. Does the government stand alone as the only agency to provide such rights?

A right to safety and security is not mentioned. Nor is the right to protection. A right to a healthy environment might have been added.

6. By nearly all criteria, except perhaps the low pay, the program seems to have been successful. Young people were pleased to be working, families benefited from the pay, and some conservation projects were completed. Such a program would be more difficult to do currently—the rights of youth, liability, the cost of bureaucracy, the pay scale, and the tasks of finding volunteers to work at such jobs and finding worthwhile projects that do not compete with other laborers must be considered.

7. The statement has to be accepted as true until the massive expenditures end. Certainly military purchase orders, filling the needs of three million military personnel, research and development of new weapons, and the costs of wars or "police actions" have stimulated the economy, encouraged production, and employed millions. But there seems to be no reason why, if the military budget were drastically reduced, the government could not spend the funds on projects beneficial to the welfare of all Americans. These alternative expenditures might be more stimulating to the economy since so many of the military products are a "dead end"; that is, they do not contribute to further production. But a sudden cut in military expenditures by 50 percent would have a shock effect on the economy.

8. No ideal president exists, only a best one for the times. What if Roosevelt had been president in 1929? Would he have acted differently than Hoover in the four subsequent years? Not understanding economic matters very well, Roosevelt left himself vulnerable to the most persuasive advisors. It is sometimes costly, both in funds and in human misery, to experiment with projects. Being physically paralyzed, Roosevelt had to rely on others to bring him eyewitness accounts. He often contradicted himself and equivocated. But most historians still list him among the great presidents.

9. Students will probably remember some of these items much longer than they will remember statistical information or textbook explanations of specific programs. Anecdotes catch the imagination and reveal the past in human terms. Yet some of the incidents are not peculiar to the depression; situations like B, E, and F have occurred at other times. Welfare programs (C) may still be insufficient in many states. Thus, these may not give as clear a picture as a simple statistic: 25 percent of the American work force was unemployed in 1932. Situations B and C are especially disturbing since they deal directly with human welfare. Anecdotes do serve to emphasize and support data offered by historians. They also add interest and historians could use more of that in their writings.

10. This is easier to document than to explain. Possibly the ingrained ideas of Horatio Alger, the Protestant ethic of hard work bringing success, and American individualism combined to lead people to look inward for failures and shortcomings. The American ideal, taught in so many different ways, was that hard work and effort inevitably paid off in rewards and success. Failure to succeed was the individual's fault, a character weakness, or a result of not taking advantage of opportunities. Would this same attitude prevail currently?

11. Imagination may be more than the "author's personality." It may be a reconstruction of the past, based on a variety of sound evidence. Imagination is necessary in order to write good history, but the historian should not depart from the data. Imagination offers insight and fleshes out the cold facts into a recognizable form. Personality does, indeed, enter into the writing of history, but one hopes that it influences style, word choice, and structure rather than the careful, accurate description of an event or development.

The study of all classes of society and of what used to be offbeat—diet, recreation, leisure time, amusement parks, architectural sites, the severity of fist fights in the early nineteenth century—now draw the attention of historians. Kazin's "man's life . . . as a whole" always should have been the subject of history. History is the integrative discipline, pulling together all facets of situations through time. No other discipline can make that claim.

CHAPTER

17

GLOBAL CONFLICT: THE SECOND WORLD WAR

"The history of the world is none other than the progress of the consciousness of freedom."

Friedrich Hegel

"Contemporary history is the least valuable of all kinds. The relative importance of events and persons cannot be fairly estimated till time has tested them and shown which is great and which is small."

S. O. McConnell

PART I
Acquiring Essential Data

ESSENTIAL DATES

Determine the correct sequence and write the approximate date for each of the following events.

1. President Roosevelt dies; Harry S Truman becomes president. _____

2. Japanese planes attack Pearl Harbor in a surprise bombing of the American fleet. _____

3. Congress passes a series of neutrality acts in an effort to keep the United States from future involvement in wars. _____

4. A naval conference in Washington sets limits on warship tonnage for five major world powers. _____

5. Atomic bombs are dropped on two Japanese cities—Hiroshima and Nagasaki—the Japanese surrendered one week later. _____

6. Allied forces successfully invade the Normandy coast of France on what is known as D-Day. _____

7. A Lend-Lease Act provides Great Britain (and later the Soviet Union) with military supplies to continue war with Germany. _____

8. Japanese armies invade China, thus beginning the Second World War in Asia. _____

9. The Yalta Conference is held between Great Britain, the United States, and the Soviet Union to settle matters after the war in Europe and Asia. _____

10. Germany invades Poland, thus beginning the Second World War in Europe. _____

11. The Battle of Midway in the Pacific turns the tide against Japan as four of its carriers are sunk, and the planned invasion is stopped. _____

12. Germany surrenders to the Allied armies, ending the war in Europe. _____

13. Okinawa is finally taken after great loss of life by Americans, Japanese, and Okinawan civilians. _____

14. Allied forces invade North Africa under the direction of General Dwight D. Eisenhower. _____

ESSENTIAL CONCEPTS

Examine each concept and write what contemporary relevance it might have.

1. *"merchants of death"* The name given to munitions corporations that supplied explosives for the armed forces of Great Britain and France during World War I, and, it was argued, dragged the United States into the war.

_____

_____

_____

2. *non-recognition* The American policy throughout the 1930s. It was a refusal to recognize what were considered aggressive acts that were against international law and proper codes of conduct. No action was to be taken, merely a nonrecognition of conquests.

_____

_____

_____

3. *fascism* A governmental system, typical of Germany and Italy in the 1930s. It was autocratic and nationalistic, regimented industry, applied rigid censorship, and suppressed all opposition.

_____

_____

_____

4. *blitzkrieg* A "lightning war" in which armored vehicles, tanks, and airborne forces concentrate on key enemy points and launch quick, massive attacks causing confusion and disrupting enemy communications.

_____

_____

_____

5. *lend-lease* A system of aid to those nations fighting against the Axis powers. Instead of selling military goods contrary to neutrality legislation, America lent or leased these supplies until after the war.

_____

_____

_____

6. *America First Committee* A group that argued for an isolationist position in foreign policy from 1939 to 1941. They felt that the European war did not call for American involvement.

_____

_____

_____

7. *"Rosie the Riveter"*   The nickname ascribed to the women who worked in war production plants during World War II.

_____

_____

_____

8. *purple code*   The name given to the German and Japanese codes that they considered unbreakable, but that the Allied governments broke at the beginning of the war, thus allowing prior knowledge of enemy plans.

_____

_____

_____

9. *Nisei*   The second-generation Japanese citizens of the United States who, nevertheless, were rounded up and placed in detention camps at the beginning of the war. None were charged with crimes and many served honorably in the American army later.

_____

_____

_____

10. *"island hopping"*   The strategy for the defeat of Japan that consisted of attacking selected islands among a group, conquering these islands, and thus moving step-by-step to the main islands of Japan.

_____

_____

_____

11. *virtues of democracy*   The concept that democracies are inherently weak in foreign policy because they are optimistic, abide by treaties, expect the best from other nations, and are not well-prepared for war.

_____

_____

_____

12. *Holocaust*   The Nazi's "final solution" to the Jewish "problem." It consisted of the wholesale extermination of some six million Jews and perhaps one million others in "death camps" scattered throughout Europe.

_____

_____

_____

ANSWERS

Correct sequence of events and their dates.

1. 4; 1921–22
2. 3; 1935–36
3. 8; 1937
4. 10; September 1, 1939
5. 7; March 1941
6. 2; December 7, 1941
7. 11; June 1942

8. 14; November 1942
9. 6; June 6, 1944
10. 9; February 1945
11. 1; April 12, 1945
12. 12; May 7, 1945
13. 13; June 1945
14. 5; August 6 and 9, 1945

PART II
Developing Thinking Skills

SKILL EXERCISE ONE: QUESTIONING

Assume you are questioning a group of retired American military officers about the United States' strategy for World War II in Europe. Examine carefully the following questions and write under each whether it is productive or unproductive.

1. Were any of you wounded seriously during the war?

2. British General Bernard Montgomery wanted to make a quick thrust into Germany in 1944, but General Eisenhower preferred a gradual movement along a broad front from the North Sea to Switzerland. Which do you believe was the best strategy?

3. What were the normal procedures for determining strategy of military operations in the war in Europe?

4. Which officer had the most courage—American General George Patton or German Field Marshal Erwin Rommel?

5. How close to success was the German thrust into the Allied lines in the Battle of the Bulge in December 1944?

6. If you could, would you reenlist in the army currently?

7. How clear is the view of what is taking place on the battlefield to those in command behind the lines?

8. Was Eisenhower worried about the Soviet advance from the East and their acquisition of so much territory in Eastern Europe?

9. Did politicians and diplomats attempt to influence strategies and the overall conduct of the war in Europe?

10. Could we have won the war without Eisenhower?

Answers and Explanations

1. Nonproductive. This does not pertain to European strategy, although it may draw out some interesting "war stories."

2. Productive. This was a major point of dispute and the former officers' opinions would be helpful.

3. Productive. As officers they may have been directly involved in or at least may have heard about developments of plans.

4. Nonproductive. This is irrelevant to the subject. Besides, some officers may have known Patton, but not known Rommel. Who can measure courage?

5. Productive. This battle was significant and the officers may have insight into the seriousness of the German threat.

6. Nonproductive. This is of no value to the topic.

7. Productive. This would yield the officers' understanding of the problems acquiring accurate and useful information in order to make reasonable strategic decisions.

8. Productive. The officers may not actually know much about this firsthand, but if they have read or talked about it with others, they might give significant strategic information.

9. Productive. It is important to prod the officers' memory of specific cases in which this occurred. If there was very little nonmilitary influence, you could follow up with a question as to why the high command was left alone.

10. Nonproductive. Their answers might be interesting, but not directly related to strategy. Of course, if Eisenhower's strategy was indispensable to victory, then the question becomes more relevant.

What other productive questions would you ask such a collection of officers? List these.

Skill Exercise Two: Evaluating and Applying Evidence

The following thesis relates to the use of the atomic bomb. Ten items of data are listed after the thesis. Under each of them, write whether the information *supports* the thesis, *challenges* the thesis, or is *neutral* data. Briefly explain your choices, then check them with those suggested.

The Thesis

"The use of the two atomic bombs on August 6 and August 9 was the proper decision in the effort to defeat Japan."

Items of Data

1. The Potsdam Declaration calling for Japanese surrender had been rejected by the Japanese government and the military.

2. A government agency estimated that the total casualties at Hiroshima would be between ten thousand and twenty thousand.

3. Many American military men wanted the Soviet Union, whom they considered a potential enemy after the war, to get the message about the power of a United States armed with atomic bombs.

4. The earliest invasion date was November 1, 1945, but the bombs were dropped in early August.

5. The sudden use of two devastating atomic bombs shocked the Japanese public as well as their leaders.

6. Many Japanese leaders claim that the Soviet Union's entrance into the war in the Pacific and its attack on Manchuria on August 8 were more important than the two bombs.

7. Japan had two million seasoned troops in China and two million troops plus a large citizen militia in Japan, all ready to resist attack.

8. Counting those who died later from the radiation effects, more than two hundred thousand humans, most of them women and children, died at Hiroshima.

_____

_____

9. Both General Dwight Eisenhower and Admiral William Leahy spoke out against the use of the atomic bomb. They maintained that it was unnecessary and that Japan was about to surrender anyway.

_____

_____

10. The use of the bombs has been called, in a recent book, the triumph of an unthinking bureaucratic system, that is, the decision went automatically, step-by-step, through the system without being seriously questioned.

_____

_____

ANSWERS AND EXPLANATIONS

1. Supports. A formal request for surrender had been made without any sign of willingness even to negotiate.

2. Supports. This relatively low number, compared to conventional bombing, indicates no unusual loss of life. Little was known about the terrible effects of radiation. Thus, the decision might be considered a minor one compared to continued fire bombing.

3. Challenges. This argument seems to disregard Japanese lives in favor of a decision primarily to scare Russians rather than to defeat Japan.

4. Challenges. It seems that the United States still had time to wait for Japanese surrender without the use of the bomb.

5. Supports. This shock effect may have actually made the Japanese decide to surrender. Otherwise a delay may have been costly, especially in Japanese lives.

6. Challenges. Perhaps the Japanese would have surrendered without the bombs if the United States had waited another two weeks.

7. Supports. It would have been costly to defeat these more than four million troops. The Japanese government and emperor's sudden, clear-cut, and forceful decision brought about the surrender of all of these troops.

8. Challenges. Of course, women and children die when military areas are bombed but in this case the number was very large and the city was not primarily a military target.

9. Challenges. Admiral Leahy was in the Pacific and had fought for three and a half years and General Eisenhower was well aware of the circumstances surrounding the use of the bomb.

10. Challenges. This is a terrible thought. Could it be that both the strategic value and the moral issue were never raised, but that the process leading to the use of the weapon had momentum all its own?

What other challenging or supporting statements or questions can you supply? Consider the following: Could the bomb have been demonstrated first over a body of water? Was racism involved (Caucasian versus Oriental), and would the atomic bomb have been used on Germany if it had been ready before Germany's surrender? Is control of atomic weapons now easier because the bomb was used once? Does the United States carry a special stigma because it was the first and only nation to use atomic weapons? Would the atomic bomb have been used in Korea or Vietnam if not on Japan? Was one bomb enough? Could domestic politics have been a factor—three years in the bomb's development and two billion dollars of the American taxpayers' money spent—so that *results* were necessary? What are your reactions to these questions?

_____

_____

_____

_____

_____

Which of the ten previous statements are the two greatest challenges to the use of the bombs? Why?

_____

_____

_____

Which are the two most significant factors supporting the use of the bombs? Why?

_____

_____

_____

Should the decision to use the bombs have been a moral issue or only a military, tactical one? Why?

_____

_____

_____

Considering the supporting and challenging statements from this exercise and other data you may have read about, would you have approved the use of the atomic bombs on Japan in August 1945? Why or why not?

_____

_____

_____

PART III
Debating Historical, Social, and Moral Issues

QUESTIONS FOR THOUGHT

1. It has been said that the weaknesses of democracies are their optimism, their expectation that people are honest and will abide by agreements, and their belief that people of all nations, and their leaders, want to live in peace. But this confidence and these hopeful expectations often have been betrayed. In the period between the two world wars, American leaders hoped that nations would behave properly, but did little to bring about this desired behavior. Meanwhile, the Japanese moved into Manchuria in 1931, the Spanish people fell under the Francisco Franco dictatorship (helped by Fascist Germany), the Italians attacked Ethiopia, and a rearmed Germany took control of Austria and Czechoslovakia.

   Examine the following possible ways the United States in the 1920s and 1930s might have helped to prevent a world war and decide whether each would have been feasible and effective in offering a better chance for peace. Write your reactions under each.

   A. Membership in and full support of the League of Nations, including a military arm attached to the League to enforce its decisions.

   _____

   _____

   B. Insist on follow-up conferences to the Washington international conference of 1921–22. These subsequent conferences would deal with other than naval weapons and would be supervised by the League of Nations. Germany and the Soviet Union would be included.

   _____

   _____

   C. Allow and encourage membership in the League for Germany and the Soviet Union.

   _____

   _____

   D. Cancel foreign debts owed the United States and drastically reduce or eliminate reparations required from Germany.

   _____

   _____

   E. A policy of strict and complete economic sanctions on any aggressor nation by all members of the League of Nations. This would include an embargo on all strategic materials such as military goods, iron ore, and oil.

   _____

   _____

F. Alliances with the major nations of Europe to guarantee their independence and a joint guarantee of the national boundaries of smaller nations in Europe.

_____

_____

G. Reciprocal agreements to lower tariffs beginning in the early 1920s among major trading nations.

_____

_____

Which of these efforts might have had the most impact? Why?

_____

_____

_____

Are these suggested actions "lessons" of history to keep in mind in current and future international affairs? Why or why not?

_____

_____

_____

Can we offer these suggestions because we have hindsight, or if we really were intent on avoiding conflict, would these steps have been obvious at the time? Explain.

_____

_____

_____

2. Consider the following suggested causes of American entry into World War II.

   A. Dislike of the political and ideological systems of Germany and Japan—dictatorships with militarism as a major feature.
   B. Fear of a threat to the ideological system that the United States advocated—democracy and the protection of human rights, especially in Europe and England.
   C. A threat to the Western Hemisphere—rumors of German agents at work in Latin American nations, along with signs that several of these nations were sympathetic toward Germany.
   D. A challenge to American markets in Europe and Asia—the Japanese control of China and Manchuria and the German domination of Europe. Possibly the French and British colonies would fall into the hands of Germany and Japan, which would reduce or end trade and investments in these areas.
   E. A threat to American possessions in the Pacific—the Philippines and Hawaii were lying exposed to Japanese pressure and attack.

F. The United States' refusal to become involved in any sort of concerted action, not even an embargo of military goods, to challenge aggression in Asia and Europe.

G. British pressure and propaganda to help support their traditional opposition to one-nation domination of Europe and their continued control over a worldwide empire.

H. A weakness inherent in a democratic ideology that espouses a faith in the essential goodness and reasonableness of people and nations, a willingness to "see the other side," and a horror of war.

I. Anger over unpaid World War I debts and Senate investigatory committee (Senator Gerald Nye's committee) data that revealed the exorbitant profits of munitions-makers in World War I. This led to a reluctance to get involved in Europe's troubles or to make the "mistake of 1917."

J. Germany's use of submarines in the Atlantic and their refusal to recognize America's "freedom of the seas" position. Eventually "incidents" occurred that made it difficult to remain neutral.

K. Misunderstandings between Japan and the United States about respective interests and demands in the western and southwestern Pacific, especially in China. The Japanese insisted on control of Manchuria and domination of China; the United States became China's mouthpiece and protector.

L. The Roosevelt administration took steps that led directly to war—ending trade with Japan, using American warships to protect shipments of goods to England, a lend-lease program to aid England and the Soviet Union, statements of moral support favoring England and China, continuing diplomatic relations with European governments in exile, and others.

M. The reckless expansion of Germany and Japan throughout Europe and Asia without regard to self-determination and recognition of human rights, and without taking note of American interests in Europe and Asia.

N. The failure of the New Deal programs to bring economic recovery and the possibility that mobilization, conversion of the economy into an "arsenal of democracy," and stimulation of the economy through military expenditures would bring prosperity.

O. Japanese and German racial and cultural doctrines of superiority, along with their need to expand and promote the interests of a "superior" people over "lesser" peoples.

P. American racists' attitudes toward the Japanese and the pro-British leanings of Roosevelt, Secretary of State Cordell Hull, and other important American leaders in government and business.

Which three of the causes do you consider the most important? Explain why for each.

_____

_____

_____

Which two of the sixteen do you consider the least important? Why?

_____

_____

Which one do you consider the most difficult to prove, that is, to gather convincing evidence to support? Why?

_____

_____

Could the United States have overcome the three causes that you consider the most important, and stayed out of the war? Why or why not?

_____

_____

_____

What "lessons" emerge from these causes, that is, what helpful advice on policy conduct so the United States can avoid future conflict?

_____

_____

_____

3. Historians disagree on the effects of the Allied policy of unconditional surrender announced shortly after the beginning of American entry into the war. Three views follow.

   A. This policy resulted in a more determined resistance by the Axis powers and took away options of a negotiated settlement perhaps as early as mid-1943 or early 1944. The great loss of life in the last one and a half years of the war might have been avoided with a "conditional" settlement. To announce such a policy is to encourage an enemy to fight harder and endure more suffering before surrendering.
   B. Wars are both military and political events. The concept of unconditional surrender was important politically in that it kept the Allies, especially the Soviet Union and the United States, together throughout the war. If unconditional surrender had been required in World War I, peace might have been more lasting.
   C. The surrender conditions were irrelevant to the Japanese and the Germans. They considered the policy propaganda and assumed that they could probably negotiate a separate surrender arrangement if they needed. Indeed, both Japan and Germany tried to come to terms with a negotiated settlement long before the war came to an end. The policy statement was not important or influential.

Which view seems most reasonable to you? Why?

_____

_____

Would unconditional surrender have been realistic in the "small" wars since World War II—Korea, Vietnam, and the Middle East? Why or why not?

_____

_____

_____

To what extent should diplomacy and politics influence decisions in a major war? Is the task to defeat the enemy and then consider diplomatic issues or to consider diplomatic factors throughout the war? Explain.

_____

_____

_____

4. Historians have debated the motivations for American involvement in the Second World War. Three interpretations follow:

   A. The traditional interpretation emphasizes a resistance to fascism, a fight against obvious evil, an effort to stop a menace to all. Democracy was in danger and the United States entry was due to Japan's military attack on the United States. The ultimate desire of the Americans was to create a better world.

   B. Some have maintained that although the war against Germany may have been inevitable, the war in Asia was unnecessary. The United States insisted on an obsolete "Open Door" policy long after it was obvious that China's market was severely limited. Popular opinion favored China over Japan, but America's realistic interest was to avoid war in the Pacific. The defeat of Japan created a power vacuum filled by Mao Tse-tung and the Communists, and brought the United States into conflicts in Korea and Vietnam. The Japanese, although brutally mistreating the Chinese, were anti-Communist and would have developed all of East Asia economically.

   C. A revisionist view maintains that economic concerns were of primary importance in America's entry into the war. The United States was worried about markets in Europe and Asia. Hitler was a threat economically, but not militarily. The liberty really sought by the United States was a liberty of the marketplace, which was achieved after the war on a worldwide scale. It was not that the Japanese and Germans mistreated the people they conquered, but that they closed markets to American goods in the conquered nations that brought the United States into the war.

   Which of these views seems most reasonable to you? Why?

   _____

   _____

   _____

   Which of these would most likely be favored by Japanese and German historians? Why?

   _____

   _____

   _____

5. Some argue that the war against Japan in the Pacific was an unnecessary war and perhaps reflects an unfair attitude on the part of the United States. In the war between China and Japan (begun in 1937), the United States assisted China

with war materials, loans, and American "volunteers." The United States condemned the Japanese colonization of China and Southeast Asia, yet did not bother about the British control of India or object to the French colonization of Vietnam (French Indochina). Japan was refused vital oil and iron ore from the United States, which also made no effort at realistic negotiation on the China problem. Do you agree with this assessment? Why or why not?

_____

_____

_____

_____

_____

6. The Yalta Conference of February 1945 was perhaps the most important meeting involving Roosevelt, British Prime Minister Winston Churchill, and Soviet Premier Joseph Stalin. Critics have argued that an ill Roosevelt allowed Stalin to take advantage of him and fix on the United States an unfair postwar arrangement. Supposedly, Roosevelt "gave away" too much. Examine the following summary of the terms of the treaty and decide whether or not you consider the treaty favorable to the Soviet Union. Write your answer after the terms.

A. Free elections to be held in all of Europe by each liberated nation; all political parties would be allowed participation.
B. Zonal occupation of Germany after the war by the victorious powers.
C. The Soviet Union to declare war on Japan two or three months after the end of war in Europe.
D. A treaty of friendship and alliance between non-Communist China and the Soviet Union.
E. The Kurile Islands north of Japan to be turned over to the Soviet Union, along with commercial interests in Manchuria.
F. Agreement to a conference in April of 1945 on the establishment of a United Nations.

_____

_____

_____

_____

_____

7. Soviet historians point out that while the United States, Great Britain, and the Soviet Union were allies against Germany in World War II, it was an unfair alliance. The Soviet Union did the brunt of the fighting until the summer of 1944 and lost more lives than all the other nations combined. Lend-lease to the Soviet Union was ended as soon as Germany surrendered; even transports on their way to the Soviet Union were turned around at sea. The United States shared technical information on war equipment with the British, but not with

the Soviet Union. Soviet requests for loans at the end of the war were denied, although loans were made to Great Britain and France. How would you react to this unfairness charge?

_____

_____

_____

_____

_____

8. In 1941, Roosevelt altered the truth to encourage anti-German feelings at home. The American destroyer, *Greer,* had trailed a German submarine for three hours and directed an attack on it before being fired upon. Roosevelt called this an act of aggression by Germany in waters "necessary for American defense." He also failed to inform the public that, although a German submarine sank the *Reuben Jones* in October 1941, that destroyer had been carrying out antisubmarine activity. Is this proper conduct for a president who said he feels that there is a dangerous enemy and that his nation needs to recognize this danger? Explain.

_____

_____

_____

_____

_____

9. In 1942, under Executive Order Number 9066, more than 110,000 people of Japanese ancestry, many of them United States citizens, were rounded up and placed in detention camps. They lost property estimated at a value of $350 million. No incidents of sabotage or any action against the United States had occurred. As a matter of fact, 17,000 of these Japanese-Americans served with great honor in the United States Army in Europe. The basis for their detention was race and ancestry. In 1944, the Supreme Court, by a vote of six to three, upheld the Executive Order. Do you agree or disagree with the detention and the subsequent Supreme Court decision? Why or why not?

_____

_____

_____

_____

_____

10. Consider carefully the two quotes at the beginning of the chapter. What does each mean? Do you agree or disagree with each quote? Explain.

_____

_____

_____

_____

_____

THOUGHTS FOR QUESTIONS

1. Items A and C would seem to have the most impact. Active membership by the United States would certainly have given more prestige to the League. Germany and the Soviet Union might have felt less resentment and been more cooperative if they had been members earlier. The military arm remained missing from the League. The United States called a disarmament conference in 1921 without involving the League. Circumventing the organization does not enhance its importance.

B. Germany was restricted in military preparations by the Treaty of Versailles. Yet no nation was willing to enforce the restrictions. Even the Washington conference's disarmament provisions depended on the good intentions of those who signed. Throughout the 1920s, nations grew less willing to disarm and might have been reluctant to meet.

D. The reparation demands certainly helped pave the way for the rise of Nazism in Germany. The debts caused resentment on the part of Great Britain and France, who had fought the Central Powers with the United States in a common effort. But the debt's greatest impact was on the American people and their attitude toward Europe; isolationism was an intent not to get involved in Europe again. A wise statesmanlike act might have been to cancel the debts immediately in 1919 and not allow this issue to poison relations between Europe and the United States for the next twenty years.

E. This policy might have been somewhat effective in the case of Japan and Italy. Could Japan have been stopped in its expansion in China with complete economic sanctions by all nations in 1931, after Japan's invasion of Manchuria? Of course, this would have reduced oil profits at a time of severe depression. But it may have been an effective policy. The United States did finally embargo oil in the summer of 1941. The Japanese followed with the attack on Pearl Harbor.

F. This alliance was an assumed function of the League of Nations and was finally asserted by Great Britain and France in 1939 when Germany invaded Poland. An alliance of European powers that included the United States to protect boundaries of smaller nations, *and* the reasonable expectation that this protection would be backed by military action, may have been effective in Europe in 1935 or 1936. But it is not reasonable to expect the United States to join such a cooperative guarantee. This concept was the part of the League of Nations' charge that drew the most criticism from the American Senate.

G. Finally put together effectively in the John Kennedy administration in the 1960s, such an agreement would have alleviated some of the consequences of the economic failure in the late twenties. Possibly, with increased trade possibilities, both Germany and Japan would have pursued different courses of action. Some of the thunder of both Hitler, needing colonial areas such as the British and French had, and the Japanese militarists, about the need for Manchuria and other parts of Asia, might have been quieted.

The world changes from decade to decade. A lesson implies ongoing wisdom and effectiveness. Variables and circumstances change over time, which is one of the lessons of history. Yet some insights and certain principles may be drawn out and considered seriously. Perhaps nations should not allow naked aggression to go unchallenged. A nation acts in a revengeful and belligerent manner if humiliated or exiled from the community of nations. These two lessons may not be profound, but they have a degree of truth.

Many people did offer advice on these actions at the time. Other considerations prevailed and other sentiments were stronger. Many political leaders have complained that they knew what was best and what should have been done, but often, for practical considerations, they could not act. Hindsight always increases this kind of confidence.

2. Items A, B, and M seem the most important. Items K, O, and P have a close relationship to item A. This answer assumes that wars are caused by attitudes and ideas rather than by economics and politics. The important issue is whether ideas and attitudes are shaped by material conditions and power considerations *or* whether the ideas and mental set produce perceptions of economic and political need.

Item J is a minor issue that only accentuates antagonisms and the general direction of policies already being developed. Possibly even without Pearl Harbor, the *Greer* or *Reuben Jones* incidents may have been used as a basis for further steps into war with Germany. Item E is weak as a cause because the exposure to attack assumes an act of war.

No evidence exists for item N.

Since Germany and Japan moved away from democracy through a process over which the United States had no direct control, it is unlikely that American action would have made a difference. The reckless expansion might have been challenged earlier. But that might have meant an earlier World War II.

A couple lessons were indicated earlier. Others might include the idea that it is much better to become involved in a situation that may lead to war long before it becomes serious and "inevitable"; that leaders must weigh carefully the economic factors in foreign affairs to see if economic interests are shaping developments and influencing political and diplomatic decisions; that the United States functions in a world in which not all nations espouse beliefs in fairness, cooperation, nonviolent solutions to problems, and an attitude of good will toward neighboring nations; that a president, for good or ill, can involve the United States in a situation that may lead to war.

3. The most reasonable view is the student's choice. One of the complaints about the armistice and settlement in 1918 and 1919 was that Germany was not completely defeated and occupied. This led to the myth spread by Hitler that German politicians had betrayed Germany and that the military could have continued to fight and could have won the First World War.

In guerrilla war it is difficult to achieve an unconditional surrender. The brutality of the war makes it unsafe to surrender or even to negotiate. Such a war has no clear-cut boundaries and an opposing army does not exist in the traditional sense. The conquest of all of Korea by United Nations troops might have been considered an unconditional surrender. Vietnam did end in a complete victory for the guerrillas, an unconditional surrender by the government of South Vietnam.

The Americans and the Japanese have tended to fight to win a war and then work at a political settlement later. European nations most often fight a war with an eye on diplomatic issues and political arrangements after the war. If the war is going to be "successful," then it seems logical to consider what the situation will be like after the war. Prudence dictates this approach.

4. Determining motivation is the most difficult historical problem. It is impossible, despite the efforts of psychohistorians, to get into the minds of past leaders. This is true even of a small group, and even more difficult when a larger number are involved in the decision-making process. Plenty of economic data exists, along with many comments by leaders, to indicate an economic motivation for war against Germany and Japan. Yet, there are obvious differences between the democratic system and the political systems of the Axis powers. A multitude of public statements emphasize this ideological struggle. Historians often end up declaring "mixed motives."

Japanese and German historians must, if they are professional, look for the truth. They might be attracted to viewpoint C, since it implies that American motives were not "pure," but tainted by a desire for economic gain.

5. Although the antagonisms between Japan and the United States may not justify a military attack on Pearl Harbor, plenty of provocations led up to the Japanese attack. Add to the ones listed earlier the American indictments of Japan, a proud and sensitive nation, for immoral action in China and Manchuria (1915 and 1931); the refusal to allow Japanese immigration into the United States (1921 and 1924 legislation); and the discrimination against Japanese students in California schools. Although people sympathized with a suffering China, becoming China's protector, and not the protector of Czechoslovakia and Poland, seems inconsistent. Was the Pacific problem a clash between two industrialized nations for trade and economic power in China and Southeast Asia? Did Japan really challenge America's Open Door policy in the Pacific rather than humiliate China and touch the sympathetic hearts of American leaders?

6. The stated provisions of the treaty do not seem unfair. Free elections were not held in Eastern Europe, but little could have been done about this in 1945–46 except perhaps a military attack by American troops, unlikely in the context of the times. Roosevelt did not *know* that the Soviet Union would not honor the agreement regarding Eastern Europe. The Soviet Union did declare war on Japan exactly three months after the war in Europe ended and did recognize Chiang Kai-shek's government in China, and not the Communist rebels. The zonal occupation took place as did the conference on the United Nations. Although the Soviet Union received the Kurile Islands and commercial interests in China, the United States did acquire complete control over the occupation of Japan and the chain of islands that include Okinawa, as well as various Pacific islands. From the Soviet viewpoint in February 1945, the agreement favored the United States.

7. Inherent within the Marxist ideology is the inevitable expansion of the Communist system as a replacement of all other systems. International organizations existed to promote this worldwide revolution. Marxist ideology had worked in the Soviet Union to produce Stalin's totalitarian dictatorship. It is not reasonable to ask

a democratic government to loan money, to give aid, and to share very important military/technological secrets with a nation whose ideology calls for the elimination of the democratic nation's government. The lost lives at the second front in Europe lay the groundwork for a successful invasion that took until 1944; there is no sign of purposeful delay of that invasion. Also, the Soviet Union had secretly signed a non-aggression pact with Hitler to allow him a free hand in Europe. In 1939, the Soviet Union took possession of a large section of eastern Poland as the Germans took western Poland. The United States did send millions in aid through the Lend-Lease Act and opened a front in Italy in 1943. The Soviet Union did not enter the war against Japan until August 1945; that is, no "second front" was opened earlier in Asia by the Soviet Union.

8. No matter what the situation is, nothing justifies condoning deceit or lying on the part of an elected leader in a democracy. Unless the whole truth is conveyed as fairly as possible, a president has betrayed a trust. As it turned out, the United States entered the war, and the destroyer incidents could have been accurately revealed. Only the preservation of national security and the saving of lives are adequate excuses for withholding disclosure of *exactly* what action the government is taking on behalf of its citizens.

9. Of course, several decades later, these actions seem unreasonable and unconstitutional. But in the context of the time, the Japanese had attacked Pearl Harbor, more than two thousand Americans had died, and Americans really feared a Japanese invasion on the West Coast. Given the anger and emotion on the West Coast, removing the Japanese-Americans to "safety" in a remote area might have been in their best interests. This is not an adequate excuse, though. Of course, their constitutional rights were denied and certainly they are owed compensation for property they lost because of the action. But, again, historians must be careful judging the behavior of decision-makers since they cannot absorb the full context of past events. Obviously racism was involved; those of recent German descent were not rounded up on the East Coast and placed in camps.

10. Hegel believed that the whole world was heading in the direction of freedom. English historians of the Whig school in the nineteenth century also, in somewhat different form, accepted the struggle for the extension of freedom as the theme of history. This seems to be a focal point of United States policy in the twentieth century, at least in the rhetoric of America's leaders. Both the world wars were fought to "extend freedom."

We are now able to see the issues and significance of the Second World War, five decades later. What seemed significant at the time pales into oblivion as the years pass. Revisions are heaped upon revisions. New files and private papers are opened. Minor decisions become turning points. Some historians consider fifty years an adequate time to wait for a serious, balanced history of an event or time period. That may be too brief a span. In the United States we seek, and often receive, instant history. A presidential administration is described, analyzed, and placed into history before the ex-president can reach his desk to write his memoirs. Only now do we begin to understand the Second World War. Much later we will understand it even better.

CHAPTER

18

ADJUSTMENT TO A DIFFERENT WORLD

"The main work of the historian is to evaluate, not to record. The facts of history do not exist for any historian until he creates them."

Carl Becker

"A complete assemblage of the smallest facts of history will tell it in the end."

J. B. Bury

PART I
Acquiring Essential Data

ESSENTIAL DATES

Determine the correct sequence and write the approximate date for each of the following events.

1. The United Nations (mostly United States) and South Korean forces fight the North Koreans, and eventually the Chinese. _____

2. Dwight D. Eisenhower is elected president over Adlai E. Stevenson. _____

3. The North Atlantic Treaty Organization (NATO) alliance is chartered. _____

4. The Nationalist forces of Chiang Kai-shek fall to the Communist forces of Mao Tse-tung in China. _____

5. The Servicemen's Readjustment Act (G.I. Bill of Rights), providing for education and housing benefits, becomes law. _____

6. The Full Employment Act is passed, granting the federal government power to act to promote a healthy economy. _____

7. The Truman Doctrine, promising help for nations being subverted by Communist rebels, is proclaimed. _____

8. A treaty is signed to end United States military occupation of Japan. _____

9. The United States Senate ratifies the United Nations charter. _____

10. The Marshall Plan granting economic aid to Europe is announced. _____

11. The Soviet Union blockades the free city of Berlin. _____

12. President Harry S. Truman orders the armed forces desegregated. _____

13. The Taft-Hartley Act is passed, limiting the power of labor unions. _____

14. Network television begins. _____

ESSENTIAL CONCEPTS

Examine each concept and write what contemporary relevance it might have.

1. *Pax Americana*   The belief, after the Second World War, that the entire world could be shaped on the model of the United States and that America could impose a peace on the world.

_____

_____

_____

2. *containment*   The policy, attributed primarily to George Kennan of the State Department and initiated by President Truman, that argued that the Soviet Union was expansive and must be restrained to its existing boundaries.

_____

_____

_____

3. *police action*   The name given to military operations in which no war was declared and in which the United States acted as police to maintain law and order among nations. It was especially connected to the war in Korea.

_____

_____

_____

4. *crimes against peace and humanity*   The charge leveled against German and Japanese leaders who were brought to trial for these "crimes" after the Second World War.

_____

_____

_____

5. *"lost China"*   The words used to indicate that the Truman administration had mishandled the situation in China and had allowed, if not encouraged, a Communist victory there.

_____

_____

_____

6. *security risk*   A type of charge leveled against government workers who seemed to have suspicious friends or who seemed to be lax in their handling of national security matters.

_____

_____

_____

7. *unsinkable aircraft carrier*   The words used to describe the value of Japan as an ally and as a strategic base for the United States military due to its presence and influence in East Asia.

_____

_____

_____

8. *Truman Doctrine*   The promise that the United States would come to the assistance of any free nation under attack by forces being aided by an outside power, especially a Communist power.

_____

_____

_____

9. *limited war*   The title given a war that is being fought in one local area. Although major powers may be actually supporting the war, neither side chooses to extend it.

_____

_____

_____

10. *"cooling off" period*   The provision of the Taft-Hartley Act that forces a union to wait eighty days before going on strike. It was considered a restriction on the freedom of union activities.

_____

_____

_____

11. *"I have names"*   The sentence uttered often by Senator Joseph McCarthy in his campaign to rid the American government of Communist influence. No actual names were ever revealed.

_____

_____

_____

12. *civil rights*   The term that became popular in the Truman period and referred to the basic rights of equal treatment for Americans from all races and backgrounds.

_____

_____

_____

ANSWERS

Correct sequence of events and their dates.

1.	5; 1944	8.	14; 1948
2.	9; 1945	9.	11; 1948–49
3.	6; 1946	10.	3; 1949
4.	7; 1947	11.	4; 1949
5.	13; 1947	12.	1; 1950–53
6.	10; 1947	13.	8; 1951
7.	12; 1948	14.	2; 1952

PART II
Developing Thinking Skills

SKILL EXERCISE ONE: FACT, INFERENCE, OR OPINION

Under each of the following statements, write whether it is a fact, an inference, or an opinion. Explain your choices and compare them with those suggested.

1. The roots of the Cold War lie in the nature of Soviet communism.

   _____

   _____

2. Capitalists are money-hungry parasites who prey on the unprotected poor nations of the world without offering any benefits.

   _____

   _____

3. In 1939, the Soviet Union invaded Poland from the east at the same time as the Germans invaded Poland from the west.

   _____

   _____

4. George Kennan was the author of the article in *Foreign Affairs* that explained and encouraged the containment policy.

   _____

   _____

5. In September 1946, Truman fired Henry Wallace, secretary of the interior, because he called for accommodation with the Soviet Union.

   _____

   _____

6. After Greece and Turkey, the Communists intended to take all the Middle East and Africa and then Asia to make the world Communist regardless of what the people chose.

   _____

   _____

7. British Prime Minister Winston Churchill called the Marshall Plan the "most unsordid act in history."

   _____

   _____

8. The Soviet Union was expansive and had a pathological fear of the West, so it was necessary to "draw lines" and contain their expansion.

   _____

   _____

9. The Soviets showed by their rejection of statesman Bernard Baruch's proposal to outlaw nuclear weapons that they wanted to blow up the United States and take it over.

   _____

   _____

10. Eastern European nations rejected the American offer of financial aid in 1947 and 1948.

   _____

   _____

Answers and Explanations

   1. Inference. This is an interpretation of the cause of the Cold War, but not a factual statement.

   2. Opinion. Some people may approve this statement, but it is a gross generalization filled with biased words and assumptions.

   3. Fact. "At the same time" here means approximately the same time.

   4. Fact. Although he signed it "x," Kennan was the author and the statement is factual.

   5. Inference. The first part is a fact and the second part is probably true, but the "because" indicates an inference.

   6. Opinion. This extreme statement is difficult to support, whatever evidence might be presented.

   7. Fact. The statement by Churchill is an inference, but that he made the statement is a fact.

   8. Inference. This was Kennan's view, but it is not a fact. It has been accepted as valid by many people, yet remains an inference.

   9. Opinion. This is not a valid inference and the conclusion does not follow the premise. The proposal's rejection could reveal many Soviet characteristics and purposes.

   10. Fact. If any reasons why it was rejected were given, they would be inferences.

Skill Exercise Two: Evaluating Arguments

   Examine the following arguments relating to the proposition that the United States was seriously threatened by subversive communism after World War II. In each, determine the primary type of appeal used and classify it in one of the following categories: *Reason, Intuition, Anecdotal, Empirical,* or *Authority.* Consider how the writer is trying to convince the reader. Check your choices with those provided afterward.

1. The Communist ideology calls for the spread of communism worldwide; there-fore, the Soviet Union will try to expand its influence whenever there is an opportunity.

   _____

   _____

2. Senator Joseph McCarthy accused people of being Communists and waved what he said were lists of 205, or 85, or 57 Communists in the State Department; he did not uncover a single Communist.

   _____

   _____

3. One gets the impression that the American people become somewhat irrational when developments do not turn out as planned and often they accuse groups of conspiracy and subversion.

   _____

   _____

4. Since Senator McCarthy was able to continue for so long without criticism from many leaders, it seems he either had their approval or that they were using him for their own purposes.

   _____

   _____

5. Journalist Whittaker Chambers, who accused Roosevelt's aide Alger Hiss of passing classified information from the State Department to him when he operated as a Communist agent in the 1930s, hid the microfilm evidence in a pumpkin on his farm.

   _____

   _____

6. President Truman required all government employees to sign an oath that they were not disloyal or Communist.

   _____

   _____

7. Alger Hiss, in the turmoil of the depression, probably did pass information to Whittaker Chambers, but he must have recovered his senses by the 1940s and maintained a loyalty to the United States thereafter.

   _____

   _____

8. Although Hiss denied even knowing Chambers, Chambers knew details about Hiss's life, a typewriter owned by Hiss had typed some of the classified papers, and Chambers produced the microfilm that Hiss had given him.

   _____

   _____

9. McCarthy kept the heat on the Democrats with his charges of their being soft on communism; therefore, the Republican Eisenhower won the election in 1952.

_____

_____

10. The Supreme Court rendered a verdict in *Dennis* v. *the United States* that it is a crime to advocate forcible overthrow of the government.

_____

_____

ANSWERS AND EXPLANATIONS

1. Authority. This is also a reasonable argument; however, the proof used here is an ideological system, an authority taken as the final word.

2. Empirical. Evidence is given of McCarthy's allegations and that he actually found no Communists.

3. Intuition. This is a judgment based on impressions or feelings without citation of evidence or authority or an appeal to reason.

4. Reason. The second half of the statement is argued on the basis of the first. The "since" is a classical reasoning word.

5. Anecdotal. This is one incident that relates to the topic, an appeal to a story of the discovery of incriminating evidence against a person in the State Department.

6. Anecdotal. This is an action taken by the president, an incident, but not enough information for an empirical argument. Nor is it a call on logic—an inference.

7. Intuition. No evidence is given here, merely a stated impression of the truth about the Hiss-Chambers case.

8. Empirical. Three items of evidence are presented to support Chambers's side.

9. Reason. The use of "therefore" indicates an argument based on reason. Other reasons, of course, might be given for Eisenhower's victory.

10. Authority. The Supreme Court is the authority in this case and the final word in interpretation of law related to the Constitution.

PART III
Debating Historical, Social, and Moral Issues

QUESTIONS FOR THOUGHT

1. As you might expect, historians disagree on the origins and responsibility for the Cold War. Consider the following three views:

   A. The Soviet Union destroyed friendly relations with the United States by attempting to spread communism throughout Europe. They supported local Communist groups in Western Europe and gave aid to rebels in Greece and Turkey. They helped Mao Tse-tung to victory in China. They stole diplomatic and technological secrets from the West. The United States was rebuffed in every effort to continue friendly relations. The Soviets set up their satellite governments in Eastern Europe and the Balkans without holding free elections. Responsibility for the Cold War lay at the feet of Soviet ambition and expansionism.

B. The United States, following a twentieth-century tradition, attempted to impose an Open Door policy in order to dominate the markets and resources of the world. An effort was made to push back the Soviet Union as far as possible and to destroy any semblance of economic equality or socialist welfare for workers and farmers. The United States took control of the economies of nations in Western Europe and completely dominated the nation of Japan, remolding it into a capitalist clone of the United States. Every effort was made by the United States to suppress the people's movement in China and to continue the rule there by the corrupt and incompetent Nationalists. United States officials, including the president, made belligerent, challenging statements that poisoned the goodwill of the war period. Hard-liners controlled United States policy. The United States used the atomic bomb as a threat to a rather moderate Soviet Union, which reacted in self-defense to American threats.

C. Both nations exhibited aggressive ambition to shape the world according to their own ideologies—communism and capitalism. The American Marshall Plan tied Western Europe to the United States economy and was a challenge to the Soviet Union. The Soviet Union, meanwhile, took control of Eastern Europe and established its totalitarian control and socialist economy there. Each nation had a deep suspicion and paranoic fear of the other. The Soviets dominated Eastern Europe and the Balkans without concern for the wishes of the people. The United States imposed its will on Western Europe, Japan, the Pacific islands, and for a while, China. Neither Country recognized the "legitimacy" of the spheres of influence of the other. Misunderstandings, false images, unfounded fears, a fanatic devotion to ideology, and a patriotic desire to advance the interests of each nation and political system caused the Cold War.

After reading the three views carefully and examining other sources of information, which view seems the most accurate to you? Explain why.

_____

_____

_____

Do views A and B still prevail in the outlook of each government in contemporary times? Explain.

_____

_____

_____

If historians read the same sources, why can they not come to an agreement on the actual causes of the Cold War? Will historians one hundred years from now, looking back after the Cold War has "passed into history," be able to agree on the causes? Why or why not?

2. A thoroughly defeated and humiliated Japan, with people accustomed to obeying authority, yielded to General Douglas MacArthur and to the American occupation forces. They accepted an effort to remold and transform their society. It seemed to work very well. The Americans reformed the education system, rewrote the Constitution, broke up large business conglomerates, gave land to farmer-tillers, promoted more democratic political practices, and established a system of equality for women. Was this success of the occupation a false signal to Americans, reinforcing the notion that what was so successful in Japan could be duplicated in Southeast Asia, in Africa, and in Latin America? If so, what might be the results of these "false signals" about American policy?

3. The domestic issues of the Truman administration are often overshadowed by his foreign-policy decisions. This can be seen by the number of paragraphs in a textbook devoted to each area: normally the Truman administration's domestic decisions receive less than one-third the space allotted to foreign policy. Examine the following domestic programs of the Truman era and explain why you agree or disagree with each:

A. The Full Employment Act of 1946 empowered the federal government to promote a healthy economy, to maintain economic prosperity.

B. The Taft-Hartley Act of 1947 provided for an injunction delaying strikes for eighty days and forbade the closed shop, secondary boycotts, jurisdictional strikes, and "featherbedding." It allowed states to pass right-to-work laws and required unions to issue financial statements. This law passed over Truman's veto.

C. Truman ordered the desegregation of the armed forces in 1948.

D. The Minimum Wage Act increased the wage from $.40 to $.75 per hour and social security was expanded to cover ten million more people.

_____

_____

E. Truman established a Loyalty Review Board to review and discuss government employees deemed disloyal.

_____

_____

Which of these decisions during the Truman years do you consider to be the most important in the long run? Why?

_____

_____

_____

If A, C, and D are considered liberal measures and B and E conservative, are you liberal or conservative in your reaction to Truman's domestic policies? Explain.

_____

_____

_____

4. The war-crimes trials against former German and Japanese leaders led to prison terms and executions. The accused were charged with ultimate responsibility for starting the war, with atrocities committed under their general supervision, and with crimes against humanity (mistreatment of civilians and special groups). Many have objected to these trials because:

A. Their legality was questionable since these were not clearly stated crimes at the time they were committed. This meant the possibility of an *ex post facto* defense.
B. The judges and the counsels were all from the side of the victors. The accused were denied the privilege of using all witnesses on their behalf.
C. The war *began* for a variety of reasons and the accused may or may not have had direct involvement in the decisions before the war.
D. Since a leader is in charge of a large number of soldiers, he cannot be held directly accountable for the conduct of all troops under him. (If so, General William C. Westmoreland could be held accountable for the massacre of Vietnamese women and children by American soldiers at My Lai in Vietnam.)
E. It is argued that those chosen to be placed on trial were a few among the many and were rather arbitrarily picked. Many more who were just as guilty were not put on trial.

React to these objections. Which, if any, have validity? Explain.

_____

_____

_____

Do you approve or disapprove of holding such trials? Why or why not?

_____

_____

_____

Is the parallel between Westmoreland and the My Lai incident and the war-crimes trials a legitimate comparison? Why or why not?

_____

_____

_____

5. United States foreign policy had long been based on the avoidance of "entangling alliances" with other nations, from the time of George Washington through the Monroe Doctrine and the rejection of membership in the League of Nations. Yet during the Truman presidency, the United States established and joined the NATO alliance in Europe and signed a bilateral alliance with Japan. Was this movement away from the historic position of the United States a wise one? Why?

_____

_____

_____

_____

6. In 1947, George F. Kennan argued that the Soviet Union would expand, if given opportunity, and that if the United States were diligent in blocking this expansion, then eventually the Soviet Union would mellow. The policy was given expression in two ways: the Marshall Plan that aided the economic recovery of Europe, thus reducing the opportunity for Soviet expansion, and the Truman Doctrine that commenced with assistance to Greece and Turkey. Do you agree with Kennan's beliefs and the action by the Truman administration? Was this an unnecessary challenge to the Soviet Union's security? Why or

why not? Is the Kennan foreign-policy statement still valid in the contemporary world? Explain.

_____

_____

_____

_____

_____

7. The Truman Doctrine states, "I believe that it must be the policy of the United States to support free peoples who are resisting attempting subjugation by armed minorities or outside pressures." Do you support this doctrine? What might be the problems with efforts to enforce the policy in actual situations? How would this policy apply to the American Revolution of 1776?

_____

_____

_____

_____

_____

8. It is sometimes said that nothing is learned from history, that we repeat the same mistakes. Yet five steps were taken at the end of World II that signified an understanding of American failures after World War I and an effort to avoid these failures after World War II. Do you agree that these were *lessons* learned, or were they merely coincidentally related to post-World War I? Write your response after each.

   A. The defeated enemy (Germany and Japan) must be rehabilitated and helped to recovery in order to begin the normal activities of a sovereign nation as soon as possible.

   _____

   _____

   _____

   B. A world organization must be put together while the major powers have a common purpose. The League of Nations was organized in 1919 *after* World War I and it was not effective. The United Nations was organized in 1945 *before* World War II ended and it was more effective.

   _____

   _____

   _____

   C. The defeated nations must be occupied to indicate that they have truly been defeated. Germany was not occupied after World War I, which led to

Hitler's charge that they had never really been militarily defeated, but were betrayed by politicians.

_____

_____

_____

D. The United States can and must influence events in Europe by being involved, rather than by remaining isolationist as after World War I.

_____

_____

_____

E. An aggressive power must be contained rather than ignored or yielded to—contrast Germany after World War I (1930s) and the Soviet Union after World War II.

_____

_____

_____

9. Truman called the Korean War a limited war to be fought only on the Korean peninsula. MacArthur objected and complained of the "privileged sanctuary" of Manchuria and, once the Chinese entered the war, wanted to extend the war into mainland China. Truman concluded that this would involve the Soviet Union and possibly bring about a third world war, so he restricted MacArthur to the Korean peninsula. MacArthur also argued that a clash with Communist China was inevitable anyway and insisted on a clear-cut victory in all of Korea, whatever the risk. Would you support MacArthur or Truman in this controversy? Why?

_____

_____

_____

_____

10. Senator Joseph McCarthy operated at a time when Americans believed that a significant internal Communist conspiracy and threat existed. He accused people of being Communists and government departments and agencies of harboring known Communists. Much of this was done by suggestion, exaggeration, innuendo, and the linking of people with organizations that he considered subversive. Careers were ruined, people lost jobs and reputations, and many who could have helped the accused were afraid to speak up or become involved. McCarthy had immunity from libel since he was a senator. What is the danger of this sort of public accusation of citizens, often without substantial and convincing evidence? Must the tolerance of his tactics be written off as the clumsy

efforts of an elected representative to protect the nation, therefore excusable? What can be done to protect the innocent? Suppose this whole process has the approval of the vast majority of the American people. Does that mean it is acceptable as the will of the people? Explain.

_____

_____

_____

_____

_____

11. Consider the quotations at the beginning of the chapter. Explain their meanings and implications and determine whether you agree or disagree. How might each quote apply to this period of history?

_____

_____

_____

_____

_____

THOUGHTS FOR QUESTIONS

1. This is the student's choice. View C seems most accurate, but perhaps it is an easy way out since it blames both sides. View A dominated the 1950s, view B prevailed in the late 1960s, and view C arose in the 1970s. Is another view possible? Use your imagination to structure another view.

The "official" version of each government follows A or B. Neither one is apt in the near future to "confess" publicly their contribution to the Cold War. But maybe today both governments have a tacit understanding, if not acceptance, of the other side's concerns in the Cold War.

Perhaps the Cold War is a clear example of how a historian's background and circumstances function in relation to the time of the writing. Conservative Cold War mentality dominated the 1950s. A rebellious questioning permeated the late 1960s. A reasoned, somewhat detached, objectivity appeared in the 1970s. Historians functioned in the milieu of the prevailing atmosphere. Or, did they help create the atmosphere? Does this mean history is a product of the times in which it is written? That history is not true or false, but a view of the past held by historians in a given historical period?

2. Although the roots of efforts to remold other societies in the American image go back at least to the Monroe Doctrine, the experience in Japan was a strong reinforcement of this attitude. What was done "with relative ease" in Japan should be possible in Vietnam or Ghana or El Salvador. Any lack of success would be then attributable to a sinister influence—Marxists or cultural flaws in the indigenous so-

ciety. On the other hand, the principles of the United Nations and statements made at other international gatherings also reinforce the validity of many principles found in American society and "imposed upon" Japan.

Nearly all nations at least proclaim acceptance of democracy and human rights. The most controversial principle is that of an open-market/free-enterprise system. Many nations reject this as unworkable or as a system that produces injustice. To many American policy-makers, this economic principle even comes before democracy and human rights, at least in practice. The real danger is that Americans will not realize that other nations' interest in human rights and democracy may correspond to the particular culture and that a type of economic equality and "justice" may be more important in some societies than in others. The American goal may be the humane treatment of all human beings, but the definition of "humane treatment" may differ from society to society.

3. A. This act officially designated the federal government instead of the 150-year-old "natural economic law" as responsible for a strong economy. What had been practiced in the New Deal was now official policy. If we conclude that the government has taken on this responsibility, then it has been relatively successful since 1946.

B. Perhaps all of the features of Taft-Hartley are "reasonable," yet they are all antilabor from a union viewpoint. Would it be unreasonable to require any person with fascist leanings or with racist attitudes to be removed from management? The eighty-day "cooling off" period benefits owners and removes the essential power from labor unions—the right to strike. Featherbedding can apply to management also. Keeping too many management personnel on the job is costly, threatening an industry's financial viability. Are corporation financial statements submitted for government review?

C. There is no reason to oppose this.

D. This seems appropriate, since the cost-of-living increased so rapidly after the war and the philosophy of Social Security requires wide application of it.

E. Certainly no one supports the retention of spies or subversives in government. Yet such a board is dangerous unless it is scrupulous in its investigation and application of the law. Evidence indicates that among the thousands who resigned when under investigation and among the hundreds who were fired, many were pressured because of sexual preference, alcoholism, unpaid debts, or close association with someone "suspicious."

Truman was a liberal president and opposed Taft-Hartley. However, he established the Loyalty Review Board and was rather hawkish in foreign policy. Traditional conservatives (the liberals of the nineteenth century) might question the loyalty board on the principle of personal liberty.

4. Item B: The fact that the judges and counsels were from the side of the victors is disturbing. The Japanese and the Germans overwhelmingly believed that the findings and decisions of the trials were foregone conclusions. In some cases, in the Japanese trials, evidence on behalf of the accused was not even admitted in the trial. Item D: Although a military commander is to set a tone and atmosphere for the conduct of his personnel, he cannot possibly be held accountable in all situations for the behavior of every detachment of men under his command.

Despite all these objections, some of which seem to have merit, it is inconceivable that no one would be punished for the enormous brutality and savage military behavior of both Germany and Japan during the Second World War. Certainly equal and absolute justice was not achieved by the trials, but an expression of anger and conscience emerged—a necessary "statement" that these acts were wrong and must not be repeated.

The My Lai incident is perhaps a much more isolated incident than the overall conduct of Japanese troops in the Philippines. The nature of the Vietnam War, guerrilla warfare without a clearly identifiable enemy, mitigates the circumstances. Yet the small babies at My Lai were not part of the guerrilla forces. The principle that a commanding officer is responsible for the behavior of his troops is still valid to some extent.

5. The postwar world posed new problems. In a world without nuclear bombs and long-range-delivery weapon systems, the United States could safely hide behind a two-ocean moat. A new power, the Soviet Union, emerged as a threatening rival to the United States. Perhaps an early involvement in the affairs of Europe—in the 1930s—could have influenced decisions that led to World War II. In other words, the historic position may have been unwise. On the other hand, NATO and the alliance with Japan were both threatening gestures to the Soviet Union and may have contributed to the fear, vigorous military preparation, and tightening of the Soviet grip on Eastern Europe and the Balkans.

6. Containment assumes a country's desire to expand everywhere. It also renders a broad interpretation of "expansion." If a revolt occurs, and its leaders had training in the Soviet Union and are equipped with Soviet weapons, is that Russian expansionism? Suppose the revolutionaries are a mixture of socialists and various other ideologies and are attempting to overthrow a dictator who has friendly ties with the United States—is this Soviet expansionism? Resistance can lead to increased aggressive activity on the opposite side. But few leaders want to take a chance and stand by while a friendly nation switches, with Soviet support, to those who are successful in a revolt. Since the Egyptians sent Soviet advisors home, the United States loaned large sums to Eastern Europe, and China warmed to the United States, perhaps the Soviet Union will want to establish a containment policy! Containment may be difficult to define.

7. The problems of the Doctrine's enforcement are many. Must the people always be free, and what exactly does "free" mean—democracy, human rights, pro-American? Is it enough that they are merely not Communist? What type of "support"—financial aid, military equipment, American troops? Is rebellion by an armed minority an internal problem to be settled between the government and the rebels? Is subjugation the goal of revolutionaries—or freedom, justice, or a turnover in government personnel? What is meant by "outside pressures"?

The American Revolution involved an armed minority that attempted to overthrow the representatives of the British government and their supporters. Both the French and Spanish applied "outside pressures" and the Dutch loaned money. Of course, the ideology of the American Revolution is quite different from that of Soviet communism, at which the Truman doctrine was obviously aimed.

8. The five statements seem valid, but it is difficult to know whether or not the policies were planned and whether they were related to an understanding of the post-World War I period. President Roosevelt believed that the United Nations should be organized before the end of the war, while the Allies were friendly. No doubt some actions were taken because they seemed appropriate at the time and not di-

rectly because of an awareness of the failures of 1919. Lessons in history, by implication, mean generalizations that cover several events. These five statements do not apply to enough cases to be called "lessons" of history, at least in the sense of similar recurring events that establish general laws.

9. Manchuria was off-limits, but so was Japan, an American supply area bristling with military bases. Great damage could have been done if the American base in Sasebo, Japan, had been bombed. With the difficulties of a land war in Asia, it is questionable if permission to attack Manchuria would have assured a United Nations victory. Defining "victory" in Korea is difficult. Is victory a United Nations occupation of all of Korea? Would constant antagonism against the Chinese along the Yalu River be part of a "victory," or the occupation of part of Manchuria? MacArthur's prediction of eventual war with China has *not* come to pass several decades later.

10. The obvious danger of such tactics is the destruction of careers and the pain caused the accused and their relatives. Beyond this, it is the intimidation of those who should speak out and support the accused. An expansion of this sort of activity could severely restrict basic American freedoms. The Senate should police its own members and speak out against false and exaggerated charges. The American education system, especially the social-studies curriculum, must teach the meaning of dissent in a free society and the ethics of responsibility as citizens.

11. Facts are on paper and in the resources. Becker is correct in that the events labeled as "facts" have all occurred in the past and are lost forever. We have only the briefest descriptions, probably inaccurate and biased, of what transpired in the past. Possibly a time traveler from an earlier time would not recognize our description of the times in which he or she lived. Yet out of this historians must make sense of the past. Becker considers this a creative act, implying originality and selection based on a personal criteria or agenda. Historians normally would like to think the process is much more objective and "scientific" than that.

Bury disagrees with Becker and has faith that, as historians and other social scientists mine the sources and establish details, the past will begin to form itself in a realistic and objective portrayal of what actually happened. The facts will speak and will be sufficient for a clear and accurate comprehension of history. What does Bury do about the gaps in knowledge, the destroyed or sequestered resources (especially in authoritarian nations), the events that leave no written records, the one-sided nature of many accounts of events, and so forth? Do you agree with Becker or with Bury? Why?

CHAPTER

19

FROM IKE TO KENNEDY

"History is the most dangerous product evolved from the chemistry of the intellect . . . History will justify anything. It teaches precisely nothing, for it contains everything and furnishes examples of everything."

Paul Valery

"Voltaire to the contrary, history is a bag of tricks the dead play upon historians." [Voltaire had said that history was *"a bag of tricks historians play on the dead."*]

Lynn White, Jr.

PART I
Acquiring Essential Data

ESSENTIAL DATES

Determine the correct sequence and write the approximate date for each of the following events.

1. The United States and the Soviet Union come into conflict over missiles in Cuba. The Port Huron statement is issued by the Students for a Democratic Society (SDS). _____

2. John F. Kennedy is elected president over Richard M. Nixon. _____

3. The boycott of buses by blacks in Montgomery, Alabama, begins. The Suez Canal crisis emerges. _____

4. A Civil Rights march on Washington takes place. Kennedy is assassinated. _____

5. The National Defense Education Act is passed, bringing federal aid to specialized education. _____

6. Dwight D. Eisenhower is inaugurated president and goes to Korea in an effort to end the Korean War. _____

7. The American Federation of Labor merges with the Congress of Industrial Organizations (CIO). _____

8. The Peace Corps is established. The Bay of Pigs invasion takes place. American military advisors are sent to Vietnam. _____

9. President Eisenhower and Soviet premier Nikita Khrushchev meet at Camp David. Alaska and Hawaii become states. Fidel Castro is victorious in Cuba. _____

10. The *Brown v. Board of Education* decision calls for school integration. Senator Joseph McCarthy is censored by the Senate. _____

ESSENTIAL CONCEPTS

Examine each concept and write what contemporary relevance it might have.

1. *"beat generation"* Groups of youth in major cities who considered Americans impersonal and materialistic and who advocated a life-style of spontaneity and of freedom from social and sexual restraints.

_____

_____

_____

2. *rollback*   Secretary of State John Foster Dulles's belief that containment was a negative policy and that the United States should attempt to make gains against communism, to roll it back rather than control expansion.

---

3. *"creeping socialism"*   The belief that programs such as those of the New Deal and the Truman era, along with many being proposed by liberals in Congress, were signs of a movement toward a socialist system in the United States.

---

4. *brinkmanship*   The willingness to challenge an enemy to the very brink of armed conflict, with the expectation that the enemy will yield before the actual conflict. It was Dulles's policy against the Soviet Union.

---

5. *domino theory*   The belief, expressed by Eisenhower in the 1950s, that if one small nation is allowed to become Communist, other surrounding nations also will be pressured to "fall" to communism, like a row of dominoes.

---

6. *spirit of Camp David*   The first sign of a slight "thaw" in the Cold War when Eisenhower and Khrushchev met cordially and arranged for some modest cultural exchanges in 1955.

---

7. *counterinsurgency*   The Kennedy policy calling for the development of forces that operate to defeat guerrilla forces in a contest for a revolutionary overthrow of a government.

---

8. *missile gap*   The Kennedy campaign term used to indicate that the Soviet Union was far ahead of the United States in missile developments. Kennedy discovered this was not true after he became president.

_____

_____

_____

9. *monolithic communism*   The belief that the Communist system emanates from one center, Moscow, and that this center controls all Communist governments, policies, and actions throughout the world.

_____

_____

_____

10. *Levittown*   The name given to small, low-cost, mass-produced, suburban houses, all very similar in style and features, that were built in the 1950s, at first along the East Coast and eventually nationwide. They illustrate an American urge for conformity.

_____

_____

_____

11. *chain of command*   The style of executive operations first used by Eisenhower. A chief of staff in the White House screens all communications and supplies the president with the essence of important matters for a final decision.

_____

_____

_____

12. *military-industrial complex*   The name Eisenhower gave to the Pentagon's cooperation and interaction with industries that produced military supplies and assisted with new technology. In Eisenhower's opinion it was an ominous combination.

_____

_____

_____

ANSWERS

Correct sequence of events and their dates.

1. 6; 1953
2. 10; 1954
3. 7; 1955
4. 3; 1956
5. 5; 1958

6. 9; 1959
7. 2; 1960
8. 8; 1961
9. 1; 1962
10. 4; 1963

PART II
Developing Thinking Skills

SKILL EXERCISE ONE: PERCEIVING SIMILARITIES AND DIFFERENCES

Two attitudes toward the Cold War between the United States and the Soviet Union follow. Read each carefully, then afterward write the similarities and differences. Compare your findings with those suggested.

The Views of John Foster Dulles, *secretary of state, 1953–1959*

Communism is evil incarnate and Communists are agents of Satan. The world is arranged in a simple division: the dark totalitarian Communists against the free world aligned with the United States. All nations must make choices of one side or the other—neutrality is an untenable position; in fact, it is immoral.

Communism is a huge monolith directed by the government in Moscow. We must not appease or even coexist with this evil force, but seek to eradicate it. Our policy must not be merely containment, but a rollback—a constriction in the area and influence of Soviet communism. We must help those people who live under the godless Communist system to revolt against their oppressors and establish free institutions. We must "actively develop hope and a resistant spirit within the captive peoples." The United States must challenge every effort of Communist influence, even if this brings us to the verge of nuclear war. Those not willing to go to the brink are not sincere in their opposition to Communist oppression. Tensions will not ease as long as world conquest is a Communist goal. The world's troubles stem primarily from Communist conspiracy, and if a serious case of Communist aggression occurs, the United States must be prepared to counter with massive retaliation against the Soviet Union and Communist China. This is the only deterrent to Communist mischief likely to be effective.

A large number of conventional forces are unnecessary, since we can rely on the threat of nuclear retaliation "instantly, by means and places of our choosing." This policy of massive retaliation avoids an economic weakening of the United States by allowing the reduction of costly conventional forces. It is our obligation to see to it that friendly governments remain in power in places we deem important to our security. Covert (secret, undercover) action by the Central Intelligence Agency or other groups may be necessary to subvert foes and to help friends. They must have a free hand to function without normal legal or moral restraints since we are in a deadly struggle with an evil and unscrupulous foe. Supporting social reforms in underdeveloped nations often leads to chaos and turmoil, which opens up opportunities for Communists to gain influence. We may have to cooperate with governments that we do not like, even with dictatorships, in order to stop Communist aggression.

The Views of John F. Kennedy, *president, 1961–1963*

"Let every nation know, whether it wishes us well or ill, that we shall pay any price, bear any burden, meet any hardship, support any friend, oppose any foe, in order to assure the survival and success of liberty." However, being civil and willing to talk and negotiate are not signs of weakness. There are limitations on American power, as "6 percent of the world's population . . . cannot impose [its] will on the other 94 percent of mankind . . . therefore there cannot be an American solution to every world problem." We must accept a "world of diversity," nations with various institutions and creeds, with each nation solving its "own problems according to its own traditions and ideas."

Communists can continue to exist as one element, but the diversity of the world will lead it away from becoming a monolithic center for communism. Moscow cannot dominate or control a pluralistic world. The world must be made "safe for diversity." Neutral countries must struggle for their own nationhood outside the framework of the Cold War. We can help Soviet leaders reach a more enlightened view of the world, one with mutual toleration and a commitment to settle disputes peacefully. Of course, a great gulf exists between the Soviet Union and the United States. Freedom and communism are in a deadly embrace and "the world cannot exist half slave and half free." But the United States must not view "conflict as inevitable" or "accommodation as impossible." "No government or social system is so evil that its people must be considered as lacking in virtue . . ."

Ways must be found to persuade the Soviet Union to end its national-liberation war strategy in underdeveloped areas. A counterinsurgency force is needed to operate in the context of social reform. Intervention abroad must be relegated to these specially-trained groups who can counter Communist revolutionary forces. Peaceful, gradual reform must be encouraged, and in many cases, it may not be exactly to our liking. If the United States relies only on a nuclear deterrent, a nuclear war will be likely in the near future. A diversified conventional force is necessary. However, the United States must build up its nuclear missile system. The Soviet Union and the United States must both rethink their policies and approaches to diplomacy.

What are the similarities in the two views?

_____

_____

_____

_____

_____

What are the differences between the two views?

_____

_____

_____

_____

_____

Which view do you agree with most? Why?

_____

_____

_____

Could part of the differences between the two views be explained by a change in circumstances? Dulles's view was coming from the recent background of the Korean War, of Communist espionage in the United States and Great Britain, of a Communist victory in China, and of a Soviet Union led by Premier Joseph Stalin. Kennedy's view emerged from Eisenhower's efforts at conciliation with Khrushchev, and the knowledge that the Soviet Union then had missiles as powerful as those of the United States. Comment.

_____

_____

_____

During the Dulles era, despite his missile rattling and brinkmanship, we were never on the verge of nuclear war. Yet Kennedy took a more conciliatory attitude and found himself in a dangerous Cuban Missile Crisis and close to a nuclear war. How can this be explained?

_____

_____

_____

Which of these two views has the strongest support in the American government at present? Explain.

_____

_____

_____

Suggested Answers

Similarities

    A. Opposition to the Communist system
    B. Seeing communism at work in the underdeveloped world
    C. Opposition to the spread of communism or the suppression of freedom
    D. Recognition of a great difference between the Soviet system and the American system
    E. Willingness to make concerted efforts to spread freedom around the world

Differences

    A. Communism is seen as totally evil/no system is so evil as to be devoid of virtue.
    B. Welcomes situation that leads to the brink of nuclear war/avoids the development of local conflicts into a nuclear war threat.
    C. The world is divided into two camps/the world is diverse with many different systems.
    D. Neutrality is immoral and cannot be accepted/some nations will remain neutral and the United States must accept that.

E. The United States must be involved in all areas of the world/there is no American solution to every world problem.

F. The Communist system is unified and monolithic/the Communist system will diversify as the ideology works its way through varied traditions and cultures.

G. Confrontation and the reduction of Soviet influence must be sought/coexistence and peaceful relations are necessary.

H. Prepare for massive retaliation should Communist uprisings appear in underdeveloped areas/meet the Soviet challenge of liberation movements by counterinsurgency.

SKILL EXERCISE TWO: DETERMINING RELEVANCE OF EVIDENCE

Examine carefully the following statements of data related to the given topic. Under each indicate whether the data is *relevant* or *irrelevant* to the topic. Then briefly explain your decision. Compare your choices with those offered.

TOPIC: OVERALL, PRESIDENT EISENHOWER PRODUCED A SUCCESSFUL FOREIGN POLICY FOR THE 1950s.

1. Eisenhower was sixty-two years old, a national hero, and beloved by his compatriots when he assumed office in 1953.

_____

_____

2. No wars took place involving the United States military during Eisenhower's eight years in office.

_____

_____

3. Eisenhower operated the presidency on the assumption that he would propose policy to Congress and then they could decide according to "their own consciences."

_____

_____

4. Eisenhower appointed businesspersons to important positions in government, so much so that one writer remarked that his cabinet consisted of "eight millionaires and a plumber."

_____

_____

5. Both the United States and the Soviet Union tested large-yield nuclear weapons in the atmosphere in 1954, thus bringing the problem of radioactive fallout to world attention.

_____

_____

6. In the U-2 Incident, Eisenhower had to publicly take responsibility for the spy plane and its disruption of relations with the Soviet Union.

_____

_____

7. During the Eisenhower administration, the CIA used covert operations to support friends of the United States and to subvert foes in Iran (1953) and in Guatemala (1954).

_____

_____

8. Eisenhower warned the American people of the military-industrial complex's undue influence on government and on society.

_____

_____

9. Both Secretary of State John Dulles and Vice-President Richard Nixon advised Eisenhower to become involved in Vietnam in 1953, with atomic bombs and with American troops.

_____

_____

10. The People's Republic of China regarded Khrushchev's policy of peaceful coexistence as a betrayal of Communist principles.

_____

_____

ANSWERS AND EXPLANATIONS

1. Irrelevant. This certainly helped him in conducting foreign policy, but did not necessarily make him successful.

2. Relevant. It may have been luck, or neglect of important issues, but one sign of success is not to be involved in wars.

3. Irrelevant. This technique has an impact on foreign policy, but does not by itself assure success or bring failure.

4. Irrelevant. This is a domestic issue, although the secretary of state was a millionaire with foreign investments.

5. Irrelevant. Of course, world opinion is related to foreign policy and nuclear testing has implications in foreign policy, but a direct relationship does not exist between this and a successful foreign policy.

6. Relevant. This is directly related to a failure in foreign policy.

7. Relevant. Both nations remained "friends" of the United States; however, the covert techniques are questionable in the long run.

8. Irrelevant. This is important and indirectly related to foreign policy, but not to Eisenhower's success or failure—merely to his insight.

9. Relevant. This relates to foreign policy and to its success or failure, depending how one reads the consequences of Eisenhower's refusal to take overt action in Vietnam in 1953.

10. Irrelevant. The United States was eventually affected by this attitude of Communist China, but Eisenhower's policy success was not related to it.

PART III
Debating Historical, Social, and Moral Issues

QUESTIONS FOR THOUGHT

1. Campaign speeches in 1952 contained the following phrases:

> "*. . . an administration which knows how to practice the wiser spending of less of the people's money . . . how to make government the more efficient servant of the people . . . bring government close to the people . . . faith in the people to act more wisely than can a bureaucrat removed a thousand miles from the scene of action.*" Dwight D. Eisenhower

> "*. . . government is an umpire, denying special privilege, ensuring equal rights, restraining monopoly and greed and bigotry . . . the role of government is . . . to remove roadblocks put in the way of people by nature and greedy men . . . government has the duty of helping people develop their country.*" Adlai E. Stevenson

What is the difference in emphasis or philosophy between the two campaign speeches?

_____

_____

_____

_____

Are you able, from these speeches, to guess what policies and approaches each of the candidates might take if elected president? Why or why not?

_____

_____

Would you have voted in 1952 for Eisenhower or Stevenson? Why?

_____

_____

2. Charles Wilson, Eisenhower's secretary of defense, said "what is good for our country is good for General Motors and vice versa," and another cabinet secretary claimed that the administration represented "business and industry." Are these quotes appropriate for a nation in which business seems so essential to society's prosperity? Explain.

_____

_____

_____

3. Eisenhower supported and was proud of the Interstate Highway Act of 1956, whereby the federal government paid 90 percent of the construction costs of a vast interstate highway system. This program produced excellent highways for efficient and rapid travel across most of the United States. On the other hand, it favored trucks over railroads and the automobile over mass transportation, and encouraged suburban sprawl. Was this progressive and beneficial legislation, or an example of government interference in the economy that cost the taxpayer while favoring some groups over others? Explain.

_____

_____

_____

_____

_____

4. Resistance to integration in the South was partially based on states' rights and state sovereignty in the field of education. Governor Orval Faubus of Arkansas resisted the effort to integrate nine black students into Central High School in Little Rock. Eisenhower, although not in agreement with the Supreme Court decision, in September 1957 sent federal troops into Little Rock to enforce the decision and allow the black students into the school. Do you agree with Eisenhower's decision? Why or why not?

_____

_____

_____

_____

5. John Foster Dulles, secretary of state under Eisenhower, espoused very controversial foreign policy. Analyze and evaluate each of the following three components of his policy:

   A. Containment of communism is too "negative." The United States must encourage the development of "hope and a resistant spirit within captive peoples." Communism must lose ground and be rolled back.
   B. The United States must not depend on conventional military action in small nations, but must rely on the atomic bomb as a deterrent power and

be prepared to go to the brink of nuclear war over military aggression (even guerrilla warfare) supported by the Soviet Union or Communist China. A willingness to use "massive retaliation" is vital.

C. Institutions must be created to carry out the mission of the United States, not only overtly, but also *covertly*—the National Security Agency and the Central Intelligence Agency. Even though we engage in a "cold" war, we must use every means available to promote our interests and to deter Soviet involvement on the world scene.

Is such a policy practical—likely to work effectively? Explain.

_____

_____

_____

_____

_____

6. Many significant diplomatic events and decisions occurred during the brief Kennedy presidency. Examine the following ones and rank them afterward from most to least important.

   A. Peace Corps—volunteers go to developing nations and offer practical assistance in various areas.
   B. Bay of Pigs—a failed attempt to encourage an uprising against Cuban premier Fidel Castro in 1961 by sending Cuban refugees ashore in Cuba as a core of leadership.
   C. Alliance for Progress—a program in 1961 to stimulate economic development and democratic reform in Latin America through loans and investments, de-emphasizing military involvement.
   D. Cuban Missile Crisis—a successful challenge in 1962 to the Soviet Union's attempt to place intermediate-range nuclear missiles in Cuba.
   E. Nuclear Test Ban Treaty—a 1963 agreement to end nuclear testing in the atmosphere, in outer space, and under water, effectively restricting testing to underground.

Your ranking: _____

Explain your choices for the first and last in importance:

_____

_____

_____

What criteria did you use for the ranking; that is, what standards did you use in judgment?

_____

_____

_____

7. React to the following quotation from Eisenhower's farewell address:

   "The conjunction of an immense military establishment and a large arms industry . . . we must not fail to comprehend its grave implications . . . [We must be alert to the] domination of the nation's scholars by Federal employment, project allocations . . . [and] to the equal and opposite danger that public policy could itself become the captive of a scientific-technological élite."

   Explain what Eisenhower means by these words.

   _____

   _____

   _____

   Do you agree with Eisenhower? Why or why not?

   _____

   _____

   _____

8. Three presidents held office in the eighteen years after World War II: Truman, Eisenhower, and Kennedy. After reading a textbook and other sources, list some of the characteristics of each president and some of their accomplishments. Which of these three do you consider the most capable and best prepared by background and experience to be president? Why?

   _____

   _____

   _____

   _____

   _____

   Which accomplished the most as president? Explain.

   _____

   _____

   _____

   Truman took a long brisk walk every morning with a group of reporters. Eisenhower played golf with friends from the business world, and Kennedy played touch football with his family. Are these activities metaphors for their attitudes and for the times in which they lived? Explain.

   _____

   _____

   _____

How would these three presidents compare to or rank with the five who followed them—Lyndon B. Johnson, Richard M. Nixon, Gerald R. Ford, Jimmy Carter, and Ronald Reagan? Explain.

_____

_____

_____

_____

_____

9. During the late 1950s and early 1960s, nationalistic uprisings began in earnest in the underdeveloped world as nation after nation struggled for freedom from European control or overthrew right-wing dictatorships often subservient to Western commercial interests. The United States faced a special dilemma. The nation was born on the basis of self-determination and opposition to colonialism. A natural sympathy for revolutionary groups seemed to be in order. Yet often many of the leaders of these revolutionary groups were Marxists; some had been trained in the Soviet Union, and a few had close connections and perhaps commitments to the Soviet Union. The United States sought to "contain" communism. How should the United States have gone about solving this dilemma?

_____

_____

_____

_____

_____

Dulles's solution was the concept of massive retaliation and nuclear war. Kennedy sought to develop counterinsurgent forces to turn revolutions away from Marxism and yet bring about needed reforms. Other leaders advised patience— allow the revolutionaries to gain power, then cooperate with them, give them support, and hope that moderate leadership prevails. Which one of these solutions seems to offer more promise of success? Why?

_____

_____

_____

_____

_____

10. After the American spy plane, the U-2, was shot down over the Soviet Union in 1960, Eisenhower at first denied that it was a spy plane. When Khrushchev presented the spy equipment, the remains of the plane, and the pilot who had confessed that the plane was a spy plane, Eisenhower then admitted it and took full responsibility. Khrushchev had offered Eisenhower a way out by saying that he was "quite willing to grant that the President knew nothing about the plane."

Because Eisenhower took full responsibility, the planned summit with Khrushchev in Paris did not take place. Should Eisenhower have pled ignorance and attended the summit? Why or why not?

_____

_____

_____

_____

_____

11. Consider the two quotations at the beginning of the chapter. Explain their meanings and implications and whether you agree or disagree with each.

_____

_____

_____

_____

THOUGHTS FOR QUESTIONS

1. Eisenhower placed emphasis on establishing a frugal government and on the people making choices without government interference. He was biased against a "big" or an active government. Stevenson's government was to be more active and involved in developing the nation, in establishing justice, and in promoting equal opportunity.

Both statements are vague enough to allow presidential support for nearly any reasonable plan or specific bill. However, Stevenson probably would follow a liberal agenda of government assistance, encouragement, and intervention to help promote the social and economic well-being of the nation. Eisenhower's policies would be to follow a course of inaction and restraint, emphasizing state and local responsibility, and with confidence that the system functions best on its own.

This author voted for Stevenson in both 1952 and 1956, a vote of the heart. Stevenson seemed more compassionate and showed a greater concern for those who needed help in America. He also seemed to be more competent and wiser than Eisenhower. But the American people decided differently.

2. To equate the overall interests of the two—the government and General Motors—certainly gives prestige, and perhaps privilege, to General Motors. What Wilson meant was that a healthy and prosperous General Motors was important for the prosperity of the United States. The rise or fall of a corporation should not be vital to the economic health of the nation. It is too limiting to view the government as only, or even primarily, representing business. Many other constituencies and government functions are not related to the health of General Motors. The government must not be the servant of business, but the servant of the people, all the people.

3. Ironically, Eisenhower opposed large expenditures of government funds and worried about "creeping socialism." Highways did stimulate the economy in areas where they were built and encouraged movement by an already mobile people. Many industries and businesses related to road-building and to the existence of these highways benefited. These roads increased the country's dependency on oil for energy, and absorbed much land, some of it rich farmland. Roads are classified as infrastructure that benefit the economy in several ways, but they replaced other infrastructure such as trains and mass-transit systems. One has to weigh their assets and liabilities carefully.

4. Normally educational matters are a state's responsibility. But the Supreme Court's decision supersedes state decisions, and if the issue relates to the Constitution, it is removed from state control to federal jurisdiction. This leaves the states unprotected from federal encroachment. In cases where human rights are at stake, federal interference may be appropriate. Eisenhower carried out the law, however reluctantly. He functioned as president in this case against his own wishes and perhaps contrary to public opinion.

5. A. When Hungarians did revolt in 1956 and requested aid from the United States, Dulles offered no support. At the risk of what consequences does the rollback take place?

B. How would government officials know that a Marxist insurgency was initiated by and is controlled by Moscow or Beijing? Should the United States retaliate against Moscow with nuclear bombs because an indigenous Communist rebel group threatens a small nation in Central America? This policy leaves few options.

C. These institutions may be necessary, but their unrestrained covert activity can get out of hand and involve the United States in counterproductive action that contradicts traditional American values and political principles.

Dulles's policy seems impractical by most standards. It is difficult to employ, involves acute judgment and unerring discrimination, and offers very few options short of catastrophe or the threat of it.

6. Suggested ranking: D, E, C, A, B.

Event D brought the United States close to nuclear war, as close as any time since 1945. It stabilized relations with Cuba, let the Soviet Union know that there were limits to their activities, and led directly to a hot line between Washington, D.C., and Moscow. Event B was a fiasco and, other than proving the difficulty of outside efforts to overthrow an entrenched ruler, had mostly negative consequences in relations with Cuba.

The criteria used to make judgments here is the "quality" of the event; that is, does it stand apart as something beyond normal diplomatic events and decisions? Some events also have symbolic importance and stand as metaphors for important principles and ideas. If we consider the number of people affected in a beneficial way, then C or A would be more significant. Of course in the long, long run, or even as a symbolic "step," item E may be the *most* important.

7. Eisenhower meant that a combination of interests pursued by the military and corporations that supply the military can have undue influence on government policy, and that the involvement of scholars with government employment or grants may compromise both the scholars' academic responsibility and the mass of people's influence on government. Large amounts of government money spent on military-

related items provides ample opportunity for collusion between the military purchasers and industrial suppliers. A continuation of the Cold War, an involvement in a conventional small war, or a war of words that creates fear and anger can sustain such military procurement. A president and Congress can be influenced by the military and can be pressured by industry. Furthermore, military suppliers donate funds to political campaigns. The government's need for scientists and technicians can easily turn into a mutual dependence that Eisenhower considered threatening.

8. All three presidents had weaknesses. Truman probably gets higher marks from historians. Eisenhower is rising in the polls and Kennedy is declining. Both Truman and Eisenhower had more experience in leadership than Kennedy. Kennedy had charisma, style, and a flair for leadership that the mundane Eisenhower and the small-town haberdasher Truman did not have.

Students must accumulate evidence to determine the presidents' accomplishments. Remember to weigh the quality of accomplishments rather than just to add numbers. Should failures somehow be deducted?

Eisenhower's golf games with business friends were symbolic. Touch football had special appeal in the 1960s and symbolized youth and vigor, a Kennedy theme of a new generation carrying the torch. Truman's simple walk is perhaps fitting for the man and the times.

The author would rank all three presidents as "greater" than the next five. Johnson, Nixon, and Carter had great failures and were not honored in retirement. Ford had only a brief time in office. Reagan did very little, and it seems, intended to do little. Nixon's trips to China and Russia, along with some progress in disarmament, may earn him high marks. Carter's reconciliation of Egypt and Israel was significant and may prove to be one of those first steps in a thousand-mile journey.

9. The use of patience is attractive, but deadly in a political sense. If it works, and friendly relations are kept with a government of socialist leanings but not within the Soviet bloc, then it should be the preferred policy. However, the erection of a totalitarian state aligned to the Soviet Union could be disastrous to an American president and his political party. China has now become a trading partner with the United States, but the charge was made that the Democratic party "lost China" to the Communists in 1949 and, as a result of this charge, lost the next election. Controlling a revolution with counterinsurgents is risky and could be counterproductive if the effort receives wide publicity.

10. As an honest man, Eisenhower felt the need to accept responsibility for the U-2 incident. Perhaps nothing was lost by not holding the summit, and it could have been counterproductive if Khrushchev had attempted to criticize Eisenhower publicly. It is better to have a cancelled meeting than a bad meeting.

11. Valery seems to support the contention that you can prove anything by history. Is the opposite true—you cannot prove anything through the use of history? Those who are set on a course of action and search through history for an example or precedent to use in support of that action are likely to find it. However, a further search will almost inevitably reveal arguments from history against the course of action. Justifying present behavior on specific historical situations and events is dangerous. Making decisions in the present on the basis of knowledge of the past and of general wisdom gleaned from the past can be productive.

To "play" a "bag of tricks" on historians implies intent. It is probably not true that the majority of those who produce historical records intend to trick historians. But that particular question must be asked of every source—is the original recorder attempting to slant, to deceive, to obscure what really happened? Some recorders of history, no doubt, get away with it. But, it is hoped that the detective-like instincts developed by historians will uncover deceptions and help produce an accurate rendition of the past.

CHAPTER

20

YEARS OF TURMOIL
AND DOUBT

"Everyone falsifies history even if it is only his own personal history. Sometimes the falsification is deliberate, sometimes unconscious; but always the past is altered to suit the needs of the present. The best we can say of any account is not that it is the real truth at last, but that this is how the story appears now."

Joseph Freeman

"In its amplest meaning History includes every trace and vestige of everything that man has done or thought since first he appeared on the earth."

James Harvey Robinson

PART I
Acquiring Essential Data

ESSENTIAL DATES

Determine the correct sequence and write the approximate date for each of the following events.

1. The *Apollo 11* crew lands on the moon. _____

2. A treaty reducing some nuclear weapons is signed between the United States and the Soviet Union. _____

3. John F. Kennedy is assassinated in Dallas, Texas. _____

4. A Civil Rights Act is passed, increasing federal power to protect voting rights and end discrimination. _____

5. The United States establishes diplomatic relations with the People's Republic of China. _____

6. President Richard M. Nixon visits the People's Republic of China. _____

7. The Vietnam War is "Americanized"; Medicare is passed. _____

8. Nixon resigns from the office of president of the United States. _____

9. The Organization of Petroleum Exporting Countries (OPEC) establishes an oil embargo. _____

10. The Tet Offensive begins in Vietnam. Martin Luther King, Jr., and Senator Robert F. Kennedy are assassinated. Nixon is elected president. _____

ESSENTIAL CONCEPTS

Examine each concept and write what contemporary relevance it might have.

1. *War on Poverty*   The effort by President Lyndon B. Johnson to get rid of poverty in the United States in a brief period of time by attacking it as if in a war, with several well-funded programs all at once.

_____

_____

_____

2. *"search and destroy"*   The strategy used in Vietnam to discover where the enemy was hidden, then to destroy the enemy and, afterward, to return to a safe base. The soldiers did not conquer and hold land.

_____

_____

_____

3. *teach-in*   A large meeting of students on college and university campuses conducted by professors or students to point out the issues about Vietnam and American foreign policy. Classes were often dismissed for these, which were most often critical and in opposition.

_____

_____

_____

4. *black power*   The words used to describe the effort by blacks to obtain power on their own, to develop a political base and cultural pride along with their own leadership, and thereby influence politics and society.

_____

_____

_____

5. *Vietnamization*   The process of allowing the South Vietnamese soldiers to take over the bulk of the fighting in Vietnam. The United States would supply material and some direction.

_____

_____

_____

6. *"enemies list"*   The names of President Richard Nixon's political opponents picked out for special scrutiny by the Internal Revenue Service or by other branches of government in order to harass them and cause them difficulty.

_____

_____

_____

7. *"détente"*   The term used for a warmer and friendlier relationship between Communist nations and the United States. It applied especially to U.S.-USSR relations, but also between China and the United States.

_____

_____

_____

8. *executive privilege*   The insistence by Nixon that the executive branch must protect its prerogatives and the traditional separation of powers by withholding information sought by Congress or the courts.

_____

_____

_____

9. *non-negotiable demands*   The term protesters used when refusing to negotiate or compromise in their efforts to establish social, political, and economic justice and equality in several institutions in society.

_____

_____

_____

10. *"great silent majority"*   The large middle class of "solid" average Americans who felt surrounded by government, crime, inflation, drugs, and protesters. They wanted to continue with the status quo and gave support to Richard Nixon.

_____

_____

_____

11. *counterculture*   Called the "Movement" from within, this described a variety of reforms or revolts against average middle-class values; it often included experimentation with drugs, protests against social injustice, rock music, and the organization of communes. Bob Dylan was the bard.

_____

_____

_____

12. *cybernetics*   The combination of the human nervous system with electronic machinery, usually involving information storage, feedback, and control.

_____

_____

_____

ANSWERS

Correct sequence of events and their dates.

1. 3; 1963
2. 4; 1964
3. 7; 1965
4. 10; 1968
5. 1; July 20, 1969

6. 6; 1972
7. 9; 1973
8. 8; 1974
9. 5; 1979
10. 2; 1987

PART II
Developing Thinking Skills

SKILL EXERCISE ONE: CATEGORIZING AND CLASSIFYING

Assume you are investigating the Vietnam War. Items of information related to this topic follow. In the space below each item, write in the appropriate *primary*

346 ★ *Years of Turmoil and Doubt*

category: *political, economic, social, diplomatic,* or *cultural.* Check your selection with those suggested.

1. The Senate voted 88–2 and the House voted 416–0 to pass the Tonkin Gulf Resolution, giving the president a free hand in Vietnam.

   _____

2. President Johnson felt, perhaps due to his southwestern upbringing, that if American power were applied in Vietnam, any problem could be solved. He encouraged troops to "nail that coonskin to the wall."

   _____

3. Johnson and Vice-President Hubert H. Humphrey dreamed of a Great Society in Asia, a Tennessee Valley Authority on the Mekong River, to reform and improve the well-being of the Vietnamese people.

   _____

4. A disproportionate number of Americans who actually fought and died in Vietnam were the poor and minorities.

   _____

5. It was found that at least a 10–1 ratio of American and South Vietnamese troops to Vietcong troops was necessary for success in a guerrilla war.

   _____

6. Both Senators J. William Fulbright and Robert F. Kennedy were persistent and outspoken critics of American involvement in Vietnam.

   _____

7. Although it is difficult to argue that a vital need for resources and markets caused American involvement in Vietnam, the concept of open markets and the existence of rubber resources and possible oil deposits must be considered.

   _____

8. Both the Soviet Union and China offered assistance to North Vietnam, but neither sent troops, nor did the Soviet Union threaten or retaliate in other ways or in other areas of the world.

   _____

9. After President Nixon ordered the invasion of Cambodia, campuses exploded in protests involving 1.5 million students on 1,200 campuses.

   _____

10. Congress soon raised questions about the invasion of Cambodia, since the invasion was carried out without authorization of or consultation with Congress and it amounted to an American invasion of an independent nation's territory, which by traditional definition was an act of war.

    _____

Answers and Explanations

1. Political. This is political information, even though the results may have influenced diplomacy.

2. Cultural. Johnson was president and he speaks of a military victory, but the main focus is on an American attitude—"can do" confidence.

3. Social. Once again, this item involves a foreign nation and its realization would require government appropriations, but the effort involves social change. It also could be economic or diplomatic, depending on the context of the sentence and the writer's purpose.

4. Social. These are class and ethnic considerations—social issues.

5. Diplomatic. War is normally in this category.

6. Political. They criticized Johnson's foreign policy, but the power struggle was two senators against a president, all Democrats.

7. Economic. Markets, resources, and trade certainly belong in the economic sphere, although they are closely tied to diplomacy as well.

8. Diplomatic. This involves the conduct of two foreign nations in relation to the United States, and is thus diplomatic.

9. Social/Political. Protests can be and most often are against a government, but the protest itself is also a social phenomenon.

10. Political. This is definitely a political issue, even though the particular object of debate is related to foreign relations (war).

It is simple to see the difficulty in classifying these statements into separate categories. Some easily fit two or more categories and nearly all impinge on more than one. However, the alternative to placing items of data into categories is chaos. Historians are forced to make some sort of meaningful design or structure from the diverse data of history. The chronological method is the most popular, but even those data need to be divided by topics and grouped into several consecutive paragraphs or a separate section of the narrative. What other ways of categorizing the above information can you imagine—for example, a breakdown of data into groups based on whether the information supports pro-American or pro-Communist views?

Skill Exercise Two: Analyzing Quantified Data

Examine carefully the following statistics related to the 1960s and the 1970s. For each of the statistics explain:

A. The "obvious" meaning and implications of the numbers.

B. Suggest what questionable interpretations or unsound inferences might be drawn from the numbers.

C. Point out what other *types* of statistics might be useful in understanding the quantities.

1. During the Vietnam War, the United States dropped twice as many bombs

on Southeast Asia as all the Allies dropped on Germany and Japan during World War II.

A. _____

_____

_____

B. _____

_____

_____

C. _____

_____

_____

2. By October 1963, President Kennedy had 16,732 American military advisors in Vietnam. None were considered combat troops, but 73 American military men had been killed by October.

A. _____

_____

_____

B. _____

_____

_____

C. _____

_____

_____

3. During the Vietnam War, it is estimated that of young men between the ages of eighteen and twenty-three, forty thousand fled to Canada; five hundred thousand deserted the armed forces; and two hundred and fifty thousand were given "less than honorable" discharges.

A. _____

_____

_____

B. _____

_____

_____

C. _____

_____

_____

4. In 1937, two-thirds of American families were below the poverty level established for that time; in 1947, one-third were below the poverty level; in 1960, one-fourth were below; and in 1970, one-fifth were below.

A. _____

_____

_____

B. _____

_____

_____

C. _____

_____

_____

5. In 1870, only 1.7 percent of young people between the ages of seventeen and twenty-one were in college. In 1970, 40 percent were in college. College enrollments increased from 3.8 million in 1960 to 8.5 million in 1970.

A. _____

_____

_____

B. _____

_____

_____

C. _____

_____

_____

SUGGESTED ANSWERS

1. A. The United States saturated Vietnam with bombs. This amount seems excessive, considering the size of the nation and the amount dropped throughout World War II.

B. More bombs were dropped than necessary, thus the United States revealed a hatred for the Vietnamese. The bombing was a very successful tactic in Vietnam. Vietnam had more targets for effective bombing than Germany or Japan.

C. The length of time the bombing took place in World War II compared to Vietnam; the enemy's resistance to bombing in each case; statistics of the impact and effectiveness of the bombing in each case; and the effectiveness of other strategies in each war all would be useful.

2. A. President Kennedy, as of October 1963, had made a strong effort to influence the outcome of the Vietnam War, but had not committed the United States to actual combat in the war.

B. Kennedy was on the way to a full commitment of American military power in Vietnam. Kennedy would have withdrawn American advisors and not have become more deeply involved in the war. This number of military advisors in 1963 is a very large commitment. Only 16,000 military advisors is a symbol or token pledge, not a commitment. Politically, the 73 American dead would have inevitably called for more involvement.

C. What was the total number of South Vietnamese troops in 1963? What amount of material and financial aid was being sent to Vietnam in 1963? Were the 16,000 troops in combat areas and secretly taking part in combat? What portion of American troops was being trained in jungle-type warfare in 1963? Did public-opinion polls indicate a willingness by the American people to escalate involvement in Vietnam?

3. A. Many young Americans did not believe that they should participate in the Vietnam War and made an active effort to avoid direct involvement.

B. Young Americans in the late 1960s did not have as much courage as those of earlier years. The war was considered immoral and illegal by most American youth. Public opinion was against the war. Brave and patriotic young men participated, but cowards tried to find a way out. Young Americans were more sensitive to the morality of foreign policy and the value of human life than in previous wars.

C. What were the desertion and less-than-honorable discharge records of previous wars? What number of the appropriate age group actually participated in World War II and the Korean War? What number actually expressed moral objections to the war? Are there different "estimates" by others who have knowledge on this subject? What are the various reasons for less-than-honorable discharges?

4. A. American standard of living improved from 1937 to 1970 for lower-income groups. The percentage of people living under poverty conditions has dropped in the thirty-three years.

B. More people lived in poverty in 1937 than in 1970. The American people should be proud of the progress over the thirty-three-year period. A trend toward economic democracy is growing in America. By 1970, the percentage living in poverty was the lowest in United States history.

C. What does the data show about the poverty level since 1970? What percentage of those living in poverty in 1937 were farmers whose income may have been supplemented by food from the farm? How many people are included in each year's percentages? What income was accepted as poverty-level income in each of the years and what was the average family income for those years?

5. A. The American interest in and participation in education has increased enormously since 1870. Many more opportunities for young people to acquire a college education exist in 1970 than in 1870.

B. Americans are more intelligent currently than they were one hundred years ago. Many young people went to college to avoid the draft in the 1960s. More young Americans are interested in a liberal-arts education currently than in the 1870s. Americans make wiser, more rational decisions than they did one hundred years ago. People were rather ignorant and incompetent back in the 1870s.

C. What percentage of youth were in college before the age of seventeen in 1870 and in 1970? What was the literacy rate in 1870 and in 1970? What are the statistics on the circulation of books, magazines, and newspapers per person in 1870 and in 1970? How many hours per day did the average youth of college age spend watching television or listening to music instead of reading?

Which of the above statistics do you consider the most insightful in understanding the 1960s and 1970s? Why?

_____

_____

_____

Which of the quantified items do you judge to be the most misleading? Why?

_____

_____

_____

PART III
Debating Historical, Social, and Moral Issues

QUESTIONS FOR THOUGHT

1. On June 17, 1972, five men with cameras and bugging equipment were arrested in the Democratic National Committee offices in the Watergate Building in Washington, D.C. President Nixon knew about this a few days afterward and took part in a cover-up conspiracy. Money was raised to buy the silence of those arrested. Nixon told reporters at a press conference that a thorough investigation indicated that no one in the White House or on his staff was involved. He "misspoke" about this involvement. Should Nixon have been impeached because he had, according to Article I of the House Judiciary Committee's articles of impeachment, "prevented, obstructed, and impeded the administration of justice . . . [thus acting] . . . contrary to his trust as President and subversive of constitutional government?" Why or why not? How serious was the Watergate affair for a democratic society? Explain.

_____

_____

_____

_____

2. A list of programs that President Johnson and Congress placed into law in the 1960s follows. Indicate under each whether you agree or disagree with the program and explain why.

   A. Large amounts of federal aid to education at all levels.

_____

_____

   B. Medicare—free or low-cost medical care for the elderly.

_____

_____

   C. Medicaid—free medical care for the poor.

_____

_____

   D. Model Cities Program—block grants to cities for urban renewal and planning, with representatives from the cities making the plans.

_____

_____

   E. Voting Rights Act—empowered the federal government to register voters who could not, for various reasons, get registered in their state of residence.

_____

_____

   F. Affirmative action—required federal contractors and institutions receiving federal funds to attempt to hire women and minorities.

_____

_____

   G. National Foundation on the Arts and Humanities—federal funds for the support of the arts and the humanities.

_____

_____

   H. Safety standards for motor vehicles set by the federal government.

_____

_____

   I. Establishment of the Office of Economic Opportunity, which organized and supervised programs such as Job Corps, Neighborhood Youth Corps, Head-Start, Upward Bound, and so forth.

_____

_____

Which two are, in your judgment, the most important programs? Why?

_____

_____

_____

Liberals supported these programs and some conservatives opposed them. Based on support of or opposition to the programs, would you consider yourself a liberal or a conservative? Explain.

_____

_____

3. The election of 1968 placed Hubert Humphrey against Richard Nixon. Humphrey was a liberal somewhat tainted by his association with the Vietnam situation, while Nixon was a conservative who had lost to John Kennedy in 1960 and lost the election for governor of California in 1962. Nixon promised to end the war and hinted at a secret plan. Humphrey said he intended to continue Johnson's liberal agenda. Who would you have voted for in 1968? Why?

_____

_____

_____

_____

_____

4. React to these two views on the Vietnam War:

> ". . . the United States in the end abandoned South Vietnam . . . Had President Johnson provided reinforcements, and had he authorized the operations I had planned in Laos and Cambodia and north of the DMZ [Demilitarized Zone dividing North and South Vietnam at the seventeenth parallel] . . . the North Vietnamese would have broken." General William C. Westmoreland, 1976

> "The picture of the world's greatest superpower killing or seriously injuring 1,000 non-combatants a week, while trying to pound a tiny backward nation into submission on an issue whose merits are hotly disputed, is not a pretty one." Secretary of Defense Robert S. McNamara, Memorandum to President Johnson, May 19, 1967

From your reading about the Vietnam War, which of these represents your understanding of the American involvement in the war? Explain.

_____

_____

_____

Could both views be correct? Explain.

_____

_____

_____

Is it possible for the historian to gather sufficient evidence to prove either of these views correct or incorrect? Why or why not?

_____

_____

_____

5. A former Pentagon official, Daniel Ellsberg, in June 1971 gave the *New York Times* classified documents (not available for the public). These documents were later labeled the *Pentagon Papers*. They revealed a pattern of deception and concealment about Vietnam by the American government. Should the *Times* have accepted and published these papers? Why or why not? What are the various issues involved in the decision to publish or not to publish? Explain.

_____

_____

_____

_____

6. In March 1968, American soldiers under the command of Lieutenant William F. Calley, Jr., massacred more than one hundred (perhaps more than four hundred) unarmed Vietnamese civilians at My Lai. The victims were mostly old men, women, and children, including babies. Should this event be considered an unfortunate incident that often occurs in the heat of battle or a symbol of the immoral nature of American involvement in Vietnam? Explain.

_____

_____

_____

Shortly after the disclosure of this information in 1971, public-opinion polls revealed that 65 percent of the American people considered it "morally wrong" for Americans to be fighting in Vietnam. Was this poll an example of the American people becoming emotionally involved in the war, developing a horror of the suffering and a sympathy for the victims, many of them women and children, *or* a reasoned judgment that, considering diplomatic factors, Cold War politics, the economic costs, and the reputation of the United States, the war was counter-productive and not in the best interests of America?

_____

_____

_____

Could this be an example of television reports to the living rooms of American families actually dictating policy of a democratic nation? Explain. If television reports of World War I battlefields and trenches had been available in Europeans' homes, would there have been great pressure to end the war after a year or so of the fighting? Why or why not?

_____

_____

_____

7. A Congress controlled by Democrats appropriated funds for programs it believed to be important. Often these programs conflicted with the priorities of President Nixon. The president resorted to the practice of impoundment, that is, of refusing to actually spend funds already appropriated by Congress. At one point in 1973, the total impounded funds reached $15 billion and involved more than a hundred federal programs. Do you agree with this impoundment as an executive right or do you consider it an infringement on the powers of the legislative branch? Explain.

_____

_____

_____

_____

_____

8. The Immigration and Nationality Act of 1965 did away with the quota system based on national origins. It provided for immigration on the basis of the reunion of families or the bringing of skills needed in the United States. An amendment in 1976 set the immigration for each country in the Western hemisphere at twenty thousand annually. Do you agree with these new criteria? Why or why not? If not, what criteria would you propose for immigration?

_____

_____

_____

_____

_____

9. Consider these two different approaches of the late 1960s to the problem of racism in American society:

> "... the point of departure is the principle that the oppressor has no rights that the oppressed is bound to respect. Kill the slavemaster, destroy him utterly, move against him with implacable fortitude. Break his oppressive power by any means necessary."
> Huey P. Newton, 1967

> "The problem with hatred and violence is that they intensify the fears of the white majority, and leave them less ashamed of their prejudices toward Negroes . . . violence only adds to the chaos . . . Through violence you may murder the liar, but you cannot murder the lie, nor establish the truth." Martin Luther King, Jr., 1967

Which viewpoint do you agree with most? Why?

_____

_____

_____

Which approach has been most successful for minorities in United States history? Explain.

_____

_____

_____

To what extent is this a major issue for people who feel oppressed in all areas of the world in contemporary times?

_____

_____

_____

10. Herbert Marcuse seemed to offer a philosophy of violence in his book, *One Dimensional Man*. He argued that the working class had surrendered its right to bring about revolutionary change because it had joined the capitalists. He maintained that violence existed in the established system; therefore, it was not morally wrong to use violence to break the established system of oppression. The voices that support this oppression must be suppressed. Do you agree with Marcuse? Why? If severe injustice exists as part of the established system, is that to be considered "inherent violence"? Explain.

_____

_____

_____

_____

11. In August 1964, North Vietnamese soldiers fired on two American destroyers that were supporting a South Vietnamese commando raid on two islands in the Gulf of Tonkin. No damage was done to the destroyers, and the second raid may not have actually occurred. Congress responded by passing a resolution to allow the president to "take all necessary steps, including the use of armed force" to assist South Vietnam. From this resolution, President Johnson early in 1965 ordered the bombing of North Vietnam and began sending American combat troops (eventually 550,000 Americans) to fight in Vietnam. Did Congress abdicate responsibility in offering the president this "blank check"? Explain. Was the pretext for the resolution sufficient? Why or why not? How does this incident relate to Americans sailing on the *Lusitania* in 1917, sending the *Maine*

to Havana in 1898, the replenishment of Fort Sumter in 1861, and the movement of troops to the disputed Rio Grande River in 1846?

_____

_____

_____

_____

_____

12. The Carter initiative on foreign affairs in 1977 involved an emphasis on human rights. Although President Carter was not always able, in the realistic atmosphere of power politics and American interests, to follow his principles on human rights, he argued, "Because we are free, we can never be indifferent to the fate of freedom elsewhere. Our moral sense dictates a clear-cut preference for those societies which share with us an abiding respect for individual human rights." Do you agree with this approach to foreign policy? Why or why not? Is this approach only an ideal or can a nation find ways to implement such a policy? Explain.

_____

_____

_____

_____

_____

13. React to the following "lessons" of history drawn out of this time period. Do you agree or disagree with them, and what are the exceptions to or problems with each? For item F, list any other "lessons" that reflect a pattern.

   A. If a president wants to become involved in assisting another nation militarily, he can manipulate affairs so that incidents occur that force Congress to support his efforts.

   _____

   _____

   _____

   B. It is difficult for an outside power, no matter how superior in military technology, to defeat a nationalist guerrilla group fighting among its own people on its own soil.

   _____

   _____

   _____

C. A lengthy military involvement cannot be sustained by a government if there are a large number of dissenters and a vocal, active opposition to it.

_____

_____

_____

D. Reform movements often end in war as fervent reformers attempt to bring reform to other areas or to people who have hitherto resisted reform.

_____

_____

_____

E. The hubris of great political success—say, an overwhelming election victory—can bring many difficulties to a president who then believes that everything can be accomplished.

_____

_____

_____

_____

F. _____

_____

_____

_____

14. Already historians and participants are applying interpretive skills to the Vietnam War. Consider the following three interpretations:

A. The war dislocated the Vietnamese people and made them dependent on the United States. The United States lacked a coherent political and economic solution to Vietnam's nonmilitary problems and tried to defeat a national revolution without adapting to the challenge of guerrilla warfare. The North Vietnamese were not really a part of any world Communist movement, so the doctrine of containment and the domino theory did not apply.

B. The war represented a breakdown in political decision-making caused by a Cold War outlook of inflexible rigidity. President Johnson had only the traditional complete victory in mind when a negotiated settlement or other alternatives might have worked. Leaders failed to recognize Vietnam's internal antagonisms such as the Catholic leadership over a Buddhist peasantry.

C. The administration in Washington, D.C., put limitations on military operations and allowed only a gradual escalation of pressure on the enemy. The press and television produced negative images of defeat and failure. If very early in the war commanders had been allowed to pursue the enemy into Laos and Cambodia and to their departure points in North Vietnam, the war could have been brought to a successful conclusion. Leaders in Washington listened to the press more than to their own military personnel and other officials on the scene.

Which of these interpretations do you agree with most? Why?

_____

_____

_____

Can the three be reconciled to offer a "complete" or unified interpretation? Why or why not?

_____

_____

_____

What specific questions would you like to ask proponents of the three interpretations?

_____

_____

_____

15. President Nixon installed a voice-activated audio tape system in his White House office. Many hours of tapes were accumulated. Nixon refused to surrender the tapes to congressional committees, arguing that such an act would infringe on the separation of powers and executive privilege. Later he argued that the tapes were private property and, therefore, did not belong in the public domain. Do you agree with either of these arguments? Why or why not?

_____

_____

_____

_____

16. In 1972, President Nixon went to the People's Republic of China (Communist China). He was graciously received by the Communist leadership, including Mao Tse-tung. Yet Nixon had been an ardent anti-Communist and throughout his career opposed any ties with this Communist giant. Which of the following are *likely* and which are *questionable* inferences derived from Nixon's visit to China? Explain your decision under each.

   A. Nixon hoped to persuade the Chinese to give up communism and establish a Western-style democratic government with a capitalist economy.

_____

_____

B. Nixon took advantage of the split between Communist USSR and Communist China and hoped to persuade the Chinese to move closer diplomatically to the United States.

_____

_____

C. Nixon believed that a president establishes his place in history from success in foreign policy and this surprising diplomatic move would enhance his prestige as innovative and astute in foreign policy.

_____

_____

D. The president needed support against a possible Communist threat in South Korea or a movement of Soviet troops into combat in Vietnam.

_____

_____

E. China needed investments and technology and would provide a market for American goods, which would not only bring profits to American corporations but tie the Chinese to the American market system.

_____

_____

Which do you consider to be the primary reason for the visit to China? Why?

_____

_____

_____

17. Dirty tricks accompanying the efforts to reelect President Nixon in 1972 included burglary, electronic surveillance, mail interception, telephone bugs, implication of opponents in sex scandals, damaging the air-conditioning facilities at the Democratic convention site, breaking into a psychiatrist's office to acquire papers, and more. Are these activities to be expected as part of an election campaign in a democratic society, or are they exceptional and dangerous to the functioning of a democracy? Explain.

_____

_____

_____

_____

_____

18. The Nixon Doctrine, proclaimed in July 1969, stated that the United States would support its friends and allies, but would not defend all free nations nor

come to the aid of every nation threatened by another nation. The United States would choose those countries that were important to its security and in which intervention would make a difference. John F. Kennedy had promised earlier that the United States would ". . . support any friend, oppose any foe, in order to insure the survival and the success of liberty." Truman had promised that the United States would "support free peoples who are resisting attempted subjugation by armed minorities or outside pressures." Which policy do you agree with—Nixon's or Truman's and Kennedy's? Why?

_____

_____

_____

_____

_____

19. Probably the most significant (Justice Earl) Warren Court decision was the 1954 *Brown* case calling for school desegregation. However, the Supreme Court made several other significant decisions in the 1960s and 1970s. Examine the following seven decisions, then under each explain whether you agree or disagree with the decision.

A. *Engle* v. *Vitale* (1962)—banned local and state laws requiring prayer in public schools.

_____

_____

B. *Baker* v. *Carr* (1962)—held that the equal-protection clause of the Fourteenth Amendment empowers the federal courts to force reapportionment of state legislatures, thus supporting the principle of one-person, one-vote. All elected legislators (both houses) were to represent approximately the same number of people.

_____

_____

C. *Gideon* v. *Wainright* (1963)—established that the Sixth Amendment requires states to provide defense counsel for indigent defendants (those who cannot afford a lawyer).

_____

_____

D. *Heart of Atlanta Motel* v. *United States* (1964)—the 1964 Civil Rights Act is upheld as constitutional; outlawed racial discrimination in public accommodations and restaurants under the regulation authority of interstate commerce.

_____

_____

E. *Escobedo* v. *Illinois* (1964)—held that the police must inform a suspect of the Fifth Amendment provisions against self-incrimination and that the suspect must be granted legal counsel.

_____

_____

F. *Miranda* v. *Arizona* (1966)—specified strict procedures to be used in attempting to extract a confession from the accused.

_____

_____

G. *Swann* v. *Charlotte-Mecklenburg Board of Education* (1971)—required cities to bus students out of their neighborhoods if necessary in order to achieve integration.

_____

_____

Rank the seven from most important to least important.

_____

For the one you chose as most important, explain why.

_____

_____

Do the effects of the above decisions make the Supreme Court into a "legislative" body?

_____

_____

_____

To what extent can it be argued that by these decisions the Supreme Court is interfering with the rights and prerogatives of states? Should the Court become involved in state matters if principles of the Constitution are involved? Was this the situation in the above seven cases? Explain.

_____

_____

_____

_____

_____

20. Consider the two quotations at the beginning of the chapter. Explain their meanings and implications and whether you agree or disagree with each.

_____

_____

_____

_____

_____

THOUGHTS FOR QUESTIONS

1. One could argue that Watergate was a minor break-in, that Nixon was not aware that it was taking place, and that the cover-up was an effort to protect the prestige of the presidency. But the break-in was a criminal act by employees of one political party against another political party. The machinery of government was employed to contain the exposure of information about the act. Nixon, as a lawyer, was certainly aware of the seriousness of his action. It was a threat to the very heart of democratic government—illegal action against the political opposition and the use of government agencies to protect the illegal act.

2. Here students must make individual choices. Items E and I are very significant. The first extends voting power to a group that then can use this power to gain justice and equal treatment. The other attempts to attack the problems of poverty and to promote the ideal of equal opportunity. One might argue that, on paper, or in the planning and theoretical stages, all look beneficial. Cost must be considered, especially as it relates to effectiveness. The affirmative-action program is probably the most controversial; all are programs that attempt to improve the human condition.

3. Nixon received 31.8 million votes; Humphrey received 31.3 million; and George Wallace received 9.9 million. If we count most of Wallace's votes with the Nixon total, then the voters seemed to favor a "law and order" leader. The war continued for four more years and the liberal program ground to a halt. Nixon did shock everyone with a proposal for a guaranteed income above the poverty level for every family in the United States. How different might the next eight years have been had Humphrey been elected president?

4. This is the student's choice. Both could be correct: it is possible that some sort of "victory" could have been won against North Vietnam, but McNamara's judgment would still stand—not a very pretty victory.

Since McNamara refers to an impression of what is happening in Vietnam, an examination of press reports, film, and videos might confirm his evaluation. We can never know the validity of Westmoreland's view. The events took place without his alternatives. At the time, many people were asking what was meant by "victory" in the context of so much death and destruction. One is reminded of the American officer's observation that he had to "destroy the village in order to save it."

5. People have faced this moral choice over and over again in history from the characters in _Antigone_ to Ellsberg. The major issue here is whether to obey the government's restriction on classified material or to pay heed to a higher moral law, that of placing the truth before the American people. The question of releasing infor-

mation that would damage the government's reputation during a crucial phase of the war also was raised. Both Ellsberg and the *Times* had to make these decisions. The information increased opposition to the war. Of course, the government's right to deceive the people on behalf of what government officials called a "higher cause" or for the people's own good is an issue.

6. "War is hell," as an American general once said. But the deliberate killing of defenseless women and children goes beyond just an unfortunate incident in the heat of battle. It may be more symbolic of the frustration of guerrilla warfare, a signal of racism, or a product of fear and uncertainty about the purpose of being in the village of My Lai or in Vietnam. Many intellectuals and many respected diplomats and congresspersons used reasoned arguments against American involvement in Vietnam. These, along with the war's emotional impact on the American public, provided a formidable opposition.

Certainly the brutality of the war was being brought into the television rooms of America. The atrocities and savagery may not have been any more frequent or more intense than in any other war. However, before, the American public could not see the death, the pain, and literally the "blood" of combat. Yet to maintain that these vivid scenes alone led to American opposition to the war is unfounded. It seems that World War I would have been shortened considerably if the horror of the trenches had been seen in German and French living rooms. Perhaps the people of all nations, and especially the leaders, should at regular intervals be required to view live scenes of the horrors of war. Would this make a difference in attitudes?

7. The courts eventually sided with Congress and required the expenditure of impounded funds. They viewed the impoundment as an effort to revoke the will of Congress, the elected representatives of the American people. The president had already signed the congressional appropriations bill into law. Efforts at economizing in government may deserve consideration, but the amount involved here impinges on overall policy. If this right of impoundment were extended without limits, it would lead to complete control of nearly all legislation and programs enacted by Congress. Without funds, government departments cease to function.

8. The immediate results of the new act and the amendment were twofold. First, Asian immigration moved from 7 percent of total immigration in 1965 to 33 percent by 1976. Also, illegal immigrants from Latin American increased. An estimate of the number of illegal aliens in the United States in 1980 was six million. Requiring an immigrant to exhibit a needed skill possibly drew out people from underdeveloped nations who possessed skills essential to those nations. Also, it removed a stabilizing element in those societies. Is there a limit on the desirable population level of the United States? Should the right of immigration be centered on humanitarian factors only—the reuniting of families or providing a haven for those fleeing political or religious persecution?

9. Students must choose from these viewpoints. Native Americans fought and then had to yield. The black-power movement seemed to instigate a white backlash with Nixon's successes in 1968 and 1972. The civil-rights movement gained success under King's leadership as Americans became aware of the degree of and the ugliness of discrimination, such as the fire hoses and attack dogs used against nonresisting blacks. But the threat of ultimate violent action on the part of many blacks may have hovered in the background. The impact of blacks standing up to white authority may have produced pride and inspiration. Does the King tradition function best in the long run?

Immediate gains by violence may be offset by a reactionary change in public attitudes. The world currently seems caught in this dilemma. Does terrorism get results? Is the pursuit of goals in a gradual, peaceful manner so slow that the limited progress is unsatisfactory? Both South Africa and the Middle East now face these choices.

10. One must distinguish between a *system* that allows for opportunity and thus inequality and the purposeful effort of those who are successful in the system to oppress those who are not. Does violence purify the system and set up a just one with benevolent leaders? Will those who gain power by opposing oppression then resort to oppression in order to maintain control? Must the voices that support oppression be *violently* suppressed? Is the only practical answer the establishment of a society in which "inherent violence" exists, but in which many opportunities are available to struggle out of the "inherent violence" of poverty, inadequate housing, and a criminal environment? Degree of "oppression" also must be considered. For example, many Americans living below the poverty line have a higher standard of living than 80 percent of the world's population.

11. Many congresspersons later indicated that the resolution vote was not meant to approve a large-scale commitment to Vietnam. The extent of involvement seemed beyond the provocation—a few torpedo boats and no damage to American ships. Of course, the incident was really only an excuse to release a planned action based on, in Johnson's opinion, a need to protect a small country from a Communist takeover. This was a "war," but Congress did not declare it with the usual meaning given the term.

The other four events were all decisions that placed an invitation to strike before a belligerent enemy. After the strike, the president had a pretext to respond in a manner of his choosing, often in a way that had been planned earlier.

12. It would seem, when noting the principles on which the United States was founded, that this approach would have to be a significant factor in foreign relations. However, its implementation is problematic, given a world of nations that might advocate other principles as superior to those of human rights—religious truth or ideological principles, for example. Some argue that a country's preservation is automatically the guiding principle for all national conduct. But taken to the extreme, self-preservation could dominate citizens' mind-set to the exclusion of any concern about human rights. It may be that a disregard for human rights beyond a nation's boundaries leads to a disregard for human rights within a nation's boundaries. We are only made whole by seeking the wholeness of others! If a powerful nation indicates that its friends are those who accept and implement the idea of human rights, this knowledge should, of itself, promote human rights. There is a risk, and often some sacrifice, in the effort.

13. A. This has historical precedent, as seen with presidents in the cases cited in question number 11—Abraham Lincoln, James Polk, William McKinley, and Woodrow Wilson. It may not always work, but the pattern has existed for more than one hundred years of American history.

B. Certainly it is difficult. Yet the Soviet Union suppressed rebellions in East Germany, Hungary, and Czechoslovakia. The United States silenced Filipino rebels from 1899 to 1902. A Polish uprising was brutally suppressed by the Germans in 1944. Yet the terrain was alien in some of the areas. Many other factors must be considered in accounting for guerrilla or interventionist success.

C. The key words are "lengthy" and "large number." The American people were divided during the War of 1812. The Copperheads dissented in the North during the Civil War. Anti-imperialists were active during the Spanish-American War. These wars were shorter in length than the American involvement in Vietnam (eight years, 1965–73); also, by 1971, the opposition had moved to majority status.

D. This pattern is intriguing. Exceptions are the War of 1812 and the Mexican War, and perhaps the war in Korea. Yet the charge that a war is a result of reform, just because it comes at the end of the reform effort, can not be proven. Certainly abolitionists influenced the Civil War and Woodrow Wilson's progressive idealism to make the world safe for democracy was a factor in American entry into World War I. Possibly President Johnson intended to extend his Great Society to Vietnam.

E. Exceptions to this lesson are in George Washington, James Madison, James Monroe, and perhaps Theodore Roosevelt. One consideration is the size of the troubles. Ronald Reagan also may be an exception, although the second term brought more problems than the first. Even with these exceptions, does the pattern still serve as a useful generalization that might be a warning to future presidents who accomplish a great electoral victory and then expect unlimited success?

14. This is the student's choice. Both A and B seem correct. Interpretation C appears to be a rationalization or excuse, to those of us who, no doubt, were influenced by the aura of that time. Military men called for a few thousand more troops and saw the "light at the end of the tunnel." With complete control of the airspace over all Vietnam; the largest navy in the world; 550,000 military personnel (plus at least as many South Vietnamese); more bombs than were used in all of World War II by all sides; and fighting in supposedly friendly territory, the United States was not able to prevail. Perhaps the war was unwinnable, at least in the traditional sense of defeating an enemy in order to establish the security of the citizens of South Vietnam. Even a victory would not have silenced critics who viewed the war from interpretations A and B.

Is Vietnam in any worse condition now than it would have been had the United States not intervened in 1965? What sort of reasonable negotiated settlement might have been available in 1965? Were there other strategic ways of fighting the war that would have brought success without the civilian casualties? Which reports were more accurate about what was really happening in Vietnam—the official military reports or the media coverage?

15. The equipment, the blank tapes, and the installation were all at public expense. The conversations recorded were, for the most part, on public issues relating to the government. This viewpoint seems to provide a sound argument for their public-domain status. However, if Nixon had taken notes, using government paper and pen, of these same conversations, would these notes be private or government property? Separating an elected official's public and private domain is difficult. However, the Senate investigation committee that demanded the tapes was seeking evidence for a case of criminal activity and impeachment proceedings.

16. A. Questionable. Nixon would have had little hope for such a drastic change, although eventually, after Mao's death, a limited free-enterprise system and a certain amount of dissent was allowed.

B. Likely. Nixon was able to play off one country against the other and began a rapprochement with the Soviet Union immediately after the visit to China.

C. Likely. Nixon had made statements to this effect earlier in his career. The opportunity was there, the time seemed right, and Nixon took the initiative. Historians already praise him for this success.

D. Questionable. There were no signs that the Soviet Union had any such plans or objectives. It is unlikely that the Chinese, in 1972, would have become involved in Vietnam.

E. Likely. A capitalist nation seeks markets and the possibility of invest-ments. This may not have been the primary purpose in the mission, but it is likely that it was one of the aims. United States policy had called for an "Open Door" for trade in China since 1899.

B seems to be the primary reason. These diplomatic ties were of great importance, far beyond economic or personal considerations. The fact that Secretary of State Henry Kissinger headed the way indicates the diplomatic objectives of the trip.

17. These activities are difficult to accept as normal political activity. Similar acts have appeared singularly in past elections, but never to this extent in quantity and in obvious illegality. These are the types of activities that keep dictatorships in power, and in expanded form, attach totalitarian regimes to a nation. Nixon's supporters used "national security" as an excuse, but a threat to national security was not evi-dent in most of the activities. The irony is that Nixon did not need these "dirty tricks" to win the election!

18. From George Washington's farewell address through the Monroe Doctrine, to the isolationism of the 1920s, American policy centered on noninvolvement in the affairs of other nations. The Truman and Kennedy statements, along with John Fos-ter Dulles's implication that even people of the Communist bloc could depend on American support, seemed to commit the United States to defend against any threat to freedom anywhere. This is a great obligation for any nation. Sometimes interven-tion exchanges one authoritarian system for another. Nixon was stating reality, a pragmatic limitation on the all-inclusive promises of Truman and Kennedy. Policing the world is not always in the best interests of the United States or of the nations being policed. However, there is a saying that the reduction of freedom anywhere in the world reduces freedom everywhere. In a complex world, America's close friends and allies are not always themselves free. Are some nations, in a Cold War context, not important?

19. Suggested ranking: B, C, F, E, D, A. The *Baker* case (B) enabled many of those who had been left out of the maintstream of American society to begin to exercise some power in urban areas that in most states were under-represented in state legislatures. This power has led to much legislation to establish justice and promote equal opportunity.

Any decision of a court has a force of law, so a court legislating is not a new phenomenon. Some of the decisions given here overturned existing law. The Court's positive function seemed to overshadow its negative function in the Warren years.

Since the rights of citizens under the Constitution are considered "sacred" and immutable, then the Court has the right to preserve these rights. The fact that primarily individual states interfered with these rights is only incidental. Federal laws and federal court decisions were also declared unconstitutional. The guarantee of equal protection under the law to all citizens is a solemn responsibility. The issue of whether a state's leaders feel that the state's sovereignty has been impinged upon pales in comparison.

20. Freeman has an insightful comment on the writing of history. Historians write history for the present surrounded by an environment impregnated with current val-ues and attitudes. No historian deliberately falsifies history, we hope. A factual de-scription of a town in New England in the seventeenth century, based on the use of

all available resources, probably will not change much over time. But Freeman is speaking primarily about the structure of history, the effort to infuse history with meaning. This is the story now; it will change in the future.

Robinson's statement is meaningless in many ways. We have no record of all that has happened. We have some hint at .00001 percent of the significant events and developments over time. Is history what the historian decides to write down as history? History is in our minds. The events of the past are lost forever. We recreate them with our own perceptions and to our own liking.

APPENDICES: SPECIAL SKILLS HISTORIANS NEED

APPENDIX 1
Thesis and Topic Selection

Research and writing are important parts of a historian's work. The research activity normally begins with a thesis. A thesis is a proposition, an educated guess, about a subject or issue that a person advances and offers to maintain by evidence and argument. It is a statement about which evidence can be gathered to encourage its acceptance as true, although sometimes doubts still exist after careful study. After settling on a thesis, the historian proceeds to gather relevent evidence and arguments. In most cases the thesis is proven, at least to the satisfaction of the historian doing the research. In some cases the evidence does not support the thesis, and the proposed article based on the thesis is not presented to the academic community.

At other times a historian's research and writing may be centered on a description of a topic or on a narrative structure. In this case the historian gathers relevant, often chronological, data about the topic and then describes the event or situation in an organized fashion.

Thus a historian may be accumulating evidence and arguments to prove or disprove a clearly stated proposition or accumulating coherent data and ideas in order to describe a topic accurately and to present significant data, often new data, on the topic. Of course, historians may use some analysis with the descriptive-narrative topic; and the thesis format has much description. So the two are not mutually exclusive.

Four precautions must be taken in selecting a thesis or topic for research. The same four caveats apply to a history student's term paper or to a written report in history. These are:

1. The thesis or topic may be too *broad.* It must be limited and related to the available time to do adequate research and writing.

2. Sometimes a thesis or topic can be too *narrow* or insignificant for research. A historian must ask if the research is important and if the results will interest those in the field.

3. Enough *resource materials* must be available to carry out the necessary research. Many topics warrant study, but lack available resource materials with satisfactory data.

4. Finally, often a thesis or topic is not *clearly stated.* This can disorient the reader and result in a collection of useless, unrelated data.

The skill of formulating a viable thesis or recognizing a suitable topic is important for history students and also for the students in other academic disciplines and even in nonacademic situations. After each of the following items, indicate whether it is primarily a thesis or a topic. Then, using the four guidelines above where appropriate, write whether you consider the thesis or topic a suitable one for an undergraduate paper in an American history course. Check your choices with those suggested.

THESIS OR TOPIC

1. The barrels used by the Portuguese to hold drinking water aboard ships were tighter than those used by the Spanish.

   _____

   _____

2. The leaders of all the voyages to the New World in the first fifty years after Columbus were men motivated primarily by greed and desire for wealth and power.

   _____

   _____

3. An examination of all the conditions in Europe from 1400 to 1600 that led to exploration and colonization in America.

   _____

   _____

4. A presentation of the content of advertisements that William Penn distributed in Europe in order to attract settlers to Pennsylvania.

   _____

   _____

5. The bills considered and the laws passed by the House of Burgesses from 1619 to 1660 dealt mostly with land policy and trade matters, that is, economic affairs.

   _____

   _____

6. A comparative study of the differences in curriculums, the libraries, the qualifications of teachers, and the methods of teaching at Harvard College and at William and Mary College in the 1750s.

   _____

   _____

7. The tobacco grown in Virginia in the 1620s was more like the current "Mixture 79" brand in texture and aroma than any other current brand.

   _____

   _____

8. A study of the world view of the Aztecs, Incas, and other native tribal groups of America prior to the arrival of Christopher Columbus.

   _____

   _____

9. God supported the Puritan settlements in the seventeenth century much more than God helped the Virginia settlements.

_____

_____

10. An analysis and report on the seventeenth-century Puritan attitudes toward the religious condition and capabilities of the American Indians.

_____

_____

Formulate one thesis and one topic suitable for a student paper on the time period being considered here:

11. _____   _____

_____

_____

12. _____

_____

_____

ANSWERS AND EXPLANATIONS

1. Thesis. Inappropriate. The statement is much too narrow and insignificant to consider seriously. Resource materials would be very difficult, perhaps impossible, to find.

2. Thesis. Inappropriate. Motivation is extremely difficult to decipher; it is often mixed, and who can say which impulse was the primary one? Besides, the sources might be in several languages and scattered in many libraries.

3. Topic. Inappropriate. This is much too broad and would require a lengthy period of intensive research by a serious, well-trained scholar.

4. Topic. Appropriate. The advertisement are limited to one man's, are probably available in printed form, and would be of interest and significance.

5. Thesis. Appropriate. This proposition is for a limited period, is centered on one geographic and subject area, and the resources are probably available.

6. Topic. Appropriate. The study is limited to specific subject areas and institutions and both primary and secondary sources would be available in academic libraries.

7. Thesis. Inappropriate. Only descriptions of tobacco odors are available for the 1620s. The proposition is not very important.

8. Topic. Inappropriate. This is too broad and may not be possible, given the scarcity of written records. Of course, secondary sources exist—products of the archaeological research of scholars.

9. Thesis. Inappropriate. Historians have difficulty determining and evaluating divine influence. The thesis is vague ("supported" in what way?) and would still be argumentative no matter how much data were collected.

10. Topic. Appropriate. The study is limited by century and by subject. It would be significant and sources are available. Perhaps it would be a challenging assignment and might best be narrowed to Boston or to a smaller time span.

QUESTIONS

1. Which is the most beneficial or productive way for historians to approach a subject—from a thesis or from a descriptive/narrative topic approach? Why?

2. Is the actual process for a historian likely to be first the selection of a thesis, followed by the gathering of data on the thesis, or first a gathering of data about a general topic and then the formation of a thesis? Explain.

3. Does the establishment of a thesis threaten a historian's objectivity; that is, does it tempt the historian to gather and use only data that support the thesis?

4. How might proving a thesis false, through the evaluation of relevant evidence, easily result in the development of another thesis—perhaps one that is the opposite of the initial thesis? Consider the following *false* thesis: "The climate and diet in Virginia enabled settlers there to live longer and healthier lives than those in New England." Could it be reversed and defended? If so, explain how.

5. Although a descriptive/narrative topic approach to writing history might result in an interesting story, why might the reader end up entertained rather than challenged to think deeply about the subject?

APPENDIX 2
Evaluating Sources

Sources for historians are people, books, documents, or material objects that supply information. Historians most often use written sources, but especially in the twentieth century, audio and visual materials and artifacts have become important. Numerical materials, although not "written" in the usual meaning of the term, are usually set on paper and are in most cases explained in written form or used in support of a written statement.

Sources can be divided into the following three categories, although some historians are more comfortable with two categories—primary and secondary:

1. *Primary sources* These are sources produced usually by a participant or observer at the time an event or development is taking place, or even at a later date. Manuscripts are primary sources preserved in their original form. Primary sources include letters, diaries, journals, newspapers, memos, descriptive accounts, memoirs, and autobiographies. They may include nonwritten sources such as taped inteviews, films, videotapes, photographs, furniture, baseball cards, tools, weapons, houses, and other items. Primary sources are sometimes referred to as "original sources."

2. *Secondary sources* When a historian uses primary sources to write about a topic or to support a thesis, a secondary source is produced. Secondary sources are monographs, professionally researched and clearly written, about events and developments in the past for which both primary and other secondary sources are normally used. They also may include arranged artifacts—for example, a specially designed room of eighteenth-century furniture. Most books in the history section of a library and the articles in history journals are secondary sources.

3. *Tertiary or popular-history sources* Some historians maintain that a further distinction can be made, a third level of written history materials, neither primary nor secondary. These materials include textbooks—collected and organized historical data based on the scholarly study of others—popular-history articles written by journalists, and writings that use history to persuade, promote, or excite interest—often found in popular magazines or newspapers.

Of course, depending on a historian's intent, some sources change their designation. For example, George Bancroft's nineteenth-century history of the United States is a secondary source; yet if the historian is writing an article on "The Techniques of Writing History in the Nineteenth Century," it becomes a primary course.

Consider the following sources. Decide whether each is normally a primary, secondary, or tertiary source, and write in your answer. Then explain it and speculate how each might be classified differently under special circumstances.

SOURCES

1. A twenty-page article analyzing the political ideas found in the diaries of John Adams.

2. A newspaper report written by an eyewitness to the Boston Massacre of 1770.

_____

_____

3. A statistical analysis of colonial divorce records from 1750 to 1770.

_____

_____

4. A copy of George Washington's last will and testament.

_____

_____

5. A biography of George Washington written in 1810.

_____

_____

6. The *Autobiography of Benjamin Franklin.*

_____

_____

7. A *National Enquirer* article listing some oddities about the Founding Fathers.

_____

_____

8. A textbook chapter describing immigration patterns in the eighteenth century.

_____

_____

9. A taped audio interview in which Samuel Eliot Morison, an authority on Christopher Columbus, is questioned about Columbus's logbook and journal.

_____

_____

10. A videotape of the Valley Forge buildings, fortifications, cannon, and battlefield, along with an interview of the site's curator or manager.

_____

_____

ANSWERS AND EXPLANATIONS

1. Secondary. The diaries are primary sources, but their analysis produces a secondary source.

2. Primary. The report may be very biased and even inaccurate, but as an eye-

witness account it is a primary source. Of course, the historian must establish that, to the best of his or her knowledge, the eyewitness was indeed at the site.

3. Secondary. The divorce records and the numbers taken from them are primary sources. But putting these together in categories with a purpose and then making comments and interpretations of the data produce a secondary source.

4. Primary. Produced by Washington during his life, the will is a primary source. It also may exist in manuscript form.

5. Secondary. The biographer would have written about Washington using primary sources—letters, diaries, and writings of contemporaries.

6. Primary. Written by Franklin about his own life, the material was probably from memory, notes, or letters.

7. Tertiary. Certainly this is not primary, nor is it secondary since it is not a scholarly study using primary sources. It is a brief list of items gathered from unknown sources that may or may not be reliable.

8. Tertiary or secondary. Did the textbook author gather data for his description exclusively from secondary sources? If so, we might consider it a tertiary source. If the author is an expert on immigration and wrote the chapter mainly from primary sources, then it becomes a secondary source.

9. Secondary. Despite the fact that the topic is about the logbook and journal, the tape is, in essence, an interview of an expert using primary sources as bases for comments.

10. Secondary. If some of the items are authentic for the time and place, the items are primary sources, but the total layout was produced later.

QUESTIONS

1. Look up the colonial period in a textbook chapter bibliography or a library card catalogue. List two primary and two secondary sources for this period.

    Primary

    (1.) _____

    _____

    (2.) _____

    _____

    Secondary

    (1.) _____

    _____

    (2.) _____

    _____

2. In our daily lives we interact with primary sources. We read newspapers and magazines, see television news, listen to eyewitness accounts, and participate in events and developments. Anything produced in writing about an event while it is taking place becomes a primary source for the historian of the future. Choose one current event of which you are an "observer" either directly through television coverage or through newspapers, news magazines, or the radio. Write a

brief paragraph of approximately forty words about this event, offering your opinion.

_____

_____

_____

_____

_____

A. Is this source that you produced a primary or a secondary source? Why?

_____

_____

B. Would a historian one hundred years from now consider your writing of any importance? Why or why not?

_____

_____

C. One difficulty with primary sources is that the usefulness of their data is uneven and they are often biased. Is this true of your paragraph? Why?

_____

_____

3. Have you ever been in a highly emotional situation where action was taking place quickly and unexpectedly, such as an accident, a fight, or a development in an athletic contest? How accurate would your report be of exactly what took place—the sequence of events, words spoken, appearance of participants, motivation of participants, and so forth? Would your account be a good primary-source description of what happened? Explain.

_____

_____

_____

_____

_____

4. Important and controversial plays in televised sports are often repeated in instant replay. Could such a device change our understanding of history? Why or why not? If more and more of "history" is videotaped and kept for posterity, will our perception of the past be more accurate and complete? Why or why not?

_____

_____

_____

_____

5. Would a videotaped session of an American Philosophical Society meeting in Philadelphia in 1758 be of more value to historians than the written minutes of the meeting, a copy of the paper presented at the meeting, and references to the meeting in the writings of those who attended? Why or why not?

---

6. Consider the following three sources. After each explain why it might be biased and why it might be very valuable to the historian in spite of the bias.

    A. Sections of the journal of Cotton Mather, a Puritan minister, in which he wrote about the Salem witch trials.

    B. A letter from a frontier settler in which he wrote about the culture of the Indians and their right to their hunting grounds.

    C. A southern plantation owner's journal describing the living conditions of the slaves on his plantation.

APPENDIX 3
Analysis of Historical Sources

When historians examine documents, especially those of philosophical or ideological content, they use analytical skills in several ways. Assuming that the document is authentic and reliable, historians attempt to find the meaning of the ideas in the document. This may involve understanding the words used in the document—their meaning in the past is not necessarily the same as in the present—and trying to discover the author's intent.

Historians are also interested in how the document was used, the impact it had on events at the time it was written, and the number and type of people who used it. If it has references to concrete events or situations, historians want to know if the description and interpretation of these events are accurate and reasonable.

After this analysis historians will often render a judgment on the validity of the ideas and proclamations in the document. As noted before, historians project their values into the debate about the validity and importance of the ideas. This is subjective, but since it arises out of a scholarly historian's research, it is worthy of consideration. The analysis process and then the personal reaction to its results become part of the enjoyment of history and lead to serious further analysis and stimulating debate. History students also must adopt this habit of analysis, followed by a personal effort to formulate meaning out of the results.

The Declaration of Independence of 1776 is one of the major documents in American history. Surprisingly few Americans have read it seriously and analyzed its concepts. Students should read carefully the following opening section of the Declaration of Independence and then answer the related questions.

> *When in the Course of human events it becomes necessary for one people to dissolve the political bands which have connected them with another, and to assume among the Powers of the earth, the separate and equal station to which the Laws of Nature and of Nature's God entitle them, a decent respect to the opinions of mankind requires that they should declare the causes which impel them to the separation.*
>
> *We hold these truths to be self-evident, that all men are created equal, that they are endowed by their Creator with certain unalienable Rights, that among these are Life, Liberty and the pursuit of Happiness. That to secure these rights, Governments are instituted among Men, deriving their just Powers from the consent of the governed. That whenever any Form of Government becomes destructive of these ends, it is the Right of the People to alter or to abolish it, and to institute new Government, laying its foundation on such principles and organizing its Powers in such form, as to them shall seem most likely to effect their Safety and Happiness. Prudence, indeed, will dictate that Governments long established should not be changed for light and transient causes; and accordingly all experience hath shewn, that mankind are more disposed to suffer, while evils are sufferable, than to right themselves by abolishing the forms to which they are accustomed. But when a long train of abuses and usurpations, pursuing invariably the same Object evinces a design to reduce them under absolute Despotism, it is their right, it is their duty, to throw off such Government, and to provide new Guards for their future security. Such has been the patient sufferance of these Colonies; and such is now the necessity which constrains them to alter their former Systems of Government. The history of the present King of Great Britain is a history of repeated injuries and usurpations, all having in direct object the establishment of an absolute Tyranny over these States. To prove this, let Facts be submitted to a candid world.*

QUESTIONS

1. What do you consider the five most important ideas in the above selection from the Declaration? Explain why for each. (See the Suggested Answers for Questions 1 and 2.

   A. _____

   _____

   _____

   _____

   B. _____

   _____

C. _____

_____

_____

D. _____

_____

_____

E. _____

_____

_____

2. Which two ideas in the document might be interpreted in more than one way? Explain these different interpretations.

A. _____

_____

_____

B. _____

_____

_____

3. Assume you are asked to be highly critical of this document, that is, to question the validity of its ideas and especially the problems involved in applying them to practical situations. What criticisms would you make or what questions would you raise about the ideas?

_____

_____

_____

_____

_____

4. For each of the following ideas, explain whether you think they have eternal validity for all mankind or whether they are particular beliefs applying only to the culture of the American colonies in July 1776.

A. ". . . that all men are created equal . . ."

_____

_____

B. ". . . Governments are instituted among Men, deriving their just Powers from the consent of the governed."

_____

_____

C. ". . . all men . . . are endowed by their Creator with certain unalienable Rights, that among these are Life, Liberty and the pursuit of Happiness."

_____

_____

5. What is meant by the phrase "should not be changed for light and transient causes"? How does one distinguish between "transient causes" and "a long train of abuses"?

_____

_____

_____

6. Do the words "Laws of Nature and of Nature's God" and "endowed by their Creator" indicate that Thomas Jefferson sees a connection between religion and basic rights? Explain.

_____

_____

_____

7. If a government exists without open protest or widespread public criticism and with no signs of rebellion by the people living under it, can we assume it rules with "the consent of the governed"? Explain.

_____

_____

_____

8. Are the ideas in the Declaration of Independence meaningful and important in the contemporary world? Are these still "truths"? Are they "self-evident"? Why or why not?

_____

_____

_____

9. While writing this document in Philadelphia, Jefferson owned 150 slaves who worked for him on his plantation in Virginia. Was Jefferson a hypocrite? Explain.

_____

_____

_____

10. Jefferson originally included a statement criticizing the king for allowing the slave trade to continue. This was removed by the Continental Congress in deference to southerners. Should it have been included regardless of the sensibilities of slaveholders? Why or why not?

_____

_____

_____

11. The Declaration was read throughout the American colonies. It was copied, translated, and spread throughout Europe. How might the historian determine the *impact* it had on the success of the American Revolution? If it was quoted from the newspaper, if people included excerpts from it in their letters and diaries, and if soldiers carried copies of it into battle, would that be convincing proof of its widespread influence? Why or why not?

_____

_____

_____

12. Examine the complete Declaration of Independence in a history textbook. Why do you think some historians have referred to it as a "propaganda" document?

_____

_____

_____

13. What other rights, if any besides "Life, Liberty, and the pursuit of Happiness," do you consider the unalienable rights of the human race? Be specific. Consider the right to adequate shelter, freedom to move and travel, and others.

_____

_____

_____

14. The original phrase from John Locke listed unalienable rights as "Life, Liberty and *Property*." Why do you think Jefferson changed "Property" to "pursuit of Happiness"?

_____

_____

_____

SUGGESTED ANSWERS FOR QUESTIONS 1 AND 2

1. A. All men are created equal.
   B. Governments exist to secure basic rights.
   C. People may abolish governments that are destructive to these rights.
   D. Government receives its power from the consent of the governed.
   E. Government should not be changed for "light and transient causes."
2. A. Distinguishing between the "light and transient causes" and the "long train of abuses and usurpation."
   B. The concept of the equality of all *men*. Are women included? In what ways are people equal—political rights, legally, conditions of life, education, wealth, and others?

APPENDIX 4
Analysis of a Textbook Chapter

Instead of outlining or "highlighting" portions of a history textbook chapter, students can develop analytical thinking skills *and* acquire significant data by an analysis approach to the chapter. Not only are you as a student likely to remember more data, but you will remember the data in a meaningful context because you will have applied reflective thinking and evaluation skills to issues and topics. The chapter analysis that follows is generic and can be applied to any chapter in a standard history textbook.

You can use this approach during self-study and review. Also, the written results from these questions could stimulate class discussion—comparing the different choices various students made. Students could explain and defend their insights and evaluations of what is important. Thus, instead of memorizing, underlining, or outlining textbook information, students can explain and argue about the chapter topics.

ANALYSIS OF A TEXTBOOK CHAPTER

1. What are the *two* most important *decisions* individuals or groups made in the chapter? Explain the consequences of each. Were these decisions beneficial or harmful? What alternatives were available to them?
2. What two items of *statistical* information are most important in understanding the chapter? What inferences and implications can be drawn from these statistics?
3. What two *ideas* seem to be major influences on developments described in the chapter? (Two examples are the idea of neutrality in the 1930s or the concept of states' rights of John C. Calhoun, Thomas Jefferson, and James Madison.) Explain these ideas in your own words. To what extent are they still viable in the contemporary world? Explain.
4. What key *words*, *terms*, and *phrases* give insight into the chapter topics? List and define in your own words several of these.
5. What were the factors of causation in the chapter; that is, what "made things happen" (for example, a desire for economic gain or for political power)? Be specific.

6. What *contemporary* events, ideas, and developments are similar to those described in the chapter? Explain their relationship.

7. What *moral or ethical* issues (such as choices between good and evil, right and wrong, harmful and beneficial) are raised by events, decisions, and ideas described in the chapter?

8. Which two *individuals or small groups* were most important in the developments and events described in the chapter? Explain.

9. In what ways did *economic* factors or developments influence the events and developments described in the chapter? Explain.

10. What two events have had the most impact on subsequent history? Why?

11. What picture or descriptive sketch from the chapter best reveals its main theme? Explain why.

12. What "ifs" appear in the chapter—if this had not happened or had happened otherwise, then what historical developments might have been very different? These should be reasonable or believable. Explain how subsequent history might have developed.

APPENDIX 5
Using Library Sources

The historian's laboratory is the library. Since historians normally interact with the written word, usually printed, the place where the words are located is most crucial. Sometimes manuscripts or even printed records can be found at other locations—church archives, museums, family estates, in business files, and even in the attics of old houses. But these are not the normal focal point for historians; in most cases the library provides the nest for historical records. Thus it behooves history students to learn how to make use of this laboratory and its equipment.

Choose a topic related to the time period being studied. Then move through the library as outlined in the following steps and in each source find an interesting or significant item of information on the topic. Write in the page number, and the volume title and number if appropriate. In some cases the topic may not be found in the source exactly as listed. Then either find an aspect of the topic or a closely-related topic, or if this seems inappropriate, ignore that resource and note that no information was available. Some of the library sources listed yield only bibliographical information rather than actual data about the topic. If so, copy some of the relevant bibliographical information.

Sources to Examine

1. Card catalogue, for information on two books related to the topic or an aspect of it.

2. Encyclopedia—*Britannica, Americana,* or another academic encyclopedia.

3. *Reader's Guide to Periodical Literature*—list two magazine or journal articles as sources about the topic.

4. Look up one periodical article listed in the guide and write some information about the topic.

5. Look in either the *Humanities Index* or the *Social Science Index* for more professional-type articles on the topic (for years before 1965 this source is titled the *International Index*). Write the titles of two articles. Look up one and write some information about the topic.

6. Walk through the history and the political-science sections of the library (the Dewey Decimal 900s and 300s). Find two books that probably contain information about the topic and write their titles and authors.

7. *New York Times Index*—find a report or article on the topic and write the title and the date. Look up one article or news report and write some information about the topic. (This source may be only on microfilm.)

8. *Dictionary of the History of Ideas*—think of an idea related to the topic, find this idea in the source, and write some information on it.

9. *Guide to Archives and Manuscripts*—this index reveals where manuscripts (non-printed sources usually on the original paper) are located. Write the location of a manuscript source related to the topic.

10. *Encyclopedia of American History*, Richard B. Morris, editor—write information on the topic from this source.

11. *Guide to the Study of the United States*, two volumes—find a book on the topic and write some information from its description.

12. *The New Cambridge Modern History*—write information on the topic from this source.

13. *Historical Statistics of the United States*, two parts, four volumes—copy some statistical data related to the topic.

14. *Oxford-English Dictionary*—choose a key word related to your topic and write information on the history of the word.

15. *Dictionary of American Biography*—look up a person related to your topic and write some information about this person.

16. *Atlas of American History*—explain what maps may reveal about the topic.

17. *Journal of American History*—look in the index (usually annual) and find an article related in some manner to your topic; read the first two pages of the article and write some information from them.

For numbers 18, 19, and 20, make use of other sources in the reference room that might yield information about your topic. Copy the name of the source and some relevant data.

18. _____

19. _____

20. _____

Examples of Other Sources

1. *Magill's Survey of Cinema*, four volumes—films on various topics

2. Nineteenth-Century Literature Criticism (and *Twentieth-Century Literary Criticism*), thirty-four volumes

3. *Encyclopedia of Science and Technology,* fifteen volumes

4. *Encyclopedia of World Art,* sixteen volumes

5. *Dictionary of Folklore*

6. *Encyclopedia of American Economic History,* three volumes

7. *History of American Presidential Elections,* four volumes

8. *Harvard Encyclopedia of American Ethnic Groups*

9. *Biographical Dictionary of American Congress—1774–1971*

10. *Encyclopedia of Education*

11. *Supreme Court Cases*

12. *Encyclopedia of Religion*

13. *International Encyclopedia of the Social Sciences*

14. *Encyclopedia of Philosophy*

15. Historical journals—*American Historical Review, William and Mary Quarterly, Journal of Economic History,* and so forth.

Use your *imagination* in finding information related to your topic. For example, if the topic is "Philadelphia in the Colonial Period," you should look in an encyclopedia or textbook and compile subjects related to the main topic. Related subjects might be Benjamin Franklin, volunteer fire companies, the American Philosophical Society, artists of Philadelphia, maps of early Philadelphia, poems about Philadelphia, and others. The relationships among subjects are many and data can be found in most of the sources listed.

APPENDIX 6
Philosophy of History and Factors Causing Changes in History

PHILOSOPHY OF HISTORY

Most historians shy away from speculation about the philosophy of history. They argue that this area of study should be left to philosophers while historians continue to do research and writing about what happened in the past and why it happened. However, the philosophy of history does have a hidden impact on the historian. It can influence the choice of research topics, overall attitude toward the selection of sources and evidence, and explanations of the meaning of past events and developments. It should not affect the commitment to accuracy and objectivity, the analytical evaluation of evidence chosen, or the search for resources.

Notice the impact a philosophical outlook has in the following example: If a researcher believes that history is or should be moving in a direction of increased freedom for individuals and more democratic governments, then often the choice of research topics would revolve around episodes in this struggle for freedom. Also, the emphasis in the search for evidence would center on examples of the success of democracy over more authoritarian systems. Analogies, quotations, statistical data, and examples would seem more relevant and noticeable when associated with the extension of democracy or the advancement of individual freedom. Thus, the subject matter, the perspective, and the conclusions all would be perceived in relation to the philosophical mind-set of that historian.

The three major approaches to the overall meaning of history, to the philosophy of history, follow:

A. History has no ultimate meaning. It is a "tale told by an idiot," as William Shakespeare wrote. It can be read for entertainment. It may offer some advice for the present. Each period of history has its particular contribution to art and literature, to beauty and creativity. However, history is going nowhere; it has no overall purpose. It has no reliable lessons or generalizations. Why human beings even developed and began to think analytically and to write is a mystery. The end of history comes with the end of the human race. Any efforts to impose a *meaningful* structure on the unfolding of history are futile. To the Greeks and the Chinese, history repeated itself in cycles—the same pattern of events and developments occurring again and again in similar structure. Some modern thinkers (such as Oswald Spengler in the 1920s) have approved this cyclical pattern, but have deduced no ultimate meaning from it all. Other modern thinkers have considered history an existential encounter—an apprehension of its meaning by fulfilling roles with dignity, honor, and energy, but not with any hope that history is imbued with significance or purpose. Historicism calls on the historian to seek understanding of an epoch within a particular culture, to interpret, to admire, to respect, and to seek insight and understanding. But meaning, purpose, or goals cannot be found.

B. The meaning of history comes from outside. History has a religious or philosophical purpose with a designed movement from beginning to end. What happens within history reveals this divine purpose and contributes to the predestined progress and end to human history. Particular historical events need to be examined and understood in light of history's overall direction and goals, goals that have been arrived at by a process unrelated to the actual data of history. This may be a "revealed" purpose in a religious context or a secular philosophical deduction. Only forces outside history can imbue the mundane events of history with meaning and purpose.

C. History has meaning, but no great design imposed from the outside. It is evolving in a progressive fashion toward a more just and equitable world. Secular progress brings constant stage-by-stage improvement in all aspects of human history. Marxists argue that the elimination of socioeconomic classes and the common ownership of the means of production will inevitably bring about a better world, a perfect society. Others envision the worldwide development of industry and the promotion of democracy, leading to a high standard of living and a free, creative atmosphere. Still others predict an increased spiritual and moral awareness with an improvement of the human race. Whatever particular pattern or design is projected for the unfolding of history, its meaning and direction come from an understanding of history itself and from foretelling future developments through past stages and trends.

Reflect on these three philosophies of history and write your reaction to them. Which most nearly fits your outlook on history? Why? Have you read about particular events and developments that seem to support your viewpoint? Explain.

_____

_____

_____

_____

_____

FACTORS CAUSING CHANGES IN HISTORY

Factors causing changes in history are numerous. Historians continually search for the influences that cause the movement from one event to another. Rank the following list of broad factors that bring historical changes from most to least important. Of course, the influence of particular factors may be different according to each event, but try to reflect on their *overall* influence, based on your study of United States history.

1. Geography—climate, physical elements, location.

2. Classes—the clash of socioeconomic classes and special-interest groups.

3. Great leaders or small groups of men and women—the appearance of a hero or event-making personality.

4. History moves in an evolutionary process predetermined by genes and natural selection.

5. God moves history through the religious beliefs of people, through supernatural manipulation of events, or in some other manner.

6. War—violent clashes of groups and nations—is a catalyst for change in history.

7. Nations, peoples, and civilizations all follow the pattern of human life—birth, growth, strength, decay, and death.

8. History is determined by the aggressive, possessive, and selfish struggle of humans as part of the animal world—a search for bread and security.

9. Ideas are the prime movers in history; people freely think and then act according to these thoughts.

10. An elite group at the top of society, through their cooperative effort and collective decisions, bring about changes in history.

11. The inner psychological needs of people—self-preservation, power, recognition—determine events. Many of these are not consciously recognized.

12. Particular challenges appear at certain times in history, and the responses of individuals, groups, and even nations to these challenges produce events and developments in history.

13. Economic drives—to acquire necessities, to produce and sell for profit, and to gain wealth.

14. Gradual alterations to the way of life of families and communities—child rearing, community decisions, and so forth—bring about lasting change.

15. Race and ethnic pride—the unequal abilities and the clash of different groups in an effort to survive and prevail.

16. Mysterious forces beyond the grasp of human beings and unrecognizable in particular events cause developments in history.

Student Ranking:

_____

What other factors not in the list above may bring about changes in history?

_____

_____

_____

Explain why you ranked the two you considered most significant.

_____

_____

_____

Which of the above factors have been most often used by historians to explain change?

_____

_____

_____

What is the difference between these explanations for changes in history and the philosophies of history described earlier?

_____

_____

_____

APPENDIX 7
Family History, a Beginning

Your family's life is filled with "history." You inherit from your family members their past, their experiences. These interact with your own experiences to become you. To know your history is to better understand yourself. Furthermore, to write a family history is to create a historical source, a document. How important is the source? If we should discover the family and personal history of an average young person who lived in the Roman Empire in A.D. 80, it would be a fascinating and remarkable contribution to our understanding of that time period. Your family history is of value to you, to your family, and possibly to some historian in the future.

Data for this brief beginning of your family history can best be obtained by interviews of your family members. You normally will find that these interviews are enjoyable and rewarding. Use the following model for acquiring information.

1. Your name and home address: _____

_____

Date: _____

2. National origins of your family—from where in Europe, Latin America, Africa, Asia, or the Pacific did your family come to the United States? When did this occur? What is known about the families at the place of origin? (Of course, several locations may be involved as your family tree spreads broadly into the past.)

3. What was the means of income or the occupations of your family members in the past?

4. Discover and describe the education and training of family members.

5. What were your family residences in the United States—location, type of dwelling, character of the community?

6. What were your family's military involvements or memories of warfare?

7. Family cultural activities—abilities; performances in art, music; memorable moments; special skills such as cabinetmaking, gardening, and so forth.

8. Family travel experiences—business, tours, national or international vacations.

9. Athletic achievements—school or college, recreation, games, exercise, and others.

10. Church and religious involvements—philosophy or outlook on life; thoughts on ethics, moral behavior, death, keys to success, purpose of life, relationship to community.

11. Political persuasion and involvement in politics—voting record and support for particular candidates, evaluation of presidents or other leaders.

12. Family traditions, habits, "folklore," customs, traditional activities, holiday customs.

13. Unusual happenings—close calls, luck, coincidences, memorable occasions, meetings with the "famous," turning points in family fortunes.

14. Old objects made or preserved by the family as heirlooms or "hand-me-downs"—antiques, old pictures of furniture. List and describe.

15. Reminiscences of living family members of what "life was like back in the . . . ," both serious and "light" experiences and memories from the past.

16. Outside events, ideas, and developments that directly or indirectly influenced your family's history—international, national, local, economic, political; for example, the depression, World Wars I and II, government programs, new industry.

17. Written family records—letters, diaries, journals, writings, newspaper articles about the family, calendars with written schedules or appointments, and so forth. List and describe.

18. Other items of interest or importance about your family background that do not fit in the above classifications.

(*Note:* No confidential information should be included in this family history if it is to be shared with the instructor or made available for other students to see.)

QUESTIONS

1. What are the difficulties in discovering and presenting an accurate history of your family?

_____

_____

_____

2. To what extent do you trust the memory of the people you interviewed? Did present concerns or viewpoints or what they have read about the past interfere with the accuracy of their memory? Explain.

_____

_____

_____

3. How did you decide what to include and what to leave out?

_____

_____

_____

4. What might be the elements of bias in your selection of which data to include, your description of the experiences, and the explanations by those you interview?

_____

_____

_____

5. Of what use might this family history be if it were discovered two hundred years from now and turned over to a historian?

_____

_____

_____

6. After completing this family history, do you intend to add to it in the future? Why or why not?

_____

_____

_____

When interviewing parents, grandparents, and other relatives, it is important to suggest topics for obtaining reactions and reminiscences. These serve to "prime the pump," to stimulate memories, and to center the interview on topics about which you want to acquire information. An audiotape is useful. The following topics may draw out responses in your interview:

SCHOOL MEMORIES

discipline
subjects
teachers, athletics
lunch, classroom
clothing, books

GAMES

types
outside
table games
exercise

RADIO/FILMS

programs
early television
music
entertainment

CHURCH

Sunday School
pastor, teachers
services, hymns
youth groups

ANIMALS/PETS

farm animals
zoos
hunting

DOCTORS

dentists
cures, remedies
hospitals, costs

SHOPPING

groceries
store design
prices
markets
home canning

COMMUNITY

circus
carnivals
parades
barbershop
soda fountain
civic clubs

JOBS

pay, spending
hours, benefits
dangers
making ends meet
rich and poor

READING

magazines
newspapers
comics
books

DATING

activities
cost
going steady
marriage

CLOTHING STYLES

weather
winters, heating
keeping cool
storms

DANGERS

disease
causes of worry

TRANSPORTATION

train, auto
airplanes
bicycle

VACATIONS

when, where
activities, cost

HOLIDAYS

birthdays
Christmas
other holidays

CHILDREARING

morality
taboos
punishments

SPORTS

participant
observer
games

• Characters in the community, unforgettable people, unusual family friends.
• Memories of Franklin Roosevelt, war, New Deal, Pearl Harbor, John F. Kennedy assassination, elections (Harry Truman victory in 1948), *Sputnik,* Charles Lindbergh, Cuban Missile Crisis, Babe Ruth, Joe DiMaggio, specific presidents, film stars, military heroes, wealthy people, notorious characters, criminals, and others.

It is helpful to read and write down specific topics appropriate to the decades of the person being interviewed.

APPENDIX 8
Personal History as Social History

Many times history seems to be a subject that deals with remote times unrelated to our present lives. Historians argue that this apparent unrelatedness is not true, even when we study the distant past. In an examination of events that took place two hundred years ago, we find valuable insights into human nature, into the realities of social behavior, and into the effectiveness of government policies and programs. History provides understanding of the totality of human behavior, of the social interactions of humans in actual situations.

Besides discovering these insights from the past, we step through history each hour of our lives. We are part of history on a day-to-day basis as each moment passes by and becomes meshed with the past. To most of us, this does not involve the participation in important political, diplomatic, or cultural events and decisions. We are not "movers and shakers" who will be written about personally in monographs, biographies, and textbooks of the future. However, we do "make history" in a small way. With the increasing interest in the new social history and its concentrated study of the lives of the average person, our own lives become important sources for historians. The growing interest among historians in the changes in family structure, diet, disease, recreation, childrearing, community celebrations, and other topics related to the ongoing lives of average people makes our decisions, behavior patterns, attitudes, and values important sources for historical study. Our personal history then becomes a primary resource.

Think, for example, of the importance of a journal kept by a Revolutionary War soldier in which he reacts to the leadership of George Washington, comments on the food and drink, reflects on the reasons for fighting, describes the treatment of a local group of Loyalists, and offers descriptions and opinions of numerous incidents and situations around him. This journal would be of immense value to historians, even though the soldier is not famous and has not been involved in significant decisions. The same could be true about a journal you might keep at a college or university—a journal containing your descriptions, reflections, and reactions to what takes place around you, both locally and on national and international developments.

Assume you are producing a record, a resource that might be used by a future historian. Answer the following questions about your personal life and about events of the times. Then analyze what you have produced by answering the questions about your record. (Do not include information that you consider very private or that might be embarrassing to you or to others.)

Name ———————————————— Birthplace ————————————

Date of Birth ———————————— Date of Writing ————————————

Location of Writing ————————————————————————————

1. What were the childrearing methods used in your family (rules, punishments, encouragements, family meetings)?

    _____

    _____

2. In what ways have grandparents and relatives influenced your life?

    _____

    _____

3. In what ways has your racial or ethnic background had an impact on you and your life experiences?

    _____

    _____

4. What three childhood memories stand out most clearly in your mind? Why are they important? Why do you remember them?

    _____

    _____

5. What family celebrations were important (holidays or other occasions)?

    _____

    _____

6. What are your travel experiences with or without the family?

    _____

    _____

7. What specific political events, elections, campaigns, speeches, incidents do you remember? Write what you remember about them.

    _____

    _____

8. What specific events in foreign affairs do you especially remember? Write your reflections about these.

    _____

    _____

9. What two nonentertainment people involved in serious responsibilities or making an important impact on society in your lifetime do you admire the most? Explain why for each.

    _____

    _____

10. What two notorious people do you dislike the most? Explain why for each.

   _____

   _____

11. List some of the ideals, wisdom, and rules for living that from your experience to this point seem best to follow in your behavior and decision-making?

   _____

   _____

12. What fads, popular customs, special words, and style of dress and grooming have you experienced or participated in during your life?

   _____

   _____

13. What are the beneficial features of American society that should be retained and encouraged? List and explain briefly.

   _____

   _____

14. What are the troublesome, harmful aspects of American society that should be restrained or overcome? List and explain what should be done.

   _____

   _____

15. What material items and artifacts from your life have you kept to this point— items that might be important to the "material history" of the future, antiques that reflect the material culture of society, documents (diaries, letters, personal writings, "official" papers such as tax returns, check stubs, legal papers, newspaper articles), or collections (stamps, recordings, photographs, tools, foreign currency)? List some of these and explain them briefly.

   _____

   _____

QUESTIONS

1. Suppose the above data and artifacts are found by a historian in the year A.D. 2190. Of what value might they be to the historian? What parts might be misunderstood?

   _____

   _____

2. How accurate are your answers to the questions? That is, are they honest, durable, carefully thought-out answers or are they temporary reflections that might

change six months later? How can historians determine the honesty and seriousness of those who produce the records they use?

_____

_____

_____

3. Would you want this information to be "used" by a historian in the future? Why or why not? If you keep a diary or write letters, would you want these to be used? Why or why not?

_____

_____

_____

A famous American author wrote letters to a friend and insisted that the letters be destroyed after his friend read them. They were not destroyed and now have been published. Was this a betrayal or is it historians' responsibility to use historical records regardless of the wishes of those who produced them? Explain.

_____

_____

_____

4. Historians must use whatever records are available, and in many cases the records are not sufficient for a completely adequate understanding of a situation. Do your answers to the fifteen questions offer a balanced, accurate portrait of *you*? Explain. What other information would help in understanding you and your life?

_____

_____

_____

5. Former president Richard M. Nixon's audiotapes were recorded in the White House while he was president. His claim has been that these are private records and should not be made public nor made available to historians without his permission. What is your reaction to his claim?

_____

_____

_____

6. Do you intend to add to this brief personal history in future years or will you be satisfied with what is here and not pursue it any further? Explain why in either case. Do you or will you ever keep a diary or journal? Why or why not?

_____

_____

_____

A 9
B 0
C 1
D 2
E 3
F 4
G 5
H 6
I 7
J 8